Hands-On Computer Vision

Wei Shen · Chongjie Si · Chen Yang · Yong Yu

Hands-On Computer Vision

人民邮电出版社
POSTS & TELECOM PRESS

Springer

Wei Shen
Shanghai Jiao Tong University
Shanghai, China

Chongjie Si
Shanghai Jiao Tong University
Shanghai, China

Chen Yang
Shanghai Jiao Tong University
Shanghai, China

Yong Yu
Shanghai Jiao Tong University
Shanghai, China

ISBN 978-981-95-4834-7 ISBN 978-981-95-4835-4 (eBook)
https://doi.org/10.1007/978-981-95-4835-4

Jointly published with Posts & Telecom Press
The print edition is not for sale in Mainland China. Customers from Mainland China please order the print book from: Posts & Telecom Press.
ISBN of the Co-Publisher's edition: 978-7-115-63575-4

The original submitted manuscript has been translated into English. The translation was done using artificial intelligence. A subsequent revision was performed by the author(s) to further refine the work and to ensure that the translation is appropriate concerning content and scientific correctness. It may, however, read stylistically different from a conventional translation.

This Springer imprint is published by the registered company Springer Nature Singapore Pte Ltd.
The registered company address is: 152 Beach Road, #21-01/04 Gateway East, Singapore 189721, Singapore

Preface

In today's digital age, it's hard to say that computer vision is a mysterious, unknown high-tech field, as applications such as selfie beautification, facial recognition, and assisted driving have long entered our daily lives. Computer vision is leading us toward the gateway to an intelligent future.

From 2019 to 2020, one of the authors of this book, Prof. Wei Shen, taught a course on computer vision in the Department of Computer Science at Johns Hopkins University in the United States. Starting from 2021, Wei Shen continues to teach the course on computer vision for the classes of Artificial Intelligence (Pilot Program for Outstanding Talents) at Shanghai Jiao Tong University. During his teaching, he found that learners face two main challenges in studying computer vision. On the one hand, computer vision encompasses knowledge from multiple fields, including image processing, pattern recognition, geometric reconstruction, and deep learning. The vast knowledge system poses a challenge for learners to master the entire knowledge system of computer vision. Many learners, even young computer vision researchers, are often only proficient in a particular subfield of computer vision and know little about other subfields. On the other hand, computer vision is a field with high requirements for engineering implementation. Understanding the principles of computer vision algorithms does not necessarily mean that they can be programmed to achieve the desired results. To help learners cope with these challenges in learning computer vision, the author has written this book, *Hands-On Computer Vision*. In response to the first challenge, the author refers to the knowledge system architecture in Prof. Richard Szeliski's book *Computer Vision: Algorithms and Applications* and combines his teaching experience to divide the content of this book into four parts: Introduction to Computer Vision, Image Processing, Visual Recognition, and Scene Reconstruction. Parts I and II are the foundation for the latter two, which represent two types of computer vision tasks. Part III is the semantic understanding of image content, and Part IV is the reconstruction of the geometric structure of the scene in the image. The author hopes to cover all the content of computer vision through the division and connection of these four parts. In response to the second challenge, the author wrote this book directly in the form of Python Notebook, presenting the algorithm principles and runnable code together. In this way, learners can quickly implement the learned computer vision algorithms, forming a closed loop of algorithm principles and experimental results.

China is not short of good computer vision textbooks. The *Computer Vision: Algorithms and Applications* translated by Prof. Haizhou Ai and the *Deep Learning and Computer Vision: Algorithm Principles, Framework Applications, and Code Implementation* compiled by Prof. Yun Ye are excellent introductory books. This book strives to make some breakthroughs in terms of the coverage of knowledge points and the combination of theory and practice. On the one hand, this book covers as many knowledge points of computer vision as possible, especially classical computer vision, because many of its ideas are still very useful today; on the other hand, this book leads readers into the world of computer vision with numerous examples and codes, improving self-learning efficiency and assisting classroom teaching. It is hoped that this book can contribute to the cultivation of computer vision talents in our country.

Content Arrangement

Computer vision is an application-oriented discipline. Different applications correspond to different computer vision tasks; thus, the organization of this book is based on these computer vision tasks. Based on the author's understanding of computer vision, computer vision tasks are divided into three categories: image processing, visual recognition, and scene reconstruction. Since the input of computer vision systems is images or videos, it is necessary to first process the images, which is also the basis for the other two types of tasks. The content of image processing in this book includes: convolution, image filtering, template matching, edge detection, corner detection, SIFT feature detection, image stitching, and image segmentation. These image processing tasks are also often referred to as low-level vision tasks. In this part, we will introduce classic image processing algorithms. Based on image processing, we can understand the semantic content in the image; these tasks are called visual recognition tasks, also known as high-level vision tasks. The content of visual recognition in this book includes: image classification, semantic segmentation, object detection, instance segmentation, human pose estimation, and action recognition. In this part, we will mainly introduce visual recognition algorithms based on deep learning. In addition, we can also reconstruct the three-dimensional structure of the scene in the image. These tasks are called scene reconstruction. The content of scene reconstruction in this book includes: camera calibration, motion field and optical flow, parallel binocular vision, and 3D reconstruction. In this part, we will introduce scene reconstruction algorithms based on geometry.

How to Use This Book

Each chapter of this book is composed of a Python Notebook, which elaborates on the definitions, theoretical analysis, algorithmic processes, and runnable code related to computer vision. Readers can choose to read the parts they are interested in according to their needs. For example, readers who only want to learn the overall ideas of each algorithm without paying attention to the specific implementation details can read only the text parts excluding the code; readers who already understand the algorithm principles and just want to practice coding can focus on the specific implementation part of the code.

This book is primarily intended for university students (both undergraduates and graduates), teachers, corporate researchers, and engineers who are interested in computer vision. Before reading this book, readers should be familiar with some basic mathematical concepts and foundational knowledge of mathematical statistics, such as matrix operations, probability distributions, and numerical analysis techniques.

This book serves as an introductory text for computer vision and can also be used as a textbook or supplementary material for computer vision courses in universities. The code provided in this book is written in Python 3, and readers need to have a certain foundation in Python programming. We provide brief explanations of the Python libraries used in this book. Each example code includes variables that readers can set themselves, making it easy for readers to modify and observe the corresponding results, thereby deepening their understanding of the algorithms. We try to comment on some key code as much as possible, but we are well aware that we cannot explain every line of code clearly. We encourage readers to think more during the code learning process, explore additional resources, and pursue full understanding. The source code of this book can be downloaded from the repository at https://github.com/boyu-ai/Hands-on-CV. We have recorded video courses for this book. Readers can scan the QR codes in the book to access them or study the materials directly on the website https://hcv.boyuai.com.

On the basis of getting started with computer vision, if readers are interested in further understanding deep learning, data structures and algorithms, machine learning, natural language processing, or reinforcement learning in a hands-on learning format, we recommend reading *Hands-on Deep Learning*, *Hands-on Data Structures and Algorithms*, *Hands-on Machine Learning*, *Hands-on Natural Language Processing*, and *Hands-on Reinforcement Learning*, respectively.

Due to limited abilities and energy, there may be some minor issues in the process of writing this book. If there are any inaccuracies, we sincerely ask readers to criticize and correct them so that we can revise and improve in the next edition. We hope that every reader can gain something after studying this book. Perhaps it can help readers understand the overall ideas and model principles of computer vision, or it can help readers practice computer vision coding more proficiently, or it can help readers open the door to interest in computer vision and conduct more in-depth computer vision research. Regardless of which one, it is a great honor for us.

Acknowledgements

We sincerely thank the students of the DeepVision Lab at the Artificial Intelligence Institute of Shanghai Jiao Tong University for their outstanding contributions to this book. We thank the students of the 2022 class of Artificial Intelligence (Pilot Class for Outstanding Talents) at Shanghai Jiao Tong University for drawing some of the illustrations in this book, including Yidan Cui, Tianxing Wu, Yuan Fang, Yunlan Li, and Zifeng Li, etc. In addition, Liang Yin and Yuan Tian from Boyu Education reviewed this book and provided very valuable suggestions, for which we express our gratitude. Wei Shen is also supported by NSFC 62322604.

Shanghai, China

Wei Shen
Chongjie Si
Chen Yang
Yong Yu

Contents

Part I
Introduction to Computer Vision

Chapter 1
Introduction to Computer Vision

1.1 What Is Computer Vision?

Dear reader, welcome to the world of computer vision. What comes to mind when you hear the term "computer vision"? You might think of intelligent robots in sci-fi movies that can automatically recognize targets, or Mars rovers that can roam autonomously, or even facial recognition access control and face payment systems that have entered our lives. Indeed, these are the technologies that computer vision aims to achieve or has already achieved.

Human exploration of computer vision originates from our understanding of biological vision and our fascination with artificial intelligence robots. As humans, we can easily perceive our surrounding three-dimensional world, understand and recognize the visual information we receive. As shown in Fig. 1.1, we humans use our eyes as visual sensors, project scenes onto the retina for imaging, and then use our brains as analyzers to analyze the images. Through the analysis of our brains, we can understand the content expressed by the scene, know that the scene is an evening view; we can recognize targets in the scene, such as white tigers, clouds, etc.; we can also perceive the three-dimensional geometric structure in the scene, knowing the distance relationship between various targets. Note that vision is not just the process of seeing, but more importantly, the process of analysis. Thanks to our unparalleled brains, the human visual system is very powerful. So, can computers also have a visual system like humans? As shown in Fig. 1.1, analogous to the human visual system, the computer vision system uses a camera as a visual sensor and a computer as an analyzer. Since the human brain is too complex and its analysis mechanism has not been fully understood, we do not require computers to completely mimic the analysis process of the human brain. Instead, we treat the entire computer vision system as a black box, requiring that under the same input, the output of the computer vision system is the same as that of the human visual system. Since the images or videos usually obtained by cameras are the input, the goal of computer vision is to analyze the properties of the real world from these images or videos, such as detecting

W. Shen et al., *Hands-On Computer Vision*,
https://doi.org/10.1007/978-981-95-4835-4_1

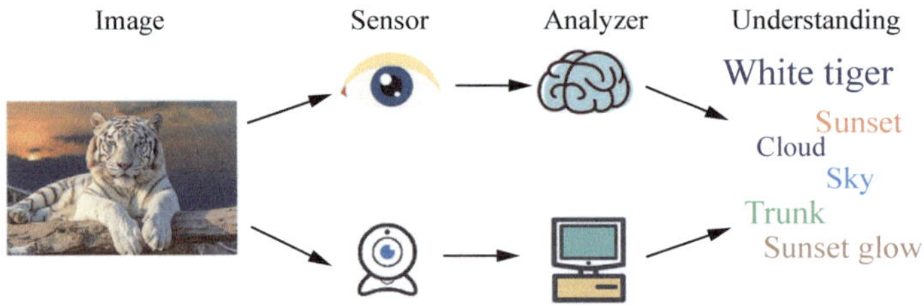

Fig. 1.1 Human visual system (above) and computer vision system (below)

and recognizing targets in the scene or reconstructing the three-dimensional structure of the scene. The analysis results need to be consistent with the analysis results of human vision.

1.2 Why Do We Need Computer Vision?

Most of the information received by humans comes from vision. As carriers of visual information, images and videos contain a huge amount of information, and each image can be said to tell a story. With the development of mobile terminals and the Internet, we can easily access and retrieve massive amounts of images and videos. If computers can have a visual system like humans and quickly analyze and understand the content of these massive images and videos, it will undoubtedly greatly improve our quality of life. Today, computer vision technology is no longer science fiction, but has been applied to our lives and has begun to play a role. Here are some typical applications of computer vision.

(1) Face detection and recognition. Face detection has long been used in digital cameras to help focus on faces. Face recognition is now widely used in train passenger ticket checking systems, personal computer and laptop login systems, etc.
(2) Optical character recognition (OCR). OCR technology is now widely used in license plate recognition (automatically and quickly determining the time a vehicle enters and leaves a site) and check recognition (scanning checks with a mobile app to deposit check amounts).
(3) Panoramic image stitching. Today's smartphones have panoramic image shooting functions. With a simple sweep of the phone, you can capture panoramic images.
(4) 3D modeling. Some mobile apps have already implemented 3D modeling functions. By taking multi-angle shots of a target with a phone, you can reconstruct the 3D model of the target.
(5) Video conference background blurring. Video conferencing software usually provides a background blurring function, which uses image segmentation technology in computer vision.

(6) Driver assistance systems. Many cars are now equipped with driver assistance systems. These systems integrate object detection, image segmentation, and other computer vision technologies to achieve lane detection, obstacle detection, distance measurement, etc., enhancing driving safety. Researchers in computer vision are now working to upgrade driver assistance systems to autonomous driving systems to achieve self-driving cars.
(7) Assisting medical imaging diagnosis. Medical imaging, such as X-rays, ultrasound, computer tomography (CT), and magnetic resonance imaging (MRI), which can help doctors diagnose patients' conditions in a non-invasive way. Today's auxiliary medical imaging diagnostic systems have integrated many computer vision technologies (such as semantic segmentation), achieving functions such as lesion area detection and disease prediction, thereby reducing the workload of doctors.

1.3 Challenges and Difficulties in Computer Vision

Although computer vision has been implemented in some specific scenarios, it remains an unsolved problem in general situations. Our requirement for general computer vision, that is, the output of the computer vision system, is consistent with the output of the human visual system under the same input, does not seem high. This is because humans have become accustomed to their ability to analyze visual information. However, we must emphasize that achieving general computer vision is very difficult, mainly because computer vision faces a semantic gap. For the same image, what we humans see is semantically meaningful content. For example, in Fig. 1.2, we can easily segment the main subject in the image, knowing that this is a camel, and part of its body is covered by a pile of weeds; but for the computer, what it "sees" is just a meaningless numerical matrix (images are stored in digital form in the computer). The association between this numerical matrix and the semantic information we see is obviously not direct, i.e., there is a huge gap between them, which is called semantic gap.

To achieve computer vision, it is necessary to narrow this semantic gap, but due to many factors, this task becomes very challenging. Figure 1.3 lists some of these challenging factors.

(1) Illumination change: Changes in illumination will change the appearance of the object after imaging, increasing the difficulty of target recognition.
(2) Viewpoint change: Changes in viewpoint will also change the appearance of the object after imaging, increasing the difficulty of target recognition.
(3) Scale variation: Human vision can adaptively capture objects of multiple scales, while computers often can only discover objects of different scales through multi-scale search.
(4) Intraclass variation: The appearance of objects within the same class may vary greatly, as shown in Fig. 1.3 with two chairs. Humans can use knowledge to infer that these two objects are chairs, but this is too difficult for computers.

(a) What humans see

254	152	154	56	72	78	96	98
120	187	192	143	176	113	131	127
162	172	196	124	175	123	122	116
223	198	230	162	159	92	27	85
83	77	73	140	144	201	240	159
165	82	76	45	18	64	165	57
	58	90	70	68	89	201	78
79	16	37	135	173	126	136	157

(b) What computers see

Fig. 1.2 Example of semantic gap

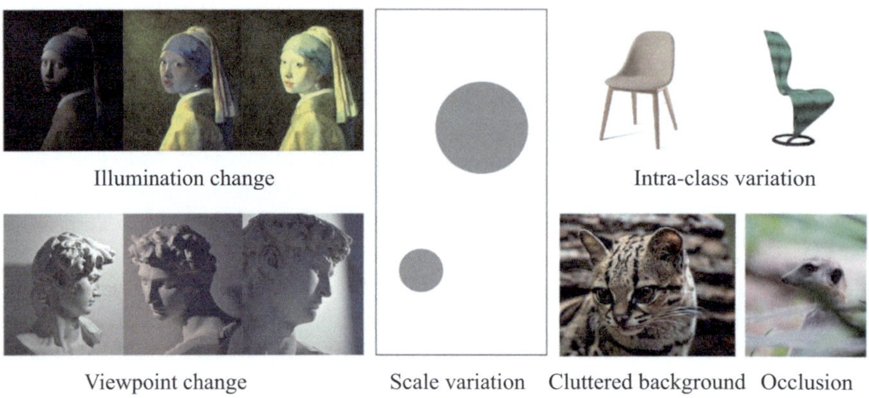

Fig. 1.3 Challenging factors affecting computer vision

(5) Cluttered background: Interference from a cluttered background can make it difficult to segment the foreground object, especially when the textures of the foreground and background are similar.

(6) Occlusion: Occlusion can cause part of the object to be missing, thereby increasing the difficulty of target recognition. Human vision will automatically "fill in" the missing parts, while it is difficult for computers to achieve this "fill in".

1.4 History and Development of Computer Vision

Figure 1.4 shows the milestones in the history of computer vision development. The upper half of the figure is the development history of theories and methods in computer vision. Since computer vision systems process visual information, that is, images, the development of computer vision cannot be separated from the support of digital image data. The lower half of Fig. 1.4 shows the development of image data.

In 1959, neurophysiologists David Hubel and Torsten Wiesel discovered through cat vision experiments that the biological visual system integrates information from simple to complex. They won the 1981 Nobel Prize in Physiology or Medicine for this research result, which also promoted the breakthrough development of computer vision technology 40 years later. In 1957, Russell Kirsch and his colleagues from the American Standards Association (ASA, now the American National Standards Institute, ANSI) developed a device that could convert images into discrete values that could be read by machines—this was the first digital image scanner, making it possible to process digital images. The first scanned digital photo was a photo of his son, which is now in the Portland Art Museum. In 1963, American engineer Lawrence Roberts described the process of extracting three-dimensional information from two-dimensional pictures in his doctoral thesis, which is considered one of the pioneers of modern computer vision, initiating computer vision research aimed at understanding three-dimensional scenes. In 1966, Professor Seymour Papert of the MIT Artificial Intelligence Laboratory decided to launch a summer vision project and solve computer vision problems within a few months. He organized students to design a platform that could automatically perform background/foreground segmentation. Although unsuccessful, this is a sign of the formal birth of computer vision as a scientific field. Among the students who participated in this summer project was a person named David Marr. In 1977, David Marr completed his work "Vision: A Computational Investigation into the Human Representation and Processing of

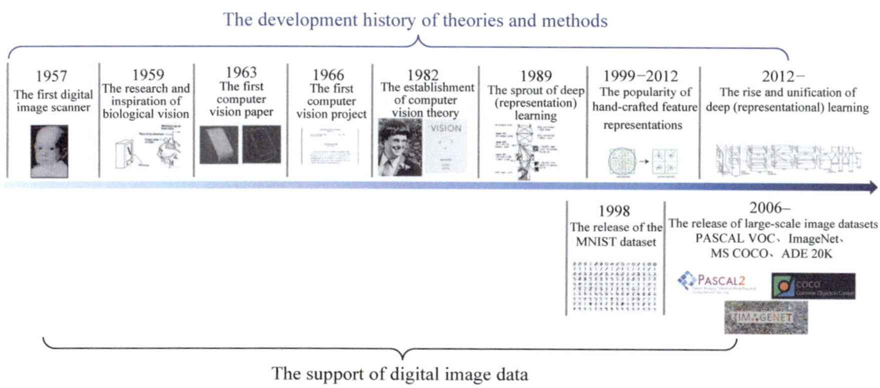

Fig. 1.4 History of computer vision development

Visual Information".[1] *Vision: A computational investigation into the human representation and processing of visual information* (see footnote 1), proposed a multi-level visual information processing framework; at the same time, proposed a three-level hypothesis for the processing process of the visual system: computational theory, representation and algorithm, and hardware implementation.

The concept of representation is very advanced, and representation is the transformation of the original image into a form that is easy for computers to understand. The research of computer vision has always been seeking better representations, and each revolutionary innovation in representation has greatly advanced computer vision technology. David Marr passed away from leukemia shortly after becoming a full professor at MIT, at the age of only 35. This was undoubtedly a major loss for the field of computer vision. Fortunately, his published works have become treasures in the field of computer vision. The highest honor in the direction of computer vision research is also named the Marr Prize. In 1989, Yann LeCun proposed a three-layer convolutional neural network (CNN) for handwritten digit recognition. This was the first deep learning method used for computer vision, sowing the seeds for such methods. Unfortunately, these methods were not given much attention for a long time. In 1998, he improved this network and integrated the SD-1 and SD-3 datasets from the National Institute of Standards and Technology (NIST), releasing the MNIST handwritten digit dataset. The improved network, known as LeNet-5, already has all the basic elements of modern convolutional neural networks. But at that time, more people were focusing on hand-crafted feature representations. In 1999, Professor David G. Lowe of the University of British Columbia proposed the Scale-Invariant Feature Transform (SIFT), designing scale-invariant, rotation-invariant image gradient histograms as representations of image keypoints for tasks such as image matching and 3D reconstruction. In 2001, Microsoft engineer Paul Viola proposed Harr features, a grayscale description of images based on multi-scale templates, combined with the Adaboost classifier, to implement the first practical face detector. In 2003, Professor Andrew Zisserman of Oxford University, inspired by the bag-of-words model in the field of text retrieval, proposed the bag of features (BoF),[2] using the frequency of visual words as a representation for tasks such as image classification and image retrieval. In 2005, Bill Triggs, a researcher at the French National Institute for Research in Computer Science and Automation (INRIA), proposed the Histogram of Oriented Gradients (HOG), similar to SIFT, for object detection. During the same period, more and more large-scale image datasets were established for computer vision tasks, including the PASCAL VOC dataset, ImageNet dataset, MS COCO dataset, and ADE20K dataset, etc. These large-scale datasets also laid the groundwork for the rise of deep representation learning methods.

In 2012, the field of computer vision underwent a revolution. Geoffrey Hinton and his students proposed AlexNet—a deep convolutional neural network consisting of 5 convolutional layers and 3 fully connected layers, which won the 2012 ImageNet

[1] The English version was published in 1982.

[2] The bag of features originates from the bag-of-words model in text processing, where words are replaced with image blocks.

competition and had an error rate 10.8% lower than the second place (non-deep learning method). This marked the beginning of the deep learning era in computer vision! Deep learning representations began to replace hand-crafted feature representations. Geoffrey Hinton and Yann LeCun jointly won the 2018 Turing Award. In 2015, Professor Trevor Darrell of the University of California, Berkeley, and his student Jonathan Long, among others, proposed the Fully Convolutional Network (FCN), extending deep learning to other visual tasks such as semantic segmentation. In 2016, Kaiming He, then a researcher at Microsoft Research Asia, proposed ResNet—a convolutional neural network that can stack a large number of layers, which won the 2015 ImageNet competition, marking the beginning of the era of deep learning dominance in the field of computer vision!

1.5 Mathematical Notation Conventions for Variables in Computer Vision

Methods in computer vision often involve various types of variables, such as scalars, vectors, matrices, etc. The mathematical symbols for these variables are not the same in different books. This book first makes a unified convention for the mathematical symbols of these variables to facilitate subsequent descriptions of methods.

In this book, scalars are represented by italicized uppercase or lowercase letters or strings, such as K and k. Vectors are represented by bold italic lowercase letters, such as $\boldsymbol{v}$; vectors are usually assumed to be column vectors, such as $\boldsymbol{v} = [x\ y]^{\mathrm{T}}$; $v(i)$ is the ith element in the vector. Matrices are represented by bold italic uppercase letters, such as $\boldsymbol{M}$; $M(i, j)$ represents the element in the ith row and jth column of the matrix; elements in the matrix can also be defined in the order of column-first indexing as $M(i)$ representing the ith element. Higher-order tensors are represented by bold italic uppercase letters, such as $\boldsymbol{T}$; the indexing of elements in tensors follows the same pattern as for vectors and matrices. Sets are represented by script uppercase letters, such as $\mathcal{S}$. Spaces are represented by double-struck uppercase letters, such as $\mathbb{R}$. Functions are represented by italic lowercase letters, with variables enclosed in parentheses and separated by commas, such as $f(x, y)$. Specifically, a point P on a two-dimensional plane is usually represented as a comma-separated list in parentheses (x, y), corresponding to a two-dimensional vector $\boldsymbol{p} = (x, y)$ originating from the origin. This correspondence can be extended to higher dimensions.

1.6 Summary

This chapter introduces the concept of computer vision by drawing analogies between human vision and computer vision; it highlights the importance of computer vision by listing its practical applications; it demonstrates the challenges of implementing a general-purpose computer vision system; and it presents the history of computer vision by introducing its milestones.

Next, we will dive in, learning about computer vision through theoretical study and coding practice according to the content arrangement. Let's get started!

Part II
Image Processing

Chapter 2
Convolution

2.1 Introduction

Nowadays in the field of computer vision, convolution is probably the most frequently appearing term. This is because convolutional neural networks are widely used to solve various computer vision tasks and have become a default tool in the field of computer vision. However, the term convolution does not come from the field of computer science, but from the field of signal processing. Convolution is an important operation in signal processing, used to calculate the output response of a linear system to an input signal. What is convolution? As the name suggests, it is to "flip" first, then "accumulate". In professional terms, the input of convolution is two functions, one is the input signal function, the other is the system function; the convolution operation first flips one function, then slides it over the other function for accumulation, and finally gets the output result, as shown in Fig. 2.1. In the case of continuous functions, superposition refers to the integration of the product of two functions, while in the discrete case it is the weighted sum of functions, for simplicity, it is collectively referred to as superposition.

So, what is the significance of such an operation as convolution? Why do we need to flip the input function first? Textbooks on signal processing usually explain it this way: the result of convolution is not only related to the current input signal response value, but also to the input response value of the signal at all past moments. This shows that convolution not only considers the current situation, but also considers the situation at past moments. It is a kind of accumulation of corresponding effects, so there is a process of "flipping" first and then "accumulating". This description is still very abstract, let's take an example from real life. Imagine you are standing by a pond, throwing stones into the pond. Throw a stone, and there will be ripples in the pond, then the ripples slowly fade away, and the water surface becomes calm again. Throwing stones is the input signal, and the resulting ripples are the response to the input. So what if you keep throwing stones into the pond at a certain speed? In this case, how to calculate the size of the water wave at a certain place on the water surface

W. Shen et al., *Hands-On Computer Vision*,
https://doi.org/10.1007/978-981-95-4835-4_2

(a) Input signal function (b) System function (c) Flipping (d) Sliding and accumulating

Fig. 2.1 Convolution of input signal function and system function

at a certain moment? According to common sense, we know that the size of the water wave at a certain place at the current moment is not only related to the water wave caused by the stone thrown at the current moment, but also related to the water waves caused by all the stones thrown before, it is the cumulative result of these water waves. This is the process of "flipping" first and then "accumulating", "flipping" considers all inputs related to the current input, and "accumulating" accumulates the effects of these inputs.

Similarly, in image processing, the calculation of convolution is to weight the pixel values in the neighborhood of each pixel. Here, the spatial neighborhood corresponds to the moments before, and after in time, the image is the input signal function, the weighted weight is the system function, and the result of convolution is the response of the system function to the input image, that is, the image feature. It can be seen that convolving an image is the process of extracting image features, which is also the basis of image recognition and other computer vision tasks.

In this chapter, we introduce the mathematical definition and code implementation of convolution with one-dimensional convolution as the lead, then extend to two-dimensional convolution, and introduce the convolution operation on images.

2.2 One-Dimensional Convolution

Mathematically speaking, convolution is an operation like addition, subtraction, multiplication, and division. The fundamental operation of its operation is to first shift one of the two functions ($f(\cdot)$ and $k(\cdot)$), then multiply it with the other function and accumulate it. In this operation process, because it involves integration or series operations, it looks very complicated. For functions defined in the continuous domain, according to the definition of convolution, the formula for one-dimensional convolution is as follows:

$$g(x) = f(x) * k(x) = \int_{-\infty}^{\infty} f(\tau)k(x-\tau)\mathrm{d}\tau.$$

In the above formula, the input of one-dimensional convolution is a one-dimensional signal $f(x)$ and a one-dimensional convolution kernel $k(x)$; in signal processing, $f(x)$ is the input signal function, $k(x)$ is the system function. It is easy to see that convolution is the integration of τ within the range of $(-\infty, \infty)$, and the object of integration is the product of $f(\tau)$ and $k(x-\tau)$. It should be noted that only $k(x-\tau)$ in the right side of the equation involves x, while the rest is only related to τ.

According to the formula of one-dimensional continuous convolution, the calculation steps of convolution operation can be obtained.

(1) Transformation: Change the horizontal axis of the input signal function, with the independent variable changing from x to τ.
(2) Flip: Flip one of the functions.
(3) Translation: The flipped function is translated with the variable τ to obtain $k(x-\tau)$. If $\tau > 0$, then move to the right, otherwise move to the left.
(4) Multiply: Multiply $f(\tau)$ and $k(x-\tau)$.
(5) Integral: The area under the curve of the product of $f(\tau)$ and $k(x-\tau)$ is the convolution value at position x.

Convolution as an operation has the following properties.

(1) Commutative law: $f(x) * k(x) = k(x) * f(x)$.∘
(2) Associative law: $[f(x) * g(x)] * k(x) = f(x) * [g(x) * k(x)]$.
(3) Distributive law: $f(x) * [g(x) + k(x)] = f(x) * g(x) + f(x) * k(x)$.

One-dimensional continuous convolution plays a pivotal role in audio processing and other areas. However, the signals that computers can usually handle are not continuous but discrete, so next, we introduce the one-dimensional convolution of discrete functions.

According to the definition of convolution, the one-dimensional convolution formula of discrete functions is as follows:

$$g(i) = f(i) * k(i) = \sum_{l} f(l)k(i-l),$$

where l traverses the definition domain of $f(i)$. Unlike one-dimensional continuous convolution, the input signal and convolution kernel are discrete functions $f(i)$ and $k(i)$ (usually represented by arrays or vectors), and the integral becomes a sum. The length of the convolution kernel is generally odd, which is designed for symmetry. In most cases, the length of the input signal function $f(i)$ is much greater than the length of the convolution kernel $k(i)$. Figure 2.2 is the calculation process of one-dimensional discrete convolution.

Based on the above definition, we can derive the calculation steps of one-dimensional discrete convolution.

(1) Transformation: Change the horizontal coordinate of the input signal function, the independent variable changes from i to l.
(2) Flip: Flip one of the functions.
(3) Translation: The flipped function moves with the variable l, resulting in $k(i-l)$. If $l > 0$, then move to the right, otherwise move to the left, and l is an integer.
(4) Multiplication: Multiply $f(l)$ and $k(i-l)$.

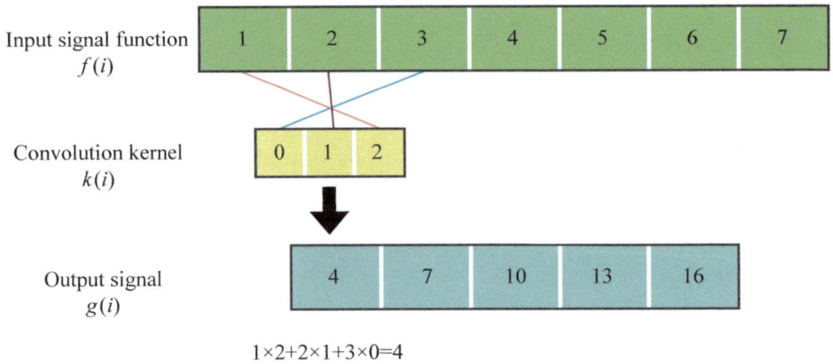

Fig. 2.2 Calculation of one-dimensional discrete convolution

(5) Accumulation: The accumulated value of the product of $f(l)$ and $k(i-l)$ is the convolution value at i the convolution value of the position.

From Fig. 2.2, it is not difficult to conclude that for discrete variables, convolution can be understood as "flipping and summing", that is, multiplying and then summing. In addition, it is important to consider how the length of the output signal relates to the length of input signal and the size of convolution kernel.

Assume the length of the input signal is m, the size of the convolution kernel is n, according to the method shown in Fig. 2.2, it is easy to get the length of the output signal is $m - n + 1$. But does this mean that the output length will get smaller and smaller with repeated convolution of an input signal?

In fact, this situation may indeed exist. Therefore, to prevent this situation, the input signal is usually subjected to a zero-padding operation. For the input, the number "0" is added to the left of "1" and the right of "7", as shown in Fig. 2.3; thus, the length of the input signal increases by 2 and the length of the corresponding output signal also increases. The zero-padding operation allows the length of the output signal to remain consistent with the input signal. Moreover, if two "0"s are added to both sides of the input signal in the figure, the length of the output signal is greater than the length of the input signal. Generally, the number of zero-padding on one side of the input signal is less than the size of the convolution kernel. This is because when the number of zeros is equal to or greater than the length of the convolution kernel, the result of the convolution is 0, which is equivalent to zero-padding the output signal, which is meaningless. A more intuitive zero-padding operation can be seen in two-dimensional convolution.

In fact, in addition to the zero-padding operation that can achieve changes in the length of the output signal, the length of the output signal can also be changed by changing the stride (stride) of the convolution kernel each time it moves. The stride here refers to the distance the convolution kernel moves each time. For example,

Fig. 2.3 Zero-padding of the input signal

using a convolution kernel with a stride of 2 to convolve the input signal in Fig. 2.3, after the convolution is completed at the position of "0", the next convolution will be performed directly at the position of "3". Obviously, a total of 4 convolution operations will be performed at this time, so the length of the output signal is 4. Assuming the stride of the convolution kernel is s, the number of zero-padding on each side of the input signal is p, the length of the output signal can be obtained as $\frac{m-n+2p}{s}+1$. This formula is also applicable in two-dimensional convolution.

Next, we will write a one-dimensional convolution function. We use an array to represent the discrete function and zero-pad the input signal. The number of zero-padding is the size of the convolution kernel minus 1. The stride of the convolution kernel is set to 1, then the length of the output signal is $m+n-1$.

```
import matplotlib.pyplot as plt
# One-dimensional convolution
class conv_1d():
    def __init__(self, a, b):
     # Input signal
     self.a = a
     # Convolution kernel
     self.b = b
     # Coordinates of the input signal, default starts from 0.
     self.ax = [i for i in range(len(a))]
    # Coordinates of the convolution kernel, default starts from 0.
     self.bx = [i for i in range(len(b))]
    def conv(self):
     lst1 = self.a
     lst2 = self.b
     l1 = len(lst1)
     l2 = len(lst2)
     lst1 = [0] * (l2 - 1) + lst1 + [0] * (l2 - 1)
     lst2.reverse()
     c = [0 for x in range(0, l1 + l2 - 1)]
     for i in range(l1 + l2 - 1):
        for j in range(l2):
          c[i] += lst1[i + j] * lst2[j]
         return c


    def plot(self):
     a = self.a
     b = self.b
     ax = self.ax
     bx = self.bx

                    #   To   view   the   results   more   intu-
itively, we plot a, b and the signal obtained
     # by their convolution separately
     plt.figure(1)
    # The figure contains 1 row and 2 columns of subplots, currently
drawing on
     # the first row and first column
     plt.subplot(1, 2, 1)
     plt.title('Input')
```

```
        plt.bar(ax, a, color='lightcoral', width=0.2)
        plt.plot(ax, a, color='lightcoral')
        plt.figure(1)
        # Currently drawing on the first row and second column
        plt.subplot(1, 2, 2)
        plt.title('Kernel')
        plt.bar(bx, b, color='lightgreen', width=0.2)
        # plt.plot(bx, b, color='lightgreen')

        # Calculate the output signal and its coordinates, and draw the
    graph
        c = self.conv()
        length = len(c)
        cx = [i for i in range(length)]
        plt.figure()
        plt.title('Output')
        plt.bar(cx, c, color='lightseagreen', width=0.2)
        plt.plot(cx, c, color='lightseagreen')
```

2.2.1 Impulse Signal

Now let's use an example to demonstrate the effect of the above convolution implementation. Convolve a triangular wave signal with different convolution kernels, and then observe the effect of the convolution.

```
# Define the input signal and convolution kernel
a = [0,1,2,3,2,1,0]

# Impulse function
k = [0,0,1,0,0]

conv = conv_1d(a, k)
conv.plot()
```

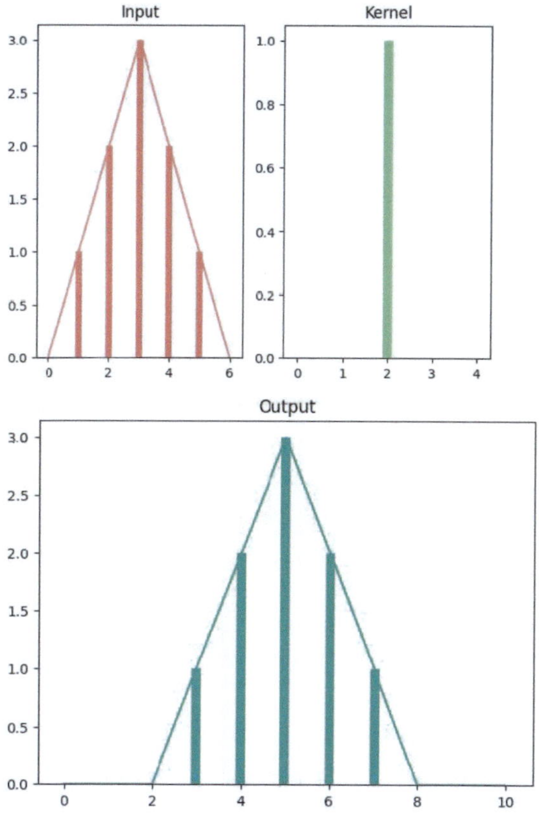

When the convolution kernel used is a unit impulse signal (the "area" equals 1, that is, a narrow pulse that only appears at one position), the input signal does not change after convolution. This is an important property of convolution.

2.2.2 *Square Wave Signal*

Let's change the convolution kernel and see what different effects the output will have.

```
# Define the input signal and convolution kernel
a = [0,1,2,3,2,1,0]
# Square wave signal
k = [1,1,1,1,1]
conv = conv_1d(a, k)
conv.plot()
```

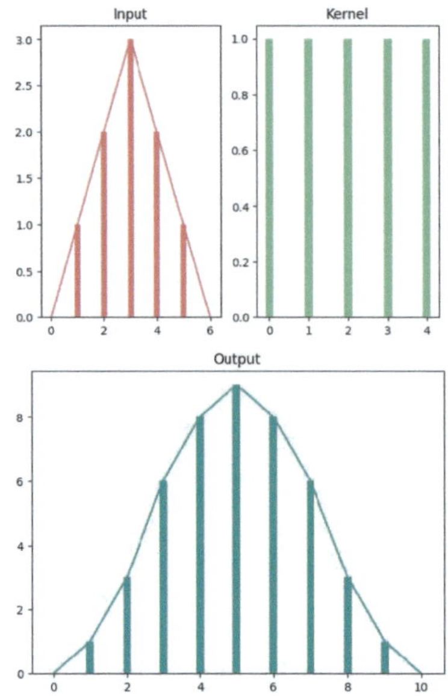

As you can see, convolving a triangular wave signal with a square wave signal has the effect of smoothing the triangular wave. Remember this phenomenon, it will be mentioned again later.

2.3 Two-Dimensional Convolution

In the field of computer vision, it is often necessary to process images, and convolution is a common image processing operation. A digital image can be regarded as a two-dimensional discrete function in space, represented as $I(i, j)$. Corresponding to a one-dimensional discrete function, a matrix can be used to represent this two-dimensional discrete function of an image. Assuming the image height is H, the width is W, and the convolution kernel is set to $K(i, j)$, the formula for two-dimensional convolution can be obtained:

$$G(i,j) = I(i,j) * K(i,j) = \sum_{i'=1}^{H} \sum_{j'=1}^{W} I\left(i',j'\right) K\left(i-i',j-j'\right).$$

The concept of convolution extends from one dimension to two dimensions, and the result is very similar, except that it becomes a "convolution" operation of matrices. Flipping then summing is the discrete version of convolution, where convolution is computed by integral, and flipping then summing is computed by the multiplication and addition of points. Here is a process of convolving a two-dimensional image (matrix) with a two-dimensional convolution kernel.

(1) Flip the matrix corresponding to the two-dimensional convolution kernel horizontally and vertically.
(2) Align this convolution kernel matrix with the top-left corner of the input image.
(3) Multiply each element of the convolution kernel matrix by each aligned element in the input image and then add up all the products to get the current convolution result. Let this convolution kernel matrix slide on the input image, with a stride of s, and repeat the above calculation.

Figure 2.4 describes part of the calculation process of two-dimensional convolution. By sliding on the input image, the convolution output of the entire image is gradually obtained.

It is not difficult to find that due to the size limitation of the convolution kernel, we cannot directly convolve the pixel "1" in the top-left corner of the input image in Fig. 2.4. Therefore, when calculating the output results of the edge row and column, zero-padding is generally performed on the original matrix, and then the convolution operation of the matrix is performed, as shown in Fig. 2.5.

For an input image of $H \times W$, the number of layers we pad with zeros is p, using a convolution kernel of stride s and size $k \times k$ to convolve it, then the number of rows in the output matrix is $\frac{H-k+2p}{s}+1$, and the number of columns is $\frac{W-k+2p}{s}+1$. Note that the above process in Fig. 2.4 of performing two-dimensional convolution on images only considers the case where the image has only two dimensions (i.e., grayscale image), while in reality, images often have a third dimension, such as common color images, which have a shape of $H \times W \times 3$, considering each pixel corresponds to R, G, B these 3 channels; and hyperspectral images, which have a shape of $H \times W \times L$ $(L > 3)$, where each pixel corresponds to L channels, containing L spectral information corresponding to wavelengths. It can be seen that the more channels each pixel corresponds to, the richer the information the image may contain, so the third dimension is also called the feature dimension of the image. So how to do two-dimensional convolution for images with channel number $L > 1$? To perform two-dimensional convolution on an input image of $H \times W \times L$, the number of channels of the convolution kernel also needs to be L, that is, the number of channels of the two-dimensional convolution kernel is by default the same as the number

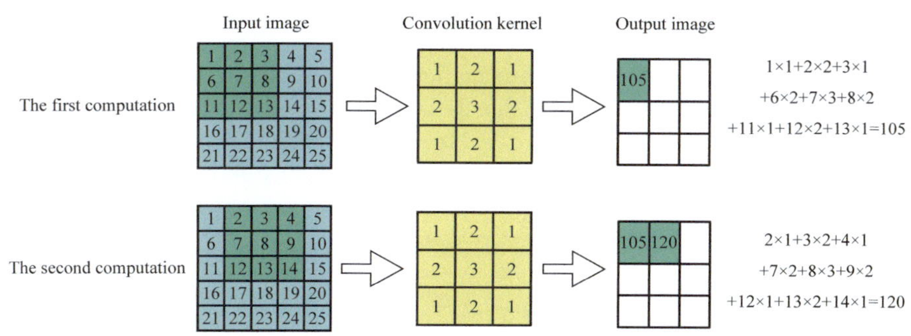

Fig. 2.4 Partial calculation process of two-dimensional convolution (stride is 1)

Fig. 2.5 Image zero-padding

Input image

0	0	0	0	0	0	0
0	1	2	3	4	5	0
0	6	7	8	9	10	0
0	11	12	13	14	15	0
0	16	17	18	19	20	0
0	21	22	23	24	25	0
0	0	0	0	0	0	0

of channels of the input image. Therefore, when we describe the size of a two-dimensional convolution kernel, we usually only mention the size of the two spatial dimensions, such as $k \times k$ convolution, but in fact the shape of the convolution kernel is $k \times k \times L$, L is determined by the number of channels of the input image. When $L > 1$, to perform $k \times k$ convolution on an input image of $H \times W \times L$, it can be achieved by the following steps: First, as previously described for two-dimensional convolution operations, for each channel corresponding to the $H \times W \times L$ input image, take the corresponding $k \times k$ The two-dimensional convolution kernel is convolved with it. This will result in L convolution results with the same spatial resolution and a channel number of 1. Then, these L convolution results are added element by element to obtain the required two-dimensional convolution result (this result is also called a feature map, a concept that will be frequently used in the second part of this book). For more content on the calculation of two-dimensional convolution of multi-channel images, please refer to "Hands-on Deep Learning".

Next, we start writing two-dimensional convolution. We will process an image and intuitively show the changes in the image before and after convolution. Similar to one-dimensional convolution, we also use impulse signals and square wave signals as convolution kernels. Note the implementation of two-dimensional impulse signals and two-dimensional square wave signals in the code. Here we directly call the library function cv2.filter2D() to perform two-dimensional convolution operations. We leave the code implementation of two-dimensional convolution as an exercise.

```
import matplotlib.pyplot as plt
import numpy as np
import cv2
import seaborn as sns
class conv_2d():
    def __init__(self, image, kernel):
     self.img = image
```

```
        self.k = kernel
      def plot(self):
        # Display input image
        plt.imshow(self.img[:, :, ::-1])
        plt.axis('off')
        plt.title('Input')
        plt.show()
        # Display convolution kernel
        fig = plt.figure(figsize=(2, 1.5))
        sns.heatmap(self.k)
        plt.axis('off')
        plt.title('Kernel')
    # Define two-dimensional convolution
      def convolution(self, data, k):
        # Directly call the library function for convolution operation
        return cv2.filter2D(data, -1, k)
    # Display two-dimensional convolution result
      def plot_conv(self):
        # Convolution process
        img_new = self.convolution(self.img, self.k)
        # Visualization of convolution result
        plt.figure()
        plt.imshow(img_new[:, :, ::-1])
        plt.title('Output')
        plt.axis('off')
return
```

For the convenience of subsequent chapters, we write a utils.py file and import the above code into this file.

2.3.1 Impulse Signal

Let's first observe the result of convolving an image with an impulse signal.

```
img = cv2.imread('lena.jpeg')
# Two-dimensional impulse convolution kernel
size = 15
k1 = np.zeros((size, size))
mid = (size-1) // 2
k1[mid][mid] = 1
# Display input image and convolution kernel
conv = conv_2d(img, k1)
conv.plot()
# Display convolution result
conv.plot_conv()
```

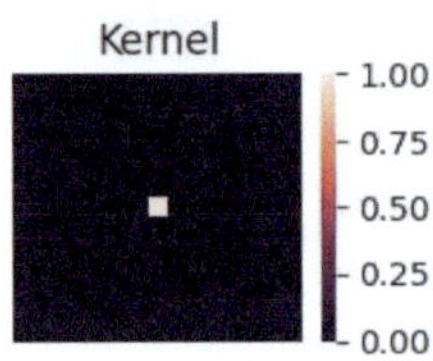

As can be seen from the results, convolving an image with a two-dimensional impulse function yields the same result as the original image. This is consistent with the results obtained from one-dimensional convolution.

2.3.2 Square Wave Signal

Let's observe the results of convolving an image with a square wave signal.

```
# Two-dimensional square wave convolution kernel
size = 15
# Because the size of the two-dimensional kernel func-
tion is n * n, we need to divide
# by (size * size) when implementing the square wave signal
k2 = 1/size/size * np.ones((size, size))
# Display the input image and the convolution kernel
conv = conv_2d(img, k2)
```

```
conv.plot()
# Display the convolution result
conv.plot_conv()
```

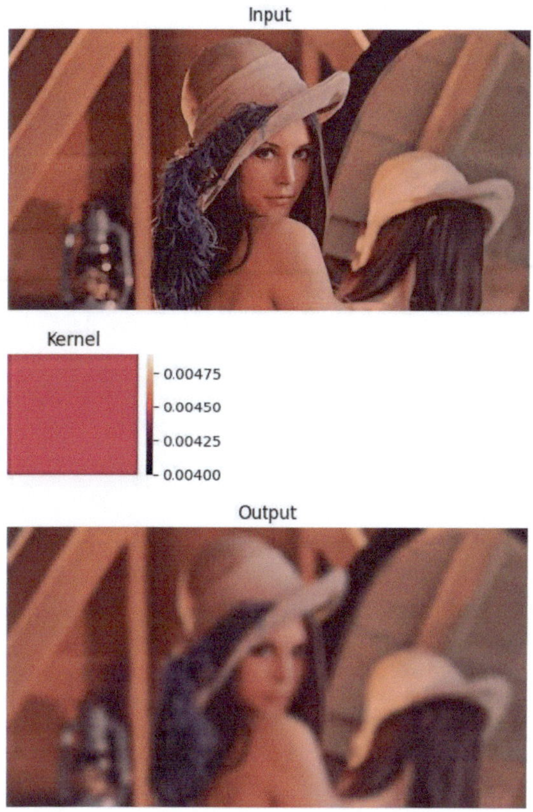

As can be seen from the results, using a square wave signal as the convolution kernel to convolve the image results in a smooth, blurred image. This is also consistent with our experimental results in one-dimensional convolution. Does this have a bit of an image processing flavor? Remember this result, we will further elaborate on its principle in later chapters.

2.4 Summary

Convolution is an important operation in the field of signal processing and is an essential technology in computer vision. In image processing, convolution not only considers the impact of a pixel but also considers the effect and influence of surrounding pixels on it, which makes the convolution operation can be the basis of filtering technology. In addition to one-dimensional and two-dimensional, convolution also has high-dimensional processing methods; interested readers can refer to relevant materials.

In the following chapters, we will further introduce the role of convolution in image processing.

Exercises

(1) Given an input sequence [1 3 4 5 4 3 1], calculate its convolution result with the convolution kernel [1 − 1].

(2) Given an input two-dimensional matrix $\begin{bmatrix} 133 & 95 & 71 & 71 & 62 \\ 133 & 92 & 62 & 71 & 62 \\ 146 & 120 & 62 & 55 & 55 \\ 139 & 146 & 117 & 112 & 117 \\ 139 & 139 & 139 & 139 & 139 \end{bmatrix}$, calculate its convolution result with the convolution kernel $\begin{bmatrix} 0 & 1 \\ -1 & 0 \end{bmatrix}$.

(3) Refer to the implementation of one-dimensional convolution, implement two-dimensional convolution, based on this implementation, complete the following tasks.

a. Calculate the convolution result of the input image and the convolution kernel in Fig. 2.4 (represented as a matrix).
b. Calculate the convolution result of the zero-padded input image and the convolution kernel in Fig. 2.5 (represented as a matrix).
c. Using the provided lena image, reproduce the image convolution experiments in Sects. 2.3.1 and 2.3.2, and compare with the experiments using library functions to see if the results are consistent.
d. Design a convolution kernel to apply a 10-pixel translation to an image in the bottom-right direction through convolution.

Chapter 3
Image Filtering

3.1 Introduction

Do you remember the result of convolving an image with a two-dimensional square wave signal in Chap. 2? Yes, the image was smoothed and blurred. This is what we call image filtering. Filtering is an important technique in image processing and has a wide range of applications in real life. Many people have used image processing software (such as Photoshop and Meitu XiuXiu) to retouch photos, beautify people in photos, and perform "skin smoothing", "acne removal", "spot removal", etc., as shown in Fig. 3.1. These retouching operations all rely on the support of image filtering technology.

The term "filtering" also comes from the field of signal processing. This term refers to the spectrum of the image, that is, the representation of the image signal in the frequency domain. You can simply understand the spectrum of the image as: areas in the image where pixel values change dramatically correspond to high-frequency information, and areas where pixel values do not change much correspond to low-frequency information. Filtering is the process of filtering out certain frequency information to change the image and achieve the desired image effect. Convolution of an image with a two-dimensional square wave signal makes the image smooth, i.e., making the changes of pixel values small, thus filtering out the high-frequency information in the image. This process is the process of image denoising. Of course, you can also do the opposite, enhance the high-frequency information in the image through filtering, thereby achieving image sharpening, that is, image deblurring. The function that implements specific filtering operations is usually called a filter.

In this chapter, we will introduce some typical filters. We will first introduce different filters from the perspective of image denoising, discuss their properties and denoising effects, and then introduce how to achieve image sharpening through filtering.

W. Shen et al., *Hands-On Computer Vision*,
https://doi.org/10.1007/978-981-95-4835-4_3

Fig. 3.1 Photo retouching by software

3.2 Image Noise

Let's first learn about two typical types of image noise—salt-and-pepper noise and Gaussian noise.

3.2.1 *Salt-and-Pepper Noise*

Salt-and-pepper noise is a common type of noise in digital images. The so-called salt and pepper refers to "pepper" as pixels with a value of 0 (black points) and "salt" as pixels with a value of 255 (white points). Salt-and-pepper noise refers to black and white pixels that randomly appear in the image, which may be caused by the image sensor suddenly being subjected to strong interference, causing errors in the analog-to-digital converter in the sensor. The algorithm for adding salt-and-pepper noise is relatively simple, just randomly add some completely black or white pixels to the image. Next, we will implement salt-and-pepper noise through programming.

```
# The utils function package file was written in Chapter 2, all func-
tions written in this book will be encapsulated into the utils func-
tion package
from utils import *
# Add salt and pepper noise
def add_Salt(img, pro):
   # img is the input image
   # pro is the ratio of salt and pepper noise
   # Add black pixels
   noise = np.random.uniform(0, 255, img[:, :, 0].shape)
   # mask is the noise adding mask
   mask = noise < pro * 255
   # Expand the dimension of mask
   mask = np.expand_dims(mask, axis=2)
   mask = np.repeat(mask, 3, axis=2)
   img = img * (1 - mask)
   # Add white pixels
```

```
    mask = noise > 255 - pro * 255
    mask = np.expand_dims(mask, axis=2)
    mask = np.repeat(mask, 3, axis=2)
    noise_img = 255 * mask + img * (1 - mask)
    return noise_img
img = cv2.imread('lenaface.jpg')
# Image with added salt and pepper noise
img_salt = add_Salt(img, 0.05)
plt.imshow(img_salt[:,:,::-1])
plt.axis('off')
plt.show()
```

3.2.2 *Gaussian Noise*

Gaussian noise refers to noise whose probability density function follows a Gaussian (normal) distribution. When taking photos at night, you may often find that the images are somewhat blurry compared to those taken in good daylight conditions. This blurriness is caused by Gaussian noise. The generation of Gaussian noise is usually due to insufficient brightness during shooting, the inherent noise and mutual influence of various components in the image sensor, or the image sensor operating at too high a temperature for a long period. Below, we will implement Gaussian noise by first randomly generating noise samples according to a two-dimensional Gaussian distribution, and then adding them to the image.

```
def add_Gaussian(img, sigma=20, mean=0):
    lab = cv2.cvtColor(img, cv2.COLOR_BGR2Lab)
    # Generate Gaussian noise
    noise = np.random.normal(mean, sigma, lab[:, :, 0].shape)
    lab = lab.astype(float)
    # Add Gaussian noise
    lab[:, :, 0] = lab[:, :, 0] + noise
    lab[:, :, 0] = np.clip(lab[:, :, 0], 0, 255)
    lab = lab.astype(np.uint8)
    noise_img = cv2.cvtColor(lab, cv2.COLOR_Lab2BGR)
    return noise_img
# Image with added Gaussian noise
```

```
img_gaussian = add_Gaussian(img)
plt.imshow(img_gaussian[:,:,::-1])
plt.axis('off')
plt.show()
```

In fact, salt-and-pepper noise and Gaussian noise can appear anywhere in our lives. In image beautification processing, facial "blemish removal" and "skin smoothing" are achieved by filtering out salt-and-pepper noise and Gaussian noise. Next, we will introduce several different filtering techniques based on practical examples.

3.3 Mean Filtering

When taking professional photos, people often request retouching, and "skin smoothing" is a common operation in this process. So how is "skin smoothing" achieved? It is done by making the face appear smoother. As mentioned in Sect. 3.1, doesn't convolving an image with a square wave signal make the image smoother? So yes, convolving a facial image with a square wave signal is one of the simplest ways to achieve "skin smoothing". But what is the underlying principle?

The mathematical form of a square wave signal as a convolution kernel is familiar to everyone, as shown in the following formula:

$$\boldsymbol{K} = \frac{1}{k^2}\begin{bmatrix} 1 & \cdots & 1 \\ \vdots & & \vdots \\ 1 & \cdots & 1 \end{bmatrix}_{k\times k},$$

where k is the size of the convolution kernel. Let the input image be $\boldsymbol{I}$, and the output image of convolving it with the above square wave signal as the convolution kernel is $\hat{\boldsymbol{I}}$. According to the convolution calculation formula in Chap. 2, we get the relationship between $\boldsymbol{I}$ and $\hat{\boldsymbol{I}}$:

$$\hat{I}(i,j) = I(i,j)*K(i,j) = \sum_{m=i-k}^{i-1}\sum_{n=j-k}^{j-1} I(m,n)K(i-m,j-n)$$

$$= \frac{1}{k^2} \sum_{m=i-k}^{i-1} \sum_{n=j-k}^{j-1} I(m, n).$$

As can be seen, convolving an image with a square wave signal is essentially averaging the pixels within each $k \times k$ neighborhood in the image. Therefore, the square wave convolution kernel is also known as a mean filter, where k is the size of the mean filter. As we know, averaging can reduce noise, and noise in images is generally where pixel values change abruptly, such as wrinkles on a face. By processing the image with mean filtering, these wrinkles can be removed, achieving "skin smoothing". The mean filter can remove high-frequency noise and only retain the low-frequency information of the image, so it is a low-pass filter, i.e., a filter that allows low-frequency information to pass. Next, we will apply mean filtering to the facial image with Gaussian noise generated in Sect. 3.2.2 and observe its effect.

```
# Mean filter size=3
size = 3
k3 = 1/size/size * np.ones((size, size))
# Display the input image and the filter kernel
conv_gaussian = conv_2d(img_gaussian, k3)
conv_gaussian.plot()
# Display the convolution result
conv_gaussian.plot_conv()
```

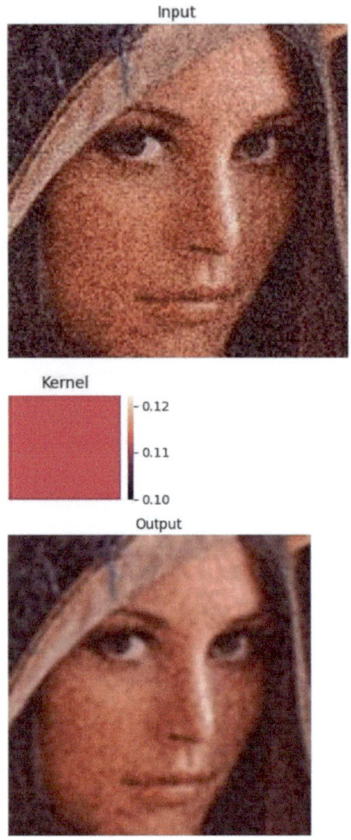

As can be seen, the image has become smoother, but the noise still exists. We increase the size of the mean filter and test again.

```
# Mean filter size=5
size = 5
k5 = 1/size/size * np.ones((size,size))
conv = conv_2d(img_gaussian, k5)
# Display the convolution result
conv.plot_conv()
# Mean filter size=9
size = 9
k9 = 1/size/size * np.ones((size, size))
conv = conv_2d(img_gaussian, k9)
# Display the convolution result
conv.plot_conv()
```

Output

Output

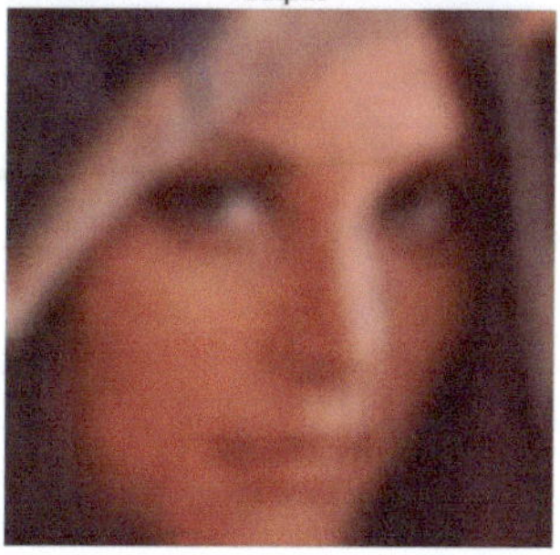

It can be clearly seen that when the size of the mean filter is 5, the noise basically disappears; but when the filter size is 9, the noise is eliminated, but the image also becomes blurry. Therefore, in the actual filtering process, it is necessary to choose an appropriate size for the mean filter to eliminate noise while retaining image features as much as possible.

Upon careful observation, it can be found that when using a mean filter to denoise an image, the output image has a very obvious "block effect", that is, there are very obvious block-like areas in the image. Is there any good way to solve this problem? This is where the Gaussian filter comes in handy.

3.4 Gaussian Filter

The Gaussian filter is widely used to eliminate image noise. Unlike the mean filter, the Gaussian filter performs a weighted average on each pixel in the neighborhood instead of a direct average, with the weights determined by the Gaussian distribution. Intuitively, the shape of the Gaussian filter is shown in Fig. 3.2.

The Gaussian kernel of the Gaussian filter is also a $k \times k$ matrix, denoted as $\boldsymbol{G}$; the value at each position (i, j) of this matrix is defined as follows:

$$G(i, j) = \frac{1}{2\pi\sigma^2} \mathrm{e}^{-\frac{i^2+j^2}{2\sigma^2}},$$

Fig. 3.2 Gaussian filter

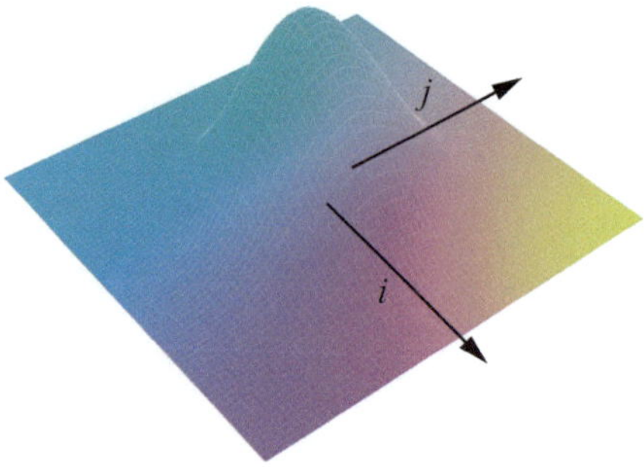

where $G(i, j)$ represents the weight of the Gaussian kernel at the displacement (i, j) from the center point of the filter; σ is the standard deviation of the Gaussian kernel. The larger the standard deviation, the larger the opening of the Gaussian kernel, and the greater the influence of distant pixels on the central pixel; the smaller the standard deviation, the smaller the opening of the Gaussian kernel, and the smaller the influence of distant pixels on the central pixel. The output image $\hat{\boldsymbol{I}}$ is obtained by Gaussian filtering the input image $\boldsymbol{I}$ with the above Gaussian kernel:

$$\hat{I}(i, j) = I(i, j) * G(i, j) = \sum_{m=i-k}^{i-1} \sum_{n=j-k}^{j-1} I(m, n) G(i - m, j - n).$$

According to the properties of the Gaussian function, we have $\sum_i \sum_j G(i, j) \approx 1$. As can be seen, the output of processing the input image with a Gaussian filter is the weighted average of the input image pixels with the Gaussian kernel as the weight, and the closer the pixel is to the center, the greater the weight. Therefore, compared with the mean filter, the smoothing effect of the Gaussian filter is softer, and it will not produce a block effect, and the entire image will become smoother.

Next, we will implement the Gaussian filter in code and test its effect.

```
# Define the Gaussian kernel
def gauss(kernel_size, sigma):
   kernel = np.zeros((kernel_size, kernel_size))
   # Define the coordinates of the center point
   center = kernel_size // 2
   s = sigma ** 2
   sum_val = 0
   # Calculate the Gaussian kernel weight for each position
   for i in range(kernel_size):
      for j in range(kernel_size):
         x, y = i-center, j-center
         kernel[i, j] = np.exp(-(x**2 + y**2) / 2 * s)
         sum_val += kernel[i, j]
   kernel = kernel/sum_val
return kernel
k_gaussian = gauss(9, 0.5)
# Display the input image and the filter kernel
```

```
conv = conv_2d(img_gaussian, k_gaussian)
conv.plot()
# Display the convolution result
conv.plot_conv()
```

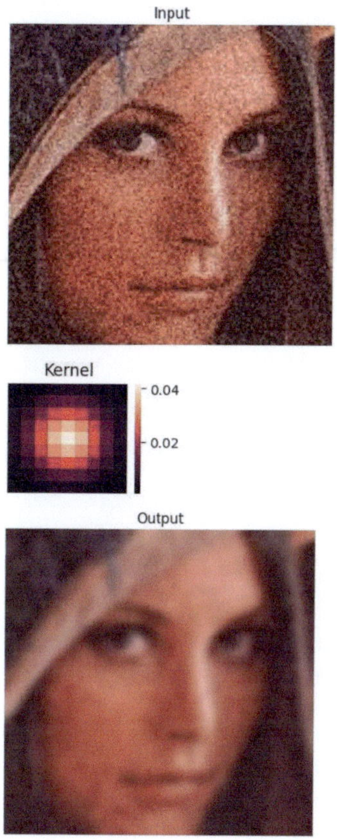

By comparing the input image and the output image, it can be clearly seen that the Gaussian noise has been effectively suppressed. We change the size of the Gaussian kernel and test again.

```
# Gaussian kernel size is 5
conv1 = conv_2d(img_gaussian, gauss(5, 0.5))
conv1.plot_conv()
# Gaussian kernel size is 7
conv2 = conv_2d(img_gaussian, gauss(7, 0.5))
conv2 plot_conv()
# Gaussian kernel size is 11
conv3 = conv_2d(img_gaussian, gauss(11, 0.5))
conv3.plot_conv()
```

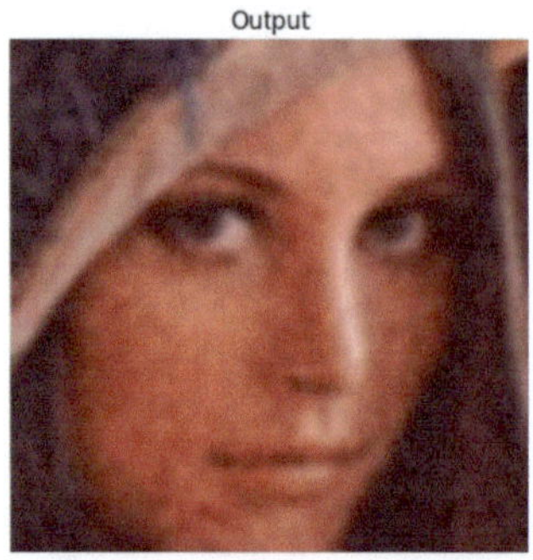

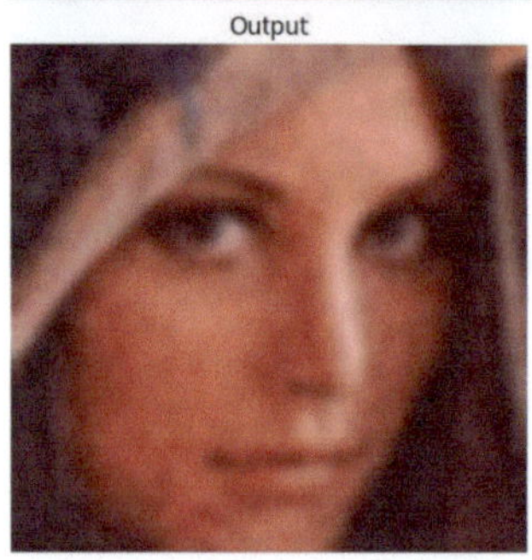

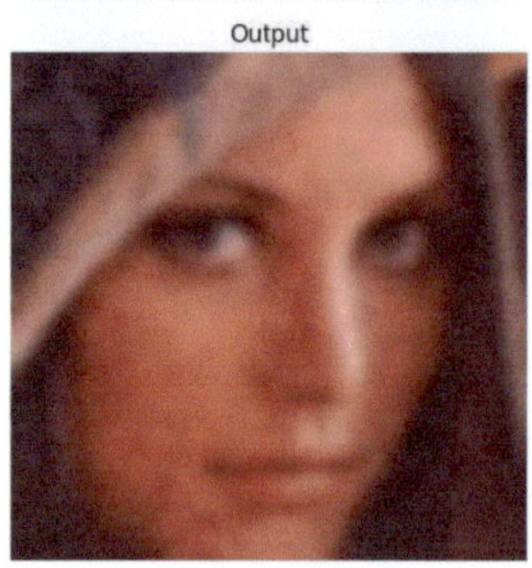

It can be seen that the Gaussian filter effectively handles Gaussian noise while avoiding the "block effect" that occurs when using mean filtering. In the following code, we can use cv2.GaussianBlur() to perform Gaussian filtering on the image.

3.5 Bilateral Filtering

Although the Gaussian filter can achieve good noise reduction results, as can be seen from the results of Sect. 3.4, the content of the image is also blurred, such as the facial features becoming blurred, and gray areas appearing between the eyeball and the white of the eye. This is caused by the Gaussian filter weighting and overlaying the white and black areas during the filtering process. So, is there any way to solve this problem? At this point, we need to introduce a new filter—the bilateral filter, which can effectively handle Gaussian noise while maintaining the clarity of the image content.

Suppose the output image after bilateral filtering of an image $\boldsymbol{I}$ is $\hat{\boldsymbol{I}}$, then their relationship is calculated by the following formula:

$$\hat{I}(i,j) = \frac{1}{W_{sb}} \sum_{m=i-k}^{i-1} \sum_{n=j-k}^{j-1} I(m,n) G_s(i-m, j-n) G_b(I(m,n) - I(i,j)),$$

where

$$\boldsymbol{G}_s(m,n) = \frac{1}{2\pi\sigma_s^2} \mathrm{e}^{-\frac{m^2+n^2}{2\sigma_s^2}}, \boldsymbol{G}_b(d) = \frac{1}{2\pi\sigma_b^2} \mathrm{e}^{-\frac{d^2}{2\sigma_b^2}}$$

$$W_{sb} = \sum_{m=i-k}^{i-1} \sum_{n=j-k}^{j-1} \boldsymbol{G}_s(i-m, j-n) \boldsymbol{G}_b(|I(m,n) - I(i,j)|).$$

$\boldsymbol{G}_s$ is the Gaussian convolution kernel in Sect. 3.4. The bilateral filter just adds a Gaussian kernel $\boldsymbol{G}_b$ on the basis of the original Gaussian filter, where $d = I(m,n) - I(i,j)$ is the difference in pixel values (brightness or color) at positions (m,n) and (i,j) of the image. Therefore, only when d is very small, that is, the pixel value at position (m, n) and the pixel value at position (i, j) are very similar, the pixel values at (m, n) will significantly influence the calculation of the pixel value $\hat{I}(i,j)$ at the output image location (i, j). Conversely, when d is large, that is, when the pixel values at location (m, n) and location (i,j) are very different, the pixel values at (m, n) will not significantly influence the calculation of the pixel value $\hat{I}(i,j)$ at the output image location (i,j). Figure 3.3 can help us understand the working principle of the bilateral filter more clearly.

In Fig. 3.3, we input an image (Fig. 3.3a) into the bilateral filter for filtering. The red dot in the figure represents the location of (i, j), and the green and orange dots represent different locations of (m, n). The height of the dots in the figure represents the size of the pixel values. It can be clearly seen that the pixel value of the red dot is close to that of the orange dot but differs significantly from the green dot. We know that the bilateral filter is composed of two Gaussian kernels (above Fig. 3.3b). When the input image passes through the bilateral filter, the influence of the green dot is suppressed due to the large difference in brightness (pixel value) between the green and red dots. In other words, after adding a Gaussian kernel to the basis of Gaussian filtering, pixels with small brightness or color differences can influence the weighted calculation of the Gaussian kernel, while pixels with large differences have a reduced impact on the weighted superposition of the Gaussian kernel, thus avoiding blurring of the image content. For example, when performing bilateral filtering on the face in the experiment, the black pixels on the eyeball will only be weighted averaged with the pixels on the black area, not with the pixels on the white of the

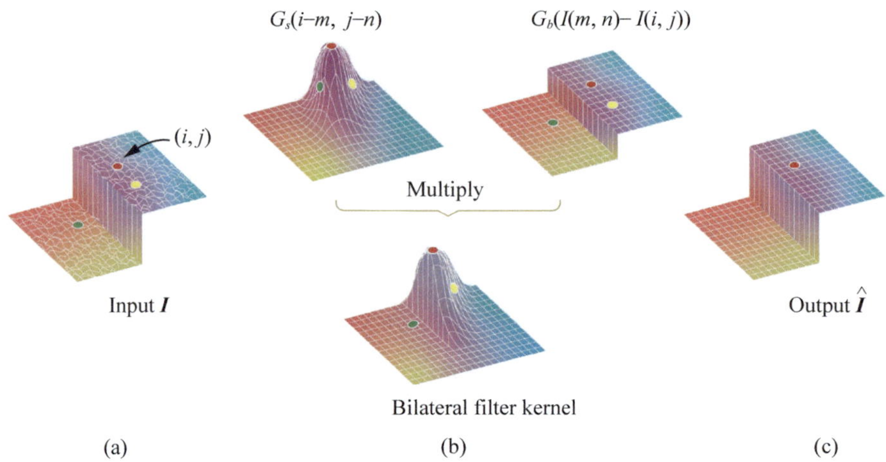

Fig. 3.3 Schematic of the filtering process by a bilateral filter

eye, ensuring the boundary between the eyeball and the white of the eye after filtering. Overall, in areas where pixel brightness or color changes are not significant, bilateral filtering has an effect similar to Gaussian filtering, while in areas where brightness or color changes dramatically, the effect of Gaussian filtering is weakened by the added term. W_{sb} is a normalization factor, $\sum_{m=i-k}^{i-1}\sum_{n=j-k}^{j-1}\frac{G_s(i-m,j-n)G_b(I(m,n)-I(i,j))}{W_{sb}}=1$, to prevent the pixel values from exceeding the value range (0–55) after the image passes through the filter. Note that the normalization factor for the mean filter is the size of the convolution kernel of the mean filter k^2, while the Gaussian filter satisfies $\sum_i\sum_j G(i,j)\approx 1$, so there is no need for specific normalization.

We leave the implementation of the bilateral filter as an exercise. Next, we call the library function cv2.bilateralFilter() to perform bilateral filtering on the image.

```
# To make image display easier later, we encapsulate this function
def plot_image(img, name, camp='gray'):
    plt.imshow(img, cmap=camp)
    plt.title(name)
    plt.axis('off')
    plt.show()
# Display the effect of the bilateral filter filtering Gaus-
sian noise
plot_image(cv2.bilateralFilter(np.uint8(img_
gaussian),30,55,45)[:, :, ::-
1], 'output')
```

As shown in the figure, the bilateral filter effectively removes noise while maintaining the clarity of the image content, such as the significant reduction of the gray blocks in the eye area.

3.6 Median Filtering

"Acne removal" is also a common operation in beauty retouching. The "acne" on the face is actually a type of salt-and-pepper noise. Let's first try the effect of Gaussian filters on salt-and-pepper noise and see if Gaussian filters can effectively "remove acne".

```
# Use Gaussian filter to filter salt-and-pepper noise
conv_salt = conv_2d(np.uint8(img_salt), gauss(5, 1))
conv_salt.plot_conv()
```

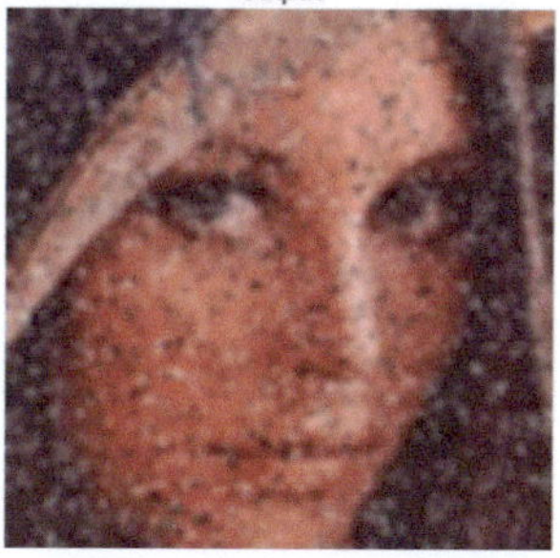

From the output, it can be seen that the Gaussian filter cannot effectively remove salt-and-pepper noise, because the Gaussian filter essentially performs a weighted sum of some pixels and cannot suppress the impact of salt-and-pepper noise. Next, we will introduce a filter that can effectively remove salt-and-pepper noise—the median filter.

The median filter is a statistical sorting filter, i.e., the image pixel value equals the median value of the surrounding pixels after sorting. For a pixel (i, j) in the image, the median filter takes the statistical median of all pixels in the neighborhood as the

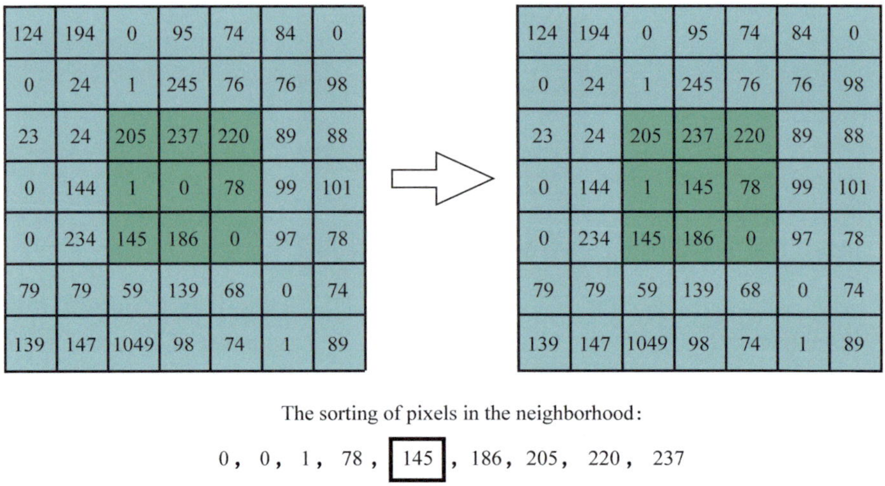

Fig. 3.4 Median filter filters salt-and-pepper noise

pixel value of this pixel. Salt-and-pepper noise is a minority in the image, and the pixel values of most pixels are normal, so the median pixel value is usually a normal pixel value. This is the principle of the median filter to remove salt-and-pepper noise. Figure 3.4 is an example of image filtering using a median filter.

As can be seen, Fig. 3.4 is scattered with salt-and-pepper noise with pixel values of 0 and 1. When the median filter slides to the center of the image, it first sorts the pixels in the area; then selects the median value of the sorted pixels as the result of the filter at the center point, i.e., replacing 0 with 145. From Fig. 3.4, it can also be seen that for the salt-and-pepper noise in the image, due to the majority of normal pixels, the statistical median is usually the pixel value of normal pixels.

We leave the implementation of the median filter as homework. Below, we call the library function cv2.medianBlur() to perform median filtering on the image and observe its suppression effect on salt-and-pepper noise.

```
conv_salt = conv_2d(img_salt, k3) plot_image(cv2.medianBlur
(np.uint8(img_salt),5)[:, :, ::-1], 'Output')
```

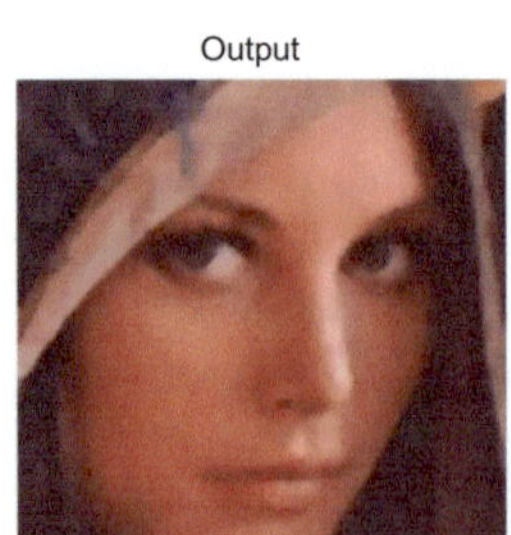

Doesn't the face in the picture look very clear? After filtering with the median filter, there is not even a shadow of salt-and-pepper noise in the image. It seems that the median filter is indeed very effective in removing salt-and-pepper noise.

3.7 Image Sharpening

Since we can make the image smooth through filtering, we can also make the image clear, which is called image sharpening. As mentioned earlier, image smoothing is to filter out the high-frequency information in the image and retain the low-frequency information. So, is image sharpening the opposite, removing low-frequency information and retaining high-frequency information? Imagine that when an image goes through Gaussian filtering, its high-frequency information is removed by the filter, leaving only low-frequency information. If we subtract the filtered image from the original image, can we get more high-frequency information in the image? Let's try it this way.

```
# Since convolution operation satisfies distribu-
tive law, we can directly calculate the stacked convolution kernel
size = 3
k0 = np.zeros((size, size))
k0[int((size-1)/2)][int((size-1)/2)] = 1
kg = gauss(size, 1)
k_shapen = 1 * (k0 - kg)
# Get the image after Gaussian filtering
img_gau = cv2.GaussianBlur(img, (9,9), 5)
shapen = conv_2d(img_gau, k_shapen)
# Show sharpening effect
shapen.plot_conv()
```

The results obtained seem to be inconsistent with the expected results. Does anyone know what the problem is? There is very little high-frequency information in the image, and the low-frequency information is the main part. Therefore, only retaining the high-frequency information results in such a "black image". We need to correct our thinking: image sharpening is about enhancing high-frequency information, not completely removing low-frequency information.

So let's try the following: add the original image back to the above "black image". This means that while retaining the low-frequency information of the original image, the high-frequency information is doubled. If we overlay this "black image" onto the original image multiple times, will the image become clearer and clearer?

```
# Build the filter kernel
k_shapen = k0 + 1 * (k0 - kg)
img_gau = cv2.GaussianBlur(img, (3,3), 1)
shapen = conv_2d(img_gau, k_shapen)
shapen.plot_conv()
```

The image has become noticeably clearer. Overlay the high-frequency information onto the original image multiple times and test its effect.

```
k_shapen = k0 + 5 * (k0 - kg)
img_gau = cv2.GaussianBlur(img, (3,3), 1)
shapen = conv_2d(img_gau, k_shapen)
shapen.plot_conv()
```

As can be seen, repeatedly overlaying the image's high-frequency information, obtained by subtracting the Gaussian filtered image from the original image, onto the original image can continuously enhance the sharpening effect.

3.8 Summary

This chapter introduces the basic concepts of filtering and several typical filters, explains their roles in image denoising and their suppression effects on different types of noise. Finally, by analogy, it introduces filters that can achieve image sharpening. For computer vision tasks, filtering is usually used for image preprocessing or post-processing, such as denoising or deblurring preprocessing, which can help us more accurately perform image recognition; it can also filter the results of recognition detection to remove some incorrect recognition detection results.

Exercises

(1) Briefly explain why Gaussian filters are more suitable for smoothing images than mean filters.
(2) Implement a bilateral filter in code, use the provided lenaface.jpg image, reproduce the denoising effect in Sect. 3.5, and compare it with the results using library functions.
(3) Implement a median filter in code, use the provided lenaface.jpg image, reproduce the denoising effect in Sect. 3.6, and compare it with the results using library functions.
(4) Based on the implementation of the median filter, try to use the median filter to denoise the lenaface.jpg image with added Gaussian noise.
(5) Refer to the image sharpening method given in this chapter, use a convolution kernel to sharpen the lenaface.jpg image.

Chapter 4
Template Matching

4.1 Introduction

Image matching, which involves finding the corresponding positions of the same or similar objects in different images, is a fundamental problem in computer vision. Based on image matching, a series of computer vision tasks such as image retrieval, image stitching, and image recognition can be accomplished. The most basic and simplest form of image matching is template matching: given a template image, find the target location in another image that has the highest similarity to the template. For example, as shown in Fig. 4.1, given a cloud as the template image, it is necessary to determine whether the image contains a cloud, and if so, the location of the cloud. Depending on the number of targets, template matching can be divided into single-target template matching and multi-target template matching. In this chapter, we will introduce the steps of template matching and the methods used to measure similarity for matching.

4.2 Implementation of Template Matching

We will first introduce the steps of template matching.

4.2.1 Matching Steps

For a template image $\boldsymbol{T}$ and an input image $\boldsymbol{I}$, let their sizes be $w \times h$ and $W \times H$ respectively ($w \leq W, h \leq H$), we follow the steps below to find the target location in image $\boldsymbol{I}$ that is most similar to image $\boldsymbol{T}$.

W. Shen et al., *Hands-On Computer Vision*,
https://doi.org/10.1007/978-981-95-4835-4_4

Fig. 4.1 Example of template matching

(1) Slide the template image over the input image, and at each sliding position (i, j), calculate the similarity between the template and the sub-image of the input image with (i, j) as the top-left vertex and size $w \times h$.
(2) After the above sliding is completed, a similarity matrix $\boldsymbol{R}$ will be obtained. Each element $R(i, j)$ of the matrix is the similarity calculated at the sliding position (i, j). It is not difficult to conclude that the size of matrix $\boldsymbol{R}$ is $(W - w + 1) \times (H - h + 1)$.
(3) After obtaining the similarity matrix, find the position (i^*, j^*) where the maximum value of the elements is located. In the input image, the area with (i^*, j^*) as the top-left vertex and w and h as the width and height is the area in the input image that is most similar to the template image, which is the target location to be found.

As shown in Fig. 4.2, to find the area most similar to Fig. 4.2a in Fig. 4.2b, first slide the template image from the top-left corner of the input image (the position of the box in the top-left corner of the right image), calculate the similarity at each position, and output the sub-image with the highest similarity. This achieves template matching in the input image.

However, how should similarity be calculated?

4.2.2 Similarity Measurement

There are many methods for measuring similarity in template matching. In this section, we mainly introduce cross-correlation and normalized cross-correlation.

(a) (b)

Fig. 4.2 Schematic of template matching

1. Cross-Correlation

The method of cross-correlation is very simple: multiply the corresponding elements of the template and the input image sub-image and sum them. At the position (i, j) [with (i, j) as the top-left vertex], the cross-correlation calculation formula of the template and the input image sub-image is

$$R(i,j) = \sum_{m=i}^{i+w-1} \sum_{n=j}^{j+h-1} I(m,n) \cdot T(m-i, n-j),$$

where (m, n) are the coordinates of any pixel point in the input image; $(m - i, n - j)$ is the coordinate on the template corresponding to this pixel point.

Do you find the above formula familiar? Looking back at the two-dimensional convolution formula in Chap. 2, the only difference between them is whether $\boldsymbol{T}$ is flipped! In mainstream deep learning development packages (such as PyTorch and Caffe), it is assumed that the convolution kernel of the convolutional neural network has been flipped. In other words, the convolutional neural network code we usually use is actually calculating cross-correlation. No wonder many researchers in artificial intelligence believe that convolutional neural networks are similar to template matching, such as Professor Alan Yuille, a student of the famous physicist Stephen Hawking, who has mentioned the relationship between convolutional neural networks and template matching more than once.

Next, we will program to implement the above cross-correlation formula and test whether it can achieve the desired template matching effect.

```
# utils is a function package written before
from utils import *
import cv2
from matplotlib import pyplot as plt
import numpy as np
# Calculate cross-correlation
```

```
def CCORR(img, temp):
    w, h = temp.shape[::-1]
    W, H = img.shape[::-1]
    img = np.array(img, dtype='float')
    temp = np.array(temp, dtype='float')
    res = np.zeros((W - w + 1, H - h + 1))
# Calculate cross-correlation using a loop
    for i in range(W - w + 1):
        for j in range(H - h + 1):
            res[i, j] = np.sum(temp * img[j:j + h, i:i + w])
    return res
# Build a single target matching class
class temp_match_single():
    def __init__(self, img, temp):
        self.img = img
        self.temp = temp
    def match(self):
        # Input target image
        img = cv2.cvtColor(self.img, cv2.COLOR_BGR2GRAY)
        # Input template image
        temp = cv2.cvtColor(self.temp, cv2.COLOR_BGR2GRAY)
        w, h = temp.shape[::-1]
        # Calculate cross-correlation
res = CCORR(img, temp)
        # Find the position with the maximum cross-correlation value
        loc = np.where(res == np.max(res))
        top_left = [int(loc[0]), int(loc[1])]
        bottom_right = (top_left[0] + w, top_left[1] + h)
        # Frame it
                        cv2.rectangle(self.img, top_left, bottom_
right, (255,255,255), 1)
        plot_image(self.img[:, :, ::-1], 'Matching Result by CCORR')
```

We import an image and a template for template matching.

```
img = cv2.imread('lena_tri.jpg')
template = cv2.imread('lena_small.png')
test = temp_match_single(img, template)
plot_image(test.temp[:, :, ::-1], 'Template Image')
plot_image(test.img[:, :, ::-1], 'Target Image')
test.match()
```

Did the result surprise you? We didn't match the correct target! Where is the problem?

By carefully observing the cross-correlation formula, you can find that it is the direct multiplication of the template image pixel values and the input image sub-image pixel values. Therefore, when the template is fixed, the larger the overall pixel value of the sub-image (that is, the brighter it is), the larger their product will be. Therefore, cross-correlation is more likely to find areas with high brightness in the input image, rather than areas most similar to the template. So how can we solve this problem? Obviously, we need the similarity measure to be independent of the overall pixel value size of each sub-image in the input image, which requires normalization. Next, we introduce another similarity measurement method—normalized cross-correlation.

2. Normalized Cross-Correlation

Normalized cross-correlation requires normalization of the template and input image sub-images, eliminating the impact of their overall pixel value size on the cross-correlation results. The calculation formula for normalized cross-correlation of the template and input image sub-images is

$$R(i,j) = \frac{\sum_m \sum_n I(m,n) \cdot T(m-i,n-j)}{\sqrt{\sum_m \sum_n I^2(m,n)}\sqrt{\sum_m \sum_n T^2(m-i,n-j)}}.$$

Here, the two parts in the denominator reflect the magnitude of the pixel values of the template and the input image sub-image themselves. After multiplication, they serve as normalization factors to eliminate their impact on cross-correlation calculation. In fact, this is also a representation of cosine similarity. According to the above formula, we can program to implement normalized cross-correlation, rewrite the CCORR() function, and try again to see if we can find the correct target area.

```
# Rewrite the original CCORR() function, define normalized cross-
correlation
def CCORR(img, temp, normalize= True ):
  w, h = temp.shape[::-1]
  W, H = img.shape[::-1]
  res = np.zeros((W-w+1, H-h+1))
  img = np.array(img, dtype='float')
  temp = np.array(temp, dtype='float')
  t = np.sqrt(np.sum(temp**2))
  for i in range(W-w+1):
    for j in range(H-h+1):
      res[i,j] = np.sum(temp*img[j:j+h, i:i+w])
      # Perform normalization operation here
      if normalize:
                                        res[i,j]  =  res[i,j]  /  t  /
np.sqrt(np.sum(img[j:j+h, i:i+w]**2))
  return res
img = cv2.imread('lena_tri.jpg')
template = cv2.imread('lena_small.png')
test = temp_match_single(img, template)
test.match()
```

As can be seen from the results, through normalization, the impact of the overall brightness of the input image sub-image on cross-correlation calculation is eliminated, enhancing the robustness of cross-correlation measurement.

4.3 Multi-target Template Matching

Different from single-target template matching, in multi-target matching tasks, a threshold needs to be set. When the similarity between the template and a certain input image sub-image is greater than this threshold, it can be considered that this input image sub-image is the object to be matched.

Here, we need to explain the choice of the threshold. If the threshold is set too low, many sub-images in the image will be considered to match the template, causing many false matches; once the threshold is set too high, perhaps no sub-images in the image can match the template. Therefore, in multi-target template matching, a suitable threshold needs to be chosen. Set the number of sub-images to be matched k, and set the threshold to the value of the $k + 1$ largest similarity.

For convenience, we will directly use normalized cross-correlation as the measurement indicator and directly call the library function cv2.TM_CCORR_NORMED() to complete the normalized cross-correlation.

```
import numpy as np
# Use quicksort algorithm to find the kth largest value in the
sequence
def findKth(s, k):
    return findKth_c(s, 0, len(s) - 1, k)
def findKth_c(s, low, high, k):
    m = partition(s, low, high)
    if m == len(s) - k:
        return s[m]
    elif m < len(s) - k:
        return findKth_c(s, m + 1, high, k)
    else:
```

```
        return findKth_c(s, low, m - 1, k)
def partition(s, low, high):
    pivot, j = s[low], low
    for i in range(low + 1, high + 1):
        if s[i] <= pivot:
            j += 1
            s[i], s[j] = s[j], s[i]
    s[j], s[low] = s[low], s[j]
    return j
# Building a multi-target template matching class
class temp_match_multi():
    def __init__(self, img, temp, k=50):
        self.img = img
        self.temp = temp
        # Define the number of sub-figures
        self.k = k
    def match(self):
        # Input template image and target image
        temp = cv2.cvtColor(self.temp, cv2.COLOR_BGR2GRAY)
        img = cv2.cvtColor(self.img, cv2.COLOR_BGR2GRAY)
        w, h = temp.shape[::-1]
        method = eval('cv2.TM_CCORR_NORMED')
        res = cv2.matchTemplate(img, temp, method)
        temp = list(np.array(res).flatten())
        # Find the kth largest value in res
        threshold = findKth(temp, self.k+1)
        print('The set threshold is:', threshold)
        loc = np.where(res >= threshold)
        # Select the found sub-images
        for pt in zip(*loc[::-1]):
                    cv2.rectangle(self.img, pt, (pt[0] + w, pt[1] +
h), (255,255,255), 1)
                                    plt.imshow(self.img[:,   :,   ::-
1]), plt.xticks([]), plt.yticks([])
        plt.show()
img = cv2.imread('img.png')
template = cv2.imread('temp.png')
test_multi = temp_match_multi(img, template, k=50)
plot_image(test_multi.temp[:, :, ::-1], 'Template Image')
plot_image(test_multi.img[:, :, ::-1], 'Target Image')
test_multi.match()
```

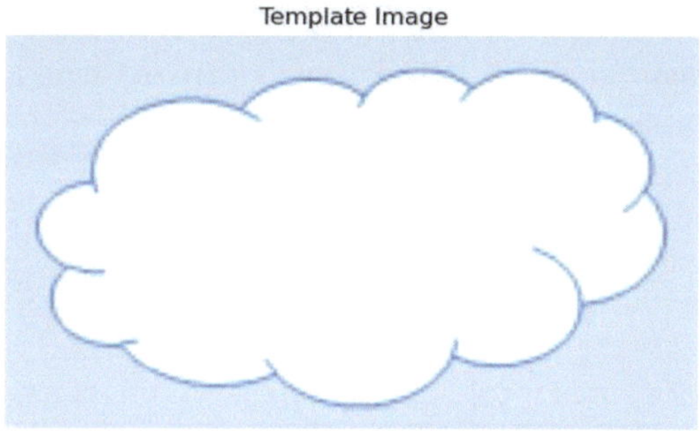

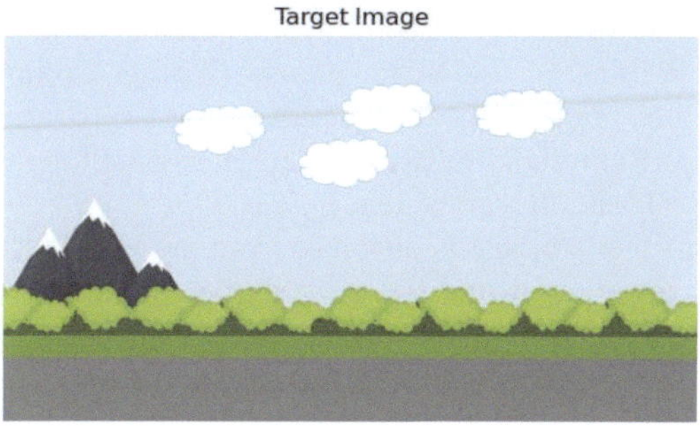

The set threshold is: 0.99798167.

4.4 Summary

This chapter introduces the most basic image matching task in computer vision—template matching. Although the template matching algorithm is simple, this sliding window-based similarity matching strategy is the basis of many computer vision methods. For example, you can glimpse a shadow of object detection from the template matching algorithm. Of course, the similarity measure required for object detection is much more complex, which we will learn in Chap. 12.

Exercises

(1) In this chapter, the experimental data we used has the same target in the template and the input image. If there are some changes in the illumination of the target in the image, such as changes in brightness, an increase in brightness for some pixels, and a decrease in brightness for others, can the normalized cross-correlation still match the target we want? If not, try to propose a similarity measurement method that can still successfully match in this situation, and verify it through programming.

(2) Calculate the computational complexity of using normalized cross-correlation as a similarity measure in template matching, where the image size is $W \times H$, and the template size is $w \times h$.

(3) If the size of the template is different from the target in the image to be matched, how should the template matching algorithm introduced in this chapter be modified to get the correct matching result? Implement and test using the provided img.png, temp.png, and temp_large.png.

Chapter 5
Edge Detection

5.1 Introduction

An edge in an image is a location where local brightness, texture, or color changes dramatically. As shown in Fig. 5.1, these changes often occur at the boundaries between objects and backgrounds, between objects, or between regions. Edges contain shape information of objects and structural information of scenes in the image, which play a crucial role in the visual system. Jitendra Malik, a member of the National Academy of Engineering in the USA, pointed out that shape provides more robust information than other features [1]. For example, the edge map on the right side of Fig. 5.1 has completely lost color information, but the semantics represented by these edges—a swan—can still be recognized. David Marr's theory of vision [2] also confirms this. According to his theory, the first step in visual information processing is based on important features such as edges extracted from images, which means edge detection is the foundation of visual information processing. In this chapter, we will introduce the mathematical model of edge detection and the implementation of several classic edge detection algorithms.

5.2 Mathematical Model of Edge Detection

Given an image $\boldsymbol{I}$, the goal of edge detection is to calculate the edge strength $E_s(i, j|\boldsymbol{I})$ and edge direction $E_\theta(i, j|\boldsymbol{I})$ at each point (i, j) in the image.

Figure 5.2 shows a one-dimensional signal, which can be regarded as the intensity of two-dimensional image pixels along one coordinate axis (the x-axis). According to the definition in Sect. 5.1, the position of the edge is where the pixel intensity changes rapidly. From calculus, we know that the change of a function can be represented by the first derivative of the function, that is, the image edge is at the maximum of the first derivative of the image.

W. Shen et al., *Hands-On Computer Vision*,
https://doi.org/10.1007/978-981-95-4835-4_5

Fig. 5.1 Schematic of edge detection

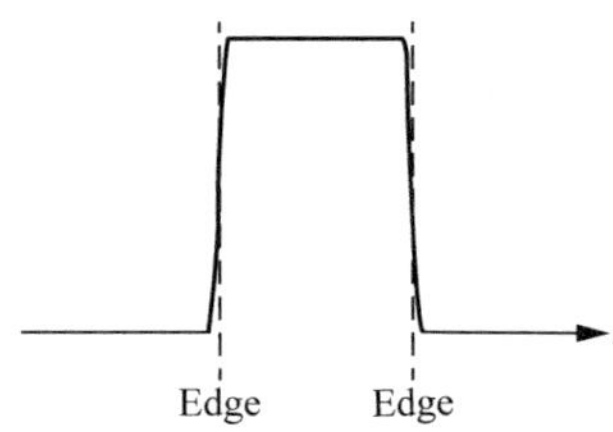

Fig. 5.2 Edge in a one-dimensional signal

Next, we introduce the calculation of the first derivative (differential) of the image.

According to calculus, the first derivative of a univariate function $f(x)$ is defined as

$$\frac{df(x)}{dx} = \lim_{\Delta x \to 0} \frac{f(x + \Delta x) - f(x - \Delta x)}{2\Delta x}.$$

We know that the image $\boldsymbol{I}$ is a matrix, where each element's value (pixel value) can be represented as the output of a bivariate function $f(x, y)$. The differential of a bivariate function can be generalized from the first derivative of a univariate function:

$$\frac{\partial f(x, y)}{\partial x} = \lim_{\varepsilon \to 0} \frac{f(x + \varepsilon, y) - f(x - \varepsilon, y)}{2\varepsilon}$$

$$\frac{\partial f(x, y)}{\partial y} = \lim_{\varepsilon \to 0} \frac{f(x, y + \varepsilon) - f(x, y - \varepsilon)}{2\varepsilon}.$$

Since digital images are discrete, the smallest position distance in digital images is 1 pixel, i.e., $\varepsilon = 1$. Therefore, in the discrete case, the continuous position coordinates (x, y) in the above formula are converted into discrete matrix element position indices (i, j), and the above formula becomes

$$I_x(i, j) = \frac{I(i + 1, j) - I(i - 1, j)}{2}$$

$$I_y(i,j) = \frac{I(i,j+1) - I(i,j-1)}{2},$$

where $I_x(i,j)$ and $I_y(i,j)$ are the first partial derivatives of the bivariate function of image pixel values at pixel (i, j) along the x-axis and the y-axis, respectively; let $\nabla I(i,j) = \left[I_x(i,j) \;\; I_y(i,j) \right]$ represent the gradient of the image at that point, so $I_x(i,j)$ and $I_y(i,j)$ are the gradient magnitudes along the x-axis and the y-axis, respectively. Therefore, in discrete digital images, the first derivative of the image is implemented through the first-order difference. The above formula is transformed into:

$$I_x(i,j) = \frac{1}{2} \sum_{m=-1}^{1} \sum_{n=-1}^{1} I(i-m, j-n) K_x(m,n)$$

$$I_y(i,j) = \frac{1}{2} \sum_{m=-1}^{1} \sum_{n=-1}^{1} I(i-m, j-n) K_y(m,n).$$

Let the matrix $\boldsymbol{K}_x = \begin{bmatrix} 0 & 0 & 0 \\ +1 & 0 & -1 \\ 0 & 0 & 0 \end{bmatrix}$, $\boldsymbol{K}_y = \begin{bmatrix} 0 & +1 & 0 \\ 0 & 0 & 0 \\ 0 & -1 & 0 \end{bmatrix}$, where the coordinates of the center position in $\boldsymbol{K}_x$ are (0,0), and the same applies to $\boldsymbol{K}_y$. Let the matrix be $\boldsymbol{I}_x = (I_x(i,j))$, where $I_x(i,j)$ is the element of the matrix, i is the row number, and j is the column number; similarly, let the matrix be $\boldsymbol{I}_y = \left(I_y(i,j)\right)$. The above equation can be written as

$$\boldsymbol{I}_x = \boldsymbol{I} * \boldsymbol{K}_x, \boldsymbol{I}_y = \boldsymbol{I} * \boldsymbol{K}_{y.}$$

What can we infer from the form of the above equation? Yes, the above equation is in the form of convolution, indicating that the first-order difference of the image can be calculated through convolution.

From this, we obtain the gradient $\nabla I(i,j) = \left[I_x(i,j) \;\; I_y(i,j) \right]$ of each pixel in the image. The edge strength $E_s(i,j|\boldsymbol{I})$ and edge direction $E_\theta(i,j|I)$ at position (i, j) in image $\boldsymbol{I}$ can be calculated based on the gradient $\nabla I(i,j)$ at that point:

$$E_s(i,j|\boldsymbol{I}) = \|\nabla I(i,j)\| = \sqrt{I_x^2(i,j) + I_y^2(i,j)}$$

$$E_\theta(i,j|\boldsymbol{I}) = \tan^{-1}\left(\frac{I_y(i,j)}{I_x(i,j)}\right) + \frac{\pi}{2}.$$

Note that the edge direction is perpendicular to the image gradient direction. It can be seen that the key to calculating the image edge is to calculate the image gradient, which is obtained by difference calculation. In the above calculation, the image difference is convolved with $\boldsymbol{K}_x$ and $\boldsymbol{K}_y$ as convolution kernels. These two convolution kernels are called difference operators and are the simplest difference operators. One of the tasks of edge detection is to design more reasonable difference operators to calculate the image gradient more accurately and robustly.

5.3 Edge Detection Algorithm

Edge detection algorithms usually have three steps.

(1) Image smoothing: Edge detection algorithms are mainly based on the derivative of image pixel intensity, but the derivative is very sensitive to image noise, because image noise can also cause abrupt changes in image pixel intensity. Therefore, the image is first filtered and smoothed to improve the robustness of the edge detection algorithm to image noise.
(2) Image gradient calculation: Convolve the smoothed image with the difference template to obtain the image gradient.
(3) Image edge positioning: Locate the edges in the image based on the edge strength and edge direction obtained from the gradient.

Since both image smoothing and difference operations can be completed through convolution, according to the associative law of convolution, the first two steps can also be combined into one step. Next, we will introduce two edge detection algorithms—the Sobel edge detection algorithm and the Canny edge detection algorithm.

5.3.1 Sobel Edge Detection Algorithm

The Sobel edge detection algorithm [3] is one of the most classic edge detection algorithms. Its core is the Sobel operator, which consists of two sets of 3×3 convolution kernels, mathematically represented as follows:

$$\boldsymbol{K}_x = \begin{bmatrix} +1 & 0 & -1 \\ +2 & 0 & -2 \\ +1 & 0 & -1 \end{bmatrix}, \quad \boldsymbol{K}_y = \begin{bmatrix} +1 & +2 & +1 \\ 0 & 0 & 0 \\ -1 & -2 & -1 \end{bmatrix}.$$

Choose the Sobel operator along the x-axis direction and decompose it into two vectors multiplied:

$$\boldsymbol{K}_x = \begin{bmatrix} +1 & 0 & -1 \\ +2 & 0 & -2 \\ +1 & 0 & -1 \end{bmatrix} = \begin{bmatrix} 1 \\ 2 \\ 1 \end{bmatrix} \begin{bmatrix} +1 & 0 & -1 \end{bmatrix}.$$

The former is similar to a Gaussian filter (larger in the middle and smaller on both sides), the purpose of which is to suppress noise in the image; according to Sect. 5.2, the latter is a difference operator, which acts on the image to obtain the gradient magnitude along the x-axis, that is, the edge strength in the vertical direction.

The Sobel operator includes the operations of image smoothing and image gradient calculation. Next, we will implement the convolution of the Sobel operator and the image in code. First, import the lena image and write the Sobel operators along the x-axis direction and along the y-axis direction.

```
import cv2
import numpy as np
import matplotlib.pyplot as plt
# Input image
img = cv2.imread('lena.jpeg')
# Sobel operator in the x direction
kx = np.array([
    [1,0,-1],
    [2,0,-2],
    [1,0,-1]
])
# Sobel operator in the y direction
ky = np.array([
    [1, 2, 1],
    [0, 0, 0],
    [-1,-2,-1]
])
# Display the input image
plt.imshow(img[:, :, ::-1])
plt.axis('off')
(-0.5, 788.5, 430.5, -0.5)
```

Next, calculate the gradient magnitude in the x direction. With the knowledge of convolution that we have learned, we can easily write the corresponding code.

```
# Convolution of the image with the Sobel operator in the x direction
conv_x = cv2.filter2D(img, -1, kx)
plt.imshow(conv_x[:, :, ::-1])
plt.axis('off')
(-0.5, 788.5, 430.5, -0.5)
```

As can be observed, the gradient magnitude in the x direction, that is, the edge information in the vertical direction (such as the lines of the arm, hat, etc.) is effectively detected. Then, calculate the gradient magnitude of the image in the y direction.

```
# Convolution of the image with the Sobel operator in the y direction
conv_y = cv2.filter2D(img, -1, ky)
plt.imshow(conv_y[:, :, ::-1])
plt.axis('off')
(-0.5, 788.5, 430.5, -0.5)
```

As shown in the figure above, the gradient magnitude in the y direction, that is, the edge information in the horizontal direction (such as the contours of the eyes, etc.) is also well extracted. Based on the image gradient (I_x, I_y), substitute into the edge strength and edge direction formulas in Sect. 5.2 to get the result of edge detection.

When calculating edge strength, in order to improve efficiency, the approximate value without square root is usually used:

$$E_s(i, j|\boldsymbol{I}) = \|I_x(i, j)\| + \|I_y(i, j)\|$$

```
E = abs(conv_x) + abs(conv_y)
plt.imshow(E[:, :, ::-1])
plt.axis('off')
(-0.5, 788.5, 430.5, -0.5)
```

5.3.2 Canny Edge Detection Algorithm

Although the Sobel operator incorporates a Gaussian-like filter, enabling it to suppress image noise to some extent, distinguishing between image noise and the edge itself is a challenging task, especially when the image often contains false edges generated by chaotic textures. Image smoothing can suppress noise to a certain degree, but it also makes the image blurry and reduces the intensity of the edges. Therefore, the degree of image smoothing should be adjustable, and the results of edge detection should also be multi-scale (such as adjustable smoothing degree). Next, we introduce a multi-scale edge detection algorithm—the Canny edge detection algorithm [4]. The Canny algorithm is perhaps the most widely used edge detection algorithm in computer vision, typically implemented in the following steps: (1) Image smoothing, i.e., noise suppression; (2) image gradient calculation; (3) non-maximum suppression (NMS) of edge intensity; (4) edge localization based on hysteresis-based thresholding.

1. Image Smoothing

Since edge detection is very sensitive to image noise, it is necessary to denoise the image before proceeding with subsequent operations. Combining the knowledge learned in Chap. 3, a Gaussian filter is generally used to denoise the image. The degree of image smoothing depends on the size of the standard deviation of the Gaussian kernel. The larger it is, the smoother and blurrier the image; the smaller it is, the more image details are retained, but the more noise there is. Different sizes represent different scales. By adjusting the size and performing edge detection on images with different degrees of smoothing, we obtain multi-scale edge detection results. In the implementation, we first set the size of the Gaussian kernel to 5, and the standard deviation to 1.5 (when the size of the Gaussian kernel is three times the standard deviation, the filtering effect is generally good).

```
from utils import *
# Set the size and variance of the Gaussian kernel kernel_
size = 5
sigma = 1.5
# Import an image
```

```
img = Image.open('lena.jpeg')
# Convert it to grayscale
img = img.convert('L')
img = np.array(img)
# Construct the Gaussian convolution kernel
kernel = gaussian_kernel(kernel_size, sigma)
# Convolve with the image
smoothed = cv2.filter2D(img, -1, kernel)
# Display the image
plot_image(img, 'Original image')
plot_image(smoothed, 'Smoothed image')
```

2. Image Gradient Calculation

Once we have the smoothed image, we can calculate the horizontal gradient magnitude I_x and the vertical gradient magnitude I_y in a manner similar to the Sobel operator. Then, we can calculate the gradient magnitude (edge intensity) at each pixel in the image $E_s(i, j|I) = \|\nabla I(i, j)\| = \sqrt{I_x^2(i, j) + I_y^2(i, j)}$, whereas well as the gradient direction $tan^{-1}\left(\frac{I_y(i,j)}{I_x(i,j)}\right)$, i.e., the direction perpendicular to the edge, as shown in Fig. 5.3.

```
# Calculate the gradient magnitude in the x-axis direction
def partial_x(img):
    # Get the size of the image
    Hi, Wi = img.shape
    out = np.zeros((Hi, Wi))
```

Fig. 5.3 Gradient direction

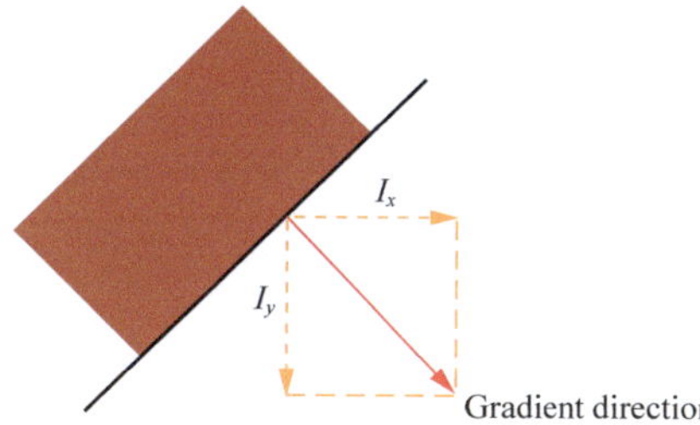


```
    # Normalize the convolution kernel
    k = np.array([[0,0,0],[0.5,0,-0.5],[0,0,0]])
    # Convolve the image
    out = cv2.filter2D(img, -1, k)
    return out
# Calculate the gradient magnitude in the y-axis direction
def partial_y(img):
    Hi, Wi = img.shape
    out = np.zeros((Hi, Wi))
    k = np.array([[0,0.5,0],[0,0,0],[0,-0.5,0]])
    out = cv2.filter2D(img, -1, k)
    return out
# Obtain the gradient magnitudes of the image in two directions
Gx = partial_x(smoothed)
Gy = partial_y(smoothed)
# Plot the image gradient
plot_image(Gx, 'Derivative in x direction')
plot_image(Gy, 'Derivative in y direction')
```

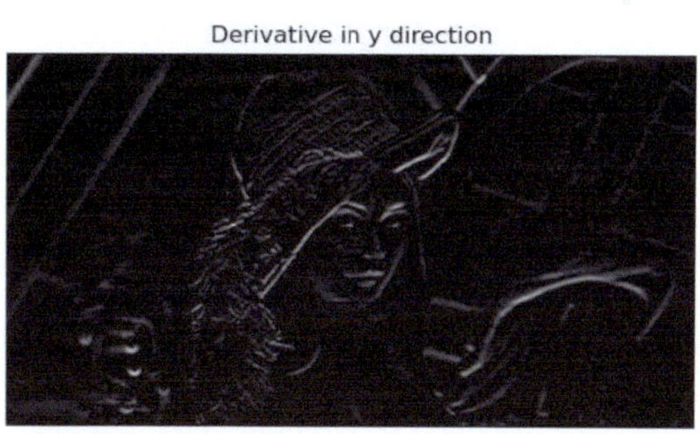


```
# Calculate gradient magnitude and direction
def gradient(img):
    G = np.zeros(img.shape)
    theta = np.zeros(img.shape)
    dx = partial_x(img)
    dy = partial_y(img)
    # Obtain the image gradient magnitude
    G = np.sqrt(dx**2 + dy**2)
    # Obtain the gradient direction
```

```
    theta = np.rad2deg(np.arctan2(dy, dx))
  # Adjust the gradient direction to be within the range of 0° to 360°
    theta %= 360
    return G, theta
  G, theta = gradient(smoothed)
  # Display the results obtained from the image gradient
  plot_image(np.uint8(G), 'Gradient magnitude')
```

3. Non-maximum Suppression of Edge Strength

As can be seen from the above results, the edge lines obtained directly from the gradient are very thick and appear blurry. Therefore, non-maximum suppression is needed to thin the edges. Non-maximum suppression preserves pixels with locally maximum edge strength along each gradient direction and removes pixels with non-locally maximum edge strength in that direction.

First, the gradient direction of each pixel in the image is quantized into 8 fixed directions, i.e., $\left\{\frac{k}{8}\pi\right\}_{k=0}^{7}$. Then, the edge strength of the current pixel is compared with the edge strength of the pixels in the neighborhood along the gradient direction (including positive and negative directions) of this pixel. If the edge strength of the current pixel is the maximum, this pixel is preserved as an edge pixel, otherwise, it is removed from the edge.

For example, in Fig. 5.4, consider the current pixel (i, j), its gradient direction is as shown by the arrow in Fig. 5.4. The two neighboring pixels (i', j') and (i'', j'') in the positive and negative directions along this gradient direction are found respectively (usually the 8 neighboring pixels of the current pixel are selected). If the edge strength of the current pixel (i, j) is the maximum among these 3 pixels, i.e., $E_s(i, j|\boldsymbol{I}) = \max\{E_s(i, j|\boldsymbol{I}), E_s(i', j'|\boldsymbol{I}), E_s(i'', j''|\boldsymbol{I})\}$, then the current pixel is preserved in the edge, otherwise, it is removed from the edge and set $E_s(i, j|\boldsymbol{I}) = 0$. Note that in the original Canny algorithm, the author uses a method of finding the zero-crossing points of the Laplacian operator along the gradient direction to determine the local maximum points of edge strength. Here, we achieve the same effect through non-maximum suppression.

```
# Non-maximum suppression algorithm
def non_maximum_suppression(G, theta):
    # Get the size of the gradient map
```

Fig. 5.4 Non-maximum suppression

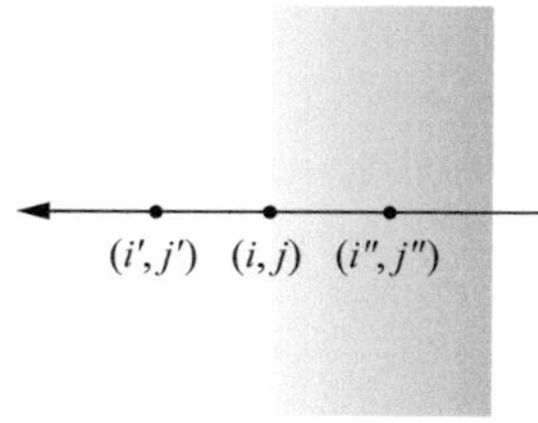


```
    H, W = G.shape
    # Project the gradient direction into the nearest 45° space
    theta = np.floor((theta + 22.5) / 45) * 45
    theta %= 360
    # The final output image gradient
    out = G.copy()
    for i in range(1, H-1):
        for j in range(1,W-1):
            # The gradient direction at the current pixel, which can be
            # divided into 4 bins
            angle = theta[i,j]
            if angle == 0 or angle == 180:
                ma = max(G[i, j-1], G[i, j+1])
            elif angle == 45 or angle == 45 + 180:
                 ma = max(G[i-1, j-1], G[i+1, j+1])
            elif angle == 90 or angle == 90 + 180:
                ma = max(G[i-1, j], G[i+1,j])
            elif angle == 135 or angle == 135 + 180:
                ma = max(G[i-1, j+1], G[i+1, j-1])
            else:
                print(angle)
                raise
            # ma is the maximum value of the pixel gradient magnitude of
the two
            # neighborhood points of the current pixel
             # If the value of ma is greater than the gradient magnitude
of the
            # current pixel, it is considered that the current pixel is
not
            # considered as an edge point
            # And set the gradient magnitude of this pixel to 0
            if ma > G[i,j]:
                out[i,j]=0
        return out
nms = non_maximum_suppression(G, theta)
plot_image(np.uint8(nms), 'Non-maximum suppressed')
```

It can be easily seen from the experimental results that the detected image edges have become clearer.

4. Edge Location Based on Hysteresis Thresholding

Through non-maximum suppression, we have refined the edges into edge lines, and next, we need to determine the final edge positions. We binarize the edge strength $\boldsymbol{E}_s$, transforming it into a binary edge map $\boldsymbol{E}_b$, i.e., if $E_b(i, j|\boldsymbol{I}) = 1$, then the pixel (i, j) is an edge point, otherwise it is not an edge point. The simplest binarization method is the single threshold method, i.e., taking a single threshold T, and binarizing it:

$$E_b(i, j|\boldsymbol{I}) = \begin{cases} 1, \ E_s(i, j|\boldsymbol{I}) \geq T \\ 0, \ E_s(i, j|\boldsymbol{I}) < T \end{cases}.$$

However, this single threshold method can easily cause broken edges. To solve this problem, the Canny edge detection algorithm uses a double threshold and proposes a method based on hysteresis thresholding. The algorithm uses two thresholds, one high and one low, denoted as T_h and T_l ($T_l < T_h$). If the edge strength of pixel (i, j) $E_s(i, j|\boldsymbol{I})$ is greater than or equal to the high threshold, this pixel is marked as a strong edge point, $E_b(i, j|\boldsymbol{I}) = 1$; if the edge strength is less than the low threshold, this pixel is marked as a non-edge point, $E_b(i, j|\boldsymbol{I}) = 0$; if the edge strength is between the two thresholds, this pixel is marked as a weak edge point, and further determination of $E_b(i, j|\boldsymbol{I})$ value is needed:

$$E_b(i, j|\boldsymbol{I}) = \begin{cases} 1, & E_s(i, j|\boldsymbol{I}) \geq T_h \\ 0, & E_s(i, j|\boldsymbol{I}) < T_l \\ \text{to be determined} & T_l \leq E_s(i, j|\boldsymbol{I}) < T_h \end{cases}.$$

This is the so-called hysteresis thresholding. Next, we will implement the determination of strong and weak edges through double thresholding.

```
# Determine strong and weak edges through double thresholding
def double_thresholding(img, high, low):
    # Initialize strong and weak edges as boolean matrices
    strong_edges = np.zeros(img.shape, dtype=np.bool_)
    weak_edges = np.zeros(img.shape, dtype=np.bool_)
    # Get the size of the input image
```

```
    a,b = img.shape
    for i in range(a):
        for j in range(b):
            # If it is greater than or equal to the Th threshold, it is a
strong edge
            # point
            if img[i,j] >= high:
                strong_edges[i,j] = 1
            # If it is less than the Th threshold and greater than or equal
to the Tl
            # threshold, it is a weak edge point
            elif img[i,j] < high and img[i,j] >= low:
                weak_edges[i, j] = 1
    return strong_edges, weak_edges
low_threshold = 3
high_threshold = 6
strong_edges, weak_edges = double_thresholding(nms, high_
threshold, low_threshold)
# Return the edge map of the superimposed strong and weak edges
edges = strong_edges * 1.0 + weak_edges * 0.5
plot_image(strong_edges, 'Strong Edges')
plot_image(edges, 'Strong+Weak Edges')
```

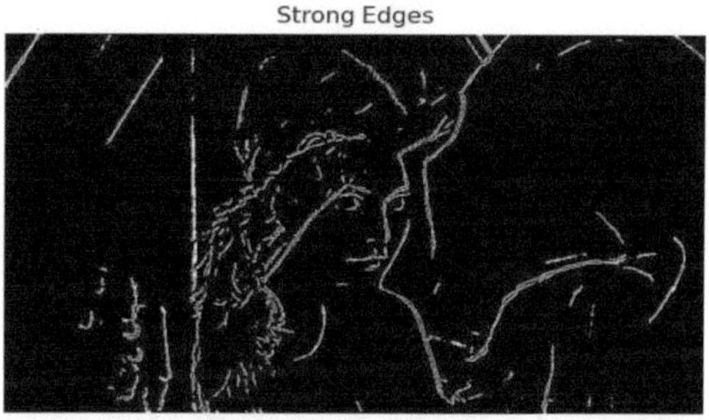

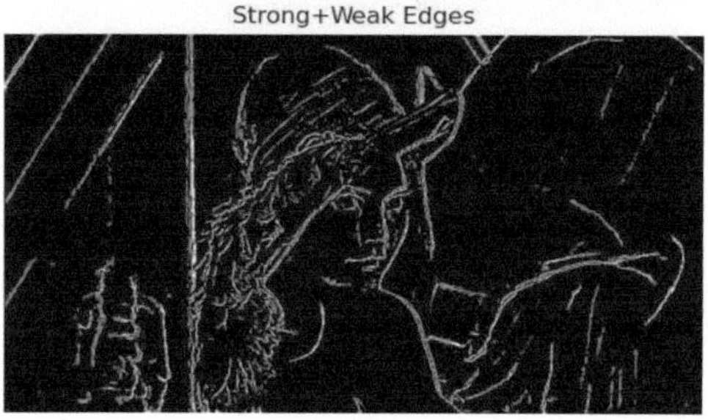

Strong edge points are confirmed edge points, while weak edge points are only confirmed as edge points when they are in the neighborhood of confirmed edge points (such as within the 8-neighborhood). Next, we will implement the determination process for weak edge points.

```
# Get the neighbors at (x, y)
def get_neighbors(x, y, H, W):
```

```
    neighbors = []
    for i in (x - 1, x, x + 1):
        for j in (y - 1, y, y + 1):
            if i >= 0 and i < H and j >= 0 and j < W:
                if (i == x and j == y):
                    continue
                neighbors.append((i, j))
    return neighbors
# Determine whether the weak edge point is an edge point
def link_edges(strong_edges, weak_edges):
    # Get the size of the graph
    H, W = strong_edges.shape
    # Get the position of strong edge points
    indices = np.stack(np.nonzero(strong_edges)).T
    # Initialize the final result as a Boolean matrix
    edges = np.zeros((H, W), dtype=np.bool_)
    weak_edges = np.copy(weak_edges)
    edges = np.copy(strong_edges)
    # Combine all the coordinates of strong edge points into a list
   q = [(i,j) for i in range(H) for j in range(W) if strong_edges[i,j]]
    while q:
     # The pop() function returns the last element in the list and
removes it from the
    # list
        i, j = q.pop()
        # (a, b) are neighbors of (i, j)
        for a, b in get_neighbors(i, j, H, W):
              # If the current point is a weak edge point and is in the
neighborhood of
            # a strong edge point, it can be considered as an edge point
            if weak_edges[a][b]:
                # To avoid repeated judgment on the same weak edge point,
its value
                is set to 0
                weak_edges[a][b] = 0
                # Add this weak edge point to the list of edge points
                edges[a][b] = 1
              # Since this weak edge point has confirmed as an edge point,
                i# t needs to be added to q
                  # By putting this point into q, it can be judged whether
there are
                # weak edge points around this point in the next iteration
                q.append((a,b))
    return edges
# Get the final edge map
edges = link_edges(strong_edges, weak_edges)
plot_image(edges, 'Final image')
```

In summary, we encapsulate the Canny edge detector as the following function.

```
def canny(img, kernel_size=5, sigma=1.5, high=6, low=3):
   # Get the Gaussian filter
   kernel = gaussian_kernel(kernel_size, sigma)
   # Apply Gaussian filtering to the image
   smoothed = cv2.filter2D(img, -1, kernel)
   # Get the gradient map of the image
   G, theta = gradient(smoothed)
   # Apply non-maximum suppression to the gradient map
   nms = non_maximum_suppression(G, theta)
   # Get the information of strong and weak edges
   strong_edges, weak_edges = double_thresholding(nms, high, low)
   # Classify weak edge points into edge points or non-edge points to
get the final
   # edge map
   edge = link_edges(strong_edges, weak_edges)
   return edge
plot_image(img, 'Original image')
canny_img = canny(img)
plot_image(canny_img, 'Edges of image')
```

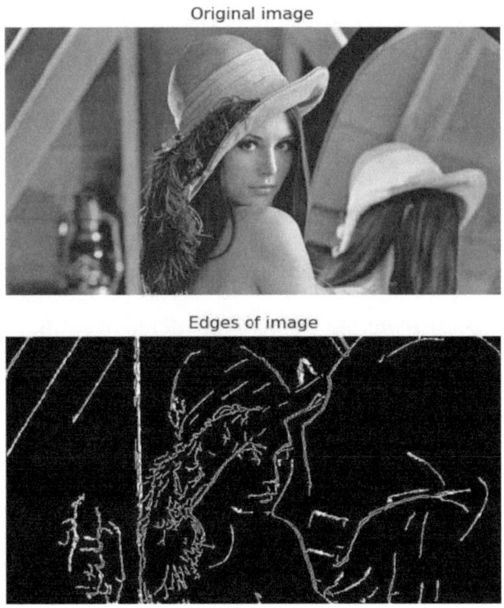

We found that in the above image, the edges of the female hair tips were detected, but it also included many edges caused by minor texture changes. As previously mentioned, the Canny operator can obtain multi-scale outputs by adjusting the standard deviation and kernel size of the Gaussian filter, making the edge detection results insensitive to minor texture changes. Next, we try to adjust the size and standard deviation of the Gaussian kernel, observe and compare the effects of different smoothing degrees on the edge detection results.

```
canny2 = canny(img, kernel_size=7, sigma=2)
plot_image(canny2, 'Kernel Size: 7, Sigma: 2')
canny2 = canny(img, kernel_size=9, sigma=2.5)
plot_image(canny2, 'Kernel Size: 9, Sigma: 2.5')
canny2 = canny(img, kernel_size=9, sigma=3)
plot_image(canny2, 'Kernel Size: 9, Sigma: 3')
```

Kernel Size: 7, Sigma: 2

Kernel Size: 9, Sigma: 2.5

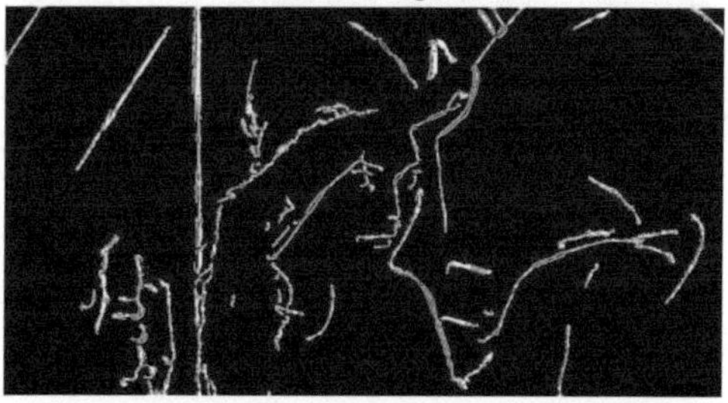

Kernel Size: 9, Sigma: 3

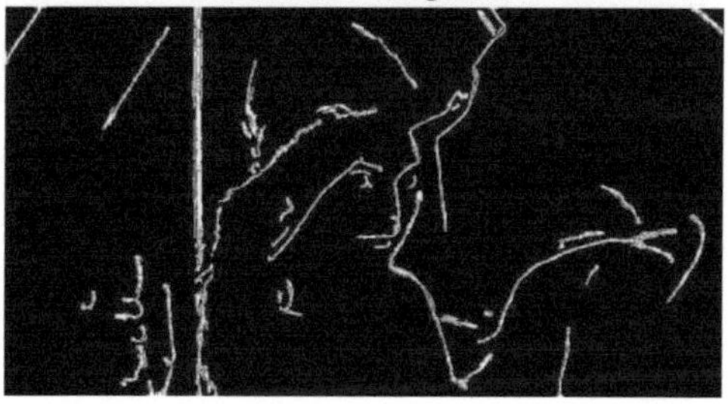

We found that as the standard deviation of the Gaussian kernel increases, the edge detection results become more robust to minor texture changes, but important edges are also lost. Therefore, we need to balance the weight between image smoothing and noise reduction. We encapsulate all the above functions into utils.py.

5.4 Summary

This chapter introduces the mathematical model of edge detection and explains two edge detection algorithms—Sobel edge detection algorithm and Canny edge detection algorithm. Both algorithms are based on the difference calculation of image gradients, and the strength and direction of the edges can be obtained through gradient calculation. Although the Sobel operator is simple, the detection results are easily affected by image noise. The Canny operator is the most widely used edge detection operator. By changing the convolution kernel size to adjust the smoothing degree of the image, it outputs multi-scale edge detection results and improves the positional accuracy of edge detection and the robustness to noise through non-maximum suppression and hysteresis thresholding methods.

Exercises

(1) The edge detection methods used in this chapter are all based on the first-order derivative of the image. Can the second-order derivative of the image also achieve edge detection? If so, try to implement an edge detection algorithm based on the second-order derivative.
(2) In this chapter, we used the Canny edge detection algorithm to detect the edges of grayscale images. So, how to use the Canny operator to implement edge detection of color images?
(3) Given an image, it is necessary to enhance the edge information in the image. How to use edge detection algorithms (such as Sobel, Canny, etc.) to achieve edge detection and enhancement?
(4) The Canny edge detection algorithm uses a double threshold strategy to judge the strong and weak edges. How to choose the thresholds?
(5) Is the Canny edge detection algorithm sensitive to noise? If it is sensitive to noise, explain why and propose a method to solve the noise problem.
(6) Compared with the Sobel edge detection algorithm, what are the differences and advantages of the Canny edge detection algorithm?

References

1. BORENSTEIN E, MALIK J. Shape guided object segmentation[C]//IEEE Conference on Computer Vision and Pattern Recognition, 2006, 1: 969–976.
2. MARR D. Vision: A computational investigation into the human representation and processing of visual information[M]. MIT press, 2010.
3. SOBEL I, FELDMAN G. An isotropic 3×3 image gradient operator[R]. Presentation at Stanford Artificial Intelligence Project, 1968.
4. CANNY J. A computational approach to edge detection[J]. IEEE Transactions on Pattern Analysis and Machine Intelligence, 1986 (6): 679-698.

Chapter 6
Corner Detection

6.1 Introduction

As mentioned in Chap. 4, template matching is the most basic and simplest form of image matching, where the template and the sub-image to be matched must have a high degree of similarity. So, how is image matching generally achieved? For example, how can we find the matching relationship between two images of a building taken from different perspectives, as shown in Fig. 6.1a? This requires detecting features in the image for matching. Speaking of features, the first thing that might come to mind are those special locations, such as the vertices of a building, as shown in Fig. 6.1b. These local features are often referred to as keypoint features or interesting point features. As keypoint features, they usually need to satisfy four properties: (1) repeatability, the same keypoint feature should be detectable in images under different geometric and photometric transformations; (2) saliency, each keypoint feature has a distinctive description that is different from other keypoint features, usually representing the image block around its location; (3) compactness, the number of keypoint features should be much less than the number of image pixels; (4) robustness, keypoint features should have a certain insensitivity to cluttered image backgrounds and occlusions. The keypoint features shown in Fig. 6.1b possess these properties, and they are all located at the intersection of two lines (edges), so they have a vivid name—corners. By matching corresponding corners in two images (Fig. 6.1c), and calculating the transformation matrix based on the matching relationship, the two images can be stitched into a larger image (Fig. 6.1d). This chapter will introduce a classic image corner detection algorithm—the Harris corner detection algorithm.

W. Shen et al., *Hands-On Computer Vision*,
https://doi.org/10.1007/978-981-95-4835-4_6

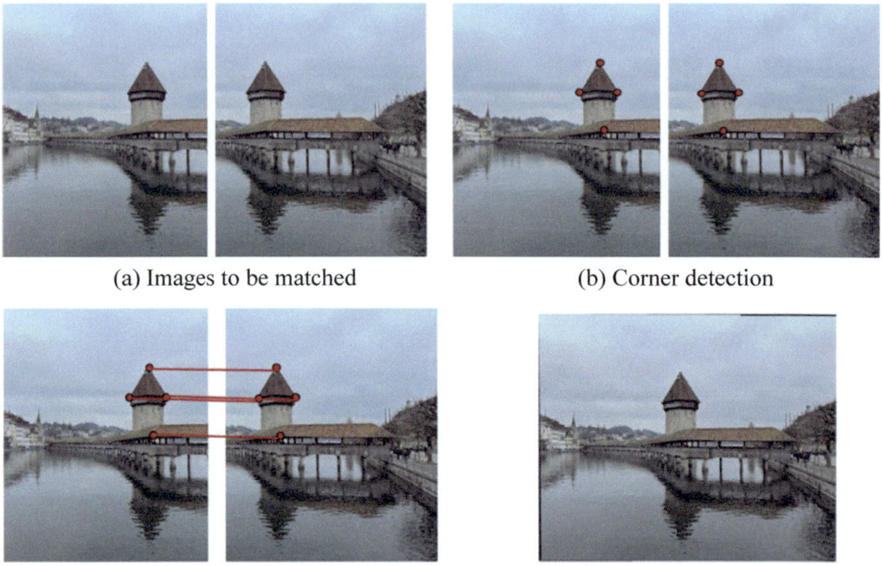

(a) Images to be matched (b) Corner detection

(c) Corner matching (d) Image stitching

Fig. 6.1 Image matching based on corners

6.2 Harris Corner Detection Algorithm

How to detect corners? Let's first analyze the characteristics of corners. Figure 6.2 shows a basic example of a corner. What patterns can we find from this example? If a small window is placed at a certain position p in the image, and then a small movement is made within the local range, and the change in pixel values in the window before and after the movement is examined, it can be found that: when p is in a flat area, no matter which direction the window is moved, the change in pixel values in the window before and after the movement is very small; when p is near the edge, if the window is moved along the edge direction, the change in pixel values in the window before and after the movement is also very small, but if it is moved in other directions, a larger change in pixel values will occur; when p is near the corner, no matter which direction the window is moved, a larger change in pixel values will occur.

Based on the above discussion, corners can be detected in the following way: use a fixed-size window to make a small movement in any direction at a certain position in the image, and compare the change in pixel values in the window before and after the movement. If a small displacement in any direction can cause a large change in pixel values in the window, then we consider that there is a corner in the window. The Harris corner detection algorithm is a representative algorithm based on this principle.

The Harris algorithm mainly includes the following two steps:

(a) Flat region (b) Edge (c) Corner

Fig. 6.2 Comparison of flat areas, edges, and corners

(1) For each position in the image, calculate the change in pixel values inside the window before and after the movement;
(2) Calculate the corner response function corresponding to the change in pixel values, and perform threshold processing on this function to extract corners.

6.2.1 Calculate Pixel Value Change

Place a window $\boldsymbol{W}$ at a certain position in the image $\boldsymbol{I}$, and move it a small displacement (u, v), as shown in Fig. 6.3, define the change in pixel values before and after the window movement $E(u, v)$ as follows:

$$E(u, v) = \sum_{(i,j)\in W} (I(i+u, j+v) - I(i,j))^2,$$

where (i, j) is a position inside the window; $I(i, j)$ is the current pixel value; $I(i + u, j + v)$ is the pixel value after displacement.

We know that when the window is in a flat region, no matter where the position (u, v) points in any direction, the value of $E(u, v)$ will be relatively small, because $I(i+u, j+v)$ and $I(i, j)$ are basically equal in flat regions. When the window is at the edge, if the direction of the displacement (u, v) is the direction of the edge normal, the calculated $E(u, v)$ will be relatively large, while if the direction of the displacement (u, v) is along the edge direction, then $E(u, v)$ will be relatively small.

Fig. 6.3 Movement of a window at a certain position

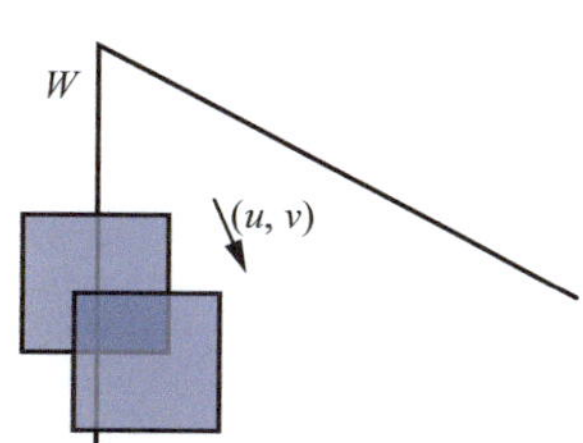

Only when the window is at the corner, no matter which direction the displacement (u, v) points to, the corresponding $E(u, v)$ will be very large. Therefore, our goal is to find such a window that can satisfy that for any (u, v), the value of $E(u, v)$ is very large. However, it is difficult to traverse all (u, v) to obtain the corresponding $E(u, v)$. Therefore, mathematical tools are needed to solve the above equation. The first-order Taylor expansion of the above formula is used to obtain its approximate form. For a two-dimensional image, its first-order Taylor expansion can be written as

$$I(i+u, j+v) \approx I(i,j) + uI_x + vI_y,$$

where I_x is the gradient magnitude of the image along the x-axis; I_y is the gradient magnitude of the image along the y-axis. That is,

$$I_x = \frac{\partial I(i,j)}{\partial x}, I_y = \frac{\partial I(i,j)}{\partial y}.$$

Therefore, $E(u, v)$ can be written as

$$\begin{aligned} E(u, v) &= \sum_{(i,j)\in W} \left(I(i,j) + uI_x + vI_y - I(i,j)\right)^2 = \sum_{(i,j)\in W} \left(uI_x + vI_y\right)^2 \\ &= \sum_{(i,j)\in W} \left(u^2 I_x^2 + v^2 I_y^2 + 2uvI_x I_y\right). \end{aligned}$$

Extracting (u, v), we get the final form:

$$E(u, v) = [u \quad v]\boldsymbol{M}\begin{bmatrix} u \\ v \end{bmatrix},$$

where the matrix $\boldsymbol{M}$ is

$$\boldsymbol{M} = \sum_{(i,j)\in W} \begin{bmatrix} I_x^2 & I_x I_y \\ I_x I_y & I_y^2 \end{bmatrix}.$$

It is not difficult to find that, $M = \sum_{(i,j)\in W} \boldsymbol{H}$, where $\boldsymbol{H}$ is the Hessian matrix of the image $\boldsymbol{I}$. Since $\boldsymbol{M}$ is a real symmetric matrix, it can be diagonalized, so it is further processed into

$$\boldsymbol{M} = \boldsymbol{R}\begin{bmatrix} \lambda_1 & 0 \\ 0 & \lambda_2 \end{bmatrix}\boldsymbol{R}^T,$$

where λ_1, λ_2 are the eigenvalues of the matrix $\boldsymbol{M}$; $\boldsymbol{R}$ is a two-dimensional rotation matrix. Substituting the above equation into the calculation of $E(u, v)$, we get

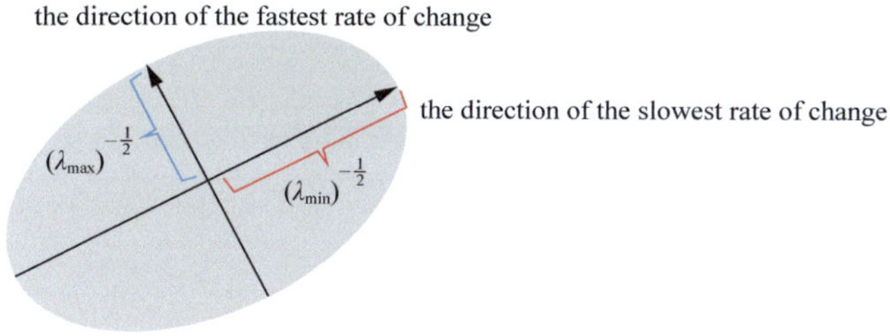

Fig. 6.4 Relationship between matrix and eigenvalues

$$E(u, v) = [u \quad v]\boldsymbol{R}\begin{bmatrix} \lambda_1 & 0 \\ 0 & \lambda_2 \end{bmatrix}\boldsymbol{R}^T\begin{bmatrix} u \\ v \end{bmatrix}.$$

Let $[m \quad n] = [u \quad v]\boldsymbol{R}$, we get

$$E(u, v) = [m \quad n]\begin{bmatrix} \lambda_1 & 0 \\ 0 & \lambda_2 \end{bmatrix}[m \quad n]^T = m^2\lambda_1 + n^2\lambda_2.$$

It can be seen that the magnitude of the pixel value change $E(u, v)$ is directly related to the two eigenvalues λ_1 and λ_2 of the matrix $\boldsymbol{M}$. $E(u, v)$. It can be represented as an ellipse determined by the eigenvalues λ_1, λ_2 which define the lengths of the long and short axes, and the direction determined by the eigenvectors, as shown in Fig. 6.4.

6.2.2 *Computing Corner Response Function*

As previously mentioned, the change in pixel values near the corner, $E(u, v)$, is significant for any small displacement (u, v). That is, if a point is a corner, the corresponding pixel value change $E(u, v)$ also has a large minimum value. How to obtain the minimum value of $E(u, v)$? Sect. 6.2.1 has already expressed $E(u, v)$ as a function of two eigenvalues λ_1, λ_2, and knowing $[m \quad n] = [u \quad v]\boldsymbol{R}$, we have

$$m^2 + n^2 = [m \quad n]\begin{bmatrix} m \\ n \end{bmatrix} = [u \quad v]\boldsymbol{R}\boldsymbol{R}^T\begin{bmatrix} u \\ v \end{bmatrix} = u^2 + v^2.$$

Here, we assume that the small displacement (u, v) is approximately a unit vector, i.e., $u^2 + v^2 \approx 1$, then we have $m^2 + n^2 \approx 1$, and it is easy to obtain the maximum and minimum values of $E(u, v)$ respectively as

$$\max_{u,v} E(u, v) = \max(\lambda_1, \lambda_2)$$

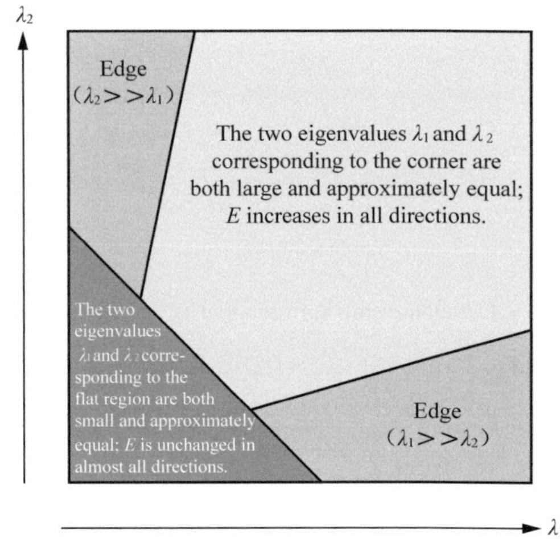

Fig. 6.5 Relationship between two eigenvalues and image region

$$\min_{u,v} E(u, v) = \min(\lambda_1, \lambda_2).$$

As shown in Fig. 6.4, because the minimum value of the pixel value change $E(u, v)$ corresponding to the corner is large, the two eigenvalues λ_1, λ_2 corresponding to the corner should also be relatively large. For edges and flat regions, similarly, they can be also determined based on the two eigenvalues λ_1, λ_2. The relationship between the two eigenvalues and the image region is shown in Fig. 6.5, summarized as follows.

(1) Both eigenvalues are small and approximately equal, indicating that the two axes of the ellipse are long and approximately equal in length; corresponding to flat regions in the image.
(2) One eigenvalue is large, the other is small, and the difference between them is large, indicating that the two axes of the ellipse are of different lengths and the difference is large; corresponding to edges in the image.
(3) Both eigenvalues are large and approximately equal, indicating that the two axes of the ellipse are short and approximately equal in length; corresponding to corners in the image.

Although the two eigenvalues λ_1, λ_2 can qualitatively determine the nature of the corner, we always hope to determine which pixels are corners through a single metric, the corner response function. Empirically, the corner response function is defined as

$$\rho = \lambda_1\lambda_2 - \alpha(\lambda_1 + \lambda_2)^2,$$

where α is a constant, usually taken as 0.04 to 0.06. You can verify whether this corner response function can reflect the relationship between the two eigenvalues and the flat regions, edges, and corners. The relationship between the corner response function and the image region is shown in Fig. 6.6, summarized as follows:

Fig. 6.6 Relationship between corner response function and image region

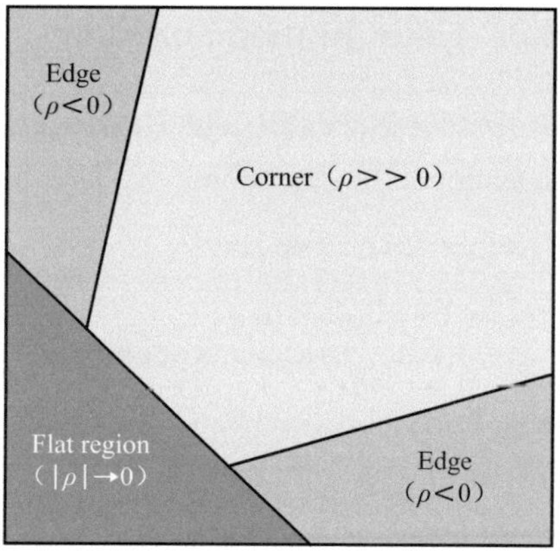

(1) If $|\rho|$ is very small, tending to zero, it corresponds to flat regions in the image.
(2) If ρ is negative, it corresponds to edges in the image.
(3) If ρ is a large positive number, it corresponds to corners in the image.

That is, if the corner response function ρ at the window location is positive and the larger it is, the more likely the window location is a corner, thus obtaining a quantifiable corner calculation method. According to linear algebra, we know:

$$\det(\boldsymbol{M}) = \lambda_1\lambda_2$$

$$\mathrm{trace}(\boldsymbol{M}) = \lambda_1 + \lambda_2.$$

Therefore, it can be directly calculated through the matrix $\boldsymbol{M}$ to calculate the corner response function, thus avoiding eigenvalue decomposition:

$$\rho = \lambda_1\lambda_2 - \alpha(\lambda_1 + \lambda_2)^2 = \det(\boldsymbol{M}) - \alpha(\mathrm{trace}(\boldsymbol{M}))^2.$$

After calculating the corner response function ρ, we judge ρ based on the set threshold γ. If $\rho > \gamma$, this location is determined to be a corner.

Let's summarize the specific steps for corner detection in an image.

(1) Calculate the gradient magnitude of each pixel in the image I_x, I_y.
(2) Slide a local window $\boldsymbol{W}$ to the position of each pixel in the image, and calculate the sum matrix of the image Hessian matrix in the window $\boldsymbol{M} = \sum_{(i,j)\in W} \boldsymbol{H}$.
(3) Calculate the corner response function $\rho = \det(\boldsymbol{M}) - \alpha(\mathrm{trace}(\boldsymbol{M}))^2_{\circ}$
(4) Perform non-maximum suppression on the corner response function of the entire image.
(5) Set the threshold γ. If $\rho > \gamma$, it is a corner.

6.3 Code Implementation

We have learned the theory of Harris corners, next, we will implement Harris corner detection in programming.

```
from utils import *
# Calculate the corner response function
def responseFunc(M):
    # Set hyperparameters
    k = 0.04
    # Calculate the determinant of M
    det = np.linalg.det(M)
    # Calculate the trace of M
    trace = np.trace(M)
    # Calculate the corner response function
    R = det - k * trace ** 2
    return R
# Harris corner detection algorithm
def harris_corners(src, NMS= False ):
    # Get the length and width of the input image
    h, w = src.shape[:2]
    # Convert the image to grayscale
    gray_image = cv2.cvtColor(src, cv2.COLOR_BGR2GRAY)
    # Initialize the corner matrix
    cornerPoint = np.zeros_like(gray_image,dtype=np.float32)
    # Calculate the gradient magnitude of the image along the x axis
and y axis
    grad = np.zeros((h, w, 2), dtype=np.float32)
    # Gradient along the x axis
    grad[:,:,0] = cv2.Sobel(gray_image, cv2.CV_16S, 1, 0)
    # Gradient along the y axis
    grad[:,:,1] = cv2.Sobel(gray_image, cv2.CV_16S, 0, 1)
    # Calculate the values of the elements in the Hessian matrix, the
values at this
    # time are the results of the sum, that is, the elements of the M
matrix
    Ixx = grad[:,:,0] ** 2
    Iyy = grad[:,:,1] ** 2
    Ixy = grad[:,:,0] * grad[:,:,1]
    # Calculate the values of the elements in the Hessian matrix in the
window,
    # using the Gaussian function as the window function
    Ixx = cv2.GaussianBlur(Ixx, (3, 3), sigmaX=2)
    Iyy = cv2.GaussianBlur(Iyy, (3, 3), sigmaX=2)
    Ixy = cv2.GaussianBlur(Ixy, (3, 3), sigmaX=2)
    for i in range(gray_image.shape[0]):
        for j in range(gray_image.shape[1]):
            # Construct M matrix
 struture_matrix = [[Ixx[i][j], Ixy[i][j]], [Ixy[i][j], Iyy[i][j]]]
            # Calculate corner response function
            R = responseFunc(struture_matrix)
            cornerPoint[i][j] = R
            # Calculate corner response function
```

```
                R = responseFunc(struture_matrix)
                cornerPoint[i][j] = R
        # Non-maximum suppression
        corners = np.zeros_like(gray_image, dtype=np.float32)
        threshold = 0.01
        # Return the maximum value of all corner responses
        maxValue = np.max(cornerPoint)
       # We set the threshold of the corner response function to threshold
    * maxValue
        for i in range(cornerPoint.shape[0]):
            for j in range(cornerPoint.shape[1]):
                # If NMS operation is performed
                if NMS:
                  # The current corner response value is greater than the
    threshold and
                # is also the maximum value of the neighboring points
                if cornerPoint[i][j] > threshold * maxValue and \
                    cornerPoint[i][j] == np.max(
                    cornerPoint[max(0, i - 1):min(i + 1, h - 1),
                    max(0, j - 1):min(j + 1, w - 1)]):
                    corners[i][j] = 255
                else :
                  # The current corner response value is greater than the
    threshold
                if cornerPoint[i][j] > threshold * maxValue:
                  corners[i][j] = 255
        # Return the detected corners
        return corners
    # Image material comes from the OpenCV-Python website
    img = cv2.imread('sudoku.png')
    plt.imshow(img[:, :, ::-1])
    plt.axis('off')
    plt.title('Original Input')
    plt.show()
    response = harris_corners(img)
    img[response == 255] = [0, 0, 255]
    plt.imshow(img[:, :, ::-1])
    plt.axis('off')
    plt.title('Harris Corner Response')
    plt.show()
```

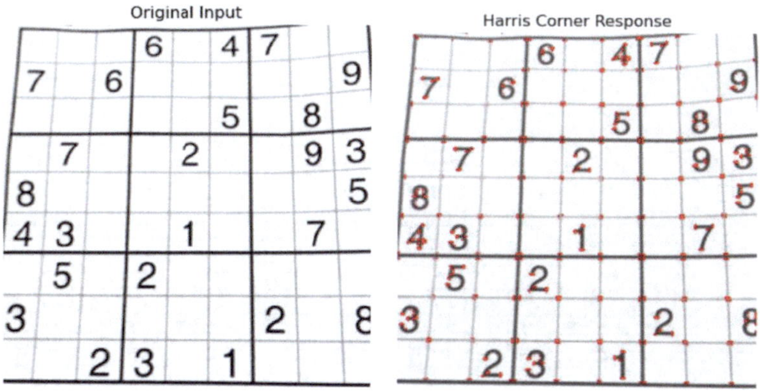

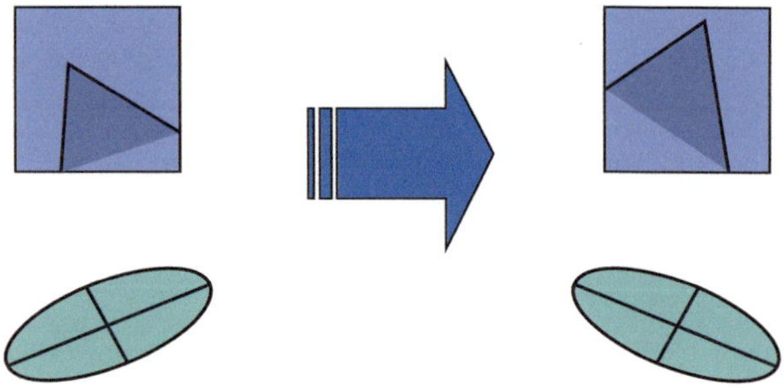

Fig. 6.7 Effect of image rotation on corner detection

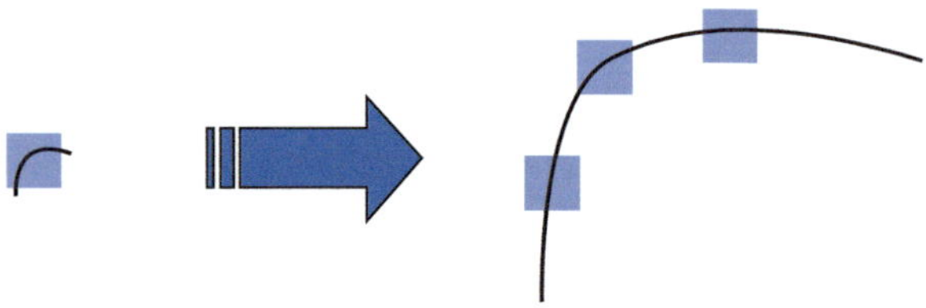

Fig. 6.8 Impact of image scaling on corner detection

6.4 The Effect of Image Transformation on Corner Detection

As mentioned in Sect. 6.1, feature points are relatively invariant (repeatability) to image transformations. Let's explore whether the corners detected are invariant when the image undergoes transformations, such as rotation, translation, and scaling?

When the image is rotated, the detected corners remain unchanged. As shown in Fig. 6.7, it can be intuitively found that the rotation of the image only changes the rotation factor $\boldsymbol{R}$ of the matrix $\boldsymbol{M}$ and does not change its corresponding eigenvalues, so it does not affect the corner detection.

Similarly, translating an image does not change the magnitude of the matrix's eigenvalues, so the Harris corner detection still maintains invariance. However, when an image is scaled, corners in the original image may be detected as edges. As shown in Fig. 6.8, after the image is enlarged, the original corners are detected as multiple edge points. Therefore, corners are not invariant to image scaling!

6.5 Summary

This chapter introduced a type of feature point in images—corners, as well as the Harris corner detection algorithm. Although corners are invariant to many image transformations and are commonly used feature points for image matching, they do not are invariant to changes in the scale of the image, which is a limitation of corners. So, are there feature points that are invariant to image scaling? The SIFT feature detection introduced in Chap. 7 will address this issue.

Exercises

(1) The Harris corner detection algorithm determines whether the current location is a corner based on the amount of pixel value changes within a fixed-size window. Does the size of this window affect the results of corner detection? Use the provided sudoku.png for this experiment and analysis.
(2) Use the provided sudoku.png for an experiment, i.e., analyzing whether three types of image transformations (rotation, translation, scaling) have any impact on corner detection.
(3) Use the provided sudoku.png for an experiment, analyzing whether the Harris corner detection algorithm is sensitive to image noise (such as Gaussian noise and salt-and-pepper noise).
(4) In Harris corner detection, what impact does the threshold value of the corner response function have on the results of corner detection? Use the provided sudoku.png, design an experiment, and analyze the impact of different thresholds on the results of corner detection.

Chapter 7
SIFT Feature Detection

7.1 Blob Detection and Scale Space

Let's return to the image matching problem mentioned in Chap. 6. How can we match sub-images 7.1a and b? Can we use the corners introduced in Chap. 6 for matching? Sub-images 7.1a and b have both rotation and scale transformations, and corners are not invariant to scale. Therefore, we need to find a new type of feature point (keypoint) for matching images under complex transformations. If we can locate some regions of interest in the image centered on this feature point, such as the windows shown in 7.1c and d, and if we know that these two regions match, we can calculate the rotation and scale transformations between them, thereby matching the two images. However, not every region in the image can be used for matching as a feature point area. Such areas need to satisfy the following properties:

(1) Rich in semantic information.
(2) Has a well-defined position in the image (locatable).
(3) Has a well-defined description, which can be used for matching or distinguishing other region of interests.

For the feature description of the region, the following two requirements are also needed:

(1) Invariant to image translation, rotation, and scaling.
(2) Robust to changes in illumination.

Based on the above properties, determine which regions in Fig. 7.2 are regions of interest for feature points. Are the edges in Fig. 7.2a and b feature point areas? It can be found that the features of edge regions at different positions are basically similar; thus, they cannot be accurately located. Consequently, the edge region is not a feature point region. The blob-like regions enclosed by closed contours in Fig. 7.2c and d have definite positions and sizes, as well as characteristic semantic information, which can be used for matching. Thus, blob-like regions are regions of interest for feature points.

W. Shen et al., *Hands-On Computer Vision*,
https://doi.org/10.1007/978-981-95-4835-4_7

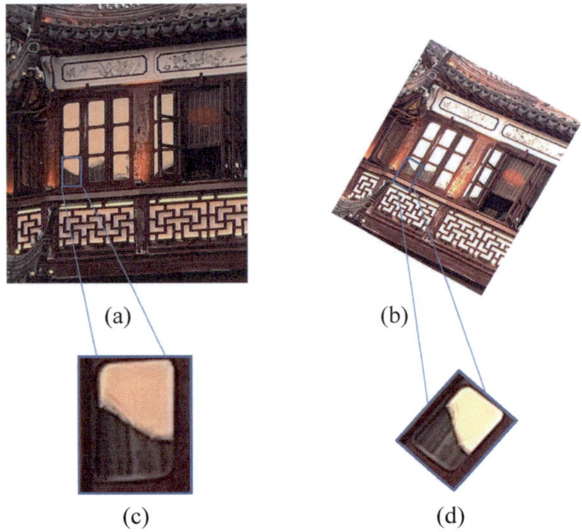

Fig. 7.1 Matching images based on features of regions of interest

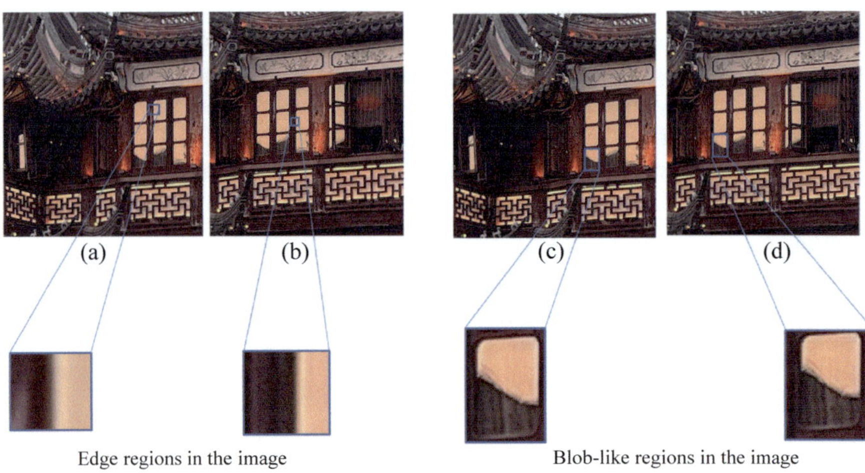

Fig. 7.2 Edge areas and block regions in the image

Therefore, detecting feature points in the image requires detecting blob-like regions in the image, determining their position, size, and direction, and finally expressing them as a feature description that is independent of size and direction. Since the blob-like region is an region with a closed contour (edge), it is natural to think of using an edge detector to detect it. Figure 7.3 shows some one-dimensional blob-like regions of different sizes, convolved with a second-order differential operator (Laplacian operator). Note that in Chap. 5, we introduced that

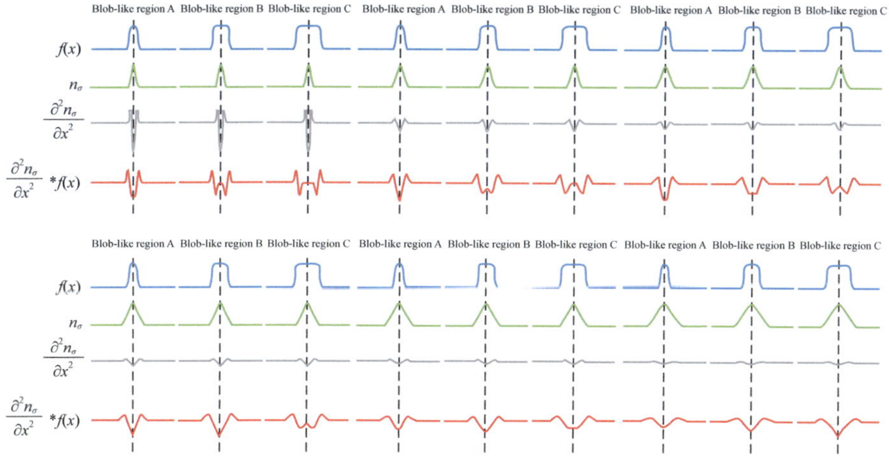

Fig. 7.3 Response of blob-like regions to the Laplacian of Gaussian operator

Gaussian smoothing should be used for denoising before edge detection, and this step is still used here. The operator that combines Gaussian smoothing and second-order differentiation is called the Laplacian of Gaussian (LoG) operator.

The bottom row of Fig. 7.3 shows the convolution results of one-dimensional blob-like regions of different sizes with the Laplacian of Gaussian operator with different standard deviations. It is not difficult to find that as the standard deviation of the LoG operator increases, when the standard deviation size of the Laplacian of Gaussian operator is the same as the size of the blob-like region, their convolution result will have a unique extremum. The standard deviation size at this time is called the characteristic scale σ^*. Since there is such an extremum of the response, can we find the blob-like regions of the input image by convolving the input image with the LoG operator with different standard deviations, and then finding the extremum of the convolution result? It's not that simple. Note that the unique extremum mentioned above is the unique extremum within the range of x values under a specific standard deviation σ (scale). If multiple scales are considered, that is, in the entire (x, σ) space (the value space composed of all value ranges of x and σ), this extremum is not a global minimum (as shown in Fig. 7.4a), which makes the above method for detecting blob-like regions unimplementable. This phenomenon occurs because the response of the LoG operator will decay as the standard deviation increases, so normalization is needed for the response, that is, it is multiplied by σ^2. The response of the normalized LoG operator is shown in Fig. 7.4b, where the extremum at the characteristic scale is the global minimum in the entire (x, σ) space. As long as the global minimum of the response of the normalized LoG operator in (x, σ) space is detected, blob-like regions can be detected and their characteristic scales can be determined simultaneously.

So far, we have learned the basic principles of blob-like region detection based on scale space. So, how can this principle be applied to images?

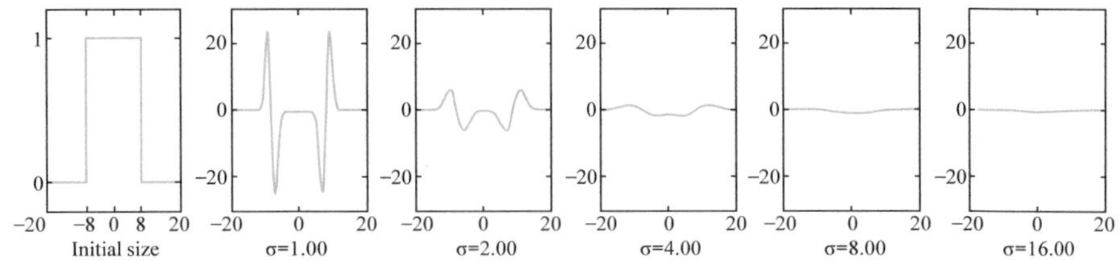

(a) The response of the non-normalized Laplacian of Gaussian (LoG) operator

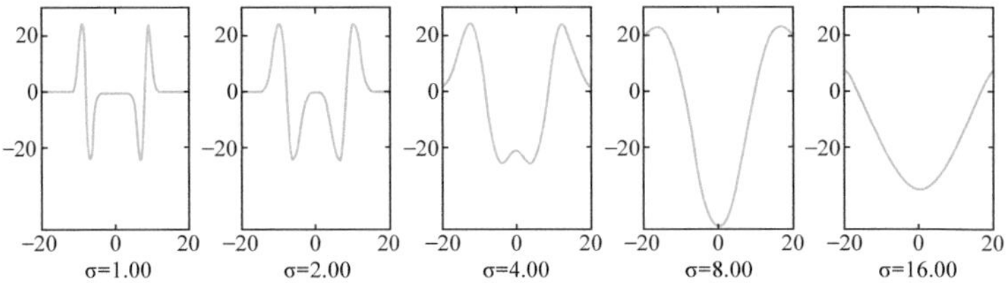

(b) The response of the normalized Laplacian of Gaussian (LoG) operator

Fig. 7.4 Response of scale-normalized Gaussian Laplacian operator

The scale space of an image $L(x, y, \sigma)$ can be obtained by convolving a Gaussian function of different scales $G(x, y, \sigma)$ with the input image (x, y). The value at this scale space (x, y, σ) is $L(x, y, \sigma)$ as follows:

$$L(x, y, \sigma) = G(x, y, \sigma) * I(x, y),$$

where (x, y) is the two-dimensional spatial coordinate, and σ is the standard deviation of the Gaussian distribution, also known as the scale space factor. From the knowledge of filtering, it is known that the smaller the σ value, i.e., the smaller the scale, the less blurred the image; the larger the σ value, i.e., the larger the scale, the more blurred the image. Large scales correspond to the overall features of the image, and small scales correspond to the detailed features of the image. By calculating the convolution of the input image with the normalized LoG operator, whether there is an extremum in the convolution result can be used to judge whether the current position is a blob-like region, i.e., whether there is a feature point. As shown in Fig. 7.5, the convolution response at the marked position (eave position) has a maximum, indicating that the marked position is a blob-like region, and the scale corresponding to this maximum is the characteristic scale of this block region. As shown in Fig. 7.6, there is no obvious extremum in the convolution response at the marked position, indicating that the marked position is not a blob-like region and there is no feature point.

If corresponding feature points are found in two images, the ratio of the characteristic scales corresponding to the feature points can be calculated to obtain the scale scaling ratio of the two images. As shown in the two images in Fig. 7.7, their corresponding scaling ratio is σ_1^* / σ_2^*.

Section 7.2 will introduce a highly efficient blob-like region detection algorithm based on scale space—the SIFT algorithm.

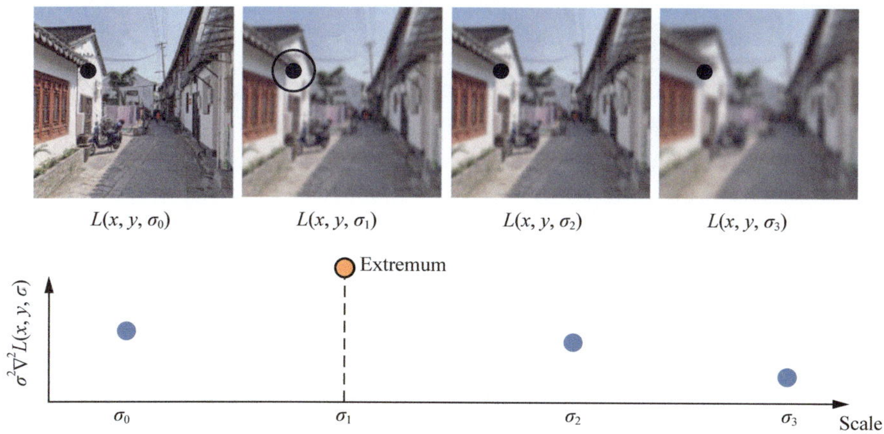

Fig. 7.5 If there is an extremum in the response of the normalized LoG operator in the image scale space, it indicates that there is a blob-like region, i.e., there is a feature point

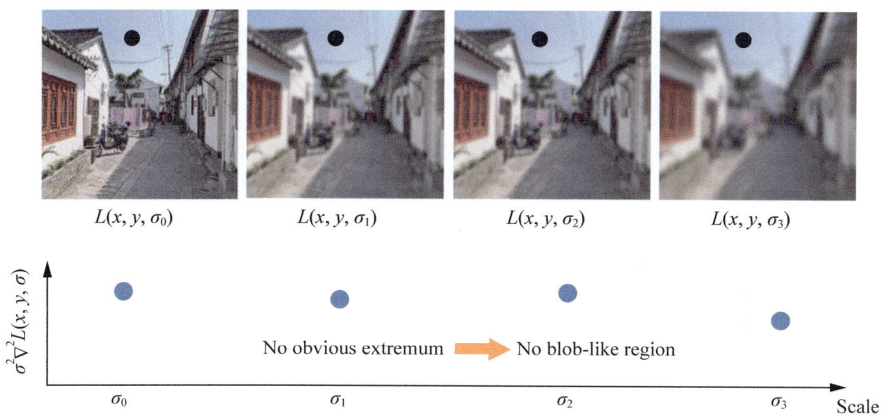

Fig. 7.6 If there is no obvious extremum in the response of the normalized LoG operator in the image scale space, it indicates that there is no blob-like region, i.e., there is no feature point

7.2 SIFT Algorithm

SIFT [1] stands for Scale Invariant Feature Transform, proposed by Professor David G. Lowe in 1999 at the IEEE International Conference on Computer Vision (ICCV). It is one of the most cited papers in the field of computer vision over the past two decades. The SIFT algorithm is a highly efficient blob-like region detection algorithm based on scale space, including blob-like region detection and blob-like description (SIFT features). Its introduction greatly promoted the development of the field of computer vision and is widely used in visual recognition and 3D reconstruction. The

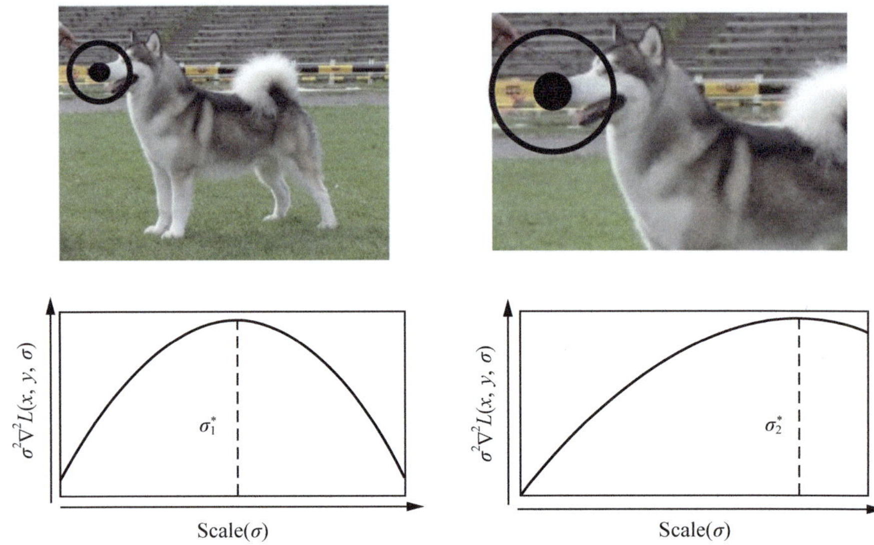

Fig. 7.7 Relationship between the ratio of feature scales and the change of image scale (illustration material from ImageNet)

main idea of the SIFT algorithm is consistent with that described in Sect. 7.1, i.e., using scale space to detect blob-like regions in images.

7.2.1 Local Extremum Detection

In Sect. 7.1, we already know how to use scale space to detect feature points, i.e., convolve the image $\boldsymbol{I}$ with the normalized LoG operator $\sigma^2\nabla^2\boldsymbol{G}$, and find the σ corresponding to the extremum in the response. To improve computational efficiency, we can use the Difference of Gaussian (DoG) operator $\boldsymbol{D}$ to approximate the normalized LoG operator. The DoG operator is defined as follows:

$$D(x, y, \sigma) = G(x, y, k\sigma) - G(x, y, \sigma).$$

Because

$$\sigma\nabla^2\boldsymbol{G} = \frac{\partial \boldsymbol{G}}{\partial \sigma} \approx \frac{G(x, y, k\sigma) - G(x, y, \sigma)}{k\sigma - \sigma}.$$

Therefore, we can get

$$D(x, y, \sigma) = G(x, y, k\sigma) - G(x, y, \sigma) \approx (k - 1)\sigma^2\nabla^2\boldsymbol{G},$$

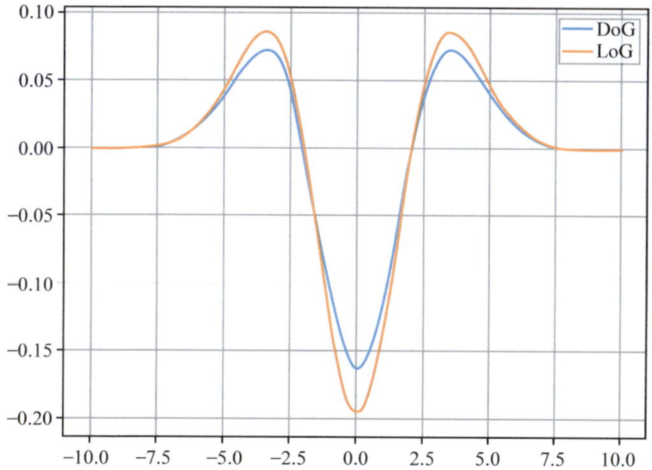

Fig. 7.8 Comparison of the normalized Gaussian Laplacian of Gaussian operator and the difference of Gaussian (DoG) operator

where k is a constant, thus the extrema will not be affected by the constant $k - 1$. As shown in Fig. 7.8, we can find that the normalized LoG operator and the DoG operator are similar.

Convolve the image $I(x, y)$ with the DoG operator $D(x, y, \sigma)$ to get

$$\begin{aligned} D(x, y, \sigma)*I(x, y) &= (G(x, y, k\sigma) - G(x, y, \sigma))*I(x, y) \\ &= L(x, y, k\sigma) - L(x, y, \sigma). \end{aligned}$$

As can be seen, the result of the convolution of the DoG operator with the image can be obtained by directly subtracting $\boldsymbol{L}$ of different scales. Therefore, the convolution of the DoG operator with the image can be calculated as shown in Fig. 7.9. First, obtain a scale space corresponding to an image, that is, obtain a series of response images by convolving a Gaussian function at varied scales with the input image, and then subtract the two response images at adjacent scales. This will yield the convolution results of the DoG operators at different scales with the input image.

As mentioned earlier, the feature points correspond to the extrema on the response map of the DoG operator. To detect the extrema on the response map, the response value of each point on the response map needs to be compared with all its neighboring points. As shown in the middle sub-figure of Fig. 7.10, the orange point to be detected in the middle needs to be compared with the response values of its 26 neighboring points (including 8 neighboring points on the same scale response map and 9×2 neighboring points on the corresponding response maps of two adjacent scales) in the entire (x, y, σ) image scale space. If the response value of this point is the largest among the 26 neighboring points, this point is considered a candidate feature point.

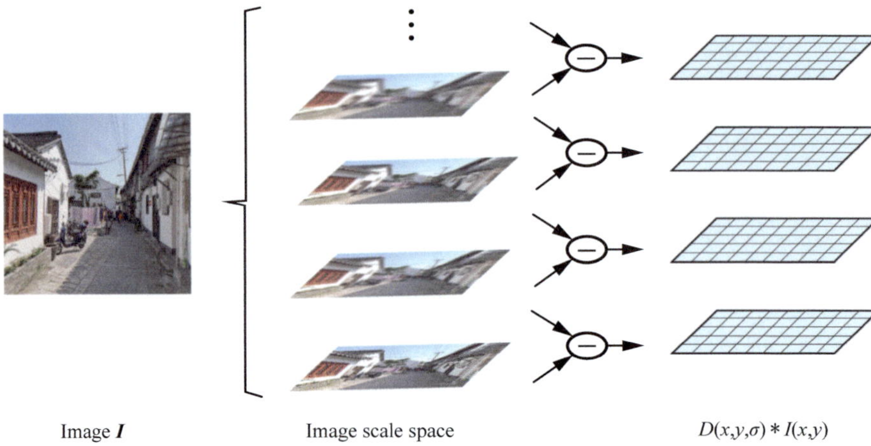

Fig. 7.9 Fast calculation of the convolution results of the DoG operator with the input image based on image scale space

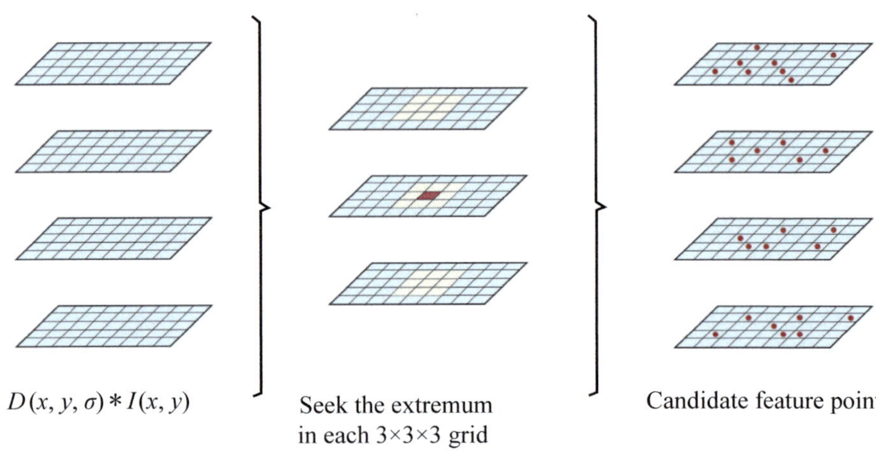

Fig. 7.10 Local extrema in the 26 neighborhoods in the image scale space are candidate feature points

7.2.2 *Feature Point Localization and Filtering*

In Sect. 7.2.1, candidate feature points are obtained through extremum detection in scale space. Note that the word "candidate" indicates that some of the detected feature points are not real feature points and need further filtering. As shown in Fig. 7.11, there is a difference between the extrema in discrete space and those in continuous space.

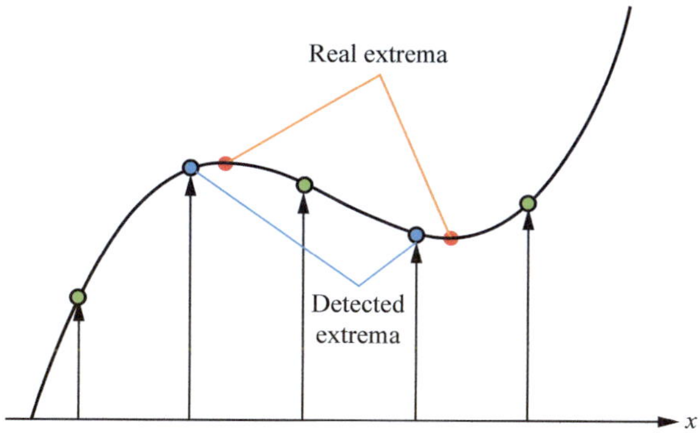

Fig. 7.11 Difference between extrema in discrete space and continuous apace

To filter out the real feature points from the candidate feature points, interpolation can be used. First, curve fitting is performed on the DoG operator. The Taylor expansion of this operator is

$$D(\boldsymbol{x}) = D(0) + \frac{\partial \boldsymbol{D}^T}{\partial \boldsymbol{x}}\boldsymbol{x} + \frac{1}{2}\boldsymbol{x}^T\frac{\partial^2 \boldsymbol{D}}{\partial x^2}\boldsymbol{x},$$

where $\mathbf{x} = (x, y, \sigma)^T$. By setting the derivative of the equation to zero, the offset of the real extremum position relative to the current position can be obtained:

$$\hat{\boldsymbol{x}} = -\frac{\partial^2 \boldsymbol{D}}{\partial \boldsymbol{x}^2}\frac{\partial \boldsymbol{D}}{\partial \boldsymbol{x}}.$$

Generally, when $\hat{\boldsymbol{x}}$ has an offset greater than 0.5 in any dimension (x, y, or σ), the interpolation center has already shifted to its neighboring point, so the current candidate feature point position must be updated, and interpolation must be repeated at the new position until convergence. In practice, this process may exceed the set number of iterations, or the updated extremum position may exceed the image boundary. Such points should be deleted. Substitute the extremal point $\boldsymbol{x}^* = \boldsymbol{x} + \hat{\boldsymbol{x}}$ into the equation to get the value

$$D(\boldsymbol{x}^*) = D(0) + \frac{1}{2}\frac{\partial \boldsymbol{D}^T}{\partial \boldsymbol{x}}\hat{\boldsymbol{x}}.$$

We call $D(\boldsymbol{x}^*)$ the contrast of this point. Since points with low contrast are easily disturbed by noise and become unstable, extrema with low contrast (less than a certain empirical value, such as 0.03) need to be deleted. In addition, candidate feature points with large edge responses need to be eliminated. As mentioned in Sect. 7.1, the edge area is not a feature point area because it cannot be accurately located. So how to eliminate candidate feature points with large edge responses? In Chap. 6, for a certain position (i,j) in the image, whether it is an edge can be determined by the corner response function. Let λ_1 and λ_2 be the Hessian matrix $\boldsymbol{H}$ corresponding to the position (i, j). The two eigenvalues, when one is much larger than the other, indicate that the position is an edge. Suppose $\lambda_1 = \gamma\lambda_2$, we have

$$\frac{\text{trace}(\boldsymbol{H})^2}{\det(\boldsymbol{H})} = \frac{(\lambda_1 + \lambda_2)^2}{\lambda_1\lambda_2} = \frac{(\gamma + 1)^2\lambda_2^2}{\gamma\lambda_2^2} = \frac{(\gamma + 1)^2}{\gamma}.$$

Based on the knowledge of inequalities, we know that the value of the above formula is smallest when $\gamma = 1$ (the two eigenvalues are equal), and it increases as γ increases. The larger γ is, the greater the difference between the two eigenvalues, and the more likely this position is an edge. Therefore, to detect whether the candidate feature point is an edge point, we only need to check whether the following formula is satisfied:

$$\frac{\text{trace}(\boldsymbol{H})^2}{\det(\boldsymbol{H})} < \frac{(\gamma + 1)^2}{\gamma}.$$

Empirically, we can set $\gamma = 10$. In this way, the feature points screened out are the final determined feature points.

7.2.3 Calculation of Feature Point Direction

In order to match similar targets at different rotation angles, feature points should be rotation invariant; thus, it is necessary to determine the main direction of the feature points. How to determine the main direction of the feature points? In Chap. 5, we introduced that image gradient can describe the direction of local structure of the image, then we can calculate the main direction of the feature points based on this idea. According to Sect. 7.2.1, we can get the position and feature scale of each feature point. According to Lowe's suggestion, the square area circumscribing the circle with the position of the feature point as the center and 4.5 times the feature scale (1.5 times the size of 3 σ principle) as the radius is the blob-like region corresponding to this feature point. After completing the gradient calculation of the feature points, use a histogram to count the gradient magnitude and direction of the pixels in the neighborhood of the feature points. The histogram is divided into bins per 10°, i.e., dividing 360° into 36 bins. The direction corresponding to each bin represents the gradient direction of the feature point, and the height of the bin represents the gradient magnitude. To compute the height of the bin, in the blob-like region, pick out the pixels whose gradient direction belong to this bin, and sum up their magnitudes as the height of the bin. Since the contributions of the gradient magnitudes of the pixels in the square area to the feature points can be different, the height of the bin can be also computed by weighted sum of the gradient magnitudes. Here, Gaussian weighting is used. If the offset of the current pixel from the feature point is (i, j), then the corresponding Gaussian weight w is

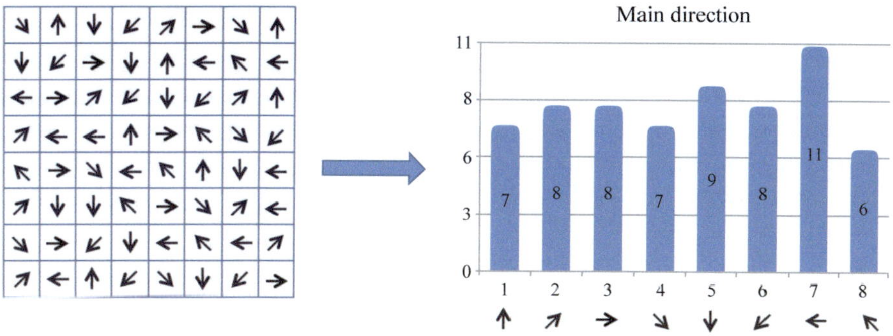

Fig. 7.12 Selecting the direction of feature points using histogram statistics

$$w = \mathrm{e}^{\left(-\frac{i^2+j^2}{2\times(1.5\sigma)^2}\right)}.$$

After counting the weighted gradient magnitudes in each direction and obtaining the histogram, in order to prevent the gradient direction angle from mutation due to noise disturbance, the gradient direction histogram also needs to be smoothed. The smoothing formula is

$$H(i) = \frac{6}{16}H(i) + \frac{4}{16}(H(i-1) + H(i+1)) + \frac{1}{16}(H(i-2) + H(i+2)).$$

Since the angle is cyclic ($0° = 360°$), if the index is out of bounds in the above formula, you can find its corresponding position between $[0°, 360°)$ through the method of circular cycling, such as $(38) = H(2)$. After smoothing, the direction of the maximum in the histogram is taken as the main direction of this feature point. As shown in Fig. 7.12, the $\leftarrow$ in the histogram represents the main direction of the feature point (the histogram in this figure divides the direction into 8 bins, each 45° as a bin).

In addition to determining a main direction for each feature point, one or more auxiliary directions may also be selected. The addition of auxiliary directions is to enhance the robustness of image matching. The definition of the auxiliary direction is that when there is another bin whose height is greater than 80% of the height of the main direction bin, the direction represented by this bin is the auxiliary direction of this feature point.

So far, the detected image SIFT feature points contain three types of information: position, scale, and direction.

7.2.4 Feature Point Description

This section establishes a descriptor for each feature point, that is, a set of vectors to represent this feature point. This descriptor needs to satisfy: (1) The descriptor is unique, that is, similar feature points have similar descriptors, and dissimilar feature points have different descriptors, so that feature points in different images can be matched based on the descriptor; (2) the descriptor is invariant to various changes (such as changes in lighting, viewing angle, etc.), thereby ensuring that the match is not affected by these changes.

In order to generate descriptors, for each feature point, take this point as the center, make a circle with a radius of $r = \frac{3\sigma\sqrt{2}(d+1)}{2}$, determine the square area circumscribing this circle, and divide this area into $d \times d$ sub-regions. Empirically, we set $d = 4$. As shown in Fig. 7.13, a histogram of the image gradient magnitudes in eight directions (east, west, south, north, southeast, northeast, southwest, northwest) is calculated within each sub-region. The gradient magnitudes can be weighted by a Gaussian function or not weighted at all. In this way, each sub-region can be represented by a histogram vector of length 8. The descriptor of the feature point, also known as the SIFT feature vector, is the 128-dimensional vector formed by concatenating the vectors of the 16 sub-regions.

However, the SIFT feature vector obtained from the above operation is not rotation invariant. Therefore, before calculating the gradient magnitude, the horizontal direction of the blob-like region where each feature point is located needs to be rotated to the principal direction (as shown in Fig. 7.14). This rotation does not change the

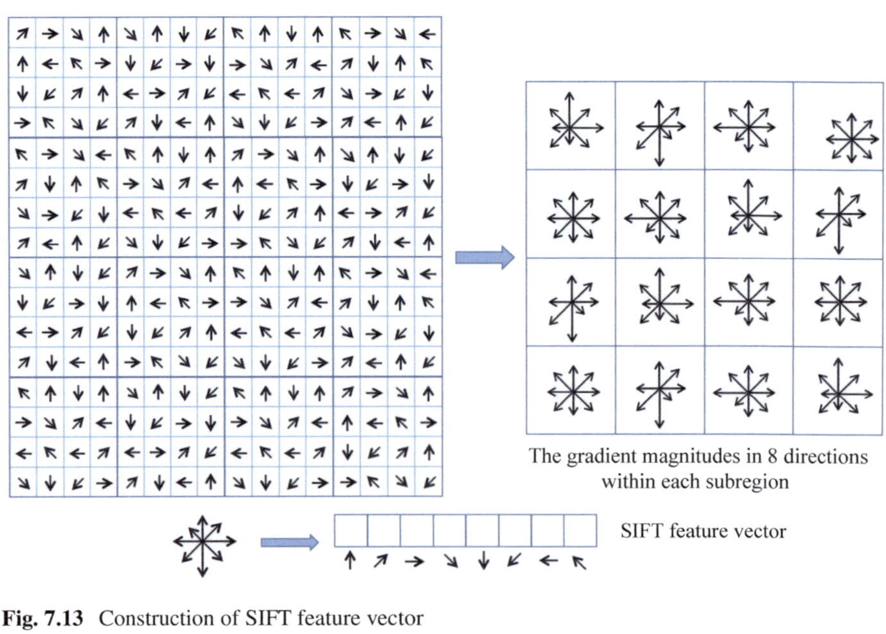

Fig. 7.13 Construction of SIFT feature vector

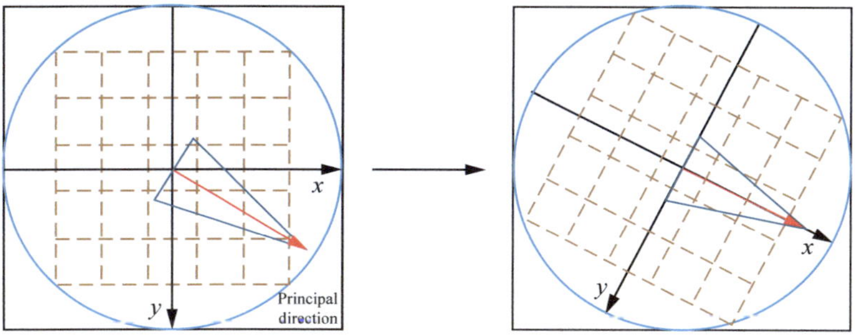

Fig. 7.14 Rotating the horizontal axis of the blob-like region where the feature point is located to the principal direction]

adjacent pixels of the feature point or the magnitude of the pixel gradient within the neighborhood. It only changes the gradient direction of each pixel. Why can the rotation invariance of the feature vector be achieved by rotating the horizontal direction of the block region to the principal direction? This is because when describing the feature point, the gradient direction needs to be determined using the horizontal and vertical axes. If this direction is related to the image itself, then when the image is rotated, this coordinate axis will also be rotated, and the descriptor obtained will be different. When this direction only depends on the principal direction of the blob-like region, no matter how much degree the image is rotated, the calculated feature descriptor will not be changed. In other words, the coordinate system relied on is not absolute, but relative.

For a point (i, j) in the blob-like region, rotate it counterclockwise by an angle α to get the coordinates of the new point (i', j'), then

$$[i' \; j']^T = \begin{bmatrix} \cos\alpha & -\sin\alpha \\ \sin\alpha & \cos\alpha \end{bmatrix} [i \; j]^T.$$

7.3 Code Implementation

In this section, we will implement the SIFT algorithm through programming. Each step of the SIFT algorithm will be written as a function. We will first implement the generation of the scale space.

```
import cv2
import numpy as np
from scipy.ndimage import maximum_filter
import matplotlib.pyplot as plt
import random
# Generate a specified number of Gaussian kernels and apply Gaus-
sian filtering to the
```

```
# image
def generateGimage(image, sigma, num_layers = 8, k_stride = 2):
    sigma_res = np.sqrt(np.max([(sigma ** 2) - ((1) ** 2), 0.01]))
      # (0,0) means the size of the convolution kernel is determined by sigma
    image = cv2.GaussianBlur(image, (0, 0), sigmaX=sigma_res,
                             sigmaY=sigma_res)
    # Generate Gaussian kernels
    k = 2 ** (1 / k_stride)
    gaussian_kernels = np.zeros(num_layers)
    # The first layer of Gaussian kernel is 1.6
    gaussian_kernels[0] = sigma
    for i in range(1, num_layers):
      # According to the properties of the Gaussian kernel, large Gaussian kernels
        # can be decomposed to reduce the amount of computation
        gaussian_old = k**(i-1) * sigma
        gaussian_new = k * gaussian_old
          gaussian_kernels[i] = np.sqrt(gaussian_new**2 - gaussian_old**2)
    # At this point, we have obtained a series of Gaussian kernels
    # Perform Gaussian filtering
    gaussian_images = [image]
    for kernel in gaussian_kernels:
        tmp_image = cv2.GaussianBlur(image, (0, 0), sigmaX=kernel,
                                     sigmaY=kernel)
        gaussian_images.append(tmp_image)
      # Return the results of image filtering with different Gaussian kernels
    return np.array(gaussian_images)
# Generate DoG (Difference of Gaussian) space
def generateDoGSpace(gaussian_images):
    dog_images = []
    for img1, img2 in zip(gaussian_images, gaussian_images[1:]):
        dog_images.append(img2 - img1)
    return dog_images
```

After generating the scale space of the image, to detect the feature points of the image, the following two steps are required: (1) Determine whether each position is a local extremum; (2) if it is an extremum, locate and screen it, and calculate the attributes of the final selected feature points.

```
# 1. Determine whether the current pixel is a local maximum
def isLocalExtremum(l1, l2, l3, threshold):
     # l1, l2, l3 are adjacent layers in the DoG scale space, all of which have been
    # sliced into 3*3
    # That is, [l1,l2,l3] is a cube
      # It is necessary to determine whether the center position of the l2 layer, i.e.,
    # the (1,1) position, is an extremum
    # threshold is a set threshold, l2[1,1] must be greater than the threshold to
    # determine the extremum
```

```
    if l2[1,1] > threshold:
        if l2[1,1] > 0:
            return np.all(l2[1,1]>=l1) and np.all(l2[1,1]>=l3) \
                and np.sum(l2[1,1]<l2)==0
        elif l2[1,1] < 0:
            return np.all(l2[1,1]<=l1) and np.all(l2[1,1]<=l3) \
                and np.sum(l2[1,1]>l2)==0
    return False
# 2. If it is an extremum, locate and screen it, and calcu-
late the attributes
# of the final selected feature points
# In this module, we will write the implementation to calcu-
late the attributes of the
# feature points
# Refer to sections 7.2.2 and 7.2.3
# Calculate the attributes of the extremum
def computeBlobAttribute(x, y, layer, dog_
images, sigma, threshold,
                border, num_layers, g_image, corners,
                scales, orientations, layers):
    # Calculate the attributes of the feature point at position (x,y)
    # At this time, it is assumed that the point at this posi-
tion is the maximum in
    # the neighborhood
    # First, it needs to be screened, and it is deter-
mined whether it is a
    # real extremum according to the Newton iteration method
    # Filter out feature points with low contrast
    # Eliminate edge response
    # After this, the information of the feature points can be obtained
    gamma = 10
    image_shape = dog_images[0].shape
    out_flag = False
    # Use the Newton iteration method to get the extremum
    # Update up to 5 times, if it does not converge, it is consid-
ered that the
    # candidate point is not an extremum
    for iter_num in range(5):
        # Get the adjacent 3 layers in the DoG space
        img1, img2, img3 = dog_images[layer-1:layer+2]
        # Slice these 3 layers to get a 3*3 cube
        cube = np.array([img1[x-1:x+2, y-1:y+2],
                    img2[x-1:x+2, y-1:y+2],
                    img3[x-1:x+2, y-1:y+2]])
        # Obtain the first and second derivatives of the cube
        grad = compute1derivative(cube)
        hessian = compute2derivative(cube)
        # Solve the equation to get the update value of Newton's iteration
        update = -np.linalg.lstsq(hessian, grad, rcond=None)[0]
        # If the moving distance is too small, it means that the current
point has
        # converged to the extremum, so we can directly return the current
point
        if abs(update[0]) < 0.5 and abs(update[1]) < 0.5 \
```

```
            and abs(update[2]) < 0.5:
            break
        # Update the current point
        y += int(round(update[0]))
        x += int(round(update[1]))
        layer += int(round(update[2]))
        # Ensure the new cube is within the DoG space
        if x < border or x >= image_shape[0] - border \
                or y < border \
                or y >= image_shape[1] - border \
                or layer < 1 or layer > num_layers - 2:
            # If it's not in the space, then out_flag = True
            out_flag = True
            break
    # If it exceeds the space size or does not converge, return directly
    if out_flag or iter_num >= 4:
        return
            # Use the following formula to calcu-
late the contrast of the extremum point
    Extremum = cube[1, 1, 1] + 0.5 * np.dot(grad, update)
    # Filter out low-contrast feature points
    if np.abs(Extremum) >= threshold:
        # Get the Hessian matrix of xy
        xy_hessian = hessian[:2, :2]
        xy_hessian_trace = np.trace(xy_hessian)
        xy_hessian_det = np.linalg.det(xy_hessian)
        # Eliminate edge response
        if xy_hessian_det > 0 and \
            (xy_hessian_trace ** 2) / xy_hessian_det < \
            ((gamma + 1) ** 2) / gamma:
            # Coordinates of the extremum point
            pt = ((y + update[0]), (x + update[1]))
            # Scale of the extremum point
            size = sigma * (2 ** ((layer + update[2])))
                        # Calculate the orienta-
tion of the feature point (main and auxiliary
            # directions)
            # Use the computeOrien() function for calculation
            orien_list = computeOrien(pt, size, layer, g_image)
            for tmp_orien in orien_list:
                # Scale
                scales.append(size)
                # Position
                layers.append(layer)
                corners.append(pt)
                # Orientation
                orientations.append(tmp_orien)
    return
```

Further implement some of the functions that appear in the above code.

```
# Write some mathematical functions
# Calculate the first derivative
def compute1derivative(cube):
```

```
    # cube is composed of 3 adjacent layers in the DoG space, each layer
is sliced
    # into 3*3
    # Need to calculate the gradient at the center of the cube
    dx = (cube[1, 1, 2] - cube[1, 1, 0]) / 2
    dy = (cube[1, 2, 1] - cube[1, 0, 1]) / 2
    ds = (cube[2, 1, 1] - cube[0, 1, 1]) / 2
    return np.array([dx, dy, ds])
# Calculate the second derivative
def compute2derivative(cube):
    # cube is composed of 3 adjacent layers in the DoG space, each layer
is sliced
    # into 3*3
    # Need to calculate the gradient at the center of the cube
        # Write out each component according to the defini-
tion of the second derivative
    center = cube[1, 1, 1]
    dxx = cube[1, 1, 2] + cube[1, 1, 0] - 2 * center
    dyy = cube[1, 2, 1] + cube[1, 0, 1] - 2 * center
    dss = cube[2, 1, 1] + cube[0, 1, 1] - 2 * center
    dxy = (cube[1, 2, 2] - cube[1, 2, 0]
      - cube[1, 0, 2] + cube[1, 0, 0]) / 4
    dxs = (cube[2, 1, 2] - cube[2, 1, 0]
      - cube[0, 1, 2] + cube[0, 1, 0]) / 4
    dys = (cube[2, 2, 1] - cube[2, 0, 1]
      - cube[0, 2, 1] + cube[0, 0, 1]) / 4
     return np.array([[dxx, dxy, dxs], [dxy, dyy, dys], dxs, dys,
dss]])
# Calculate the direction of the feature point
def computeOrien(pt, size, layer, g_image):
    # pt is the position of the feature point
    # size is the corresponding scale size
    # layer is the level where the feature point is located
      # g_image is a layer of the Gaussian scale space, i.e., g_
images[layer]
                # 1.5 times the 3sigma rule, deter-
mining the size of the circle radius
    radius = int(round(3 * size * 1.5))
    image_shape = g_image.shape
# Set the number of histogram bins
    num_bins = 36
    histogram = np.zeros(num_bins)
    smooth_histogram = np.zeros(num_bins)
    orien_list = []
    # Traverse the block area centered on the feature point, the side
length of the
    # block area is 2*radius
    for i in range(-radius, radius + 1):
        y = int(round(pt[1])) + i
        # Check if the coordinates are out of bounds
        if y > 0 and y < image_shape[0] - 1:
            for j in range(-radius, radius + 1):
                x = int(round(pt[0])) + j
                # Determine if the coordinates are out of bounds
```

```
            if x > 0 and x < image_shape[1] - 1:
                # Calculate dx and dy at the current position
                dx = 0.5 * (g_image[y, x + 1] - g_image[y, x - 1])
                dy = 0.5 * (g_image[y + 1, x] - g_image[y - 1, x])
                                            # Calculate the magni-
tude of the gradient at the current position
                value = np.sqrt(dx * dx + dy * dy)
                                            # Calculate the direc-
tion of the gradient at the current position
                orien = np.rad2deg(np.arctan2(dy, dx))
                # Gaussian weighting
                weight = np.exp(
                -0.5 / ((size*1.5) ** 2)
                * (i ** 2 + j ** 2)
                )
                histogram_index = int(
                    round(orien * num_bins / 360.)
                    )
                histogram[histogram_index % num_bins] += \
                        weight * value
    # Smooth the histogram with a Gaussian filter
    for n in range(num_bins):
        smooth_histogram[n] = (6 * histogram[n]
            + 4 * (histogram[n-1] + histogram[(n+1) % num_bins])
            + histogram[n-2] + histogram[(n+2) % num_bins]) / 16.
# Select the main direction
    orien_max = np.max(smooth_histogram)
    orien_local_max = list(i for i in range(len(smooth_histogram))
        if smooth_histogram[i] > smooth_histogram[i-1] and
        smooth_histogram[i] > smooth_histogram[(i+1) % num_bins])
    # Select the secondary direction
    for index in orien_local_max:
        if smooth_histogram[index] >= 0.8 * orien_max:
            orien_list.append(index * 360. / num_bins)
    return orien_list
```

With this, we can write the function module to determine the feature points.

```
# Detect feature points in an image
def detect_blobs(image):
    sigma = 1.6
    num_layers = 4
    border = 5
    k_stride = 1
    # Generate Gaussian scale space
    g_images = generateGimage(image, sigma, num_layers, k_stride)
    # Generate DoG space
    dog_images = generateDoGSpace(g_images)
    # Start searching for block regions
    threshold = 0.02
    corners = []
    scales = []
    orientations = []
    layers = []
```

```
    for layer, (image1, image2, image3) in \
      enumerate(zip(dog_images, dog_images[1:], dog_images[2:])):
      # Ignore points too close to the edge
      for x in range(border, image1.shape[0]-border):
        for y in range(border, image2.shape[1]-border):
          # Check if the current position is a local extremum
          if isLocalExtremum(image1[x-1:x+2, y-1:y+2],
                             image2[x-1:x+2, y-1:y+2],
                             image3[x-1:x+2, y-1:y+2],
                             threshold):
          # If it is a candidate point, further locate and screen it,
            # and return its attributes
            computeBlobAttribute(x, y, layer+1, dog_images,
                                 sigma, threshold, border,
                                 num_layers, g_images[layer],
                                 corners, scales, orientations,
                                 layers)
   return g_images, corners, scales, orientations, layers
```

Next, generate descriptors for the detected feature points.

```
# Generation of SIFT feature point descriptors
def compute_descriptors(g_images, corners, scales,
                orientations, layers):
   if len(corners) != len(scales) \
       or len(corners) != len(orientations):
       raise ValueError(
     ''corners', 'scales' and 'orientations' \
     must all have the same length.')
  descriptors_list = []
   for pt, size, orien, layer in \
    zip(corners, scales, orientations, layers):
    # Read the information of the feature point
    g_image = g_images[layer]
    x, y = np.round(np.array(pt)).astype(np.int32)
    orien = 360 - orien
    # Calculate the size of the block region
    win_s = 3 * size
    win_l = int(round(min(2**0.5 * win_s * (4+1) / 2,
      nnp.sqrt(g_image.shape[0]**2+g_image.shape[1]**2))))
   # Store the information of all points in the block region in a list
    i_index = []
    j_index = []
    value_list = []
    orien_index = []
           # A three-dimensional array stores 8 direc-
tions of 16 windows, to prevent
    # boundary overflow during calculation,
    # Expand once at the beginning and end of the row and column
    result_cube = np.zeros((4 + 2, 4 + 2, 8))
          # Build the pixel gradient histogram of 16 sub-
regions in a block region
    for i in range(-win_l, win_l+1):
      for j in range(-win_l, win_l+1):
```

```
            # Get the coordinates after rotation
            i_rotate = j * np.sin(np.deg2rad(orien)) \
                + i * np.cos(np.deg2rad(orien))
            j_rotate = j * np.cos(np.deg2rad(orien)) \
                - i * np.sin(np.deg2rad(orien))
            # Calculate the index corresponding to the 4*4 sub-region
            tmp_i = (i_rotate / win_s) + 2 - 0.5
            tmp_j = (j_rotate / win_s) + 2 - 0.5
                                # The points in the neighbor-
hood are still within the 4*4 region after rotation
            if tmp_i > -1 and tmp_j > -1 \
              and tmp_i < 4 and tmp_j < 4:
              # Position of the feature point in the original image
              i_inimg = int(round(y + i))
              j_inimg = int(round(x + j))
              if i_inimg > 0 and j_inimg > 0 \
                and i_inimg < g_image.shape[0]-1 \
                and j_inimg < g_image.shape[1]-1:
                # Calculate the gradient magnitude
                dx = g_image[i_inimg, j_inimg + 1] \
                  - g_image[i_inimg, j_inimg - 1]
                dy = g_image[i_inimg - 1, j_inimg] \
                  - g_image[i_inimg + 1, j_inimg]
                grad_value = np.sqrt(dx**2 + dy**2)
                # Calculate the gradient direction
                grad_orien = np.rad2deg(
                  np.arctan2(dy, dx)) % 360
                i_index.append(tmp_i)
                j_index.append(tmp_j)
                # Apply Gaussian weighting
                g_weight = np.exp(-1 / 8 * (
                  (i_rotate / win_s) ** 2 +
                  (j_rotate / win_s) ** 2)
)
                value_list.append(g_weight * grad_value)
                # Project the gradient direction onto 8 directions
            # The grad_orien here is the gradient in the original image
                # We need to add the angle after rotation
                orien_index.append(
                  (grad_orien - orien) * 8 / 360)
        # Insert the magnitude of each direction into the matrix result_
cube
          for i, j, value, orien1 in zip(i_index, j_index, value_
list, orien_index):
          tirlinearInterpolation(i, j, value, orien1, result_cube)
      descriptor = result_cube[1:-1, 1:-1, :].flatten()
      # Calculate the size of the descriptor
      l2norm = np.linalg.norm(descriptor)
# Set the threshold
      threshold = l2norm * 0.2
        # Truncate the descriptor, setting values greater than the
threshold to the
      # threshold
      descriptor[descriptor > threshold] = threshold
```

```
        # Perform normalization to ensure the descriptor is scale
invariant
        descriptor /= l2norm
        # Append the descriptor
        descriptors_list.append(descriptor)
    return descriptors_list
# Insert the magnitude of each direction into the matrix result_cube
def tirlinearInterpolation(i, j, value, orien, result_cube):
    # Since the position coordinates (i,j,orien) are floating point
numbers, they
    # cannot be directly assigned in result_cube
    # Considering that this floating point posi-
tion will contribute to the adjacent 8
    # integer coordinates
    # (You can imagine this floating point coordi-
nate as a point in a cube,
    # it contributes to the 8 vertices of the cube)
    # We can use trilinear interpolation to assign values to the adja-
cent 8 vertices
    # based on the distance from this point to each vertex
    # Interested readers can learn about trilinear interpola-
tion on their own
    # Quantize the coordinates first, converting them into integers
    i_quant = int(np.floor(i))
    j_quant = int(np.floor(j))
    orien_quant = int(np.floor(orien)) % 8
    # Calculate the offset before and after quantization
    i_residual = i - i_quant
    j_residual = j - j_quant
    orien_residual = (orien - orien_quant) % 8
    # Compute the weight of the current posi-
tion for each vertex according to
    # the trilinear interpolation method
    c0 = (1 - i_residual) * value
    c1 = i_residual * value
    c11 = c1 * j_residual
    c10 = c1 * (1 - j_residual)
    c01 = c0 * j_residual
    c00 = c0 * (1 - j_residual)
    c111 = c11 * orien_residual
    c110 = c11 * (1 - orien_residual)
    c101 = c10 * orien_residual
    c100 = c10 * (1 - orien_residual)
    c011 = c01 * orien_residual
    c010 = c01 * (1 - orien_residual)
    c001 = c00 * orien_residual
    c000 = c00 * (1 - orien_residual)
    # Perform assignment
    result_cube[i_quant + 1, j_quant + 1, (orien_quant + 1) % 8] +=
c001
    result_cube[i_quant + 1, j_quant + 2, orien_quant] += c010
    result_cube[i_quant + 1, j_quant + 2, (orien_quant + 1) % 8] +=
c011
    result_cube[i_quant + 2, j_quant + 1, orien_quant] += c100
```

```
    result_cube[i_quant + 2, j_quant + 1, (orien_quant + 1) % 8] +=
c101
    result_cube[i_quant + 2, j_quant + 2, orien_quant] += c110
    result_cube[i_quant + 2, j_quant + 2, (orien_quant + 1) % 8] +=
c111
    return
```

At this point, we have completed the implementation of SIFT features. Next, we import two images and find the feature points in them.

```
# Display the feature points in the image
def draw(img, corners):
    # corners are the coordinates of the feature points
    img1 = img.copy()
    for m in corners:
        pt = (int(m[0]), int(m[1]))
        cv2.circle(img1, pt, 1, (0,255,0), 2)
    return img1
# Read the image
img1 = cv2.imread('sift1.png', cv2.IMREAD_COLOR)
img2 = cv2.imread('sift2.png', cv2.IMREAD_COLOR)
gray1 = cv2.cvtColor(img1, cv2.COLOR_BGR2GRAY) / 255.0
gray2 = cv2.cvtColor(img2, cv2.COLOR_BGR2GRAY) / 255.0
# Get various information about the feature points of the two images
g_images1, corners1, scales1, orientations1, layers1 = \
                         detect_blobs(gray1)
g_images2, corners2, scales2, orientations2, layers2 = \
                         detect_blobs(gray2)
# Obtain the SIFT feature points of two images
descriptors1 = compute_descriptors(g_images1, corners1, scales1,
                         orientations1, layers1)
descriptors2 = compute_descriptors(g_images2, corners2, scales2,
                         orientations2, layers2)
img1_detect = draw(img1, corners1)
img2_detect = draw(img2, corners2)
# Display the feature points of the two images
plt.title('Output1')
plt.axis('off')
plt.imshow(img1_detect[:, :, ::-1])
plt.show()
plt.title('Output2')
plt.axis('off')
plt.imshow(img2_detect[:, :, ::-1])
plt.show()
```

It is easy to find the feature points in the image using the SIFT algorithm. Next, the found feature points need to be matched. The sets of feature points in the two images are defined as $\mathcal{S}$ and $\mathcal{R}$. For a certain feature point s_i in $\mathcal{S}$, we use the $L2$ norm to measure the distance between its corresponding feature vector $\boldsymbol{V}_{s_i}$ and the feature vectors $\boldsymbol{V}_{r_j}$ corresponding to each feature point r_j in the set $\mathcal{R}$, and then determine the feature point r_k with the shortest distance s_i and the second shortest feature point r_d. If

$$\frac{\ell_2(s_i, r_k)}{\ell_2(s_i, r_d)} < \theta,$$

it can be considered that s_i matches r_k where, $\ell_2(\cdot, \cdot)$ is the L2 norm; θ is the set threshold.

```
# Feature point matching
def match_descriptors(descriptors1, descriptors2):
   max_index = np.zeros((len(descriptors1))) - 1
   # Initialize the arrays for the closest and second closest feature
point pairs
   maxmatch = np.zeros((len(descriptors1))) + 1e10
   secmatch = np.zeros((len(descriptors1))) + 1e10
   # Set the threshold
   threshold = 0.8
   for vec1_index in range(len(descriptors1)):
      for vec2_index in range(len(descriptors2)):
         # Calculate the distance between feature point pairs
         distance = np.linalg.norm(descriptors1[vec1_index] \
                           - descriptors2[vec2_index])
         if distance < maxmatch[vec1_index]:
            # Update the currently best matching feature point
            maxmatch[vec1_index] = distance
            # Record the distance of the current feature point pair
            max_index[vec1_index] = vec2_index
         elif distance < secmatch[vec1_index]:
         # Update the distance of the second closest feature point pair
            # Here, only the distance needs to be updated, because we
don't care
```

```
            # which point is the second closest
            secmatch[vec1_index] = distance
    matches = []
    # Return the coordinates of the matched feature point pairs
    for i in range(len(descriptors1)):
        if maxmatch[i] / secmatch[i] < threshold:
            matches.append((i, int(max_index[i])))
    return matches
def draw_matches(image1, image2, corners1, corners2, matches):
# Get the resolution of the two images
    h1, w1 = image1.shape
    h2, w2 = image2.shape
    hres = 0
    if h1 >= h2:
        hres = int((h1 - h2) / 2)
            # Stitch the two images into an image with consis-
tent height for easy
        # comparison of feature point pairs
        match_image = np.zeros((h1, w1 + w2, 3), np.uint8)
        # Process R, G, B images separately
        for i in range(3):
            match_image[: h1, : w1, i] = image1
            match_image[hres: hres + h2, w1: w1 + w2, i] = image2
        for i in range(len(matches)):
            m = matches[i]
            # Get the coordinates of the matched feature point pairs in
the image
            pt1 = (int(corners1[m[0]][0]), int(corners1[m[0]][1]))
            pt2 = (int(corners2[m[1]][0] + w1),
                int(corners2[m[1]][1] + hres))
            # Circle them
            cv2.circle(match_image, pt1, 1, (0,255,0), 2)
            cv2.circle(match_image, (pt2[0], pt2[1]), 1, (0,255,0), 2)
            # Connect with a line
            cv2.line(match_image, pt1, pt2, (0, 0, 255))
    else:
        hres = int((h2 - h1) / 2)
            # Stitch the two images into an image with consis-
tent height for easy
        # comparison of feature point pairs
            match_image = np.zeros((h2, w1 + w2, 3), np.uint8)
        # Process R, G, B images separately
        for i in range(3):
            match_image[hres: hres + h1, : w1, i] = image1
            match_image[: h2, w1: w1 + w2, i] = image2
        for i in range(len(matches)):
            m = matches[i]
            # Get the coordinates of the matched feature point pairs in
the image
            pt1 = (int(corners1[m[0]][0]),
                int(corners1[m[0]][1] + hres))
            pt2 = (int(corners2[m[1]][0] + w1),
                int(corners2[m[1]][1]))
            # Circle them
```

```
        cv2.circle(match_image, pt1, 1, (0,255,0), 2)
        cv2.circle(match_image, (pt2[0], pt2[1]), 1, (0,255,0), 2)
        # Connect with a line
        cv2.line(match_image, pt1, pt2, (0, 0, 255))
    return match_image
# Perform image matching
matches = match_descriptors(descriptors1, descriptors2)
image1 = cv2.imread('sift1.png', cv2.IMREAD_GRAYSCALE)
image2 = cv2.imread('sift2.png', cv2.IMREAD_GRAYSCALE)
# Draw matching lines
match_image = draw_matches(image1, image2, corners1, corners2,
matches)
plt.title('Match')
plt.imshow(match_image)
plt.axis('off')
(-0.5, 471.5, 171.5, -0.5)
```

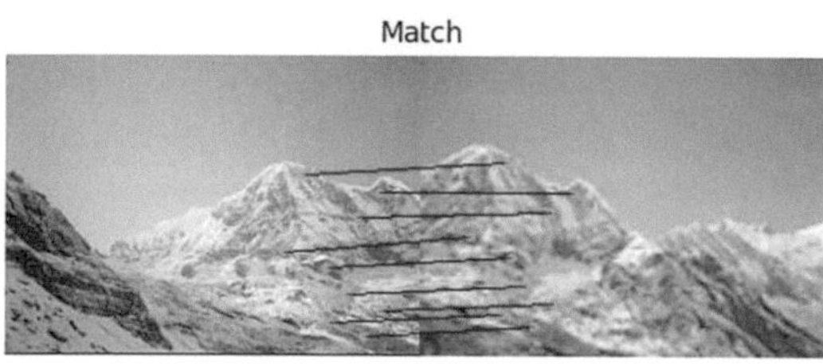

Clearly, the same features in the two images are perfectly matched. Subsequently, a series of follow-up operations such as image stitching can be performed.

7.4 Summary

This chapter introduces the basic principles of the SIFT algorithm and implements the SIFT algorithm. The SIFT feature has many advantages: it is stable, invariant to rotation, scale changes, brightness changes, etc.; it has good uniqueness and rich information. Therefore, SIFT features have become the basis for performing many computer vision tasks. In Chap. 8, we will introduce a practical application of SIFT—image stitching.

Exercises

(1) The SIFT feature descriptor is designed to have a certain degree of invariance to illumination, rotation, and scale. Analyze how the SIFT algorithm achieves this characteristic, including its principles and specific implementation steps.

(2) The SIFT algorithm and Harris corner detection are common methods for image feature detection. Compare these two methods and point out the main advantages of the SIFT algorithm over Harris corner detection.

(3) In the SIFT algorithm, in order to construct the descriptor of the feature point, it is usually necessary to divide the area around the feature point into blocks and rotate it according to the main direction. What is the purpose of this processing method?
(4) Analyze the computational complexity of the SIFT algorithm. Discuss in detail the most time-consuming steps in the algorithm, and propose possible optimization strategies or alternatives to improve the efficiency of the algorithm.
(5) Use the provided sift1.png and sift2.png to test the effects of different γ (the ratio of eigenvalues in Sect. 7.2.2) and θ (the threshold of the ratio of the nearest feature point pair to the second nearest feature point pair) on the SIFT algorithm.

Reference

1. LOWE D G. Object recognition from local scale-invariant features[C]//IEEE International Conference on Computer Vision, 1999, 2:1150–1157.

Chapter 8
Image Stitching

8.1 Introduction

When touring the magnificent landscapes of our homeland, we often marvel at the grandeur of the mountains and rivers, while regretting that we do not have the equipment to take a panoramic photo, and can only take separate photos from different perspectives. Through studying this chapter, perhaps you can create panoramic images yourself.

Image stitching refers to the technique of stitching multiple overlapping images of the same scene (which may be obtained at different times, from different perspectives, or by different sensors) into a seamless large-scale panoramic image. Image stitching has many applications in computer vision tasks such as motion detection and tracking, augmented reality, resolution enhancement, video compression, and image stabilization. Figures 8.1 and 8.2 show an example of image stitching.

8.2 Image Transformation

If you carefully observe the series of images in Fig. 8.1 and the stitched panoramic image in Fig. 8.2, do they have any geometric similarities? That's right, the panoramic image in Fig. 8.2 can be obtained by stitching the sub-images in Fig. 8.1 after operations such as scaling, rotation, and projection. These operations performed on the image are collectively referred to as image transformations. Let's first introduce a few commonly used image transformations.

(1) Translation: If image $\boldsymbol{I}$ is translated by vector $\left(t_x, t_y\right)$, then a point (i, j) on the image, corresponding to vector $\boldsymbol{p} = (i, j)$, after translation, the new point is $\left(i', j'\right)$, corresponding to vector $\boldsymbol{p}' = \left(i', j'\right)$, with $\boldsymbol{p}' = \boldsymbol{p} + \boldsymbol{t}$, where the direction of $\boldsymbol{t} = \left(t_x, t_y\right)$ is the direction of translation, and the magnitude of $\boldsymbol{t}$ is the translation distance.

W. Shen et al., *Hands-On Computer Vision*,
https://doi.org/10.1007/978-981-95-4835-4_8

Fig. 8.1 Different images of the same scene taken from different perspectives

Fig. 8.2 Image stitching

(2) Rotation: If the image is rotated counterclockwise around the origin (0, 0) by θ, then a point (i, j) on the image, corresponding to vector $\boldsymbol{p} = (i, j)$, after rotation, the new point corresponds to vector $\boldsymbol{p}' = \boldsymbol{Rp}$, where $\boldsymbol{R} = \begin{bmatrix} \cos\theta & -\sin\theta \\ \sin\theta & \cos\theta \end{bmatrix}$ is the rotation matrix.

(3) Scaling: With the origin (0, 0) as the scaling center, if the image is scaled by s_x times along the x-axis, and by s_y times along the y-axis, then a point (i, j) on the image, corresponding to vector $\boldsymbol{p} = (i, j)$, after scaling, the new point corresponds to vector $\boldsymbol{p}' = \boldsymbol{Sp}$, where $\boldsymbol{S} = \begin{bmatrix} s_x & 0 \\ 0 & s_y \end{bmatrix}$ is the scaling matrix.

(4) Symmetry: If the image is mirrored around the y-axis, it is not difficult to find that a point (i, j) on the image, corresponding to vector $\boldsymbol{p} = (i, j)$, the point symmetric to the y-axis corresponds to vector $\boldsymbol{p}' = (-i, j)$, then $\boldsymbol{p}' = \begin{bmatrix} -1 & 0 \\ 0 & 1 \end{bmatrix}\boldsymbol{p}$; if the image is mirrored around the line $y = x$, then $\boldsymbol{p}' = (j, i)$, that is $\boldsymbol{p}' = \begin{bmatrix} 0 & 1 \\ 1 & 0 \end{bmatrix}\boldsymbol{p}$.

It is not difficult to find that the correspondence before and after the image transformations in (2)–(4) above is linear, that is, it can be written in the matrix form of $\boldsymbol{p}' = \boldsymbol{Tp}$, but translation cannot be represented by such a linear transformation. As the linear transformation form of matrix multiplication is easy to calculate, can translation also be represented in the form of matrix multiplication?

Of course, it can. However, it requires extending the commonly used Cartesian coordinate system to the homogeneous coordinate system. Let λ is a constant. In

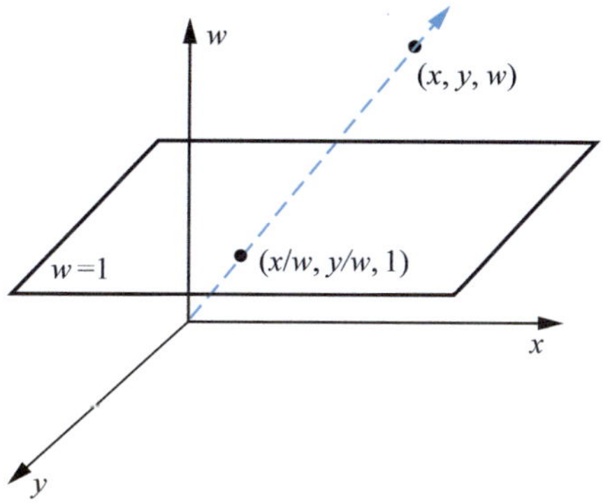

Fig. 8.3 Homogeneous coordinate system

Cartesian coordinates, for a vector $\boldsymbol{v}$, it generally holds that $\boldsymbol{v} \neq \lambda\boldsymbol{v}$, while in homogeneous coordinates, it always holds that $\boldsymbol{v} = \lambda\boldsymbol{v}$. So how do we convert between Cartesian and homogeneous coordinates? As shown in Fig. 8.3, we add the w axis based on the x-axis and the y-axis and represent the point (i, j) in the Cartesian coordinate system as $(i, j, 1)$; we call such a coordinate system a homogeneous coordinate system. For any point (x, y, w) in the homogeneous coordinate system, its corresponding coordinates in the Cartesian coordinate system are $(x/w, y/w)$.

On this basis, the points before and after translation can be represented as

$$\begin{bmatrix} i' \\ j' \\ 1 \end{bmatrix} = \begin{bmatrix} 1 & 0 & t_x \\ 0 & 1 & t_y \\ 0 & 0 & 1 \end{bmatrix} \begin{bmatrix} i \\ j \\ 1 \end{bmatrix}.$$

Similarly, for rotation and scaling, they can be represented as $\begin{bmatrix} i' \\ j' \\ 1 \end{bmatrix} = \begin{bmatrix} \cos\theta & -\sin\theta & 0 \\ \sin\theta & \cos\theta & 0 \\ 0 & 0 & 1 \end{bmatrix} \begin{bmatrix} i \\ j \\ 1 \end{bmatrix}$ and $\begin{bmatrix} i' \\ j' \\ 1 \end{bmatrix} = \begin{bmatrix} s_x & 0 & 0 \\ 0 & s_y & 0 \\ 0 & 0 & 1 \end{bmatrix} \begin{bmatrix} i \\ j \\ 1 \end{bmatrix}$. So far, in the homogeneous coordinate system, the above image transformation operations can all be represented by a 3×3 matrix $\boldsymbol{T}$. As can be seen, the last row of the matrix $\boldsymbol{T}$ corresponding to translation, rotation, and scaling operations is all $[0\ 0\ 1]$. We call image transformations corresponding to matrices of the form $\boldsymbol{T} = \begin{bmatrix} a & b & c \\ d & e & f \\ 0 & 0 & 1 \end{bmatrix}$ affine transformations. So, what kind of changes will occur to the image if the last row of the transformation matrix $\boldsymbol{T}$ is not $[0\ 0\ 1]$, but any $[g\ h\ 1]$? Experiments can yield results similar to Fig. 8.4. Clearly, when the last row of $\boldsymbol{T}$ is not $[0\ 0\ 1]$, the image undergoes some deformation, and the originally parallel image borders are no longer parallel. We call image transformation operations corresponding to matrices of the

Fig. 8.4 Projective transformation

form $\boldsymbol{T} = \begin{bmatrix} a & b & c \\ d & e & f \\ g & h & 1 \end{bmatrix}$ projective transformations, and such transformation matrices $\boldsymbol{T}$ are called homography matrices. In the 3×3 matrix, the form of the homography matrix is the most general, so the projective transformation includes all the above image transformations. Images captured by photographing a planar target from different viewpoints and images captured by photographing an arbitrary target with the camera fixed in position and only rotating its angle both satisfy the projective transformation. The situation of taking multiple images of the same scene can usually be approximated to the above two situations, so panoramic image stitching can be achieved through projective transformation.

8.3 Image Stitching Algorithm

This section explains how to implement the image stitching algorithm by calculating the projective transformation matrix.

8.3.1 Computing the Transformation Matrix

Image stitching is to stitch a set of images into a large panoramic image. The most basic problem in this task is how to stitch two images together. Given two images, to stitch them together, we need to calculate the transformation matrix between them. To calculate the transformation matrix $\boldsymbol{T}$, we need to find the matching relationship between the two images. By using the SIFT feature point detection algorithm introduced in Chap. 7, we can find the feature points on the two images, and then based on the SIFT feature description, we can determine the matching relationship between these feature points, as shown in Fig. 8.5.

Let (x, y) and $\left(x', y'\right)$ be a pair of matching feature points in the two images, represented in homogeneous coordinates as $(x, y, 1)$ and $(x', y', 1)$, respectively, and the corresponding vectors are $\boldsymbol{p} = (x, y, 1)^{\mathrm{T}}$ and $\boldsymbol{p'} = \left(x', y', 1\right)^{\mathrm{T}}$, then we have

Fig. 8.5 Image matching based on feature points

$\boldsymbol{p}' = \boldsymbol{T}\boldsymbol{p}$, that is,

$$\begin{bmatrix} x' \\ y' \\ 1 \end{bmatrix} = \begin{bmatrix} a \ b \ c \\ d \ e \ f \\ g \ h \ i \end{bmatrix} \begin{bmatrix} x \\ y \\ 1 \end{bmatrix}.$$

The relationship between x, y and x', y' can be obtained as follows:

$$x' = \frac{ax + by + c}{gx + hy + i}, \quad y' = \frac{dx + ey + f}{gx + hy + i}.$$

To more conveniently solve for the unknowns in matrix $\boldsymbol{T}$, the above equation is rewritten as:

$$x'(gx + hy + i) = ax + by + c,$$
$$y'(gx + hy + i) = dx + ey + f.$$

That is,

$$\begin{bmatrix} x \ y \ 1 \ 0 \ 0 \ 0 \ -x'x \ -x'y \ -x' \\ 0 \ 0 \ 0 \ x \ y \ 1 \ -y'x \ -y'y \ -y' \end{bmatrix} \begin{bmatrix} a \\ b \\ c \\ d \\ e \\ f \\ g \\ h \\ i \end{bmatrix} = \begin{bmatrix} 0 \\ 0 \end{bmatrix}.$$

Assuming that there are n matching feature points between the two images, the following equation can be obtained:

$$\begin{bmatrix} x_1 & y_1 & 1 & 0 & 0 & 0 & -x_1'x_1 & -x_1'y_1 & -x_1' \\ 0 & 0 & 0 & x_1 & y_1 & 1 & -y_1'x_1 & -y_1'y_1 & -y_1' \\ \vdots & & & & & & & & \vdots \\ x_n & y_n & 1 & 0 & 0 & 0 & -x_n'x_n & -x_n'y_n & -x_n' \\ 0 & 0 & 0 & x_n & y_n & 1 & -y_n'x_n & -y_n'y_n & -y_n' \end{bmatrix} \begin{bmatrix} a \\ b \\ c \\ d \\ e \\ f \\ g \\ h \\ i \end{bmatrix} = \begin{bmatrix} 0 \\ 0 \\ \vdots \\ 0 \end{bmatrix}_{2n}.$$

Let matrix $A = \begin{bmatrix} x_1 & y_1 & 1 & 0 & 0 & 0 & -x_1'x_1 & -x_1'y_1 & -x_1' \\ 0 & 0 & 0 & x_1 & y_1 & 1 & -y_1'x_1 & -y_1'y_1 & -y_1' \\ \vdots & & & & & & & & \vdots \\ x_n & y_n & 1 & 0 & 0 & 0 & -x_n'x_n & -x_n'y_n & -x_n' \\ 0 & 0 & 0 & x_n & y_n & 1 & -y_n'x_n & -y_n'y_n & -y_n' \end{bmatrix}_{2n\times 9}$, $\boldsymbol{t} = [a\ b\ c\ d\ e\ f\ g\ h\ i]^{\mathrm{T}}$, the above equation can be simplified as:

$$\boldsymbol{At} = 0.$$

Generally, the number of feature point pairs that can be obtained is far more than the number of unknowns in the equation, and due to the error in the position of some feature point pairs, the above equation may not have a unique closed-form solution. Therefore, the solution for $\boldsymbol{t}$ is often obtained by optimizing the following problem:

$$\min \|\boldsymbol{At} - 0\|_F^2 \quad s.t. \quad \|\boldsymbol{t}\|^2 = 1.$$

By solving the above equation to get $\boldsymbol{t}$, the transformation matrix $\boldsymbol{T}$ can be obtained. Note that the transformation matrix $\boldsymbol{T}$ is defined in the homogeneous coordinate system, so the scale has no effect on it. Therefore, it is only necessary to solve for the unit vector $\hat{\boldsymbol{t}}$, i.e., the eigenvector corresponding to the smallest eigenvalue of the matrix $\boldsymbol{A}^{\mathrm{T}}\boldsymbol{A}$ (the proof process is detailed in Sect. 8.6).

We summarize the process of image stitching into the following three steps:

(1) Calculate the feature points of the two images.
(2) Match the feature points of the two images.
(3) Calculate the image transformation matrix based on the matched feature point pairs.

8.3.2 Removing Mismatches Using the RANSAC Algorithm

When using SIFT for feature matching, situations like Fig. 8.6 may occur. In Fig. 8.6, the feature points in the green circle in the right image are the feature points matched

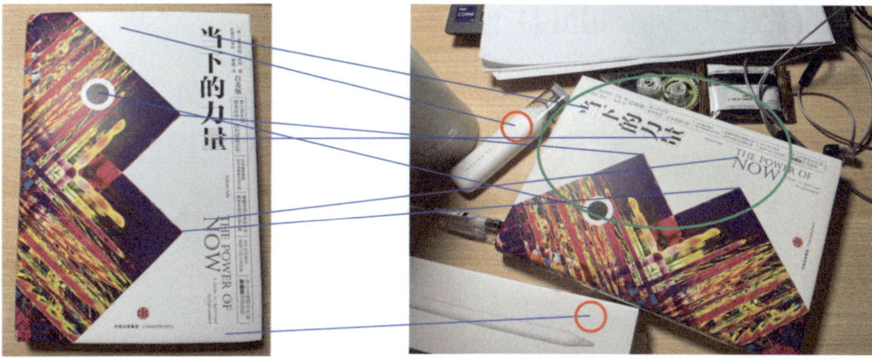

Fig. 8.6 Matching feature point pairs in two images obtained based on SIFT feature description

with the left image. However, when using SIFT to match feature points, some feature points in the left image are matched to feature points outside the green circle in the right image (such as the feature points in the red circle). These feature point matches are incorrect and should be removed to ensure the robustness of the transformation matrix calculation. How to remove these incorrect match pairs?

Let's put aside the matching problem and start with a simpler example. Figure 8.7a shows a set of data points, and we hope to fit these data points with a straight line. However, these data points are not on a straight line, so we don't know which part of the points should be used to fit the line. But intuitively, we would think that the line in Fig. 8.7c fits better than the line in Fig. 8.7b because more data points are distributed near the line. Upon further thinking, normal data points are the majority of data points with similar distribution patterns, while abnormal data points are scattered. We usually call points that conform to the model of the overall samples as inliers and points that deviate from the model or are inconsistent with the model as outliers. If a line is fitted with any two data points, the more data points are consistent with this line, i.e., distributed near it, the more inliers this line has, and the more likely this line is the one we want to fit, while data points that do not conform to this line are abnormal samples.

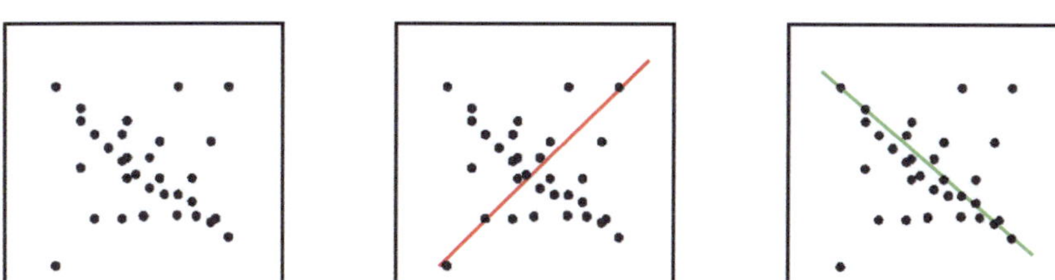

(a) Data points used for line fitting

(b) A small number of data points are consistent with the line

(c) A large number of data points are consistent with the line

Fig. 8.7 Line fitting

The Random Sample Consensus (RANSAC) algorithm is an iterative method that uses the above idea to fit a mathematical model from a set of observed data. RANSAC is a robust parameter estimation algorithm, with the following steps:

(1) Randomly select s samples (where s is the minimum sample size that can be used to fit the model).
(2) Fit the model with these samples.
(3) Count the number of inliers that are consistent with the model.
(4) Repeat the above process N times.
(5) Choose the model with the most inliers as the final fitting result.

For the problem of line fitting, a sample refers to a data point, so here $s = 2$, because two data points determine a line. Returning to the problem of matching image feature points, a sample refers to a pair of matched feature points. Matched feature points that are normal samples have consistent geometric transformation relationships, while mismatched feature points that are abnormal samples each have their own differences. For different image transformations, s is different. For translation transformations, $s = 1$, because just one pair of matched points is needed to determine the parameters of the translation transformation; for projection transformations, $s = 4$, can you explain why?

Figure 8.8 shows an experiment using the RANSAC algorithm to fit a translation transformation. In Fig. 8.8a, the translation fitting model represented by the blue arrow is first selected, and the number of inliers (blue arrows) for this translation model is 4, while the number of outliers inconsistent with it (yellow arrows and red arrows) is 3. In the next attempt (as shown in Fig. 8.8b), randomly select data (yellow arrow) to fit the corresponding model and count the number of inliers (only one). Finally, the model with the most inliers (in Fig. 8.8, the feature points corresponding to the blue arrow) is selected as the final fitting result. The feature points that are mismatched (such as the feature points corresponding to the red arrow) are not used, that is, these abnormal samples are "removed".

(a) (b)

Fig. 8.8 Removing mismatched feature points using the RANSAC algorithm

It should be noted that the RANSAC algorithm cannot guarantee the optimal solution, as it only approximates the optimal solution with a certain probability. However, as the number of iterations increases, the probability of approaching the optimal solution will increase.

8.3.3 Image Transformation and Stitching

The final step in image stitching is to transform and stitch the input images into one image. For two images $\boldsymbol{A}$ and $\boldsymbol{B}$, after detecting the corresponding feature points and calculating the transformation matrix $\boldsymbol{T}$ using the RANSAC algorithm, image $\boldsymbol{B}$ is transformed into $\boldsymbol{TB}$. Then, for the transformed image, i.e., $\boldsymbol{TB}$, the pixel values in the overlapping parts with image $\boldsymbol{A}$ are averaged to optimize the boundaries of image stitching. In this way, the final stitched image can be obtained.

In summary, we summarize the entire process of image stitching into the following four steps:

(1) Calculate the feature points of the two images.
(2) Match the feature points of the two images.
(3) Calculate the image transformation matrix using the RANSAC algorithm based on the matched feature points.
(4) Stitch the images.

8.4 Code Implementation

In this section, we will implement image stitching in code. First, import the SIFT-related functions written in Chap. 7, and then implement the RANSAC algorithm based on the process described in Sect. 8.3.

```
from utils import *
# Use the RANSAC algorithm to remove invalid points
def compute_affine_xform(corners1, corners2, matches):
    # Set the maximum number of iterations
    iteration = 50
    M_list = []
    # Store the number of normal samples for each model
    inlier_num_list = []
    for _ in range(iteration):
        # Randomly select 4 feature point pairs to fit the model
        sample_index = random.sample(range(len(matches)), 4)
        x1_s, y1_s = corners1[matches[sample_index[0]][0]]
        x1_t, y1_t = corners2[matches[sample_index[0]][1]]
        x2_s, y2_s = corners1[matches[sample_index[1]][0]]
        x2_t, y2_t = corners2[matches[sample_index[1]][1]]
        x3_s, y3_s = corners1[matches[sample_index[2]][0]]
        x3_t, y3_t = corners2[matches[sample_index[2]][1]]
```

```
        x4_s, y4_s = corners1[matches[sample_index[3]][0]]
        x4_t, y4_t = corners2[matches[sample_index[3]][1]]
        # Construct matrix A
        A = np.array([[x1_s, y1_s, 1, 0, 0, 0,
                    -x1_t*x1_s, -x1_t*y1_s, -x1_t],
                    [0, 0, 0, x1_s, y1_s, 1,
                    -y1_t*x1_s, -y1_t*y1_s, -y1_t],
                    [x2_s, y2_s, 1, 0, 0, 0,
                    -x2_t*x2_s, -x2_t*y2_s, -x2_t],
                    [0, 0, 0, x2_s, y2_s, 1,
                    -y2_t*x2_s, -y2_t*y2_s, -y2_t],
                    [x3_s, y3_s, 1, 0, 0, 0,
                    -x3_t*x3_s, -x3_t*y3_s, -x3_t],
                    [0, 0, 0, x3_s, y3_s, 1,
                    -y3_t*x3_s, -y3_t*y3_s, -y3_t],
                    [x4_s, y4_s, 1, 0, 0, 0,
                    x4_t*x4_s, -x4_t*y4_s, -x4_t],
                    [0, 0, 0, x4_s, y4_s, 1,
                    -y4_t*x4_s, -y4_t*y4_s, -y4_t]
                    ])
        # Calculate the eigenvectors of A
        _,_, v = np.linalg.svd(A)
         # Take the eigenvector corresponding to the smallest eigen-
value as the
        # final result
        M = np.reshape(v[-1], (3, 3))
        inlier_num = 0
        # Count the number of normal samples
        for (index1, index2) in matches:
         # coord is the coordinate in the homogeneous coordinate system
           coord1 = [corners1[index1][0], corners1[index1][1], 1]
           coord2 = [corners2[index2][0], corners2[index2][1], 1]
             # Calculate the coordinate after homogeneous transforma-
tion of coord1
           mapcoor = np.dot(M, coord1)
           # Set w in the homogeneous coordinate system to 1
           mapcoor = mapcoor / mapcoor[-1]
           if np.linalg.norm(coord2 - mapcoor) < 5:
              inlier_num += 1
         # Record the number of normal samples and the corresponding
transformation
        # matrix M in the list
        M_list.append(M)
        inlier_num_list.append(inlier_num)
     # Get the index of the element with the maximum normal sample value
in the list
     best_index = np.argmax(inlier_num_list)
     # Get the corresponding transformation matrix
     xform = M_list[best_index].astype(np.float64)
     # Count the feature point pairs of the model's abnormal samples
     utlier_labels = []
     for (index1, index2) in matches:
        coord1 = [corners1[index1][0], corners1[index1][1], 1]
        coord2 = [corners2[index2][0], corners2[index2][1], 1]
```

```
        mapcoor = np.dot(xform, coord1)
        mapcoor = mapcoor/mapcoor[-1]
        if np.linalg.norm(coord2 - mapcoor) < 12:
            outlier_labels.append(1)
        else:
            outlier_labels.append(0)
    return xform, outlier_labels
```

To reflect the pairs of outliers when plotting, we rewrite the draw_matches() function from Chap. 7.

```
def draw_matches(image1, image2, corners1, corners2,
              matches, outliers=None):
    # Get the resolution of the two images
    h1, w1 = image1.shape
    h2, w2 = image2.shape
    hres = 0
    if h1 >= h2:
        hres = int((h1 - h2) / 2)
       # Stitch the two images into an image of the same height for easy
comparison
        # of feature point pairs
        match_image = np.zeros((h1, w1 + w2, 3), np.uint8)
        # Process R, G, B images separately
        for i in range(3):
            match_image[: h1, : w1, i] = image1
            match_image[hres: hres + h2, w1: w1 + w2, i] = image2
        for i in range(len(matches)):
            m = matches[i]
             # Get the coordinates of the matched feature point pairs in
the image
            pt1 = (int(corners1[m[0]][0]), int(corners1[m[0]][1]))
            pt2 = (int(corners2[m[1]][0] + w1),
                  int(corners2[m[1]][1] + hres))
            # Circle them
            cv2.circle(match_image, pt1, 1, (0,255,0), 2)
            cv2.circle(match_image, (pt2[0], pt2[1]), 1, (0,255,0), 2)
            # Draw lines to connect
            if outliers:
                cv2.line(match_image, pt1, pt2, (255, 0, 0))
            else:
                cv2.line(match_image, pt1, pt2, (0, 0, 255))
    else:
        hres = int((h2 - h1) / 2)
        # Stitch the two images into an image of the same height for easy
         comparison
         # of feature point pairs
        match_image = np.zeros((h2, w1 + w2, 3), np.uint8)
        # Process R, G, B images separately
        for i in range(3):
            match_image[hres: hres + h1, : w1, i] = image1
            match_image[: h2, w1: w1 + w2, i] = image2
        for i in range(len(matches)):
        m = matches[i]
```

```
    # Get the coordinates of the matched feature point pairs in the
image
    pt1 = (int(corners1[m[0]][0]),
           int(corners1[m[0]][1] + hres))
    pt2 = (int(corners2[m[1]][0] + w1),
           int(corners2[m[1]][1]))
    # Circle them
    cv2.circle(match_image, pt1, 1, (0,255,0), 2)
    cv2.circle(match_image, (pt2[0], pt2[1]), 1, (0,255,0), 2)
    # Draw lines to connect
    if outliers:
        cv2.line(match_image, pt1, pt2, (255, 0, 0))
    else:
        cv2.line(match_image, pt1, pt2, (0, 0, 255))
  return match_image
```

Next, write the relevant functions for image transformation and stitching.

```
def stitch_images(image1, image2, xform):
  # Get image dimensions
  h1, w1, _ = image1.shape
  h2, w2, _ = image2.shape
  # Calculate the boundaries of the transformed image
  corners1 = np.float32([[0, 0], [0, h1], [w1, h1], [w1, 0]])
  .reshape(-1, 1, 2)
  corners2 = np.float32([[0, 0], [0, h2], [w2, h2], [w2, 0]])
  .reshape(-1, 1, 2)
  dst_corners1 = cv2.perspectiveTransform(corners1, xform)
  all_corners = np.vstack((dst_corners1, corners2))
  x_min, y_min = np.int32(all_corners.min(axis=0).flatten())
  x_max, y_max = np.int32(all_corners.max(axis=0).flatten())
  # Calculate the size of the new image and the translation matrix
  new_w, new_h = x_max - x_min, y_max - y_min
  translation_matrix = np.array([[1, 0, -x_min], [0, 1, -y_min],
[0, 0, 1]])
  new_xform = translation_matrix @ xform
  # Create the result image and perform perspective transformation
  result = np.zeros((new_h, new_w, 3), dtype=np.uint8) # Initialize
with a black
                                              # background
  cv2.warpPerspective(image1, new_xform, (new_w, new_h),
               dst=result, borderMode=cv2.BORDER_TRANSPARENT)
  # Create an overlay layer and fill in the right image
  overlay = np.zeros_like(result, dtype=np.uint8)
  y_start, x_start = max(-y_min, 0), max(-x_min, 0)
  overlay[y_start:y_start+h2, x_start:x_start+w2] = image2
  # Stitch the two images using a mask
  mask = overlay > 0
  for c in range(3): # Process each channel separately to avoid color
channel
               # confusion
    result[..., c] = np.where(mask[..., c], overlay[..., c],
    result[..., c])
  return result
```

Then, import two images ***A*** and ***B***, and calculate the transformation matrix of the images.

```
# Read the images
img1 = cv2.imread('stitch1.jpg', cv2.IMREAD_COLOR)
img2 = cv2.imread('stitch2.jpg', cv2.IMREAD_COLOR)
gray1 = cv2.cvtColor(img1, cv2.COLOR_BGR2GRAY) / 255.0
gray2 = cv2.cvtColor(img2, cv2.COLOR_BGR2GRAY) / 255.0
g_images1, corners1, scales1, orientations1, layers1 = \
                              detect_blobs(gray1)
g_images2, corners2, scales2, orientations2, layers2 = \
                              detect_blobs(gray2)
# Calculate the feature points of the two images
descriptors1 = compute_descriptors(g_images1, corners1, scales1,
                           orientations1, layers1)
descriptors2 = compute_descriptors (g_images2, corners2, scales2,
                           orientations2, layers2)
# Match the feature points in the two images
matches = match_descriptors(descriptors1, descriptors2)
image1 = cv2.imread('stitch1.jpg', cv2.IMREAD_GRAYSCALE)
image2 = cv2.imread('stitch2.jpg', cv2.IMREAD_GRAYSCALE)
#    xform    is    the    transformation    matrix,    outlier_
labels are the outliers of the model
xform, outlier_labels = compute_affine_xform(corners1, corners2,
                                matches)
# Display the matching feature points of the two  images
match_image = draw_matches(image1, image2, corners1, corners2,
                     matches, outliers=outlier_labels)
plt.imshow(match_image)
plt.axis('off')
plt.plot()
[]
```

Finally, transform one of the images and stitch it with the other.

```
image = stitch_images(img1, img2, xform)
plt.imshow(image.astype(np.uint8))
plt.axis('off')
plt.plot()
[]
```

8.5 Summary

This chapter introduced the image stitching method based on SIFT feature detection and RANSAC algorithm. The practical application scenarios of image stitching are wide, such as post-processing of drone aerial photography and remote sensing images. These scenarios usually have a large field of view and require image stitching technology to stitch multiple images into a large one for subsequent image processing. As a representative example, the "Zhu Rong" Mars rover took a panoramic view of Mars through image stitching technology.

8.6 Further Reading

Solving with least squares method

$$\min_p \boldsymbol{A}\boldsymbol{p}^2 \quad \text{s.t. } \bar{\boldsymbol{p}}_2 = 1.$$

Given

$$\|\boldsymbol{A}\boldsymbol{p}\|^2 = (\boldsymbol{A}\boldsymbol{p})^{\mathrm{T}}(\boldsymbol{A}\boldsymbol{p}) = \boldsymbol{p}^{\mathrm{T}}\boldsymbol{A}^{\mathrm{T}}\boldsymbol{A}\boldsymbol{p} \quad \text{s.t. } \|\boldsymbol{p}\|^2 = \boldsymbol{p}^{\mathrm{T}}\boldsymbol{p} = 1.$$

Then, a loss function $l(\boldsymbol{p})$ can be constructed to iteratively find a solution that satisfies the equation group:

$$\min_p \left\{ l(\boldsymbol{p}) = \boldsymbol{p}^{\mathrm{T}}\boldsymbol{A}^{\mathrm{T}}\boldsymbol{A}\boldsymbol{p} + \lambda\left(\boldsymbol{p}^{\mathrm{T}}\boldsymbol{p} - 1\right) \right\}.$$

Differentiating with respect to $\boldsymbol{p}$, we get

$$\boldsymbol{A}^{\mathrm{T}}\boldsymbol{A}\boldsymbol{p} + \lambda\boldsymbol{p} = 0.$$

Obviously, the smallest eigenvalue $A^{T}A$ of the matrix corresponds to the eigenvector p, which is an approximate solution to this equation group.

Exercises

(1) Why do we need at least 4 pairs of feature points to fit a projective transformation?

(2) When stitching images, you can use the SIFT algorithm to extract feature points and perform preliminary matching, then use the RANSAC algorithm to eliminate incorrect matches, solve the homography matrix, and transform one image to the coordinate system of another image, and finally stitch them. Using the provided stitch1.jpg and stitch2.jpg, design an experiment to compare the effects of stitching with/without the RANSAC algorithm.

(3) When fitting a model using the RANSAC algorithm, suppose that at least 3 data samples are needed for each iteration to fit the model, and about 50% of the data samples are normal samples. Based on these assumptions, if you want the probability of fitting the correct model to be 99%, how many iterations are needed at least?

(4) At the end of stitching two images, the two images need to be seamed, and the pixel values of the seamed part are obtained by averaging the pixel values of the overlapping parts of the two images. However, in practical applications, considering changes in image contrast, exposure, etc., directly averaging will make the stitched image have obvious seaming borders. Is there a better stitching method?

(5) Given the homography matrix of the projective transformation $\begin{bmatrix} 1 & 0 & 2 \\ 1 & 0 & 1 \\ 0 & -2 & 2 \end{bmatrix}$ and the point A with coordinates (10, –2), and the point at coordinates (2, 2), denoted as *B*, find the coordinates after applying a projective transformation to points *A* and *B*.

Chapter 9
Image Segmentation

9.1 Introduction

Graphic designers often need to extract a specific object from an image (as shown in Fig. 9.1), a technique vividly referred to as "cutting out". "Cutting out" is a practical application of image segmentation. In the field of computer vision, image segmentation is one of the oldest and most researched problems. Depending on whether it is based on human-given semantic supervision, image segmentation can be divided into unsupervised image segmentation and supervised image segmentation. This chapter will focus on unsupervised image segmentation, while supervised image segmentation (including semantic segmentation, instance segmentation, etc.) should be classified as an image recognition problem and will be introduced in subsequent chapters. The goal of unsupervised image segmentation is to divide the image into several non-overlapping regions, so that pixels with similar features are divided into the same region, and pixels with different features are divided into different regions (as shown in Fig. 9.2). This goal is fully achieved by mining the inherent structural information of the image, not based on human-annotated semantic categories, so unsupervised image segmentation is a universal problem, and its results can provide a basis or initial conditions for solving high-level visual recognition tasks (such as semantic segmentation, object detection, and instance segmentation).

In this chapter, we will introduce two representative unsupervised image segmentation algorithms—the image segmentation algorithm based on k-means and the image segmentation algorithm based on normalized cuts.

W. Shen et al., *Hands-On Computer Vision*,
https://doi.org/10.1007/978-981-95-4835-4_9

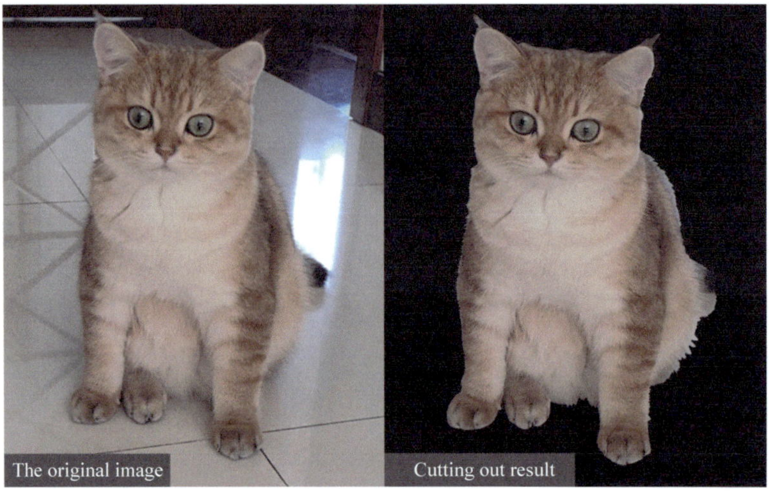

Fig. 9.1 "Cutting out"

Fig. 9.2 Example of unsupervised image segmentation

9.2 Image Segmentation Algorithm

This chapter focuses on unsupervised image segmentation, so we first need to know what unsupervised learning is. Unsupervised learning is a type of machine learning, where each training sample only has its own information, without any label information, that is, without "supervision". Clustering is a commonly used method of unsupervised learning, which refers to dividing data into clusters based on the mined relationships between data samples, so that the data samples within a cluster are similar (related) to each other, and the data samples in different clusters are different (unrelated). The greater the similarity within a cluster and the greater the difference between clusters, the better is the clustering performance. As a method of unsupervised learning, clustering is a commonly used machine learning technique in many fields. The essence of image segmentation is to cluster pixels, so image segmentation algorithms are generally based on clustering algorithms.

9.2.1 Image Segmentation Algorithm Based on k-Means Clustering

K-means [1, 2] is a clustering algorithm widely used in the field of machine learning and data analysis. It aims to divide the dataset into k different, non-overlapping subsets or clusters, with each data sample belonging to the cluster closest to it. Specifically, the k-means algorithm iterates through the following key steps:

(1) Initialization: Randomly select k data samples from the dataset and consider them as the initial cluster centers.
(2) Assignment: Assign each data sample to the cluster that belongs to the cluster center closest to it.
(3) Update: Once all data samples are assigned, calculate the mean of all data samples in each cluster and use it as the new cluster center.
(4) Repeat: Repeat the assignment and update steps until the cluster centers no longer change significantly, or the preset number of iterations is reached.

The k-means algorithm is widely used due to its simple calculation and fast convergence. It is not only used in traditional data analysis but also widely used in the field of image processing. If the pixels of an image are viewed as data points, and the k-means algorithm is used to cluster them, image segmentation can be achieved. So, for an image, how should we define pixel information? We know that each pixel contains the values of the R, G, B channels (as shown in Fig. 9.3), so we can cluster pixels based on RGB values as features.

Let's write the k-means algorithm and use RGB values to cluster pixels to complete image segmentation. First, import an image.

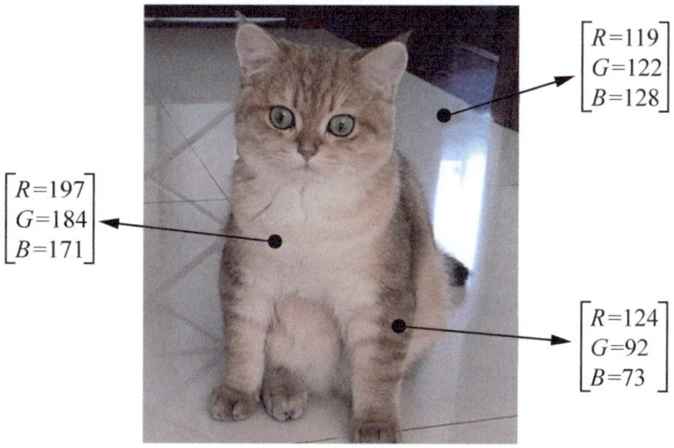

Fig. 9.3 Clustering pixels based on RGB values as features

```
from sklearn.cluster import KMeans
from matplotlib.image import imread
import matplotlib.pyplot as plt
import numpy as np
from PIL import Image
# Import an image
image = imread('segmentation.jpeg')[:,:,:3]
# Normalize RGB values to 0~1
if np.max(image)>1:
   image = image / 255
X = image.reshape(-1, image.shape[2])
# Use k-means algorithm for clustering
segmented_imgs = []
# Set the number of cluster centers
n_cluster= 4
kmeans = KMeans(n_clusters=n_cluster, random_state=42).fit(X)
print(np.unique(kmeans.labels_))
[0 1 2 3]
# Assign a corresponding color to each category for display
def decode_segmap(label_mask, plot= False ):
   label_colours = np.asarray([[79, 103, 67], [143, 146, 126],
                     [129, 94, 64], [52, 53, 55],
                     [96, 84, 70], [164, 149, 129]])
   r = label_mask.copy()
   g = label_mask.copy()
   b = label_mask.copy()
   # Assign corresponding R, G, B values to each category
   for ll in range(0, 6):
      r[label_mask == ll] = label_colours[ll, 0]
      g[label_mask == ll] = label_colours[ll, 1]
      b[label_mask == ll] = label_colours[ll, 2]
   rgb = np.zeros((label_mask.shape[0], label_mask.shape[1], 3))
   rgb[:, :, 0] = r
   rgb[:, :, 1] = g
   rgb[:, :, 2] = b
return rgb
# Get the predicted labels
segmented_img = kmeans.cluster_centers_[kmeans.labels_]
segmented_imgs = decode_segmap(kmeans.labels_.reshape(
               image.shape[0],image.shape[1]))
# Display the results
plt.imshow(image[:,:,:3])
plt.title('Original image')
plt.axis('off')
plt.show()
plt.imshow(segmented_imgs.astype(np.uint8))
plt.title('{} centers'.format(n_cluster))
plt.axis('off')
plt.show()
```

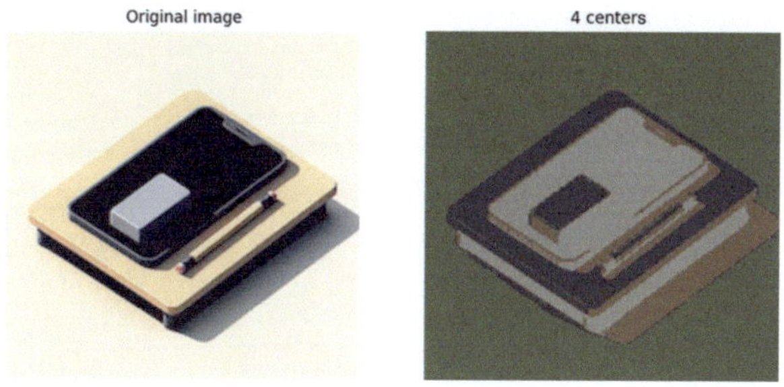

Observing the experimental results, it can be seen that using only RGB values as features may result in some isolated pixels during segmentation. In fact, since pixel coordinates inherently contain spatial information, in addition to selecting RGB values as features, coordinate information can also be incorporated. Including coordinates in the feature set allows these isolated pixels in the image to be segmented into surrounding objects. This approach considers both color similarity and spatial distribution. We attempt to perform image segmentation again, comparing the effects of setting different numbers of cluster centers on image segmentation.

```
image = imread('segmentation.jpeg')[:,:,:3]
# Normalize RGB values to 0-1
if np.max(image)>1:
   image = image / 255
sp = image.shape
# Set a weight to weight the coordinate  information
weight = 2
y = weight * np.array([[i for i in range(sp[1])]
                  for j in range(sp[0])]) / sp[0] / sp[1]
x = weight * np.array([[j for i in range(sp[1])]
                  for j in range(sp[0])])/ sp[0] / sp[1]
image = np.append(image, x.reshape(sp[0], sp[1], 1), axis=2)
image = np.append(image, y.reshape(sp[0], sp[1], 1), axis=2)
X = image.reshape(-1, image.shape[2])
segmented_imgs = []
# Set k to 6, 5, 4, 3, 2
n_colors = (6, 5, 4, 3, 2)
for n_cluster in n_colors:
   kmeans = KMeans(n_clusters=n_cluster, random_state=42).fit(X)
   segmented_img = kmeans.cluster_centers_[kmeans.labels_]
   segmented_imgs.append(decode_segmap(
      kmeans.labels_.reshape(image.shape[0],
                       image.shape[1])).astype(np.uint8))
# Display results
plt.figure(figsize=(12,8))
plt.subplot(231)
plt.imshow(image[:,:,:3])
plt.title('Original image')
plt.axis('off')
for idx,n_clusters in enumerate(n_colors):
   plt.subplot(232+idx)
   plt.imshow(segmented_imgs[idx])
```

```
plt.title('{} centers'.format(n_clusters))
plt.axis('off')
```

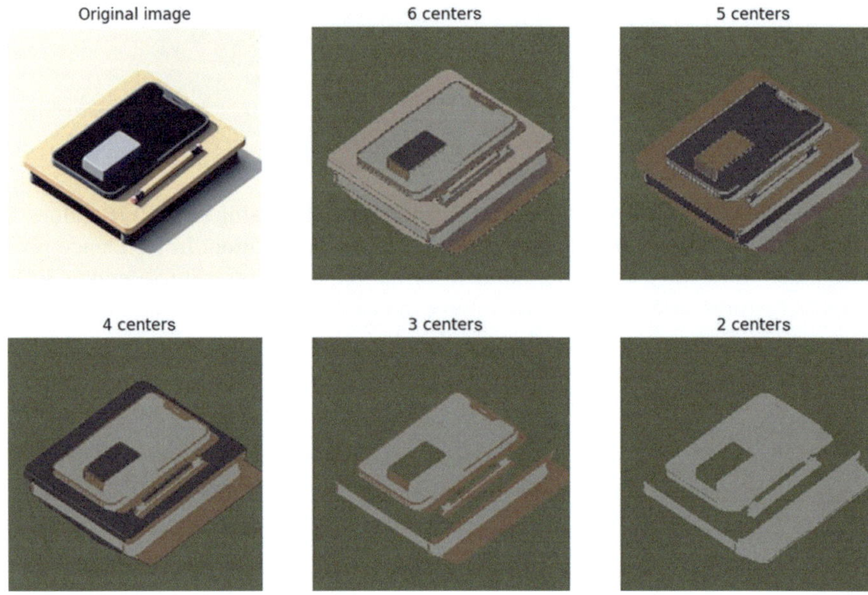

A comparison with segmentation results without coordinate information reveals that incorporating coordinates yields visibly smoother segmentation. Moreover, experimental outcomes clearly demonstrate that as the k value increases, the segmentation becomes progressively finer. In fact, the choice of k value is critical—selecting an appropriate k significantly improves the effectiveness of the image segmentation algorithm.

9.2.2 Image Segmentation Algorithm

The image segmentation algorithm based on graph cut utilizes the theory and methods of graph theory. The standard approach involves mapping the input image to a weighted undirected graph $\boldsymbol{G} = (\mathcal{V}, \mathcal{E})$, where $\mathcal{V} = \{v_1, v_2, \cdots, v_n\}$ is the set of vertices, and $\mathcal{E}$ is the set of edges. The vertices $v_i \in \mathcal{V}$ in the graph correspond to the pixels in the image, the edge $e \in \mathcal{E}$ connects a pair of adjacent pixels, and the weight of the edge $w(v_i, v_j)$ represents the non-negative similarity of adjacent pixels in terms of grayscale, color, or texture, where v_i and v_j are connected by the edge $\langle v_i, v_j \rangle \in \mathcal{E}$. Consequently, the problem of image segmentation is transformed into the problem of graph cut, where each subgraph corresponds to the segmented region in the original image, as shown in Fig. 9.4.

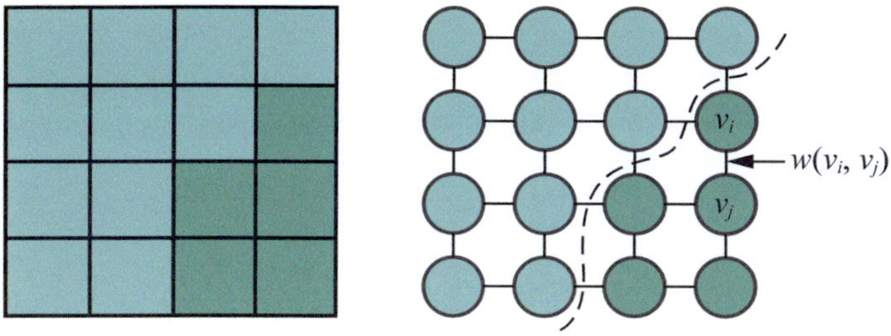

(a) The orginal image (b) G=(v, ε)corresponding to the image

Fig. 9.4 Image segmentation and graph cut

How to cut a graph? Similar to the core concept of the k-means algorithm, we hope that the similarity between vertices within the subgraphs after cutting is maximized, while the similarity between vertex pairs across different subgraphs is minimized. Taking the example of cutting an image into two subgraphs (as shown in Fig. 9.5), we divide the vertices of $\boldsymbol{G} = (\mathcal{V}, \mathcal{E})$ into two subsets $\mathcal{A}$ and $\mathcal{B}$, satisfying $\mathcal{A} \cup \mathcal{B} = \mathcal{V}$ and $\mathcal{A} \cap \mathcal{B} = \emptyset$. We define $\mathrm{cut}(\mathcal{A}, \mathcal{B}) = \sum_{u \in \mathcal{A}, v \in \mathcal{B}, \langle u, v \rangle \in \varepsilon} w(u, v)$. The minimum cut (min-cut) [3] algorithm minimizes $\mathrm{cut}(\mathcal{A}, \mathcal{B})$ to make the sum of the edge weights between the two subgraphs the smallest.

However, when using min-cut to cut the graph, the actual cutting situation is often as shown in Fig. 9.6, and the result is not ideal.

Fig. 9.5 Cutting graph nodes by min-cut

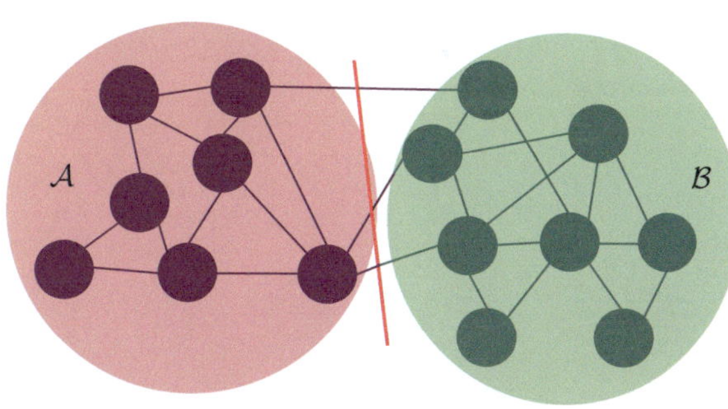

Fig. 9.6 Possible issue with min-cut

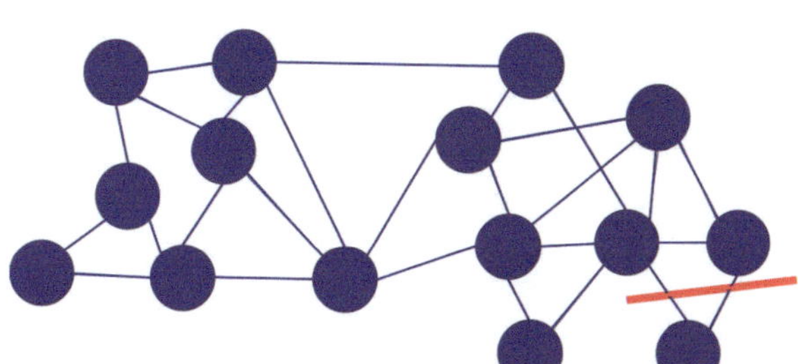

This situation is easy to explain because min-cut is achieved by minimizing $\text{cut}(\mathcal{A}, \mathcal{B})$. When there is only one vertex in one of the subgraphs, $\text{cut}(\mathcal{A}, \mathcal{B})$ is likely to be the smallest. To solve this extreme cutting situation, the normalized cut (Ncut) [4] algorithm was proposed.

The normalized cut algorithm minimizes the following formula to cut vertices:

$$\text{Ncut}(\mathcal{A}, \mathcal{B}) = \frac{\text{cut}(\mathcal{A}, \mathcal{B})}{\text{assoc}(\mathcal{A}, \mathcal{V})} + \frac{\text{cut}(\mathcal{A}, \mathcal{B})}{\text{assoc}(\mathcal{B}, \mathcal{V})},$$

where $\text{assoc}(\mathcal{A}, \mathcal{V})$ represents the sum of the weights of the edges connected to all vertices in $\mathcal{A}$ and all vertices in the graph, that is,

$$\text{assoc}(\mathcal{A}, \mathcal{V}) = \sum_{u \in \mathcal{A}, v \in \mathcal{V}, \langle u,v \rangle \in \varepsilon} w(u, v).$$

It is not difficult to find that if the set $\mathcal{A}$ contains only one point, $\text{assoc}(\mathcal{A}, \mathcal{V})$ and $\text{cut}(\mathcal{A}, \mathcal{B})$ are equal, and at this time $\text{Ncut}(\mathcal{A}, \mathcal{B})$ is larger; when the set $\mathcal{A}$ contains multiple points, the value of $\text{assoc}(\mathcal{A}, \mathcal{V})$ is larger than $\text{cut}(\mathcal{A}, \mathcal{B})$, and at this time $\text{Ncut}(\mathcal{A}, \mathcal{B})$ is smaller. This is why normalized cut can avoid the issue of min-cut.

In order to better represent $\text{Ncut}(\mathcal{A}, \mathcal{B})$, as shown in Fig. 9.7, a binary vector $\boldsymbol{x}[x_i \in \{-1, 1\}]$ is used to represent the distribution of vertices. If the vertex is at the black position, the corresponding x_i value is 1; if the vertex is at the gray position, the corresponding x_i value is -1.

In this way, $\text{Ncut}(\mathcal{A}, B)$ can be rewritten as

$$\text{Ncut}(\mathcal{A}, \mathcal{B}) = \frac{\sum_{(x_i>0, x_j<0)} -w_{ij} x_i x_j}{\sum_{x_i>0} d_i} + \frac{\sum_{(x_i<0, x_j>0)} -w_{ij} x_i x_j}{\sum_{x_i<0} d_i},$$

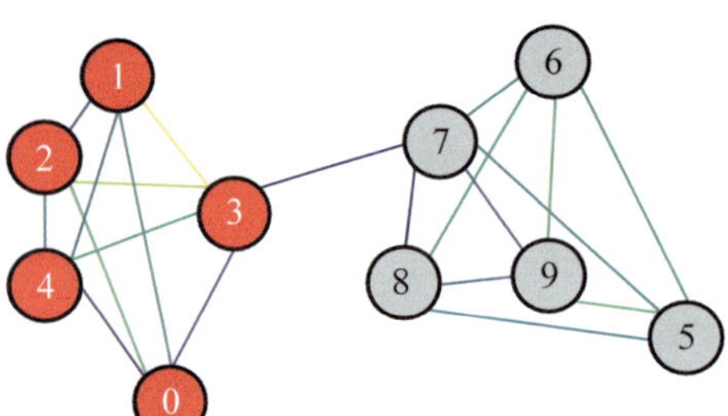

vector $\boldsymbol{x}$

0:	1
1:	1
2:	1
3:	1
4:	1
5:	−1
6:	−1
7:	−1
8:	−1
9:	−1

(a) Two types of vertices (b) The value corresponding to each vertex

Fig. 9.7 Vector representation of vertex clustering

where i and j represent vertices; $_{ij} = w\ (i, j)$; $d_i = \sum_j w(i, j)$. Let $\boldsymbol{D}$ be the diagonal matrix, $D_{ii} = d_i$; Let $\boldsymbol{W}$ be the weight matrix, $W_{ij} = w_{ij}$. Let

$$\boldsymbol{y} = \frac{1}{2}[(1 + \boldsymbol{x}) - b(1 - \boldsymbol{x})],$$

where $b = \frac{\sum_{x_i > 0} d_i}{\sum_{x_i < 0} d_i}$, we have

$$\min_{x} \mathrm{Ncut}(\boldsymbol{x}) = \min_{y} \frac{\boldsymbol{y}^{\mathrm{T}}(\boldsymbol{D} - \boldsymbol{W})\boldsymbol{y}}{\boldsymbol{y}^{\mathrm{T}}\boldsymbol{D}\boldsymbol{y}}.$$

The optimal solution to the above optimization problem can be obtained through the following formula:

$$(\boldsymbol{D} - \boldsymbol{W})\boldsymbol{y} = \lambda \boldsymbol{D}\boldsymbol{y}.$$

That is,

$$\boldsymbol{D}^{-\frac{1}{2}}(\boldsymbol{D} - \boldsymbol{W})\boldsymbol{D}^{-\frac{1}{2}}\boldsymbol{D}^{\frac{1}{2}}\boldsymbol{y} = \lambda \boldsymbol{D}^{\frac{1}{2}}\boldsymbol{y}.$$

Let $z = \boldsymbol{D}^{\frac{1}{2}}\boldsymbol{y}$, then we have

$$\boldsymbol{D}^{-\frac{1}{2}}(\boldsymbol{D} - \boldsymbol{W})\boldsymbol{D}^{-\frac{1}{2}}z = \lambda \mathbf{z}.$$

Clearly, here z and λ are the eigenvectors and eigenvalues of $\boldsymbol{D}^{-\frac{1}{2}}(\boldsymbol{D} - \boldsymbol{W})\boldsymbol{D}^{-\frac{1}{2}}$, respectively. Therefore, we only need to solve for these eigenvalues. It should be noted that using the eigenvector corresponding to the smallest eigenvalue as the basis for segmentation will cluster all vertices in the graph into one category, which is meaningless. Therefore, the basis for cutting we need is the eigenvector corresponding to the second smallest eigenvalue.

The calculation process of the normalized cut algorithm can be summarized in the following steps.

(1) Input the image, construct a graph with pixels as vertices, and define the weight function for the edges. Here, we define the weight function as

$$W_{ij} = \exp\left(\frac{-\|I_i - I_j\|_2^2}{\sigma_I^2}\right) \cdot \begin{cases} \exp\left(\frac{-\|x_i - x_j\|_2^2}{\sigma_x^2}\right), & \|x_i - x_j\|_2 < r \\ 0, & |otherwise \end{cases},$$

where σ_I, σ_x, and r are three hyperparameters.

(2) Calculate the weight matrix $\boldsymbol{W}$ and the diagonal matrix $\boldsymbol{D}$.

(3) Calculate the eigenvalues and eigenvectors of $\boldsymbol{D}^{-\frac{1}{2}}(\boldsymbol{D}-\boldsymbol{W})\boldsymbol{D}^{-\frac{1}{2}}$, and determine the eigenvector corresponding to the second smallest eigenvalue.

Next, we will implement the normalized cut algorithm in code. We first input the original image.

```
import numpy as np
import cv2
from PIL import Image
import matplotlib.pyplot as plt
sample_img = cv2.imread('segmentation.jpeg', cv2.IMREAD_
GRAYSCALE).astype(
            np.float32) / 255
plt.imshow(sample_img, cmap='gray')
<matplotlib.image.AxesImage at 0x162442580>
```

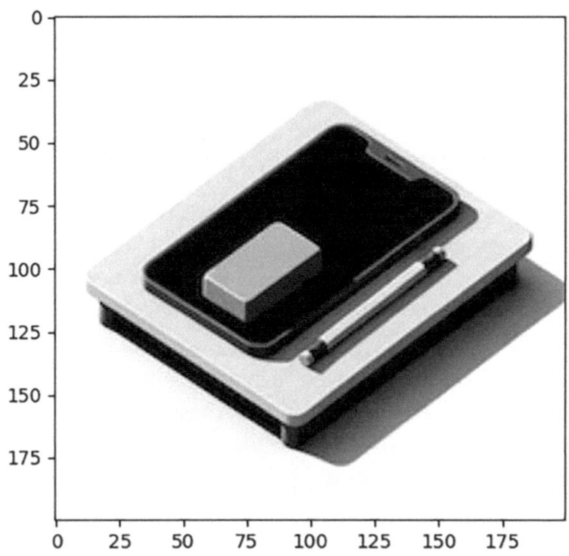

Then, we write the weight matrix.

```
def cal_dist_weighted_matrix(size, r, sig_X):
    h, w = size
    X_matrix = np.zeros((h*w, h*w))
    for i in range(h*w):
        for j in range(h*w):
            i_row, i_col = i // w, i % w
            j_row, j_col = j // w, j % w
            dist = np.power(i_row - j_row, 2) + \
                np.power(i_col - j_col, 2)
            if np.sqrt(dist) < r:
                X_matrix[i, j] = np.exp(-dist / sig_X)
    return X_matrix
def set_weighted_matrix(img, sig_I=0.01, sig_X=5, r=10):
```

```
    vec_img = img.flatten()
    F_matrix = np.power(vec_img[None, :] - vec_img[:, None], 2)
    F_matrix /= sig_I
    F_matrix = np.exp(-F_matrix)
    X_matrix = cal_dist_weighted_matrix(img.shape, r, sig_X)
    return F_matrix * X_matrix
weighted_matrix = set_weighted_matrix(sample_img)
weighted_matrix
```

```
[[1.         0.8137098  0.44657341 ... 0.         0.         0.        ]
 [0.8137098  1.         0.81873075 ... 0.         0.         0.        ]
 [0.44657341 0.81873075 1.         ... 0.         0.         0.        ]
 ...
 [0.         0.         0.         ... 1.         0.81747264 0.44863849]
 [0.         0.         0.         ... 0.81747264 1.         0.81873075]
 [0.         0.         0.         ... 0.44863849 0.81873075 1.        ]]
```

Next, solve the eigenvectors corresponding to each eigenvalue.

```
from scipy import sparse
from scipy.sparse.linalg import eigs, svds
import skimage
def n_cuts(W, image):
    n = W.shape[0]
    s_D = sparse.csr_matrix((n, n))
    d_i = W.sum(axis=0)
    for i in range(n):
        s_D[i, i] = d_i[i]
    s_W = sparse.csr_matrix(W)
    # print(s_W.shape)
    s_D_nhalf = np.sqrt(s_D).power(-1)
    # print(s_D.shape)
    L = s_D_nhalf @ (s_D - s_W) @ s_D_nhalf
    # print(L.shape)
    _, eigenvalues, eigenvectors = svds(L, which='SM')
    print(eigenvectors.shape)
    for i in range(1, 5):
        print(eigenvectors[i].shape)
        Partition = eigenvectors[i] > \
            np.sum(eigenvectors[i])/len(eigenvectors[i])
        print(Partition.shape)
        skimage.io.imshow(Partition.reshape(image.shape))
        plt.title('Ncut')
        plt.show()
```

Finally, display the corresponding segmentation results.

```
n_cuts(weighted_matrix, sample_img)
```

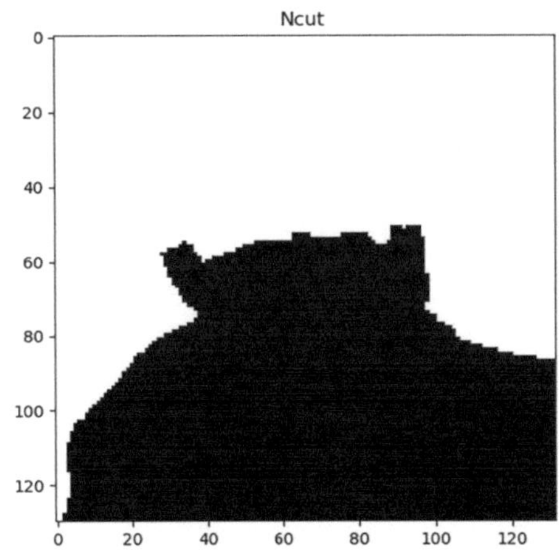

9.3 Summary

This chapter introduced unsupervised image segmentation methods. Although the results of unsupervised image segmentation methods may not seem ideal, they can serve as the basis or auxiliary work for image semantic understanding based on supervised learning (such as object detection and instance segmentation). So far, the methods we have introduced are based on unsupervised learning and do not involve image semantics. In the following chapters, we will focus on image semantic understanding based on supervised learning.

Exercises

(1) Design and implement a method for dynamically selecting the value of k so that the k-means algorithm can automatically determine the optimal k value for image segmentation. Discuss the effectiveness of the designed method.
(2) Add Gaussian noise to an image, and then use the k-means algorithm to segment the image. Observe and discuss the effect of the k-means-based image segmentation algorithm when dealing with noisy images.
(3) To reduce the computational burden of the Ncut algorithm, we can divide the input image into small sub-images. Based on this idea, implement an accelerated Ncut algorithm, and use the provided segmentation.jpeg to test the speed improvement of the improved algorithm.
(4) For the Ncut algorithm, can a more effective weight matrix $\boldsymbol{W}$ be designed by combining the edge information of the image? Use the provided segmentation.jpeg to test the impact of different weight matrices on the results.
(5) In Sect. 9.2.2, we used the Ncut algorithm to divide an image into two sub-images. Using the provided segmentation.jpeg, divide the image into multiple sub-images based on the Ncut algorithm.

References

1. JAIN A K, DUBES R C. Algorithms for clustering data[M]. Prentice-Hall, Inc., 1988.
2. MACQUEEN J. Some methods for classification and analysis of multivariate observations[C]// Berkeley Symposium on Mathematical Statistics and Probability, 1967, 1(14):281–297.
3. STOER M, WAGNER F. A simple min-cut algorithm[J]. Journal of the ACM, 1997, 44(4): 585–591.
4. SHI J, MALIK J. Normalized cuts and image segmentation[J]. IEEE Transactions on Pattern Analysis and Machine Intelligence, 2000, 22(8):888–905.

Part III
Visual Recognition

Chapter 10
Image Classification

10.1 Introduction

In previous chapters, we introduced a series of image processing algorithms. These image processing algorithms can help us extract the required information from images, laying the foundation for subsequent computer vision tasks. Starting from this chapter, we will delve into the part of visual recognition in the field of computer vision. The goal of visual recognition is to make the computer's image recognition consistent with human recognition. Therefore, visual recognition usually requires a (machine) learning process. Since the rise of deep learning in 2012, most tasks in the field of visual recognition have been accomplished using deep learning based methods. Therefore, in this part of visual recognition, we will mainly introduce visual recognition algorithms based on deep learning.

Image classification is one of the most basic problems in visual recognition, and research on this problem is the basis for studying other visual recognition problems. Image classification, as the name suggests, is to divide images into predefined categories according to certain classification rules. As shown in Fig. 10.1, simple image classification is to label these images as "cat", "camel", "tiger", etc. To describe the image classification problem in mathematical language, define the image space $\mathbb{I}$ and the predefined category set $\mathcal{C}$, given the dataset $\mathcal{D} = \{(\boldsymbol{I}^{(n)}, y^{(n)})\}_{n=1}^{N}\mathcal{D} = \{(\boldsymbol{I}^{(n)}, y^{(n)})\}_{n=1}^{N}$, where $\boldsymbol{I}^{(n)} \in \mathbb{I}$ is the nth image in the dataset, and $y^{(n)} \in \mathcal{C}$ is its corresponding label; the task of image classification is to learn a mapping from the image space to the category set from $\mathcal{D}$, so that given any image $\boldsymbol{I}$, its label can be predicted using the learned mapping function f, that is, $\hat{y} = f(\boldsymbol{I})$. Usually, this learning process needs to model the conditional probability $P(y|\boldsymbol{I})$, then $\hat{y} = f(\boldsymbol{I}) = \arg\max_{y \in \mathcal{C}} P(y|\boldsymbol{I})$.

The traditional image classification process is shown in Fig. 10.2. First, extract the image representations from the images used for training, and train an image classification model (classifier) with the corresponding labels. For each testing image, use the same representation extraction process to obtain its representation, and use the trained classifier to predict its category.

W. Shen et al., *Hands-On Computer Vision*,
https://doi.org/10.1007/978-981-95-4835-4_10

Fig. 10.1 Example of image classification

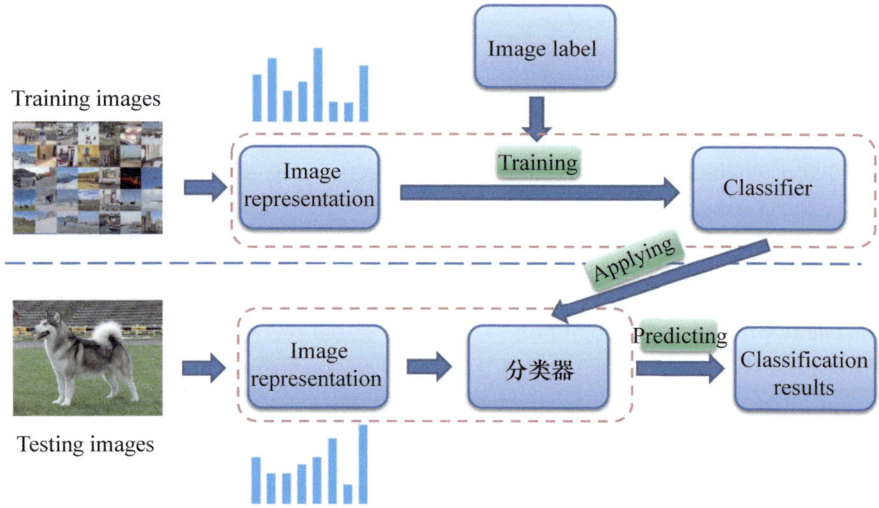

Fig. 10.2 Image classification process (training images are from the MS COCO dataset, testing images are from the ImageNet dataset)

The extraction of image representation is a key step in image classification. The performance difference between different classifiers in machine learning is not significant, so the quality of image representation directly determines the performance of image classification. Traditional image representation extraction algorithms are mainly based on manually designed image feature vectors. For example, the SIFT feature descriptor introduced in Chap. 7 is a typical manually designed image feature vector. The culmination of traditional image representation is the bag of features (BoF) [1–4] model, inspired by the bag-of-words model in the field of text retrieval, proposed by Andrew Zisserman et al. This representation model first detects and extracts multiple feature points from images, then uses clustering algorithms to cluster the feature vectors of these feature points to obtain a "dictionary", and then encodes the feature vectors in each image based on the constructed dictionary to build the representation of each image, i.e., the bag of features representation. The traditional image classification process can train image classifiers based on the bag of features representation. As can be seen, the traditional image representation extraction and image classifier training are carried out separately (as shown in Fig. 10.2), manually designed image representation often discards useful information prematurely, and the classification results cannot feedback to the image representation extraction stage; thus the classification performance will be somewhat limited.

With the rise of deep learning, joint learning of image representation and classifier through deep convolutional neural networks (DCNN) has gradually become mainstream, because through joint learning, the classification results and the extraction of image representations can mutually influence each other, thereby greatly improving the performance of image classification. The first deep convolutional neural network was proposed by Yann LeCun in 1989 [5], which was designed for handwritten character recognition. Later in 1998, he improved this network. The improved network is called LeNet-5 [6], which has all the elements of modern convolutional neural networks. In 2012, Geoffrey Hinton and his students built AlexNet [7] Model. AlexNet is an 8-layer convolutional neural network that won the ImageNet image classification competition, marking the beginning of the deep learning era for image classification. In 2015, researchers from Microsoft Asia Research Institute, including Kaiming He, proposed ResNet [8]. ResNet is a convolutional neural network that can be stacked up to thousands of layers. It set a new record in the ImageNet image classification competition, and since then, deep learning has dominated the entire field of visual recognition.

In this chapter, we will introduce image classification algorithms based on the traditional Bag-of-Visual-Words model and the deep convolutional network ResNet. Before introducing the algorithms, we need to understand some commonly used datasets and metrics in image classification.

10.2 Datasets and Metrics

In image classification tasks, we usually choose the following datasets for model training and testing.

(1) MNIST [9]: MNIST is a dataset of handwritten digits, each sample is a black and white image, and the corresponding label is one of the digits 0-9. It contains 60,000 training images and 10,000 testing images.
(2) Caltech-101 [10]: Caltech-101 was released by Li Fei-Fei and others in 2003. The dataset contains 102 categories (101 target categories and 1 background category), with 9144 images for training and testing.
(3) CIFAR-10 [11]: CIFAR-10 is a small dataset for recognizing common categories, compiled by Geoffrey Hinton and his students Alex Krizhevsky and Ilya Sutskever. It contains 10 categories, 50,000 training images, and 10,000 testing images.

(4) ImageNet [12]: ImageNet is a large-scale image recognition dataset, collected by Li Fei-Fei's team since 2007. The ImageNet dataset contains more than 20,000 categories and over 14 million images.

In this chapter, we use Caltech-101 as the dataset for the experiment, randomly selecting 60% of the data as training samples. Of the remaining data, 50% is randomly selected as validation samples, and the other 50% as test samples.

In image classification, the top-k error rate is often used as one of the model's metrics. For n testing image samples, if the number of testing images whose true category is included in the top k categories predicted by the model is m, then the top-k error rate of the model is defined as

$$\text{Top - }k\text{ error rate} = \left(1 - \frac{m}{n}\right) \times 100\%.$$

In this chapter, we use the top-1 error rate as the metric.

10.3 Image Classification Algorithm Based on Bag-of-Visual-Words Model

The Bag-of-Visual-Words model is a method for extracting image representations, which can be roughly divided into the following four steps:

(1) Extract features from the training image set to form a feature library.
(2) Cluster the feature vectors in the feature library to build a "visual dictionary".
(3) Encode each image's features using the learned visual dictionary.
(4) Represent the image based on feature encoding.

Specifically, the process begins by extracting features from the given training images, typically utilizing SIFT features. As introduced in Chap. 7, each SIFT feature descriptor is a 128-dimensional vector. All the SIFT features extracted from the training image set are collected to form an image feature bank. Then, these image features are clustered into k cluster centers using methods like k-mean clustering. These cluster centers are called "visual words", and the set of all visual words is the visual dictionary. In the visual dictionary shown in Fig. 10.3, each small block represents a visual word.

Next, visual dictionary is used to encode image features. Each feature of the image can be represented by a visual word in the dictionary that is most similar to it. This is a process we call "assigning the feature to the most similar visual word". The more times a visual word is assigned, the more frequently the semantics it represents appear in the image. As shown in Fig. 10.4, a histogram can be used to count the frequency of visual words in an image. Finally, this histogram is used to form the representation of the image.

Based on the representation of images, image classification can be achieved by training a common multi-classifier (such as SVM). Next, we will implement an image

Fig. 10.3 Clustering feature vectors to build a visual dictionary (illustration material from Ref. [13])

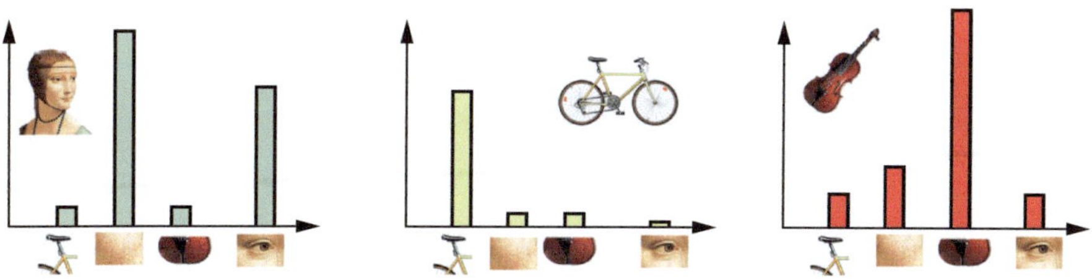

Fig. 10.4 Building image representation based on feature encoding

classification algorithm based on the visual bag-of-words model. We first import the necessary libraries and the Caltech-101 dataset.

```
from PIL import Image
import cv2
import numpy as np
import os
from sklearn.model_selection import train_test_split
from sklearn.kernel_approximation import AdditiveChi2Sampler
import random
import math
from imutils import paths
# Image data
data = []
# Corresponding labels of the images
labels = []
# Temporary variable for storing label information
 labels_tep = []
# Address of the dataset
# Download the dataset on your own and place it in the same directory
as the code
image_paths = list(paths.list_images('./caltech-101'))
for image_path in image_paths:
   # Get the category of the image
   label = image_path.split(os.path.sep)[-2]
   # Read each category of image
   image = cv2.imread(image_path)
   # Convert the image channel from BGR to RGB
   image = cv2.cvtColor(image, cv2.COLOR_BGR2RGB)
   # Standardize the size of the input image
    image = cv2.resize(image, (200,200), interpolation=cv2.INTER_
AREA)
```

```
    data.append(image)
    labels_tep.append(label)
name2label = {}
tep = {}
for idx, name in enumerate(labels_tep):
    tep[name] = idx
for idx, name in enumerate(tep):
    name2label[name] = idx
for idx, image_path in enumerate(image_paths):
    labels.append(name2label[image_path.split(os.path.sep)[-2]])
data = np.array(data)
labels = np.array(labels)
```

Then, divide the dataset into training, validation, and testing sets.

```
(x_train, X, y_train, Y) = train_test_split(data, labels,
     test_size=0.4, stratify=labels, random_state=42)
(x_val, x_test, y_val, y_test) = train_test_split(X, Y,
     test_size=0.5, random_state=42)
print(f"x_train examples: {x_train.shape}\n\
    x_test examples: {x_test.shape}\n\
     x_val examples: {x_val.shape}")
x_train examples: (5486, 200, 200, 3)
x_test examples: (1829, 200, 200, 3)
x_val examples: (1829, 200, 200, 3)
```

Next, construct a visual dictionary. To obtain the visual dictionary, we first need to extract the representations of input images. Here, we extract SIFT features from the images.

```
# Construct a dictionary to store the SIFT features of each category
vec_dict = {i:{'kp':[], 'des':{}} for i in range(102)}
sift = cv2.SIFT_create()
for i in range(x_train.shape[0]):
    # Normalize the image
    tep = cv2.normalize(x_train[i], None, 0, 255,
                cv2.NORM_MINMAX).astype('uint8')
    # Compute the SIFT features of the image
    kp_vector, des_vector = sift.detectAndCompute(tep, None)
    # Store the keypoint and descriptor information in the dictionary
    vec_dict[y_train[i]]['kp'] += list(kp_vector)
    for k in range(len(kp_vector)):
      # The 'des' uses kp_vector for one-to-one correspondence
      vec_dict[y_train[i]]['des'][kp_vector[k]] = des_vector[k]
```

To maintain balance between categories, an equal number of features is selected from each category for subsequent clustering. First, the quantity of SIFT image features per category is counted. The category with the fewest features is identified, and its feature count is used as the standard number. Features are then sampled from each category according to this standard number for the clustering task.

```
# Set the standard number of keypoints
bneck_value = float("inf")
```

```
# Use the smallest number of keypoints as the value of bneck_value
for i in range(102):
  if len(vec_dict[i]['kp']) < bneck_value:
    bneck_value = len(vec_dict[i]['kp'])
# Sort the SIFT keypoints of each category in descending order of
response value
for i in range(102):
   kp_list = vec_dict[i]['kp'] = sorted((vec_dict[i]['kp']),
                        key=lambda x: x.response,
                        reverse=True)
# Select the same number of keypoints from each category for clus-
tering, with the
# standard number of keypoints being bneck_value
vec_list=[]
for i in range(bneck_value):
   vec_list.append(vec_dict[0]['des'][vec_dict[0]['kp'][i]])
for i in range(1, 102):
   for j in range(bneck_value):
     vec_list.append(vec_dict[i]['des'][vec_dict[i]['kp'][j]])
vec_list = np.float64(vec_list)
```

Use the k-means clustering algorithm to cluster these features. The cluster centers are obtained from the visual dictionary. Here, the number of cluster centers is set to 200.

```
from sklearn.cluster import KMeans
N_clusters = 200
kmeans = KMeans(n_clusters=N_clusters, random_state=0).fit(vec_
list)
```

The visual dictionary is used to encode the features in the image, and the histogram is used to count the results of the encoding. The histogram is then normalized to obtain the representation of the image. Note that this histogram representation based on the encoding of the entire image feature will lose the position information of the image feature, that is, changing the position of the feature arbitrarily will not change the representation of the bag-of-words model. To overcome this problem, we introduce the spatial pyramid matching (SPM) [1] algorithm to enhance the representation ability of the bag-of-words model. SPM first divides the image into different levels (as shown in Fig. 10.5), and in each level, the image is divided into several blocks (the number of blocks is 1×1, 2×2, 4×4), then each divided image block in each level is represented by the above-mentioned bag-of-words model histogram, and finally, the histograms of the image blocks at all levels are connected to form a vector, which is the representation of the entire image.

```
def extract_SIFT(img):
  sift = cv2.SIFT_create()
  descriptors = []
  for disft_step_size in DSIFT_STEP_SIZE:
    keypoints = [cv2.KeyPoint(x, y, disft_step_size)
       for y in range(0, img.shape[0], disft_step_size)
         for x in range(0, img.shape[1], disft_step_size)]
```

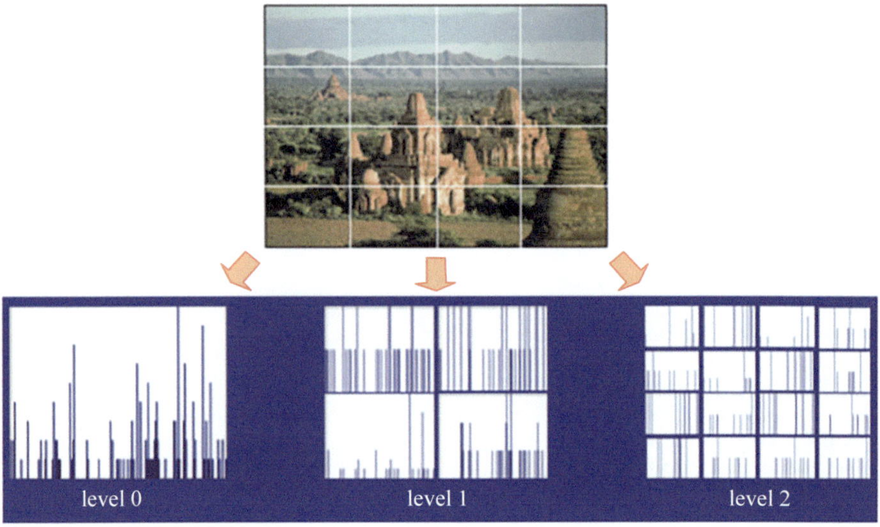

Fig. 10.5 Dividing an image by spatial pyramid matching (illustration material from Svetlana Lazebnik's personal homepage)

```
        descriptors.append(sift.compute(img, keypoints)[1])
    return np.concatenate(descriptors, axis=0).astype('float64')
# Get the SPM features of the image
def getImageFeaturesSPM(L, img, kmeans, k):
    W = img.shape[1]
    H = img.shape[0]
    h = []
    for l in range(L+1):
        w_step = math.floor(W/(2**l))
        h_step = math.floor(H/(2**l))
        x, y = 0, 0
        for _ in range(2**l):
            x = 0
            for _ in range(2**l):
                desc = extract_SIFT(img[y:y+h_step, x:x+w_step])
                predict = kmeans.predict(desc)
                histo = np.bincount(predict,
                    minlength=k).reshape(1,-1).ravel()
                weight = 2**(l-L)
                h.append(weight*histo)
                x = x + w_step
            y = y + h_step
    hist = np.array(h).ravel()
    hist /= np.sum(hist)
    return hist
```

Use SPM to extract the features of the images in the training set and the testing set.

```
# Some hyperparameters of SPM
pyramid_level = 2
DSIFT_STEP_SIZE = [4, 8]
hist_vector = []
for i in range(x_train.shape[0]):
  tep = cv2.normalize(x_train[i], None, 0,
          255, cv2.NORM_MINMAX).astype('uint8')
  # Extract SPM features of the image
  hist_SPM = getImageFeaturesSPM(pyramid_level, tep,
             kmeans, N_clusters)
  # Append the extracted features to the histogram
  hist_vector.append(hist_SPM)
hist_vector = np.array(hist_vector)
hist_test_vector = []
for i in range(x_test.shape[0]):
  tep = cv2.normalize(x_test[i], None, 0,
          255, cv2.NORM_MINMAX).astype('uint8')
  hist_SPM = getImageFeaturesSPM(pyramid_level, tep,
             kmeans, N_clusters)
  hist_test_vector.append(hist_SPM)
hist_test_vector = np.array(hist_test_vector)
```

Train an SVM classifier for image classification.

```
from sklearn import svm
# transform uses a feature mapping method
transformer = AdditiveChi2Sampler()
transformer = transformer.fit(np.concatenate(
[hist_vector, hist_test_vector], axis=0))
# Build the SVM classifier
classifier = svm.LinearSVC()
# Perform feature mapping on the trained histogram
hist_vector = transformer.transform(hist_vector)
# Fit the data
classifier.fit(hist_vector, y_train)
LinearSVC()
```

Finally, evaluate the classifier on the testing set and calculate the top-1 error rate.

```
# Perform feature mapping on the histogram of the testing image
hist_test_vector = transformer.transform(hist_test_vector)
# Calculate top-1 error rate
top1_error = classifier.predict(hist_test_vector)-y_test
tep = len(top1_error[top1_error != 0])
print('Top-1 Error', tep/len(y_test))
Top-1 Error 0.3001640240568617
```

It can be seen that using the bag-of-words model for image classification on the Caltech-101 dataset, the top-1 error rate is about 30%. Of course, the top-1 error rate of the model can be reduced on the existing basis in other ways, such as using Dense SIFT to replace SIFT to extract features from images. Dense SIFT is an improved version of the SIFT algorithm, which first processes the input image in blocks, then performs SIFT operations on each block, and extracts features.

10.4 Image Classification Algorithm Based on Deep Convolutional Network

In 2012, with the advent of AlexNet, methods based on deep convolutional neural networks gradually became the mainstream in the field of computer vision. For image classification tasks, deep convolutional neural networks can achieve end-to-end prediction from images to classification labels, eliminating the need for phased feature extraction and classifier training.

The ResNet was proposed in 2015 by researchers such as Kaiming He from Microsoft Research Asia, and it won first place in both the image classification and object detection tasks of the ImageNet Large Scale Visual Recognition Competition that year. Before the introduction of ResNet, all neural networks were composed of stacked convolutional and pooling layers (for related knowledge about neural networks, refer to "Hands-On Deep Learning"). It was believed that the more layers of convolution and pooling, the stronger the image representation information obtained, and the better the learning effectiveness. However, in experiments, researchers found that with the stacking of convolutional and pooling layers, not only did the learning effectiveness not improve, but gradient vanishing, gradient explosion, and degradation problems also occurred. In the backpropagation of neural networks, each forward propagation layer multiplies the error gradient of each layer. If the error gradient is a number less than 1, the gradient will become smaller as the number of network layers increases, resulting in gradient vanishing; if the error gradient is a number greater than 1, the gradient will become larger as the number of network layers increases, resulting in gradient explosion. These issues of gradient vanishing or gradient explosion can be solved by preprocessing the data and using batch normalization (BN) layers in the network. The degradation problem refers to the fact that networks with more layers do not perform as well on training and testing sets as networks with fewer layers. To address the degradation problem, ResNet introduced residual blocks (as shown in Fig. 10.6), adding identity mapping as a shortcut connection, skipping several layers, and adding the input to the output.

The architecture of ResNet is shown in Fig. 10.7.

We take the use of ResNet18 for image classification as an example to further illustrate the architecture of ResNet. An RGB image with a resolution of 224 pixels ×

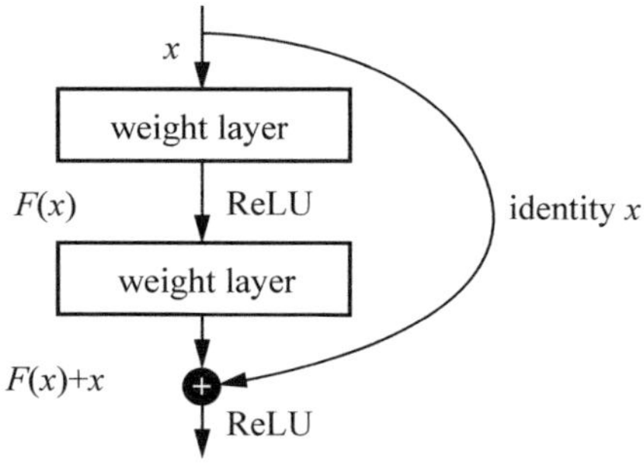

Fig. 10.6 Residual block in ResNet (illustration from Ref. [8])

Layer name	Output size	18-layer	34-layer	50-layer	101-layer	152-layer
conv 1	112×112	7×7, 64, stride-2				
conv2_x	56×56	3×3Max pool, stride-2				
		$\begin{bmatrix} 3\times3, 64 \\ 3\times3, 64 \end{bmatrix}\times2$	$\begin{bmatrix} 3\times3, 64 \\ 3\times3, 64 \end{bmatrix}\times3$	$\begin{bmatrix} 1\times1, 64 \\ 3\times3, 64 \\ 1\times1, 256 \end{bmatrix}\times3$	$\begin{bmatrix} 1\times1, 64 \\ 3\times3, 64 \\ 1\times1, 256 \end{bmatrix}\times3$	$\begin{bmatrix} 1\times1, 64 \\ 3\times3, 64 \\ 1\times1, 256 \end{bmatrix}\times3$
conv3_x	28×28	$\begin{bmatrix} 3\times3, 128 \\ 3\times3, 128 \end{bmatrix}\times2$	$\begin{bmatrix} 3\times3, 128 \\ 3\times3, 128 \end{bmatrix}\times4$	$\begin{bmatrix} 1\times1, 128 \\ 3\times3, 128 \\ 1\times1, 512 \end{bmatrix}\times4$	$\begin{bmatrix} 1\times1, 128 \\ 3\times3, 128 \\ 1\times1, 512 \end{bmatrix}\times4$	$\begin{bmatrix} 1\times1, 128 \\ 3\times3, 128 \\ 1\times1, 512 \end{bmatrix}\times8$
conv4_x	14×14	$\begin{bmatrix} 3\times3, 256 \\ 3\times3, 256 \end{bmatrix}\times2$	$\begin{bmatrix} 3\times3, 256 \\ 3\times3, 256 \end{bmatrix}\times6$	$\begin{bmatrix} 1\times1, 256 \\ 3\times3, 256 \\ 1\times1, 1024 \end{bmatrix}\times6$	$\begin{bmatrix} 1\times1, 256 \\ 3\times3, 256 \\ 1\times1, 1024 \end{bmatrix}\times23$	$\begin{bmatrix} 1\times1, 256 \\ 3\times3, 256 \\ 1\times1, 1024 \end{bmatrix}\times36$
conv5_x	7×7	$\begin{bmatrix} 3\times3, 512 \\ 3\times3, 512 \end{bmatrix}\times2$	$\begin{bmatrix} 3\times3, 512 \\ 3\times3, 512 \end{bmatrix}\times3$	$\begin{bmatrix} 1\times1, 512 \\ 3\times3, 512 \\ 1\times1, 2048 \end{bmatrix}\times3$	$\begin{bmatrix} 1\times1, 512 \\ 3\times3, 512 \\ 1\times1, 2048 \end{bmatrix}\times3$	$\begin{bmatrix} 1\times1, 512 \\ 3\times3, 512 \\ 1\times1, 2048 \end{bmatrix}\times3$
	1×1	Average pool,1000-dimensional fully-connected, softmax				
FLOPS		1.8×10^9	3.6×10^9	3.8×10^9	7.6×10^9	11.3×10^9

Fig. 10.7 ResNet architecture (illustration from Ref. [8])

224 pixels is input into ResNet, and ResNet convolves it through the conv1 layer to obtain a feature map with a spatial resolution of 112 pixels × 112 pixels and 64 channels. As we introduced in Chap. 2, the spatial resolution of the feature map is only 1/4 of the input image because the stride of the convolution in the conv1 layer is set to 2. How is the feature map with 64 channels obtained? In Chap. 2, we introduced that convolving an input image with a $k \times k$ convolution kernel will result in a feature map with one channel. Therefore, a feature map with 64 channels is obtained by convolving the input image with 64 $k \times k$ convolution kernels and then concatenating the 64 feature maps with one channel along the feature dimension. Note that a feature map can also be seen as an image, and thus we can change the number of channels of the feature map, i.e., the feature dimension, through convolution. Generally, for a feature map with t channels and a spatial resolution of $H \times W$, using s convolution kernels to convolve the feature map at the same time can output a feature map with s channels. It can be seen that the dimension of the feature map can be increased and decreased through convolution, which is very useful. After the conv1 layer, ResNet processes the feature map through four modules in sequence. Each module contains multiple convolutional layers with the same setting and reduces the spatial resolution of the feature map by 1/4. The final output of conv5_x is a 512-channel feature map with a resolution of 7 pixels × 7 pixels. After that, the feature map is input into a global average pooling layer and a fully connected layer with 1000 neurons using the softmax activation function. The fully connected layer maps a feature map with any number of channels to a vector with a dimension equal to the number of categories, which represents the probability distribution of the categories predicted by the model. Finally, the category of the image can be predicted based on this probability distribution.

To understand ResNet more deeply, let's write the network architecture of ResNet34.

```
import torch as t
from torch import nn
from torch.nn import functional as F
# Residual block
class ResidualBlock(nn.Module):
  # Images and feature maps extracted using models in deep learning
often have many
  # channels
  # For example, the channels of an RGB image are 3, namely R channel,
B channel,
  # and G channel
      def  __init__(self,  inchannel,  outchannel,  stride=1,
shortcut=None):
    super(ResidualBlock, self).__init__()
    # Observing Figure 10.6, it's not hard to see that the residual
block can be
    # roughly divided into two parts: left and right
    # The left side consists of a series of network layers, while the
right side
    # is a shortcut connection
    # Define the left side
```

```
      self.left = nn.Sequential(
        # Corresponds to the first weight layer in Figure 10.6
        nn.Conv2d(inchannel, outchannel, 3, stride, 1, bias=False),
        nn.BatchNorm2d(outchannel),
        # Corresponds to the ReLU in Figure 10.6
        nn.ReLU(inplace=True),
        # Corresponds to the second weight layer in Figure 10.6
        nn.Conv2d(outchannel, outchannel, 3, 1, 1, bias=False),
        nn.BatchNorm2d(outchannel))
      # Define the right side
      self.right = shortcut
      # The forward() function plays a crucial role in the network
structure,
    # determining how the network propagates data
    def forward(self, x):
      out = self.left(x)
      # Construct the residual block
      residual = x if self.right is None else self.right(x)
      out += residual
      return F.relu(out)
# In this module, we will implement ResNet34, the corresponding
architecture can be
# seen in Figure 10.7
class ResNet(nn.Module):
  def __init__(self, num_classes=102):
    super(ResNet, self).__init__()
    # Initial layers for image transformation
    self.pre = nn.Sequential(
      nn.Conv2d(3, 64, 7, 2, 3, bias=False),
      nn.BatchNorm2d(64),
      nn.ReLU(inplace=True),
      nn.MaxPool2d(3, 2, 1),
    )
    # The repeating network layers consist of 3, 4, 6, and 3 residual
blocks
    # respectively
    self.layer1 = self._make_layer(64, 128, 3)
    self.layer2 = self._make_layer(128, 256, 4, stride=2)
    self.layer3 = self._make_layer(256, 512, 6, stride=2)
    self.layer4 = self._make_layer(512, 512, 3, stride=2)
     # Fully connected layer for classification, mapping a multi-
channel feature
    # map to a vector with dimensions equal to the number of classes
    self.fc = nn.Linear(512, num_classes)
     def _make_layer(self, inchannel, outchannel, block_num,
stride=1):
    # Define the shortcut connection
    shortcut = nn.Sequential(
     nn.Conv2d(inchannel, outchannel, 1, stride, bias=False),
     nn.BatchNorm2d(outchannel))
    layers = []
    # Add residual blocks to the current network layer
    layers.append(ResidualBlock(inchannel, outchannel,
             stride, shortcut))
```

```
        for I in range(1, block_num):
          layers.append(ResidualBlock(outchannel, outchannel))
        return nn.Sequential(*layers)
      def forward(self, x):
        x = self.pre(x)
        x = self.layer1(x)
        x = self.layer2(x)
        x = self.layer3(x)
        x = self.layer4(x)
        x = F.avg_pool2d(x, 7)
        x = x.view(x.size(0), -1)
        return self.fc(x)
```

The convolution operation is implemented using the nn.Conv2d() function, which is defined as follows.

```
nn.Conv2d(
    in_channels,     # Number of input channels
    out_channels,     # Number of output channels
    kernel_size,     # Size of the convolution kernel
    stride=1,     # Stride of the convolution kernel
    padding=0      # Number of padding layers for the convolution
kernel
    )
```

Next, we will write an image classification task based on ResNet34. First, import the necessary libraries.

```
import torch.optim as optim
import torch
import torch.optim
import torch.utils.data as Data
import torchvision.transforms as transforms
import torchvision.datasets as datasets
import torchvision.models
from torch.utils.data import DataLoader, Dataset
import matplotlib.pyplot as plt
```

Generally speaking, in deep learning, to make the information learned by the deep network more robust, we usually perform "data augmentation" on the images. Simply put, data augmentation refers to a technique that, while keeping the dataset size relatively fixed increases the effective data volume by applying a series of transformations to original data—such as grayscaling, cropping, rotation, mirroring, brightness, hue, and saturation adjustments—thereby enhancing neural network performance. We also augmented the image data in our experiment.

```
# Define the method for image augmentation (transformation) during
training
train_transform = transforms.Compose(
  [transforms.ToPILImage(),
   # transforms.Resize((224, 224)),
   transforms.ToTensor(),
   transforms.Normalize(mean=[0.485, 0.456, 0.406],
```

```
            std=[0.229, 0.224, 0.225])])
```

Wrap the Caltech-101 dataset into a class, and generate training set class, validation set class, and testing set class.

```
# Dataset
class ImageDataset(Dataset):
  def __init__(self, images, labels=None, transforms=None):
    self.X = images
    self.y = labels
    self.transforms = transforms
  def __len__(self):
    return (len(self.X))
 # In the data class built for deep learning training, the __getitem_
_() function
  # is very important
  # __getitem__() determines how data is fed into the model
  # In the following code, you can see that when transforms are not
void,the data
  # will first go through transforms for data augmentation, and then
return for
  # subsequent operations
  def __getitem__(self, i):
    data = self.X[i][:]
    if self.transforms:
      data = self.transforms(data)
    if self.y is not None:
      return (data, self.y[i])
    else:
      return data
# Generate different classes for training, validation, and testing
train_data = ImageDataset(x_train, y_train, train_transform)
val_data = ImageDataset(x_val, y_val, val_transform)
test_data = ImageDataset(x_test, y_test, val_transform)
```

Pass the generated classes into the data loader. When training deep networks, data loaders are typically used to feed data into the network. A data loader is much like an iterator, which returns a batch of images along with their corresponding labels each iteration, with the batch size specified by batch_size. Why not return all images at once? What is batch_size?

batch_size refers to the number of data items passed to the program for training at a time. Generally, due to limitations in GPU resources and memory, it is not feasible to input all image data in the dataset into the model for training at once. Therefore, a parameter batch_size is set to input a portion of the data for training each time. This can reduce memory consumption and increase training speed, as the model becomes more accurate after each training session. For example, if there are 5486 images in the training set and batch_size=100, the model will first call the first 100 images in the training set, i.e., the 1st to 100th data, to train the model. After the training is completed, the 101st to 200th data will be used for training and so on until all data in the training set has been input into the model.

In the experiment, we set the batch_size to 2048. If your computing resources are insufficient, you can reduce it.

```
BATCH_SIZE = 2048
trainloader = DataLoader(train_data, batch_size=BATCH_SIZE,
shuffle= True)
valloader = DataLoader(val_data, batch_size=BATCH_SIZE, shuffle=
True)
testloader = DataLoader(test_data, batch_size=BATCH_SIZE,
shuffle= False)
```

Load the ResNet34 model, which will directly call the prepackaged library.

```
# Choose to use CPU or GPU training based on the current device
device = torch.device('cuda' if torch.cuda.is_available() else
'cpu')
# Load the model pretrained on ImageNet
model = torchvision.models.resnet34(pretrained='imagenet')
num_ftrs = model.fc.in_features
model.fc = nn.Linear(num_ftrs, 102)
model.to(device)
# Parallel training on multiple GPUs
model = nn.DataParallel(model)
```

Note that the parameter pretrained appears in the above code, which is an important operation in neural networks—pretraining. In most cases, the computational power and data available for training models are limited, so we hope to reuse well-trained neural networks as much as possible to save training and data resources. When performing a prediction task, if one can identify a large-scale architecture previously trained on a similar task with high performance, the shallower layers of this architecture may be leveraged to construct your target network. The technique of using a well-trained model to build a new architecture is called pretraining. Specifically, the weights on the well-trained model can be directly borrowed to initialize our model. Here, the ResNet34 is initialized with the network parameters pretrained on the ImageNet dataset.

Define the optimizer and loss function to be used during training.

```
# Define the optimizer
optimizer = optim.Adam(model.parameters(), lr=1e-4)
# Define the loss function
criterion = nn.CrossEntropyLoss()
```

For knowledge about optimizers, you can refer to "Dive into Deep Learning". We use the common cross-entropy loss to calculate the error between the model's predicted labels and the actual labels, which is defined as follows:

$$\ell = -\frac{1}{N} \sum_{n=1}^{N \overset{(n)}{\Sigma}(n)} \log\left(y^{(n)} | I^{(n)}\right)$$

Next, we write functions for training the model, validating the model, and testing the model's top-1 error rate.

```
# Define the training function
```

```
def fit(model, dataloader):
  model.train()
  # Initialize model loss and model top-1 error rate
  running_loss = 0.0
  running_top1_error = 0
  # Start iteration
  for i, data in enumerate(dataloader):
    # Prepare training images and labels, the amount of data fed into
the model
    # in each time is batch_size
    x, y = data[0].to(device), data[1].to(device)
    # The gradient needs to be set to zero before starting backprop-
agation
      # Because PyTorch will accumulate gradients in subsequent
backpropagation
    optimizer.zero_grad()
    # Feed the data into the model to get the output predicted labels
    outputs = model(x)
   # Compare the predicted labels with the actual labels to calculate
the loss
    loss = criterion(outputs, y)
    # Record the current loss
    running_loss += loss.item()
    # Record the current top-1 error rate
    _, preds = torch.max(outputs.data, 1)
    running_top1_error += torch.sum(preds != y)
    # Backpropagation
    loss.backward()
    optimizer.step()
  loss = running_loss / len(dataloader.dataset)
  top1_error = running_top1_error / len(dataloader.dataset)
    print(f"Train Loss: {loss:.4f}, Train Top-1 Error: {top1_
error:.4f}")
  return loss, top1_error
# Define the validation function, which can adjust the model param-
eters through the
# validation set
def validate(model, dataloader):
  model.eval()
  # Initialize model loss and model top-1 error rate
  running_loss = 0.0
  running_top1_error = 0
  with torch.no_grad():
    for i, data in enumerate(dataloader):
      # The process is the same as training
      x, y = data[0].to(device), data[1].to(device)
      outputs = model(x)
      loss = criterion(outputs, y)
      running_loss += loss.item()
      _, preds = torch.max(outputs.data, 1)
      correct += torch.sum(preds == y)
    loss = running_loss / len(dataloader.dataset)
    top1_error = running_top1_error / len(dataloader.dataset)
```

```
        print(f'Val Loss: {loss:.4f}, Val Top-1 Error: {top1_
error:.4f}')
    return loss, top1_error
# Define the test function to evaluate the model's performance
def test(model, dataloader):
   top1_error = 0
   total = 0
   with torch.no_grad():
     for data in dataloader:
       x, y = data[0].to(device), data[1].to(device)
       outputs = model(x)
       _, predicted = torch.max(outputs.data, 1)
       total += y.size(0)
       top1_error += torch.sum(predicted == y)
   return top1_error, total
```

Start training the model.

```
# Start training the model
# Set the number of iterations
epochs = 25
# Set the training and validation loss and top-1 error rate
train_loss , train_top1_error = [], []
val_loss , val_top1_error = [], []
print(f"Training on {len(train_data)} examples, \
    validating on {len(val_data)} examples...")
# Start iteration
for epoch in range(epochs):
   # Output iteration information
   print(f"\nEpoch {epoch+1} of {epochs}")
    train_epoch_loss, train_epoch_top1_error = fit(model, train-
loader)
         val_epoch_loss, val_epoch_top1_error = validate(model,
valloader)
   train_loss.append(train_epoch_loss)
   train_top1_error.append(train_epoch_top1_error.cpu())
   val_loss.append(val_epoch_loss)
   val_top1_error.append(val_epoch_top1_error.cpu())
# You can save the trained model
# torch.save(model.state_dict(), model.pth")
Training on 5486 examples, validating on 1829 examples...
Epoch 1 of 25
Train Loss: 0.0024, Train Top-1 Error: 0.9160 Val Loss: 0.0019, Val
Top-1 Error: 0.6900
Epoch 2 of 25
Train Loss: 0.0017, Train Top-1 Error: 0.6172 Val Loss: 0.0015, Val
Top-1 Error: 0.5648
Epoch 3 of 25
Train Loss: 0.0014, Train Top-1 Error: 0.4686 Val Loss: 0.0013, Val
Top-1 Error: 0.4855
Epoch 4 of 25
Train Loss: 0.0012, Train Top-1 Error: 0.2531 Val Loss: 0.0011, Val
Top-1 Error: 0.4106
Epoch 5 of 25
```

```
Train Loss: 0.0009, Train Top-1 Error: 0.2789 Val Loss: 0.0010, Val
Top-1 Error: 0.3302
Epoch 6 of 25
Train Loss: 0.0008, Train Top-1 Error: 0.2087 Val Loss: 0.0008, Val
Top-1 Error: 0.2477
Epoch 7 of 25
Train Loss: 0.0006, Train Top-1 Error: 0.1518 Val Loss: 0.0007, Val
Top-1 Error: 0.2078
Epoch 8 of 25
Train Loss: 0.0005, Train Top-1 Error: 0.1059 Val Loss: 0.0006, Val
Top-1 Error: 0.1613
Epoch 9 of 25
Train Loss: 0.0004, Train Top-1 Error: 0.0694 Val Loss: 0.0005, Val
Top-1 Error: 0.1263
Epoch 10 of 25
Train Loss: 0.0003, Train Top-1 Error: 0.0436 Val Loss: 0.0004, Val
Top-1 Error: 0.1039
Epoch 11 of 25
Train Loss: 0.0002, Train Top-1 Error: 0.0250 Val Loss: 0.0004, Val
Top-1 Error: 0.0897
Epoch 12 of 25
Train Loss: 0.0002, Train Top-1 Error: 0.0131 Val Loss: 0.0003, Val
Top-1 Error: 0.0798
Epoch 13 of 25
Train Loss: 0.0001, Train Top-1 Error: 0.0067 Val Loss: 0.0003, Val
Top-1 Error: 0.0672
Epoch 14 of 25
Train Loss: 0.0001, Train Top-1 Error: 0.0042 Val Loss: 0.0003, Val
Top-1 Error: 0.0689
Epoch 15 of 25
Train Loss: 0.0001, Train Top-1 Error: 0.0027 Val Loss: 0.0002, Val
Top-1 Error: 0.0645
Epoch 16 of 25
Train Loss: 0.0001, Train Top-1 Error: 0.0015 Val Loss: 0.0002, Val
Top-1 Error: 0.0640
Epoch 17 of 25
Train Loss: 0.0000, Train Top-1 Error: 0.0011 Val Loss: 0.0002, Val
Top-1 Error: 0.0640
Epoch 18 of 25
Train Loss: 0.0000, Train Top-1 Error: 0.0013 Val Loss: 0.0002, Val
Top-1 Error: 0.0623
Epoch 19 of 25
Train Loss: 0.0000, Train Top-1 Error: 0.0007 Val Loss: 0.0002, Val
Top-1 Error: 0.0601
Epoch 20 of 25
Train Loss: 0.0000, Train Top-1 Error: 0.0004 Val Loss: 0.0002, Val
Top-1 Error: 0.0590
Epoch 21 of 25
Train Loss: 0.0000, Train Top-1 Error: 0.0004 Val Loss: 0.0002, Val
Top-1 Error: 0.0596
Epoch 22 of 25
Train Loss: 0.0000, Train Top-1 Error: 0.0002 Val Loss: 0.0002, Val
Top-1 Error: 0.0585
Epoch 23 of 25
```

```
Train Loss: 0.0000, Train Top-1 Error: 0.0002 Val Loss: 0.0002, Val
Top-1 Error: 0.0574
Epoch 24 of 25
Train Loss: 0.0000, Train Top-1 Error: 0.0002 Val Loss: 0.0002, Val
Top-1 Error: 0.0580
Epoch 25 of 25
Train Loss: 0.0000, Train Top-1 Error: 0.0000 Val Loss: 0.0002, Val
Top-1 Error: 0.0580
```

Plot and observe the top-1 error rate curve and the loss curve.

```
# Plot the top-1 error rate curve
plt.figure(figsize=(10, 7))
# Top-1 error rate curve for the training set
plt.plot(train_top1_error, label='train top-1 error')
# Top-1 error rate curve for the validation set
plt.plot(val_top1_error, label='validation top-1 error')
plt.xlabel('Epoch')
plt.ylabel('top-1 Error')
plt.legend()
# Plot the loss function curve
plt.figure(figsize=(10, 7))
plt.plot(train_loss, label='train loss')
plt.plot(val_loss, label='validation loss')
plt.xlabel('Epoch')
plt.ylabel('Loss')
plt.legend()
<matplotlib.legend.Legend at 0x7ff9ae7ba350>
```

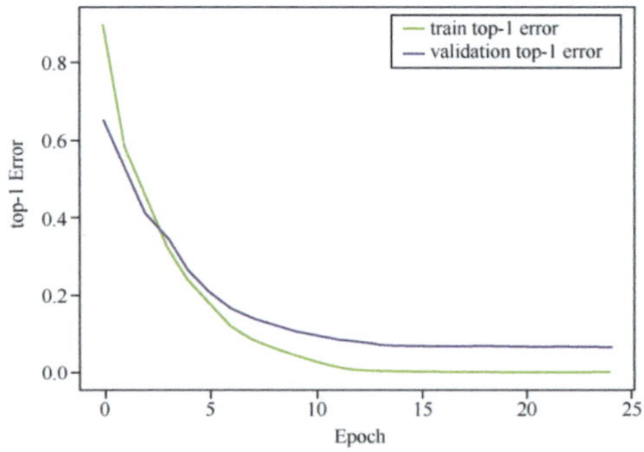

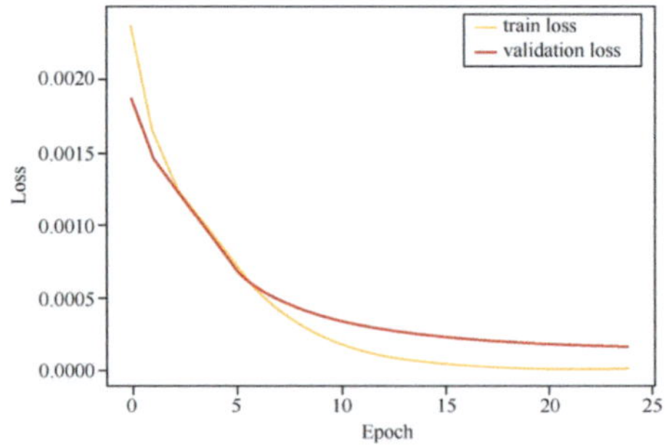

Finally, evaluate the top-1 error rate of the model.

```
top1_error, total = test(model, testloader)
print('Top-1 Error of the network on testing images: %0.3f %%' \
    % (100 * top1_error / total))
Top-1 Error of the network on testing images: 6.889 %
```

10.5 Summary

This chapter introduced one of the most fundamental problems in visual recognition—image classification. We discussed image classification algorithms based on manually designed image representations (visual bag-of-words model) and those based on deep convolutional neural networks. In subsequent chapters, we will discuss how to extend image classification algorithms based on deep convolutional neural networks to other visual recognition problems.

Exercises

(1) In the visual bag-of-words model, the size of the visual dictionary, i.e., the number of visual words, is determined by the hyperparameter k. What is the impact on the image representation capability of the visual bag-of-words model if k is set too small or too large?
(2) In the visual bag-of-words model introduced in this chapter, the encoding of each image feature uses nearest neighbor encoding, i.e., this feature is assigned to the most similar visual word in the visual dictionary. Other encoding strategies can also be used, such as assigning this feature to the n most similar visual words in the visual dictionary, with the assignment weights determined by their similarities. Try to implement a visual bag-of-words model based on the nearest neighbor encoding strategy.
(3) In the image classification algorithm based on deep convolutional neural networks, we have done a lot of data augmentation. Try to verify the impact of data augmentation on the classification results through experiments.
(4) In the image classification algorithm based on deep convolutional neural networks, we pretrained the network model. Try to verify the impact of pretraining on the classification results through experiments.

References

1. LAZEBNIK S, SCHMID C, PONCE J. Beyond bags of features: Spatial pyramid matching for recognizing natural scene categories[C]//IEEE Conference on Computer Vision and Pattern Recognition, 2006, 2:2169–2178.

2. SIVIC, ZISSERMAN. Video Google: A text retrieval approach to object matching in videos[C]// IEEE International Conference on Computer Vision, 2003, 2:1470–1477.
3. O'HARA S, DRAPER B A. Introduction to the bag of features paradigm for image classification and retrieval[EB/OL]. (2011-01-17)[2023-09-24].
4. TSAI C F. Bag-of-words representation in image annotation: A review[J/OL]. International Scholarly Research Notices, 2012(1), [2012-11-29].
5. LECUN Y, BOSER B, DENKER J S, et al. Backpropagation applied to handwritten zip code recognition[J]. Neural Computation, 1989, 1(4):541–551.
6. LECUN Y, BOTTOU L, BENGIO Y, et al. Gradient-based learning applied to document recognition[J]. Proceedings of the IEEE, 1998, 86(11):2278–2324.
7. KRIZHEVSKY A, SUTSKEVER I, HINTON G E. Imagenet classification with deep convolutional neural networks[J]. Advances in Neural Information Processing Systems, 2012, 25:1097–1105.
8. HE K, ZHANG X, REN S, et al. Deep residual learning for image recognition[C]//IEEE Conference on Computer Vision and Pattern Recognition, 2016:770–778.
9. LECUN Y. The MNIST database of handwritten digits[OL]. (1998)[2023-11-21].
10. LI F, FERGUS R, PERONA P. Learning generative visual models from few training examples: An incremental bayesian approach tested on 101 object categories[C]//IEEE Conference on Computer Vision and Pattern Recognition Workshop, 2004:178.
11. KRIZHEVSKY A, HINTON G. Learning multiple layers of features from tiny images[R]. Toronto: University of Toronto, 2009.
12. DENG J, DONG W, SOCHER R, et al. Imagenet: A large-scale hierarchical image database[C]//IEEE Conference on Computer Vision and Pattern Recognition, 2009:248–255.
13. WAN C, SHEN X, ZHANG Y, et al. Meta Convolutional Neural Networks for Single Domain Generalization[C]//IEEE/CVF Conference on Computer Vision and Pattern Recognition, 2022:4682–4691.

Chapter 11
Semantic Segmentation

11.1 Introduction

Semantic segmentation is a fundamental problem in the field of computer vision and a challenging visual recognition task. Simply put, the goal of semantic segmentation is to predict a label for each pixel in an image, which can be considered as a pixel-level "image classification", as shown in Fig. 11.1. It should be noted that, unlike the unsupervised image segmentation introduced in Chap. 9, the segmentation obtained by semantic segmentation is semantic, with each segmentation corresponding to a category in the given annotation set. As shown in Fig. 11.2, the pink and magenta segmentations correspond to the categories "person" and "horse", respectively. To describe the problem of semantic segmentation mathematically, we define the image space $\mathbb{I}$ and the predefined category set $\mathcal{C}$, given the dataset $\mathcal{D} = \{(\boldsymbol{I}^{(n)}, \boldsymbol{Y}^{(n)})\}_{n=1}^{N}$, where $\boldsymbol{I}^{(n)} \in \mathbb{I}$ is the nth image in the dataset, $\boldsymbol{Y}^{(n)}$ is the label map corresponding to this image, and the ith element $y_i^{(n)} \in \mathcal{C}$ in the label map is the label of the ith pixel in the nth image; the task of semantic segmentation is to learn a mapping from the image space to the label map space $f : \mathbb{I} \to \mathcal{Y}$ from $\mathcal{D}$, where $\forall n,\ \boldsymbol{Y}^{(n)} \in \mathcal{Y}$, so that given any test image $\boldsymbol{I}$, the learned mapping function f can be used to predict its label, i.e., $\hat{\boldsymbol{Y}} = f(\boldsymbol{I})$. Similar to image classification, this learning process needs to model the conditional probability $P(\boldsymbol{Y}|\boldsymbol{I})$, then $\hat{\boldsymbol{Y}} = f(\boldsymbol{I}) = \arg\max_{\boldsymbol{Y} \in \mathcal{Y}} P(\boldsymbol{Y}|\boldsymbol{I})$. Semantic segmentation can provide pixel-level category information, and thus it has many applications in real scenarios, such as autonomous driving, defect detection, and medical imaging auxiliary diagnosis.

In this chapter, we will implement semantic segmentation based on deep learning image classification.

W. Shen et al., *Hands-On Computer Vision*,
https://doi.org/10.1007/978-981-95-4835-4_11

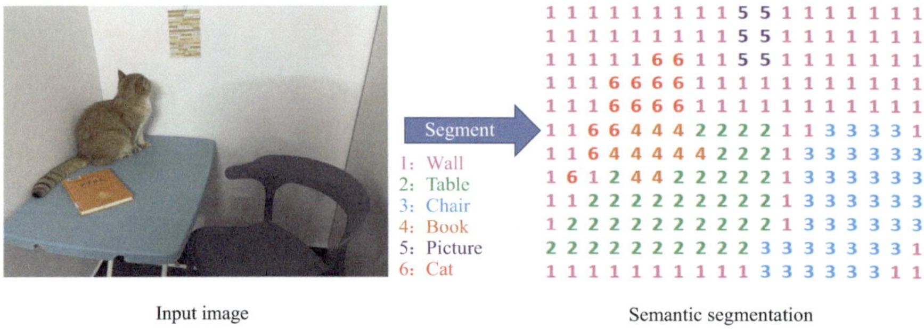

Fig. 11.1 Semantic segmentation is a kind of pixel-level image classification

Fig. 11.2 Example of semantic segmentation (image material from PASCAL VOC 2012 dataset)

11.2 Dataset and Metrics

The standard datasets used for semantic segmentation evaluation mainly include the following three.

(1) PASCAL VOC [1]: The PASCAL VOC dataset is used by the official PASCAL VOC challenge. This dataset contains about 10,000 images of 20 classes, each with complete labels.
(2) Cityscapes [2]: The Cityscapes dataset is collected from 50 cities in Germany and its neighboring countries, including street scenes from spring, summer, and autumn. The dataset is divided into two volumes, one of which contains 5000 images with high-quality pixel-level labels, covering 19 categories.

(3) ADE20K [3]: The ADE20K dataset is a scene understanding dataset released by MIT, containing over 20,000 fully annotated images, covering more than 3000 categories.

In semantic segmentation, the mean intersection over union (mIoU) is usually used as the evaluation metric. Let c represent the true category and l represent the predicted category ($c, l \in \mathcal{C}$), then mIoU is defined as follows:

$$\text{mIoU} = \frac{1}{|\mathcal{C}|} \sum\nolimits_{c \in \mathcal{C}} \frac{n_{cc}}{\sum\nolimits_{l \in \mathcal{C}} n_{cl} + \sum\nolimits_{l \in \mathcal{C}} n_{lc} - n_{cc}},$$

where $|\mathcal{C}|$ represents the number of elements in the set; n_{cl} denotes the number of pixels of class c predicted to belong to class l; n_{lc} denotes the number of pixels of class l predicted to belong to class c; n_{cc} denotes the number of pixels of class c correctly predicted to belong to class c.

11.3 Fully Convolutional Networks

We know that semantic segmentation is essentially pixel-by-pixel classification. Therefore, an intuitive method of semantic segmentation is to train a CNN model that can classify each pixel. As shown in Fig. 11.3, a fixed-size image patch centered at each pixel of the image is extracted, and its class label is assigned based on the corresponding pixel's label in the label map, thus constructing a training dataset for the CNN model. Then, the trained CNN model is used to classify these image patches. After predicting the class of each pixel in the image, we obtain the semantic segmentation result of the entire image, as shown in the far right of Fig. 11.3.

Although the above method is intuitive, it has many problems in practice.

(1) Since there may be thousands or even tens of thousands of pixels in an image, and the image patches of adjacent pixels overlap significantly, this method is computationally intensive and inefficient.
(2) Compared to the entire image, the image patches are relatively small and only local features of the image can be extracted from them, which limits the performance of the classification.
(3) The whole process is not end-to-end. It requires preprocessing and post-processing stages.

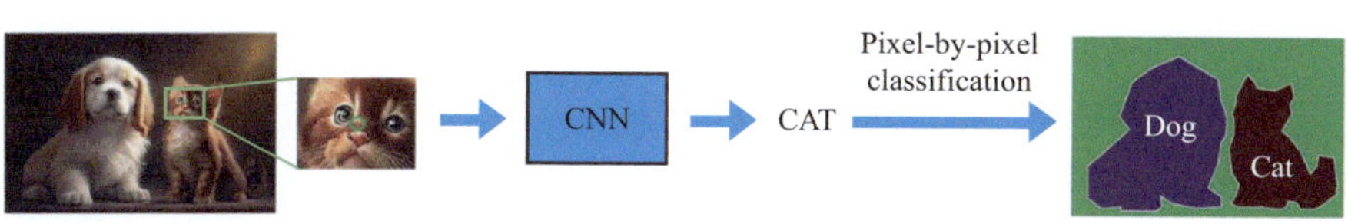

Fig. 11.3 Intuitive semantic segmentation model

To address these issues, Jonathan Long et al. proposed a new segmentation network in 2015—the Fully Convolutional Network (FCN) [4]. Unlike traditional CNN networks (such as AlexNet), in FCN, the fully connected layer of the network output is replaced with a convolutional layer with a kernel size of 1×1, as shown in Fig. 11.4. According to Chap. 10, for image classification, a fully connected layer can be used to map the multi-channel image feature map output by the convolutional layer to a vector with a dimension of $|\mathcal{C}|$, where each element's value represents the confidence of belonging to the corresponding category, thus achieving image classification. However, in semantic segmentation, it is necessary to classify each pixel of an image, and thus the fully connected layer is not applicable. To achieve end-to-end prediction, a 1×1 convolutional layer is used to replace the fully connected layer, mapping the multi-channel feature map output by the convolutional layer to a class confidence map with the same spatial resolution and a channel number of $|\mathcal{C}|$. In this way, each spatial position on the feature map output by the convolutional layer corresponds to a vector with a dimension of $|\mathcal{C}|$, indicating the confidence of the original image area corresponding to this position belonging to each category in $\mathcal{C}$, thus achieving image semantic segmentation. We call the class confidence map a heatmap, in which, the higher the confidence of belonging to a certain class, the higher the heat. By adjusting the spatial resolution of the heatmap to match the original image, we can obtain the desired semantic segmentation result.

However, two obvious problems can still be found in Fig. 11.4: As the convolution progresses, the feature map becomes smaller and smaller, and the final output heatmap is much smaller than the original image; since the final output heatmap is small, the boundary information it contains becomes very rough and cannot accurately outline the contours of the objects in the original image. To solve these two

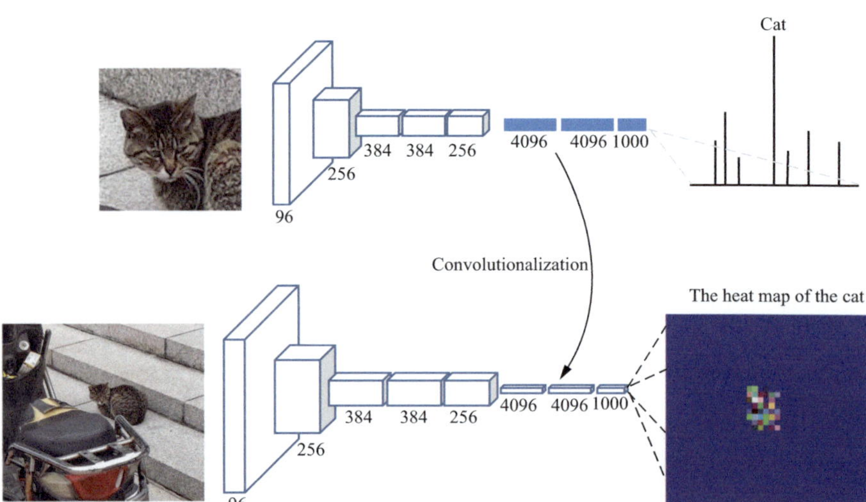

Fig. 11.4 Replace all fully connected layers with 1×1 convolutional layers

problems, the FCN network introduces two effective architectures: upsampling and skip connection.

11.3.1 Upsampling

To solve the problem of the output heatmap having a lower resolution than the original image, FCN upsamples the feature map to maintain the same spatial resolution as the original image. Upsampling can generally be achieved through bilinear interpolation. As shown in Fig. 11.5, let g be a two-dimensional signal. If we know the values of g at points Q_{11} (with coordinates (x_1, y_1)), Q_{12} (with coordinates (x_1, y_2)), Q_{21} (with coordinates (x_2, y_1)), and Q_{22} (with coordinates (x_2, y_2)), we want to find the value of g at point P(with coordinates (x, y)). The process of finding this value is actually the process of bilinear interpolation. First, perform interpolation along the x direction:

$$
\begin{aligned}
g(x, y_1) &\approx \frac{x - x_1}{x_2 - x_1}\left[g(Q_{21}) - g(Q_{11})\right] + g(Q_{11}) \\
&= \frac{x_2 - x}{x_2 - x_1} g(Q_{11}) + \frac{x - x_1}{x_2 - x_1} g(Q_{21}),
\end{aligned}
$$

$$
\begin{aligned}
g(x, y_2) &\approx \frac{x - x_1}{x_2 - x_1}\left[g(Q_{22}) - g(Q_{12})\right] + g(Q_{12}) \\
&= \frac{x_2 - x}{x_2 - x_1} g(Q_{12}) + \frac{x - x_1}{x_2 - x_1} g(Q_{22}).
\end{aligned}
$$

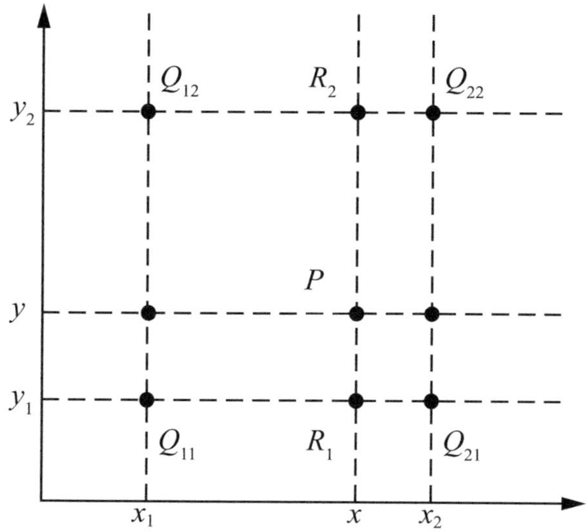

Fig. 11.5 Example of bilinear interpolation

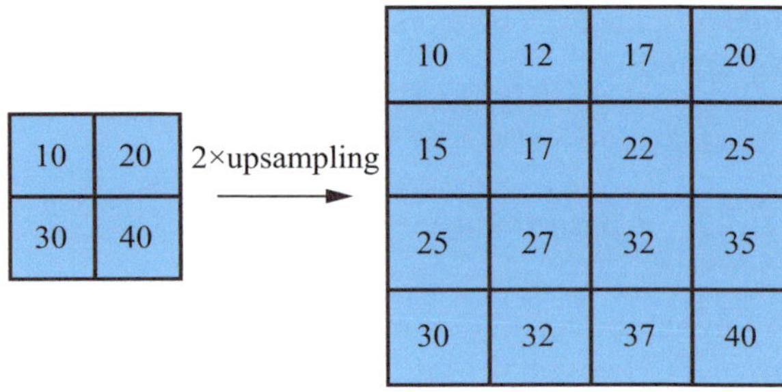

Fig. 11.6 Upsampling an image

Then perform interpolation along the y direction:

$$g(x, y) \approx g(x, y_1) + \frac{y - y_1}{y_2 - y_1}\left[g(x, y_2) - g(x, y_1)\right]$$

$$= \frac{y_2 - y}{y_2 - y_1} g(x, y_1) + \frac{y - y_1}{y_2 - y_1} g(x, y_2)$$

$$= \frac{1}{(x_2 - x_1)(y_2 - y_1)} \begin{bmatrix} x_2 - x & x - x_1 \end{bmatrix} \begin{bmatrix} g(Q_{11}) & g(Q_{12}) \\ g(Q_{21}) & g(Q_{22}) \end{bmatrix} \begin{bmatrix} y_2 - y \\ y - y_1 \end{bmatrix}.$$

In this way, we can find the value at point P. It can be seen that bilinear interpolation is actually interpolation in two directions, and the "interpolation" process in each direction is similar to the process of calculating the function value of a linear function at a certain point. Once we have studied bilinear interpolation, we can upsample an image with a resolution of 2 pixels × 2 pixels to a resolution of 4 pixels × 4 pixels, as shown in Fig. 11.6.

Observing the above mathematical form, we can see that bilinear interpolation can be implemented through convolution. Therefore, the upsampling of feature maps in deep networks can be implemented using convolutional layers, except that the convolution kernel of this layer is fixed. So, can we use a learnable convolution kernel to implement feature map upsampling? Of course, we can. This learnable convolution is called transposed convolution or deconvolution, which is a convolution with a stride less than 1. In fact, when the stride of the convolution is $s < 1$, convolving the image is equivalent to inserting $\frac{1}{s} - 1$ zeros between adjacent pixels of the image and then performing a convolution with a stride of 1. As shown in Fig. 11.7, upsampling of the input image is achieved by performing a convolution with a stride of 0.5: First, a pixel with a value of zero is inserted between every two adjacent pixels of the image, and zero padding is applied to the boundary with 2 pixels × 2 pixels; then, a convolution with a stride of 1 and a convolution kernel of 3 × 3 is performed. Finally, the image is upsampled from 2 pixels × 2 pixels to 5 pixels × 5 pixels. In actual operation, upsampling is performed on each channel of the feature map in turn to obtain the final result.

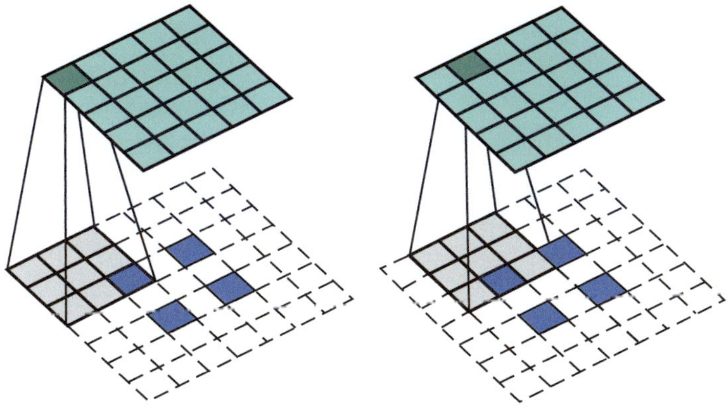

Fig. 11.7 Upsampling implemented through transposed convolution (illustration material sourced from Ref. [5])

In the code, the following function is called to implement transposed convolution.

```
import torch
torch.nn.ConvTranspose2d(
  in_channels=3, # Number of input data channels
  out_channels=3, # Number of output data channels
  kernel_size=3, # Size of the convolution kernel
  stride=2, # Convolution stride
  padding=0, # Pixels to be padded around the original image
  output_padding=0, # Pixels to be padded around the border of the
output
          # feature map, generally not set
  groups=1,     # Number of groups for group convolution, generally
set to 1
          # by default
  bias= True    # Convolution bias, generally set to False, setting
to True
          # can enhance the model's generalization ability
)
ConvTranspose2d(3, 3, kernel_size=(3, 3), stride=(2, 2))
```

Since it is a transposed convolution, the actual stride is 1/stride. Also, in actual operation, the parameters of the convolution kernel can be obtained through learning, or they can be fixed using bilinear interpolation. The code for fixing the convolution kernel weights using bilinear interpolation is as follows:

```
# Setting convolution kernel weights using bilinear interpolation
def bilinear_kernel(in_channels, out_channels, kernel_size):
  # Find the center position of the convolution kernel
  factor = (kernel_size + 1) // 2
  if kernel_size % 2 == 1:
    center = factor - 1
  else:
    center = factor - 0.5
```

```
    # np.ogrid() function to construct a two-dimensional matrix
    og = np.ogrid[:kernel_size, :kernel_size]
    print('og', og)
    # Construct convolution kernel weights
   filt = (1 - abs(og[0] - center) / factor) * (1 - abs(og[1] - center) /
factor)
    print('filt:\n', filt)
    weight = np.zeros((in_channels, out_channels,
            kernel_size, kernel_size), dtype='float32')
    weight[range(in_channels), range(out_channels),:,:] = filt
     return torch.from_numpy(weight)
```

Let's further explain some of the variables in the above code with a simple example.

```
import numpy as np
bilinear_kernel(1, 1, 3)
og [array([[0],
   [1],
   [2]]), array([[0, 1, 2]])]
filt [[0.25 0.5 0.25]
 [0.5 1. 0.5 ]
 [0.25 0.5 0.25]]
tensor([[[[0.2500, 0.5000, 0.2500],
[0.5000, 1.0000, 0.5000],
[0.2500, 0.5000, 0.2500]]]])
```

11.3.2 Skip Connections

For traditional classification networks, the spatial resolution of the feature map output by the last layer of the backbone network is too low (as shown in Fig. 11.4). After upsampling, the predicted label map is coarse and cannot accurately outline the object in the original image. Generally, the feature maps of shallow convolutional layers are larger and can accurately locate the boundaries of objects, but they lack semantic richness; the feature maps of deep convolutional layers are smaller, but they are semantically strong. Is there a way to obtain a larger feature map while also enriching it with semantic information? FCN solves this problem by fusing features from different levels of convolutional layers through skip connections. As shown in Fig. 11.8, we can connect feature maps from different levels. The connected feature map contains both local and global information, as well as shallow and deep information. Through skip connections, we can construct a feature map that is both semantically rich and contains precise object location information, thereby achieving precise semantic segmentation.

Specifically, as shown in Fig. 11.9, from the backbone network of FCN, we can obtain five feature maps with spatial resolutions of 1/2, 1/4, 1/8, 1/16, and 1/32 of the original image, respectively. There are various ways to connect feature maps.

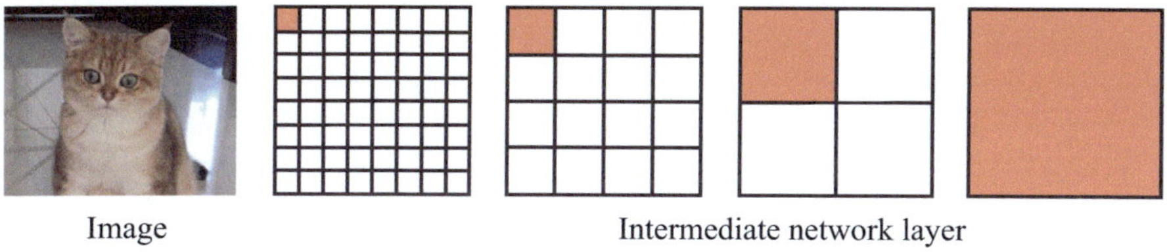

Fig. 11.8 Fusion of features from intermediate convolutional layers. These features contain both local and global information, as well as shallow and deep information

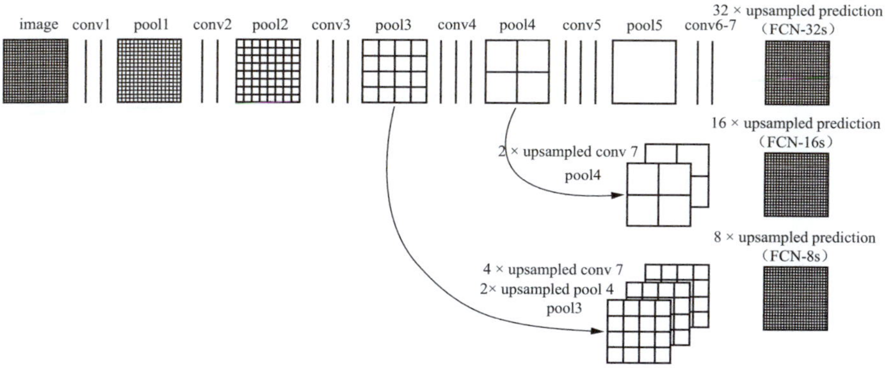

Fig. 11.9 Skip connections in FCN (illustration source: Ref. [4])

Depending on the level of the connected feature map, FCN has different variants, including FCN-8s, FCN-16s, and FCN-32s. Feature maps of different levels not only have different spatial resolutions, but also different numbers of channels. Therefore, when connecting them, we need to first adjust their channel numbers to be consistent. How can we change the number of channels of the feature map without changing its spatial resolution? Yes, the 1×1 convolution we just introduced can achieve this function. We use 1×1 convolution to adjust the channel numbers of feature maps at different levels to $|\mathcal{C}|$. For the feature map output by the fifth pooling layer (pool5) of the backbone network, after adjusting the channel number through 1×1 convolution, we directly upsample it by 32 times to obtain a feature map with the same spatial resolution as the original image. This model is called FCN-32s. We can also upsample the feature map output by pool5 by 2 times, add it element-wise to the feature map output by the fourth pooling layer (pool4) of the backbone network, and then upsample the resulting feature map by 16 times to obtain a feature map with the same spatial resolution as the original image. This model is called FCN-16s. Similarly, we can first upsample the aforementioned added feature map by 2 times, add it element-wise to the feature map output by the third pooling layer (pool3) of the backbone network to obtain a new feature map, and then upsample this feature map by 8 times to obtain a feature map with the same spatial resolution as the original image. This model is called FCN-8s.

To better illustrate this process, let's look at the code implementation of FCN-8s. Here, we choose ResNet101 as the backbone network of the model.

```
from torchvision import models
# Use ResNet101 as the backbone network, which was pretrained on
ImageNet
pretrained_net = models.resnet101(pretrained='imagenet')
import torch.nn as nn
# FCN-8s Model
class FCN8s(nn.Module):
    def __init__(self, num_classes):
    super(FCN8s, self).__init__()
    # Here we use children() to call part of the ResNet101 network
    # The spatial resolution of this deep feature map is 1/8 of the
input image
                self.stage1   =   nn.Sequential(*list(pretrained_
net.children())[:-4])
    # The spatial resolution of this deep feature map is 1/16 of the
input image
    self.stage2 = list(pretrained_net.children())[-4]
    # The spatial resolution of this deep feature map is 1/32 of the
input image
    self.stage3 = list(pretrained_net.children())[-3]
    # Adjust the number of channels output by stage3
    self.scores1 = nn.Conv2d(2048, num_classes, 1)
    # Adjust the number of channels output by stage2
    self.scores2 = nn.Conv2d(1024, num_classes, 1)
    # Adjust the number of channels output by stage1
    self.scores3 = nn.Conv2d(512, num_classes, 1)
    # Upsample by a factor of 8
    self.upsample_8x = nn.ConvTranspose2d(
      num_classes, num_classes, 16, 8, 4, bias= False )
    self.upsample_8x.weight.data = bilinear_kernel(
      num_classes, num_classes, 16) # Use bilinear kernel
    # Upsample by a factor of 2
    self.upsample_2x = nn.ConvTranspose2d(
      num_classes, num_classes, 4, 2, 1, bias= False )
    self.upsample_2x.weight.data = bilinear_kernel(
      num_classes, num_classes, 4) # Use bilinear kernel
    def forward(self, x):
    x = self.stage1(x)
    # s1 1/8
    s1 = x
    x = self.stage2(x)
    # s2 1/16
    s2 = x
    x = self.stage3(x)
    # s3 1/32
    s3 = x
    # Adjust the number of channels in the pool5 output feature map
    s3 = self.scores1(s3)
    # Perform 2x upsampling
    s3 = self.upsample_2x(s3)
    # Adjust the number of channels in the pool4 output feature map
```

```
        s2 = self.scores2(s2)
        # Fuse the feature maps of pool5 and pool4
        s2 = s2 + s3
        # Adjust the number of channels in the pool3 output feature map
        s1 = self.scores3(s1)
        # Upsample s2 by a factor of 2
        s2 = self.upsample_2x(s2)
        # Fuse the feature maps
        s = s1 + s2
        # Upsample by a factor of 8 to obtain a feature map of the same
    size as the
        # original image
        s = self.upsample_8x(s2)
        return s
```

The above code can deepen our understanding of FCN. The feature map obtained by upsampling has the same spatial resolution as the original image. Based on this feature map, we can perform pixel-wise class prediction and thus calculate the cross-entropy loss function between the predicted labels and the true labels for each pixel to train the FCN:

$$\ell(\mathcal{D}) = -\frac{1}{N}\sum_{n=1}^{N}\sum_{i}^{\Sigma}\log\left(p\left(y_i^{(n)}|i^{(n)}\right)\right),$$

where $P\left(y_i^{(n)}|\boldsymbol{I}^{(n)}\right)$ denotes the probability that the label corresponding to the ith pixel of the nth image in training dataset $\mathcal{D}$ is predicted as $y_i^{(n)} \in \mathcal{C}$ by FCN.

Now let's summarize the process of semantic segmentation using FCN: First, the backbone network is used to extract features from the image, and the different levels of the backbone network can output feature maps with different spatial resolutions; then, 1×1 convolutional layers are used to adjust the number of channels of the feature maps at different levels to $|\mathcal{C}|$; then, skip connections are used to merge the feature maps at different levels, and upsampling is used to increase the spatial resolution of the feature maps to match the original image; finally, pixel-wise category prediction is performed based on the upsampled feature maps. The overall framework of the FCN semantic segmentation process is shown in Fig. 11.10.

11.4 FCN Code Implementation

Next, we will implement the code of FCN. Let's first import the necessary libraries.

```
import os
import random
import cv2
import d2l.torch as d2l
from PIL import Image
import matplotlib.pyplot as plt
import torch.nn.functional as F
```

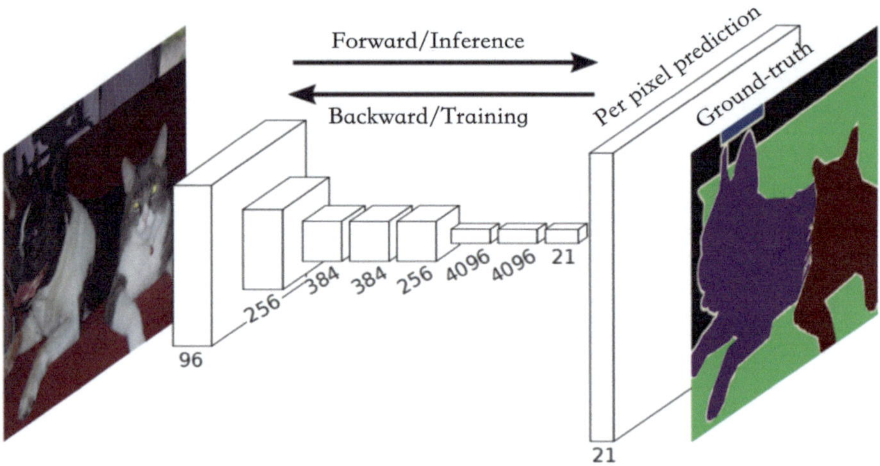

Fig. 11.10 Overall framework of FCN for semantic segmentation (illustration source: Ref. [4])

```
from torch.utils.data import DataLoader
from torch.utils.data import Dataset
from torch.autograd import Variable
from torchvision.transforms import transforms as tfs
```

We will use PASCAL VOC as the dataset for our experiment.

```
# Dataset location
# You can download the dataset yourself
voc_root = './voc/VOCdevkit/VOC2012'
# Define PASCAL VOC class
class VOCSegDataset(Dataset):
   def __init__(self, train, crop_size, transforms):
   # Define data size
   self.crop_size = crop_size
   # Define data augmentation type
   self.transforms = transforms
   # Read data and corresponding labels
   data_list, label_list = read_images(voc_root, train=train)
   self.data_list = self._filter(data_list)
   self.label_list = self._filter(label_list)
   print('Read'+str(len(self.data_list))+'images')
   def _filter(self, images):
     return [im for im in images if
      (Image.open(im).size[1] >= self.crop_size[0] and
      Image.open(im).size[0] >= self.crop_size[1])]
  # Define how data is transmitted
   def __getitem__(self,idx):
   img = self.data_list[idx]
   label = self.label_list[idx]
   # Read image
   img = cv2.imread(img)
   # Convert image channels from BGR to RGB
```

```
        img = cv2.cvtColor(img, cv2.COLOR_BGR2RGB)
        label = cv2.imread(label)
        # Since the labels correspond one-to-one with the pixels, they
also need to
        # be converted
        label = cv2.cvtColor(label, cv2.COLOR_BGR2RGB)
        # Perform data augmentation
        img, label = self.transforms(img, label, self.crop_size)
        return img, label
    def __len__(self):
        return len(self.data list)
```

Implement some of the functions that appear in the above class.

```
# Implement the methods of the above dataset class
# Read the dataset
def read_images(root, train=True):
    txt_filename = root + "/ImageSets/Segmentation/" \
        + ('train.txt' if train else 'val.txt')
    with open(txt_filename, 'r') as f:
        images = f.read().split()
    data = [os.path.join(root, 'JPEGImages', i + '.jpg')
                                for i in images]
    label = [os.path.join(root, 'SegmentationClass', i+'.png')
                                for i in images]
    return data, label
# Perform random cropping
def rand_crop(data, label, height,width):
    h, w, _ = data.shape
    top = random.randint(0, h - height)
    left = random.randint(0, w - width)
    # Crop the data
    data = data[top:top + height, left:left + width]
    # Crop the labels
    label = label[top:top + height, left:left + width]
    return data, label
# Establish corresponding labels for pixels during image enhance-
ment
def image2label(im):
    data = np.array(im, dtype='int32')
    idx = (data[:,:,0] * 256 + data[:,:,1]) * 256 + data[:,:,2]
    return np.array(cm2lbl[idx], dtype='int64')
# Define data augmentation methods
def img_transforms(im, label, crop_size):
    im,label = rand_crop(im, label, *crop_size)
    im_tfs = tfs.Compose([
        tfs.ToTensor(),
        tfs.Normalize([0.485, 0.456, 0.406], [0.229, 0.224, 0.225])
    ])
    im = im_tfs(im)
    label = image2label(label)
    label = torch.from_numpy(label)
    return im, label
# Remove the output in the bilinear interpolation function
```

```
def bilinear_kernel(in_channels, out_channels, kernel_size):
  factor = (kernel_size + 1) // 2
   if kernel_size % 2 == 1:
    center = factor - 1
   else:
    center = factor - 0.5
  og = np.ogrid[:kernel_size, :kernel_size]
  filt = (1 - abs(og[0] - center) / factor) * \
    (1 - abs(og[1] - center) / factor)
  weight = np.zeros((in_channels, out_channels,
         kernel_size, kernel_size), dtype='float32')
  weight[range(in_channels), range(out_channels),:,:] = filt
   return torch.from_numpy(weight)
```

Define some global variables that will be used (such as class information), and start loading the dataset to build the data loader.

```
# Categories in PASCAL VOC
classes = ['background','aeroplane','bicycle','bird','boat',
    'bottle','bus','car','cat','chair','cow','diningtable',
    'dog','horse','motorbike','person','potted plant',
    'sheep','sofa','train','tv/monitor']
# The number of colormaps corresponds to the number of categories,
each category has
# its unique color, which is convenient for observation when drawing
images
colormap = [[0,0,0], [128,0,0], [0,128,0], [128,128,0], [0,0,128],
   [128,0,128], [0,128,128], [128,128,128], [64,0,0],
   [192,0,0], [64,128,0], [192,128,0], [64,0,128],
   [192,0,128], [64,128,128], [192,128,128], [0,64,0],
   [128,64,0], [0,192,0], [128,192,0], [0,64,128]]
# Read data and labels
data, label = read_images(voc_root)
num_classes = len(classes)
# Convert colormap to categories
cm2lbl = np.zeros(256**3)
for i, cm in enumerate(colormap):
  cm2lbl[(cm[0]*256+cm[1])*256+cm[2]]=i
# Set input image size
input_shape = (320,480)
voc_train = VOCSegDataset( True , input_shape, img_transforms)
voc_test = VOCSegDataset( False , input_shape, img_transforms)
Read1114images
Read1078images
# Set batch_size, generate data loader
BATCH_SIZE = 64
train_data  =  DataLoader(voc_train,  batch_size=BATCH_SIZE,
shuffle= True )
test_data = DataLoader(voc_test, batch_size=BATCH_SIZE)
```

Display some images from the dataset and their corresponding labels.

```
for i, (img, label) in enumerate(voc_train):
  plt.figure(figsize=(10, 10))
```

```
  plt.subplot(221)
  plt.imshow(img.moveaxis(0, 2))
  plt.subplot(222)
  plt.imshow(label)
  plt.show()
  plt.close()
  if i ==1:
    break
Clipping input data to the valid range for imshow with RGB
data ([0..1] for floats
or [0..255] for integers).
```

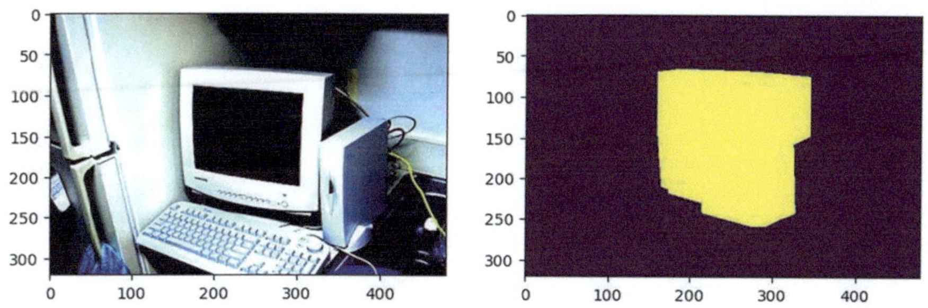

```
Clipping input data to the valid range for imshow with RGB data
([0..1] for floats
or [0..255] for integers).
```

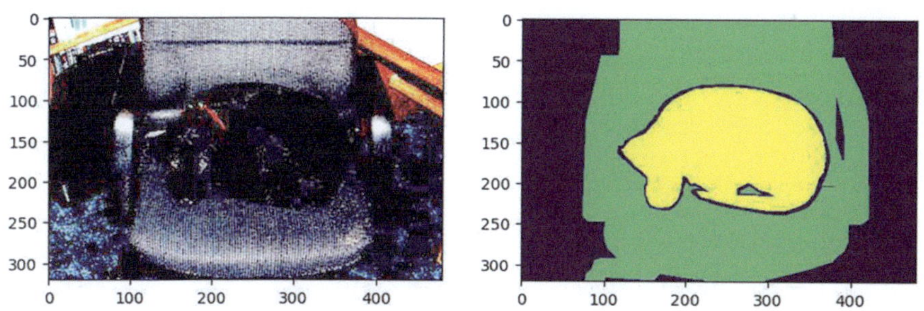

Write a function to calculate mIoU.

```
def _fast_hist(label_true, label_pred, n_class):
  mask = (label_true >= 0) & (label_true < n_class)
   hist = np.bincount(n_class * label_true[mask].astype(int) +
label_pred[mask],
           minlength=n_class ** 2).reshape(n_class, n_class)
   return hist
def mIoU(label_trues, label_preds, n_class):
# Calculate mIoU
  hist = np.zeros((n_class, n_class))
   for lt, lp in zip(label_trues, label_preds):
```

```
    hist += _fast_hist(lt.flatten(), lp.flatten(), n_class)
  iu = np.diag(hist) / (hist.sum(axis=1) +
          hist.sum(axis=0) - np.diag(hist))
  mean_iu = np.nanmean(iu)
   return mean_iu
```

Load the FCN-8s model and train it.

```
device = device = torch.device('cuda' if torch.cuda.is_
available()
                       else 'cpu')
# Load the model
model = FCN8s(num_classes)
model.to(device)
model = nn.DataParallel(model)
# Set the optimizer
optimizer = torch.optim.SGD(model.parameters(), lr=1e-2,
             weight_decay=1e-4)
# Set the loss function
criterion = nn.NLLLoss()
# Since there is no validation set, test the model on the test set
after each
# training session
# Do not display irrelevant information
np.seterr(divide='ignore',invalid='ignore')
Epoch = 120
for epoch in range(Epoch):
  # Training loss
  train_loss = 0
  # Training mIoU
  train_mean_iu = 0
  # Start training
  model = model.train()
   for data in train_data:
    x = data[0].to(device)
    y = data[1].to(device)
    # Clear gradients
    optimizer.zero_grad()
    # Get the model's predicted probability distribution
    outputs = model(x)
    # Get the model's predicted labels, size is (b,n,h,w)
    outputs = F.log_softmax(outputs, dim=1)
    # Calculate loss
    loss = criterion(outputs, y)
    # Backpropagation
    loss.backward()
    optimizer.step()
    # Record loss
    train_loss += loss.item()
    # Obtain predicted labels
    label_pred = outputs.max(dim=1)[1].data.cpu().numpy()
    label_true = y.data.cpu().numpy()
       for lbt, lbp in zip(label_true, label_pred):
     # Return the pred and gt labels for each image, calculate mIoU
```

```
        mean_iu = mIoU(lbt, lbp, num_classes)
        train_mean_iu += mean_iu
    # Test loss
    eval_loss = 0
    # Test mIoU
    eval_mean_iu = 0
    # Perform model testing
    model = model.eval()
    for data in test_data:
        x_test = data[0].to(device)
        y_test = data[1].to(device)
        outputs_test = model(x_test)
        outputs_test = F.log_softmax(outputs_test, dim=1)
        loss = criterion(outputs_test, y_test)
        eval_loss += loss.item()
        label_pred = outputs_test.max(dim=1)[1].data.cpu().numpy()
        label_true = y_test.data.cpu().numpy()
        for lbt, lbp in zip(label_true, label_pred):
            mean_iu = mIoU(lbt, lbp, num_classes)
            eval_mean_iu += mean_iu
    epoch_str = ('Epoch: {}, Train Loss: {:.5f}, Train Mean IU: {:.5f},\
        Valid Loss: {:.5f}, Valid Mean IU: {:.5f} '.format(
            epoch, train_loss / len(train_data),
            train_mean_iu / len(voc_train),
            eval_loss / len(test_data),
            eval_mean_iu / len(voc_test)))
    print(epoch_str)
```

For convenience, specific training information output is not displayed here. We randomly select some images and display their real labels and the labels predicted by the FCN-8s model.

```
# Map the predicted labels to the colormap
cm = np.array(colormap).astype('uint8')
def predict(im, label):
    im = Variable(im.unsqueeze(0)).cuda()
    out = model(im)
    pred = out.max(1)[1].squeeze().cpu().data.numpy()
    pred = cm[pred]
    return pred, cm[label.numpy()]
_, figs = plt.subplots(10, 3, figsize=(12, 10))
for i in range(10):
    x, y = voc_test[i]
    x.to(device)
    y.to(device)
    pred, label = predict(x, y)
    figs[i, 0].imshow(Image.open(voc_test.data_list[i]))
    figs[i, 0].axes.get_xaxis().set_visible(False)
    figs[i, 0].axes.get_yaxis().set_visible(False)
    figs[i, 1].imshow(label)
    figs[i, 1].axes.get_xaxis().set_visible(False)
    figs[i, 1].axes.get_yaxis().set_visible(False)
    figs[i, 2].imshow(pred)
    figs[i, 2].axes.get_xaxis().set_visible(False)
    figs[i, 2].axes.get_yaxis().set_visible(False)
```

11.5 Summary

This chapter introduced semantic segmentation. We discussed the differences between segmentation networks and classification networks, explained the network used for semantic segmentation, i.e., FCN, and implemented the corresponding functions of FCN, as well as trained and tested it on the PASCAL VOC dataset. As one of the important research contents of computer vision, semantic segmentation lays a certain foundation for subsequent image semantic understanding, such as object detection and instance segmentation.

Exercises

(1) In FCN, the feature maps of different levels of the backbone network are fused by pixel-wise addition after skip connections. Can you think of other fusion methods? Implement the fusion method you thought of and compare it with the original fusion method.

(2) If there is a large difference in the number of pixels of different categories, what problems might arise when training FCN for semantic segmentation using the pixel-wise cross-entropy loss function introduced in this chapter? If there is a problem, how should the pixel-wise cross-entropy loss function be modified?

(3) In Section 11.1, we said that semantic segmentation needs to model the conditional probability $P(\boldsymbol{Y}|\boldsymbol{I})$, but in FCN, only the conditional probability of each pixel $P(y_i|\boldsymbol{I})$ is modeled. This is an approximate solution to avoid the solution space of $\boldsymbol{Y}$ being too large. What problems might this approximation cause in the segmentation results of FCN?

(4) In Chap. 9, we introduced unsupervised image segmentation. Can the ideas or methods in unsupervised image segmentation help improve FCN and enhance the results of semantic segmentation? Provide a solution and implement it for verification.

References

1. EVERINGHAM M, VAN GOOL L, WILLIAMS C K I, et al. The pascal visual object classes (voc) challenge[J]. International Journal of Computer Vision, 2010, 88:303–338.
2. CORDTS M, OMRAN M, RAMOS S, et al. The cityscapes dataset for semantic urban scene understanding[C]//IEEE Conference on Computer Vision and Pattern Recognition, 2016:3213–3223.
3. ZHOU B, ZHAO H, PUIG X, et al. Semantic understanding of scenes through the ade20k dataset[J]. International Journal of Computer Vision, 2019, 127:302–321.
4. LONG J, SHELHAMER E, DARRELL T. Fully convolutional networks for semantic segmentation [C]//IEEE Conference on Computer Vision and Pattern Recognition, 2015: 3431–3440.
5. DUMOULIN V, VISIN F. A guide to convolution arithmetic for deep learning[EB/OL]. (2016-03-23)[2024-09-25]. arXiv: 1603.07285.

Chapter 12
Object Detection

12.1 Introduction

Object detection is a core problem in computer vision, aiming to identify the category of each object in an image and locate them. Localization refers to determining the position and size of the object, usually by outlining a bounding box around the object's contour, and determining the coordinates of the center point of this bounding box as well as its width and height.

To describe the problem of object detection in mathematical terms, we define the image space $\mathbb{I}$ and a predefined set of categories $\mathcal{C}$, given a dataset $\mathcal{D} = \{(\boldsymbol{I}^{(n)}, \mathcal{Y}^{(n)})\}_{n=1}^{N}$, where $\boldsymbol{I}^{(n)} \in \mathbb{I}$ is the n-th image in the dataset, $\mathcal{Y}^{(n)} = \left\{\left\langle c^{(n,m)}, \boldsymbol{b}^{(n,m)}\right\rangle\right\}_{m=1}^{M^{(n)}}$ is its corresponding bounding box label, $M^{(n)}$ is the number of objects in this image, the tuple $\left\langle c^{(n,m)}, \boldsymbol{b}^{(n,m)}\right\rangle$ is the bounding box label of the m-th object in this image, $c^{(n,m)} \in \mathcal{C}$ is the category label, $\boldsymbol{b}^{(n,m)} = \left(b_x, b_y, b_h, b_w\right)^{(n,m)}$ is a quadruple, representing the bounding box coordinates (since this quadruple $\boldsymbol{b}^{(n,m)}$ represents a uniquely determined bounding box, we call it the bounding box coordinates, all bounding box coordinates mentioned in this chapter refer to this quadruple), including the center coordinates of the bounding box $\left(b_x, b_y\right)$ as well as the height b_h and width b_w of the bounding box; the task of object detection is to learn a mapping from the image space to the set of bounding boxes $\mathcal{D}$, so that given any test image $\boldsymbol{I}$, the learned mapping function f can be used to predict the set of object bounding boxes in the image: $\hat{\mathcal{Y}} = f(\boldsymbol{I})$.

Figure 12.1 shows an example of object detection, where the "person", "toy", and "chair" in the image are identified, and their bounding boxes are outlined. Since the output of object detection is bounding boxes, which are regular rectangles, it is widely used in industrial fields due to its high applicability to downstream applications. For example, the output of the perception module in an assisted driving system is the bounding boxes of detected objects. In this chapter, we will introduce object detection

W. Shen et al., *Hands-On Computer Vision*,
https://doi.org/10.1007/978-981-95-4835-4_12

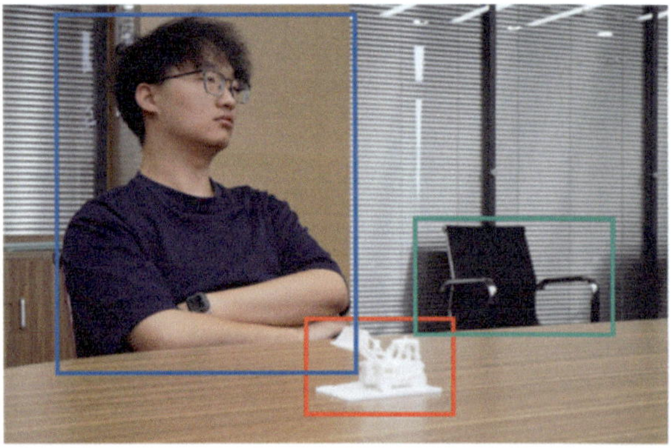

Fig. 12.1 Example of object detection

methods based on deep learning and implement the corresponding object detection framework.

12.2 Dataset and Metrics

Datasets commonly used for object detection include: PASCAL VOC, MS COCO, and ImageNet. The PASCAL VOC and ImageNet datasets have been introduced in previous chapters and will not be repeated here.

The MS COCO (Microsoft common objects in context) dataset is a large-scale dataset widely used for computer vision tasks, released by Microsoft in 2014. It is mainly used for tasks such as object detection, segmentation, keypoint detection, and image caption generation. The goal of the MS COCO dataset is to promote the development of computer vision technology in more complex scenarios. The MS COCO dataset has the following features.

(1) Large number of images: The dataset contains about 200,000 annotated images and about 130,000 unannotated images.
(2) Rich categories and sources: The images cover 80 categories of objects, such as animals, vehicles, furniture, etc., and the images come from a variety of sources, including images scraped from the Internet, street view images, and indoor images.
(3) Complex scenes: The images in the dataset contain various complex scenes, such as crowded markets, congested roads, etc., which pose a high challenge to computer vision models.

The most commonly used evaluation metric for object detection is mean average precision (mAP). As can be seen from the name of mAP, this is a precision metric defined for each category. Therefore, before defining mAP, a criterion for whether an object has been detected needs to be defined. As shown in Fig. 12.2, for an object in an image, let the set of pixels inside its ground-truth bounding box be $\mathcal{A}$, and the set of pixels inside a predicted bounding box be $\mathcal{B}$, , the overlap of the two bounding boxes is defined by the intersection over union (IoU) of the sets of pixels inside these two bounding boxes, where, $\text{IoU}(\mathcal{A}, \mathcal{B}) = \frac{\mathcal{A} \cap \mathcal{B}}{\mathcal{A} \cup \mathcal{B}}$, i.e., the area of the gray part in Fig. 12.2a divided by the area of the gray part in Fig. 12.2b. Note that the definition of IoU here is mathematically equivalent to the definition of IoU in Chap. 11. In object detection, IoU is also known as Box IoU. Given a threshold, if $\text{IoU}(\mathcal{A}, \mathcal{B}) > \theta$, it is considered that the predicted bounding box to which $\mathcal{B}$ belongs has hit the object; otherwise, it is considered that the predicted bounding box to which $\mathcal{B}$ belongs has not hit the object. According to this IoU-based criterion, given a category, for each predicted bounding box of this given category, if the IoU between its internal pixel set and the internal pixel set of a ground-truth bounding box with the given category label is greater than the given threshold, then this predicted bounding box is a true positive (TP); if the IoU between its internal pixel set and the internal pixel set of any ground-truth bounding box with the given category label is less than the given threshold, then this predicted bounding box is a false positive (FP); if an object in a ground-truth bounding box with the given category label is not hit by any predicted bounding box, then this is a false negative (FN). In this way, for the detection results of each image, the recall rate for the given category can be calculated, i.e., the proportion of correct detection relative to all ground-truth bounding boxes, as well as the precision rate (also known as accuracy), i.e., the proportion of correct detection relative to all predicted bounding boxes:

$$\text{Recall} = \frac{\text{TP}}{\text{TP} + \text{FN}}$$

$$\text{Precision} = \frac{\text{TP}}{\text{TP} + \text{FP}}.$$

Note that since whether the predicted bounding box hits the object in the ground-truth bounding box is determined by the IoU threshold, by adjusting the IoU threshold, different recall rates and precision rates will be obtained. By gradually increasing the IoU threshold from 0 to 1, a sequence of recall rate and precision rate pairs can be obtained. Based on such a sequence of recall rate and precision rate pairs, a precision-recall (PR) curve can be drawn, as shown in Fig. 12.3. The area of the region enclosed by the PR curve and the two coordinate axes is defined as the average precision (AP), and mAP refers to the average value of the APs of all categories.

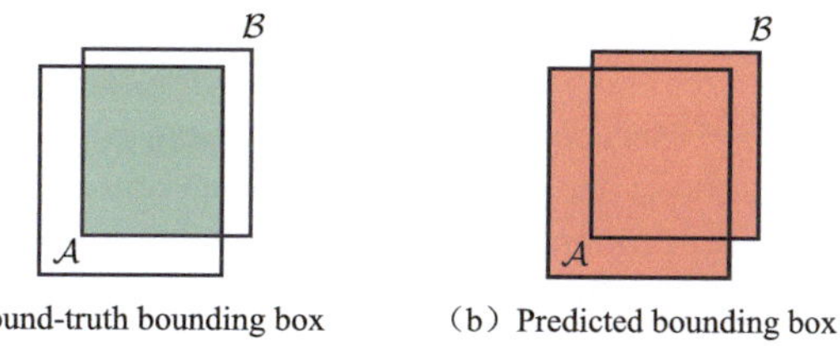

(a) Ground-truth bounding box (b) Predicted bounding box

Fig. 12.2 Measuring the overlap of two bounding boxes through IoU

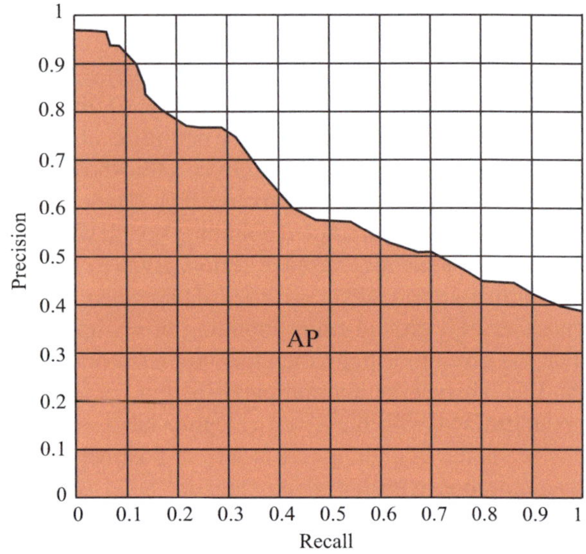

Fig. 12.3 Precision-recall (PR) curve, the area of the region enclosed by the curve and the two coordinate axes is defined as the average precision (AP)

12.3 Object Detection Models

Although Geoffrey Hinton and his students proposed AlexNet in 2012 (see Chap. 11), demonstrating the outstanding performance of deep convolutional neural networks in image classification and ushering in the era of deep learning in computer vision, researchers did not find an effective deep learning model to solve the visual recognition task of object detection in the next one or two years. This is because the process of object detection is usually based on a sliding window strategy, i.e., using a window (a kind of predicted bounding box) to slide on the image, and when it slides to a position, a classifier is used to judge whether there is an object in the window at this position. Since the size of the object is unknown, this sliding window strategy needs to try windows of various sizes at each position on the image, and the total number of windows that need to be tried for each image may be as high as hundreds of thousands or even millions. If a convolutional neural network is used as the window classifier, the processing time for an image may take several hours. This processing speed is unacceptable.

Is there a way to improve the speed of this sliding window-based object detection? In 2014, Ross Girshick et al. provided a solution—region convolutional neural network (R-CNN) [1]. They proposed that it is not necessary to traverse all windows of all sizes and positions, but only to find candidate windows where objects may exist, and then use a convolutional neural network to classify these candidate windows. So, how to find candidate windows where objects may exist? Around 2010, the problem of object proposal detection [2] was proposed, i.e., not caring about what category the object is, but quickly finding possible regions where objects exist from images. These regions are called region proposals. The bounding boxes to which the region proposals belong are candidate windows (usually the region proposals are rectangular areas; in this case, the region proposals are equivalent to candidate windows; in this chapter, by default, these two are equivalent). The confidence that a region proposal may contain an object is called objectness. Based on object proposal detection, candidate windows where objects may exist can be found, and the number of these candidate windows is far less than the number of all sliding windows. This is the basic idea of R-CNN to improve detection speed. In 2014, R-CNN won the first place in the PASCAL VOC detection dataset with an absolute advantage, marking a new milestone for object detection. Subsequently, Girshick et al. further improved and optimized R-CNN, proposing Fast R-CNN [3] and Faster R-CNN [4], which not only further improved the detection speed, but also improved the detection accuracy.

12.3.1 R-CNN

R-CNN is a pioneering work in object detection based on deep learning, as shown in Fig. 12.4. It can be roughly divided into the following steps:

(1) Extract 1000 to 2000 region proposals from the input image.
(2) Use a deep convolutional neural network (CNN) to extract features from each region proposal.
(3) Based on the extracted deep convolutional features, use an SVM classifier to recognize the object category for each region proposals.
(4) Based on the extracted deep convolutional features, use a bounding box regressor to adjust the position and size of the region proposals.

R-CNN is a method based on deep learning, so it includes both training and testing phases. The two phases of R-CNN generally follow the above steps, but there are slight differences. Next, we will introduce the training and testing phases of R-CNN in detail.

In the training phase, first an object proposal detection method, such as Selective Search [5], is used to extract 1000 to 2000 object proposals from each training image; then, all object proposals are warped to the same spatial resolution, such as 227 pixels by 227 pixels, and then a CNN is trained to extract features from these region proposals. The Selective Search used in this stage is a classic region proposal detection method. It obtains some segmented regions in the image through the image

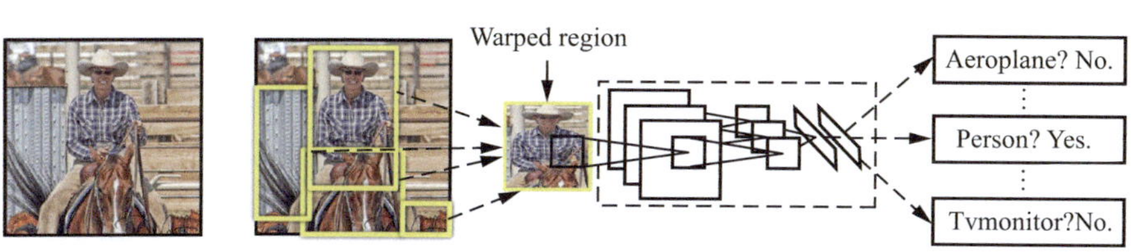

Fig. 12.4 R-CNN (illustration material from reference [1])

segmentation method introduced in Chap. 9, and then merges regions hierarchically based on region features such as color, brightness, and texture, to extract region proposals that may contain objects from the image.

The CNN used to extract the features of region proposals is generally a commonly used backbone network, such as AlexNet, VGG, ResNet, etc. These backbone networks have been pretrained on the ImageNet dataset, and need to be retrained during the training phase of R-CNN. During training, it is necessary to first assign a class label $u \in \mathcal{C}$ to each region proposal. Let the set of pixels in a region proposal in the n-th training image $\boldsymbol{I}^{(n)}$ be denoted as, first find the ground-truth bounding box $m^* = \text{argmax}_m \text{IoU}(\mathcal{R}, \mathcal{B}^{(n,m)}$ with the highest overlap with the region proposal $\mathcal{R}$, where $\mathcal{B}^{(n,m)}$ denotes the set of pixels in the ground-truth bounding box $\boldsymbol{b}^{(n,m)}$. The category label of the region proposal is determined by the following criteria:

$$u = \begin{cases} c^{(n,m^*)}, & \text{IoU}\left(\mathcal{R}, \mathcal{B}^{(n,m^*)}\right) > 0.5 \\ 0, & \text{otherwise} \end{cases}$$

$u = 0$ indicates that the region proposal corresponds to the background, because no ground-truth bounding box has a large enough overlap with it. After assigning category labels to each region proposal, the backbone network can be trained with image classification as the target task (the training method refers to the image classification algorithm introduced in Sect. 10.4). After training, use the trained backbone network to extract features from each region proposal. Finally, an SVM classifier is trained for each category based on the features extracted by the backbone network, for predicting the category label of each region proposal.

In addition, R-CNN also introduces a bounding box regressor to adjust the position and size of the region proposals. The reason for adjusting the position and size is that the initial position and size of the region proposals often deviate from the ground-truth bounding boxes. Figure 12.5 shows an intuitive example: the solid box is the ground-truth bounding box of the target toy and the dashed box is the predicted bounding box; the dashed box needs to be adjusted to make its final position and size closer to the solid box. Specifically, for the above region proposal, let the coordinates of the bounding box to which this region proposal belongs be $\boldsymbol{r} = \left(r_x, r_y, r_h, r_w\right)$, where $\left(r_x, r_y\right)$ represents the coordinates of the center of the bounding box, r_h and and r_w represent the height and width of the bounding box, respectively. The ground-truth bounding box which has the highest overlap with it is $\boldsymbol{b} = \left(b_x^{(n,m^*)}, b_y^{(n,m^*)}, b_h^{(n,m^*)}, b_w^{(n,m^*)}\right)$ (for the sake of symbol simplicity, we omit the superscript (n, m^*) in the following expressions). The coordinate offsets of the bounding box $\boldsymbol{r}$ to which this region proposal belongs relative to the ground-truth bounding box $\boldsymbol{b}$ are defined as:

$$v_x = \frac{b_x - r_x}{r_w}$$

$$v_y = \frac{b_y - r_y}{r_h}$$

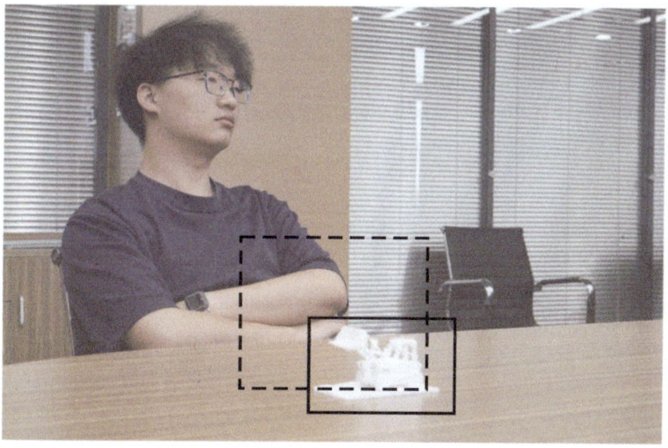

Fig. 12.5 Predicted bounding box (dashed line) and ground-truth bounding box (solid line)

$$v_h = \log \frac{b_h}{r_h}$$

$$v_w = \log \frac{b_w}{r_w}$$

By definition, the coordinate offset of this bounding box includes the relative coordinate difference between the center of the region proposal and the center of the ground-truth bounding box v_x and v_y as well as the logarithm of the scale ratio of height and width v_h and v_w. This regression task can be accomplished by a linear regressor. Let the features of the region proposal extracted by the well-trained backbone network be $\Phi(\mathbf{r})$, then $\mathbf{w}^{\mathrm{T}}\Phi(\mathbf{r})$ can be used to fit the coordinate offsets of the bounding box to which the region proposal belongs relative to the ground-truth bounding box $\boldsymbol{v}$, where $\boldsymbol{w}$ is a learnable parameter. The loss function of this bounding box regression task is defined as

$$L = \left\| \boldsymbol{w}^{\mathrm{T}}\Phi(\boldsymbol{r}) - \boldsymbol{v} \right\|^2 + \|\boldsymbol{w}\|^2.$$

The steps in the testing phase of R-CNN are similar to those in the training phase. Given a test image, the same object proposal detection method is used to extract 1000 to 2000 candidate regions, and then their spatial resolution is normalized to 227 pixels $\times$ 227 pixels. The features of these region proposals are then extracted using the well-trained backbone network. Based on the extracted features of the candidate regions, the well-trained SVM classifier and bounding box regressor are used to predict the target category of each region proposal and fine-tune its position and size. Since the number of predicted bounding boxes is usually very large, and there are many false detections, there is an additional key step in the testing phase compared to the training phase—non-maximum suppression (NMS), which is used to remove redundant predicted bounding boxes: for each category, first, the predicted bounding box with the highest confidence (this confidence can be the category probability output by the SVM classifier) is selected, set its internal pixel set to $\mathcal{A}$, and calculate

Fig. 12.6 Using NMS to remove redundant predicted bounding boxes

the overlap IoU($\mathcal{A}$, $\mathcal{B}$) with the internal pixel sets of other predicted bounding boxes (such as $\mathcal{B}$). If IoU($\mathcal{A}$, $\mathcal{B}$) is greater than a given threshold, then delete the predicted bounding box to which $\mathcal{B}$ belongs. Then the next predicted bounding box with the highest confidence is selected, and the above process is repeated. In this way, all remaining predicted bounding boxes belonging to this object category are traversed, resulting in the final detection results for that category, as shown in Fig. 12.6.

12.3.2 Fast R-CNN

Although the idea of R-CNN is straightforward, it clearly has many problems:

(1) For each region proposal in each image, the backbone network is required to use for feature computation. Since a single image usually has 2000 region proposals, computational efficiency becomes an issue.
(2) There is a lot of overlap between region proposals, leading to redundant computation during feature extraction.
(3) The training phase of R-CNN includes multiple training processes (training of the backbone network, SVM classifier, and bounding box regressor), and these training processes are not end-to-end; i.e., the results of object category classification and bounding box regression cannot be fed back to the front-end backbone network for updating network parameters.

To solve these problems, Ross Girshick proposed Fast R-CNN in 2015 [3]. The design of Fast R-CNN is more compact and greatly improves the speed of object detection. When using VGG16 as the backbone network, compared with R-CNN, the training time on PASCAL VOC 2007 is reduced from 84 h to 9.5 h, and the test time per image is reduced from 47 s to 0.32 s.

Compared to R-CNN, Fast R-CNN has two major improvements:

(1) Instead of extracting features for each region proposal individually, it extracts the feature map of the entire image first, and then directly extracts the features of each region proposal from the feature map, avoiding the process of computing features with the backbone network multiple times.
(2) In Fast R-CNN, feature extraction for region proposals, along with the training of the classifier and regressor, forms an end-to-end process. The classification and regression results can be backpropagated to update the parameters of the backbone network.

The key to implementing these two improvements is the introduction of a region of interest (ROI) feature extractor. The so-called ROI is the corresponding region in the feature map that is projected from a region proposal in the original image.

The corresponding region on the feature map where the region proposal is mapped on the image. This feature extractor needs to extract features for each Region of Interest (ROI) from the entire image's feature map (thus obtaining features for each region proposal based on the spatial correspondence between the proposals and the ROIs). Furthermore, ROIs with different spatial resolutions must be converted into a uniform fixed-size feature representation to feed seamlessly into the subsequent classifier and regressor for training. The ROI feature extractor proposed in Fast R-CNN is called ROI pooling. Simply put, the ROI pooling layer divides each ROI into $M \times N$ sub-windows and then pools the features within each sub-window. If the dimension of the feature vector in the feature map of the entire image is, then regardless of the spatial resolution of the ROI, the dimension of the ROI feature map produced by the ROI pooling layer is uniformly $M \times N \times d$.

Specifically, the overall process of Fast R-CNN is shown in Fig. 12.7 and can be divided into three steps:

(1) Extract region proposals from the input image.
(2) Use the backbone network to compute the feature map of the entire input image.
(3) Extract the features of each region proposal directly from the feature map of the entire image through ROI pooling, enabling both object category classification and bounding box regression for the region proposals.

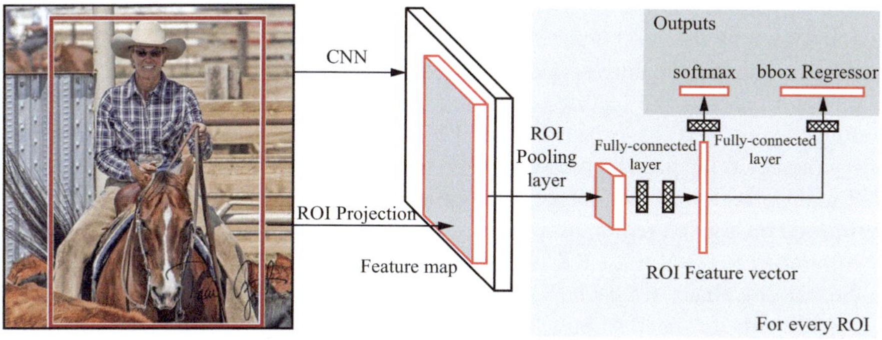

Fig. 12.7 Fast R-CNN (illustration material from reference [3])

Since ROI pooling is performed on the feature map of the entire image, implementing this operation requires computing the mapping relationship between the region proposal and the ROI. This requires understanding how the operations of the convolutional and pooling layers in the backbone network (such as ResNet or VGG, etc.) affect the spatial resolution of the feature map. For example, after processing by a convolutional layer or pooling layer with a stride of 2, the width and height of the output feature map become $\frac{1}{2}$ of the width and height of the input image. By extension, after processing by l convolutional or pooling layers with a stride of 2, the width and height of the output feature map are $\frac{1}{2^l}$ of the width and height of the original image. Therefore, there is a ratio relationship between the current feature map and the original input image in terms of spatial resolution, which is called the spatial downsampling factor. For example, when using VGG16 as the backbone network, the spatial downsampling factor of the feature map output by its last convolutional layer is $S = 32$ (because it has been downsampled 5 times). For a given region proposal on the original image, the corresponding ROI in the feature map can be found through the following calculation process.

Suppose the coordinates of the top-left corner of the region proposal in the original image are (x_1, y_1), and the coordinates of the bottom-right corner are (x_2, y_2). First, divide the original coordinates by the spatial downsampling factor S. Then apply floor operation to the top-left coordinates and ceiling operation to the bottom-right coordinates to obtain the quantized coordinates $\left(\left\lfloor \frac{x_1}{S} \right\rfloor, \left\lfloor \frac{y_1}{S} \right\rfloor\right)$ and $\left(\left\lceil \frac{x_2}{S} \right\rceil, \left\lceil \frac{y_2}{S} \right\rceil\right)$, respectively. Quantization is applied because division by the spatial downsampling factor may result in non-integer coordinates. Here we give an example: Assuming that the coordinates of the top-left corner and the bottom-right corner of the original region proposal are (50, 50) and (200, 200) respectively, and the spatial downsampling factor is 16, as shown in Fig. 12.8; then, the coordinates of the top-left corner and the lower-right corner of the corresponding region in the feature map are $\left(\frac{50}{16}, \frac{50}{16}\right)$ and $\left(\frac{200}{16}, \frac{200}{16}\right)$ (the dashed box in the figure); thus, the quantized coordinates are $\left(\left\lfloor \frac{50}{16} \right\rfloor, \left\lfloor \frac{50}{16} \right\rfloor\right)$ and $\left(\left\lceil \frac{200}{16} \right\rceil, \left\lceil \frac{200}{16} \right\rceil\right)$. Based on the quantized coordinates, the corresponding region in the feature map that maps to the region proposal in the original image can be located. In the above example, after quantization, the coordinates of the top-left corner and the bottom-right corner of the corresponding region in the feature map are (3, 3) and (13, 13), respectively; i.e., the corresponding region is the region shown by the solid box.

After obtaining the corresponding region in the feature map based on the above calculation process, the features of these regions can be extracted through the ROI pooling layer. Next, as shown in Fig. 12.7, each ROI feature map is fed to two fully connected layers which results in an ROI feature vector; finally, based on the ROI feature vector, object category classification and bounding box regression are performed on a given region proposal.

Similar to R-CNN, Fast R-CNN also includes two phases: training and testing. In the training phase, for each ROI, a ground-truth class label u and a bounding box regression offset $\boldsymbol{v}$ need to be assigned. The assignment method is the same as in R-CNN. The loss function on this ROI in Fast R-CNN is defined as

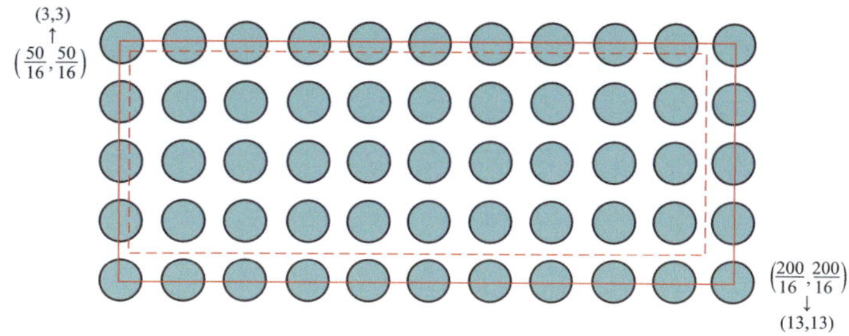

Fig. 12.8 Coordinates of the ROI are quantized in the feature map

$$L(\boldsymbol{q}, u, \boldsymbol{t}, \boldsymbol{v}) = L_{\text{cls}}(\boldsymbol{q}, u) + \lambda 1(u) L_{\text{loc}}(\boldsymbol{t}, \boldsymbol{v})$$

where $\boldsymbol{q}$ is the softmax layer's class classification output for this ROI in Fig. 12.7, which is a probability distribution defined on $|\mathcal{C}| + 1$ categories (+1 represents the background category); $\boldsymbol{t}$ is the bounding box regression offset output for the ROI by the bounding box regression layer in Fig. 12.7; *1* is an indicator function, which returns 1 when $u \geq 1$ and 0 otherwise, because bounding box regression is not required when the region proposal is considered as the background category.

The loss function consists of two parts, one is the classification loss L_{cls} and the other is the bounding box regression loss L_{loc}. $L_{\text{cls}}(\boldsymbol{q}, u) = -\log(q_u)$, q_u represents the probability value of the predicted distribution $\boldsymbol{q}$ on the ground-truth category u. L_{loc} is the smooth L1 norm loss, defined as follows:

$$L_{\text{loc}}(t, v) = \sum_{j \in \{x, y, w, h\}} \text{smooth}_{L_1}(t_j - v_j)$$

where

$$\text{smooth}_{L_1}(x) = \begin{cases} 0.5x^2, & |x| < 1 \\ |x| - 0.5, & \text{otherwise} \end{cases}$$

The steps of Fast R-CNN in the testing phase are similar to those in the training phase, which also include the above three steps. Similar to the testing phase of R-CNN, non-maximum suppression is finally needed to merge multiple highly overlapping predicted bounding boxes.

Next, let's learn about the code implementation of the core module of ROI pooling in Fast R-CNN.

```
import numpy as np


def ROI_pooling(feature_map, ROIs, output_size):
    # feature_map: input feature map, shape is (H, W, C)
    # ROIs: contains the position coordinates, height, and width of
the ROI,
```

```
    # shape is (num_ROIs, 4)
    # output_size: the size of the output after ROI pooling

    # # Convert the position coordinates, height, and width of the ROI
to integers
    # ROIs = np.round(ROIs).astype(np.int32)

    # # Calculate the height and width of each ROI
    # ROI_heights = ROIs[:, 2] - ROIs[:, 0] # (num_ROIs,)
    # ROI_widths = ROIs[:, 3] - ROIs[:, 1] # (num_ROIs,)

    # # Calculate the vertical and horizontal stride of each ROI
    # stride_y = ROI_heights / output_size[0]
    # stride_x = ROI_widths / output_size[1]

    # # Initialize the output array
    pooled_ROIs = np.zeros((ROIs.shape[0], output_size[0], output_
size[1],
            feature_map.shape[2])).

    # Perform pooling operation on the features within each ROI
    for i, ROI in enumerate(ROIs):
      # Get the coordinates of the ROI
      y1, × 1, y2, × 2 = ROI

      # Calculate the vertical and horizontal pooling stride of each
ROI
      dy = (y2 - y1) / output_size[0]
      dx = (×2 - × 1) / output_size[1]

      # Perform pooling on the features of each channel
        for c in range(feature_map.shape[2]):
       for y in range(output_size[0]):
           for x in range(output_size[1]):
              # Calculate the coordinates of the current sub-window
              y_start = int(np.floor(y1 + y * dy))
              x_start = int(np.floor(×1 + x * dx))
              y_end = int(np.ceil(y_start + dy))
              x_end = int(np.ceil(x_start + dx))

              # Extract the region on the feature map corresponding
to the
              # current sub-window
              patch = feature_map[y_start:y_end, x_start:x_end, c]

              # Perform pooling on the current sub-window
              pooled_ROIs[i, y, x, c] = np.max(patch)

    return pooled_ROIs
```

12.3.3 *Faster R-CNN*

Although Fast R-CNN significantly improved the testing time compared to R-CNN, reducing it from 47 s per image to 0.32 s, a 146-fold increase in speed, it should be noted that this testing time does not include the time used for region proposal extraction. In fact, the process of region proposal extraction is the bottleneck of object detection speed.

To further improve the speed of object detection, Shaoqing Ren, Kaiming He, Ross Girshick, and Jian Sun proposed Faster R-CNN in 2015 [4]. This method introduced a region proposal network (RPN) for efficient region proposal extraction, reducing the testing time of object detection to 0.2 s per image (including the process of region proposal extraction), nearly a 250-fold speed increase compared to R-CNN. Compared to Fast R-CNN, Faster R-CNN generates several region proposals directly from the feature map of the image through the RPN, replacing the traditional object detection methods (such as Selective Search), and achieving end-to-end training. Simply put, Faster R-CNN can be understood as "RPN + Fast R-CNN". The overall process is shown in Fig. 12.9 and mainly includes the following two steps:

(1) Extract region proposals from the input image through the RPN.
(2) Classify the object categories and perform bounding box regression on these region proposals based on the Fast R-CNN framework.

RPN is the core module introduced in Faster R-CNN. It employs a lightweight convolutional neural network operating directly on the feature map. By leveraging the inherent sliding window nature of convolutional operations, the RPN implements

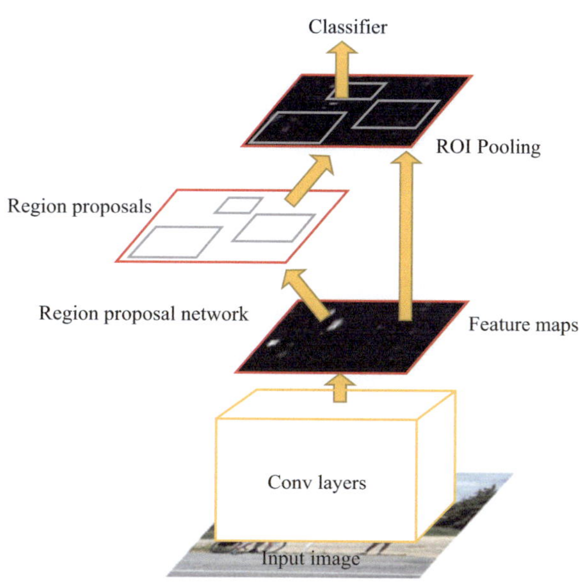

Fig. 12.9 Faster R-CNN (illustration material from reference [4])

a sliding window detection strategy, thereby replacing traditional region proposal generation methods. The process is shown in Fig. 12.10. The RPN takes the feature map output from the convolutional layers of the backbone network as input and employs a lightweight convolutional neural network that slides across the feature map. At each position, it maps the features within the sliding window centered on the current point (typically of spatial resolution $s \times s$ pixels, where s = 3) into a d-dimensional feature vector (commonly, $d = 256$ or 512). This feature vector is input to two parallel fully connected layers—a classification layer and a regression layer—to generate region proposals. Note that we have so far only mentioned the position of the region proposal, i.e., the center of the current sliding window, while the size of the region proposal remains undetermined. For this, RPN introduces an important concept—anchor. An anchor is a rectangular region centered on the current sliding window, with its spatial dimensions defined by predefined scales (sizes) and aspect ratios. Thus, the aforementioned classification layer outputs two scores, namely the confidence of the presence and absence of an object in the current anchor; the regression layer outputs four bounding box coordinate offset parameters, namely the coordinate offsets between the current anchor (an anchor is a rectangular region, also a bounding box) and its corresponding ground-truth bounding box. Since the size of the object in the image is unknown, to achieve multi-scale object detection, RPN generates multiple region proposals at each point on the feature map. The number of region proposals generated k is determined by the predefined types of anchors, i.e., by the types of anchors with basic spatial resolution. Typically, the RPN uses 3 anchor box sizes and 3 anchor box aspect ratios, resulting in a total of $k = 9$ predefined anchor boxes. Because k types of anchors are defined, the aforementioned classification layer and regression layer output 2 k confidence scores and 4 k bounding box coordinate offset parameters, respectively, at each sliding window location. If the size of the feature map output by the backbone network convolutional layer is $H \times W$ (generally about 2400), where H and W are the height and width of the feature map, respectively, then the total number of anchors in this image is $H \times W \times k$.

Faster R-CNN also includes two phases: training and testing. In the training phase, compared to the training stage of Fast R-CNN, Faster R-CNN includes the training of RPN. Similar to R-CNN and Fast R-CNN, in the training process of Faster R-CNN, to train the RPN, each anchor box needs to be assigned a ground-truth class label. This ground-truth class label is a binary label, indicating whether the anchor box contains an object that needs to be detected. The assignment of the ground-truth class label is still based on the Intersection over Union (IoU) criterion. An anchor box can be assigned a positive ground-truth class label (i.e., the anchor box is a positive anchor box containing an object to be detected) if it meets one of the following two conditions:

(1) The IoU between the pixel set inside the anchor box and the pixel set inside a ground-truth bounding box is the largest among all anchor boxes.
(2) The IoU between the pixel set inside the anchor box and the pixel set inside any ground-truth bounding box is greater than 0.7.

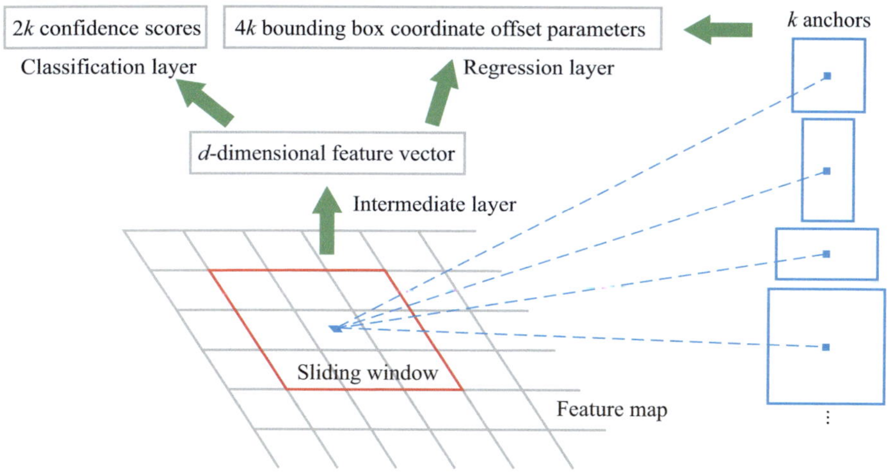

Fig. 12.10 RPN network structure (illustration from reference [4])

Generally, condition 2 is sufficient to determine a positive ground-truth class label for an anchor box. However, in some extreme cases, no anchor box can meet condition 2 for a ground-truth bounding box. In such case, condition 1 is needed as a supplement. If an anchor box does not meet either of the above conditions, and the IoU between the pixel set inside the anchor box and the pixel set inside each ground-truth bounding box is less than 0.3, then this anchor box will be assigned a negative ground-truth class label (i.e., the anchor box is a negative anchor box without an object to be detected). If an anchor box is not assigned either a positive or negative label, then this anchor box will not participate in the RPN training process.

RPN also assigns a ground-truth bounding box to each anchor box for the subsequent bounding box regression tasks. Specifically, the assignment (matching) process proceeds as follows: First, for each ground-truth bounding box, calculate the IoU between its pixel set and the pixel set of every anchor box. Then, identify the pair (ground-truth bounding box and anchor box) with the highest IoU and match them. Next, for the remaining unmatched anchor boxes, find the ground-truth bounding box whose pixel set has the highest IoU with the pixel set of the current unmatched anchor box. If this IoU exceeds a predefined threshold (typically 0.5), assign (match) that ground-truth bounding box to this anchor box; otherwise, leave the anchor box unmatched.

Based on the above definitions, the loss function of RPN for an image is defined as follows:

$$L(q^i, u^i, \boldsymbol{t}^i, \boldsymbol{v}^i) = \frac{1}{N_{\text{cls}}} \sum_i L_{\text{cls}}(q^i, u^i) + \frac{\lambda}{N_{\text{reg}}} \sum_i u^i L_{\text{reg}}(\boldsymbol{t}^i, \boldsymbol{v}^i)$$

where i is an index of the anchor boxes in the mini-batch composed of the anchor boxes in this image. Theoretically, this mini-batch can contain all the anchor boxes in this image, but this would lead to an imbalance in the number of class samples, as the number of negative anchor boxes in an image is usually much larger than the number of positive anchor boxes. Therefore, RPN randomly samples 256 anchor boxes in an image to calculate the loss function, with a maximum positive-to-negative anchor box ratio of 1:1. These 256 anchor boxes are the "mini-batch" generated by this image. If the number of positive anchor boxes in an image is less than 128, then negative anchor boxes will be used to fill this mini-batch. q^i is the predicted score of the anchor box being a positive anchor box, u^i is the ground-truth class label assigned to the anchor box. If the anchor box is a positive anchor box, then $u^i = 1$, otherwise if the anchor box is a negative anchor box, $u^i = 0$. $\boldsymbol{t}^i$ and $\boldsymbol{v}^i$ are the predicted and ground-truth coordinate offsets of the ground-truth bounding box relative to the anchor box, respectively. The bounding box regression loss is calculated using the smooth function smooth_{L_1}. In addition, $u^i L_{\text{reg}}$ indicates that only positive anchor boxes need to perform bounding box regression. N_{cls} is the size of the mini-batch, i.e., $N_{\text{cls}} = 256$, N_{reg} is the total number of points on the feature map, N_{reg} is approximately 2400; λ is a hyperparameter, default $\lambda = 10$, so the weights of the classification loss and bounding box regression loss are approximately equal.

RPN generates some region proposals with high overlap. To reduce redundancy, RPN uses non-maximum suppression (NMS) based on their confidence scores to reduce overlapping region proposals. The IoU threshold of NMS is fixed at 0.7, so about 2000 candidate regions are retained for each image. NMS not only does not reduce the final detection accuracy, but also reduces the number of region proposals. After performing NMS, RPN selects the top N region proposals for Fast R-CNN training. Since the separate training of RPN and Fast R-CNN will affect the parameters of the backbone network in different ways, Faster R-CNN adopts a "four-step alternating training" strategy to share the parameters of the backbone network during training, instead of learning two sets of separate backbone network parameters. The four-step alternating training process is as follows:

(1) The parameters of the backbone network connected to the RPN are initialized by the backbone network parameters pretrained on the ImageNet dataset. Both the RPN and the connected backbone network are trained according to the above process.
(2) The backbone network parameters of Fast R-CNN are also initialized by the backbone network parameters pretrained on the ImageNet dataset. Then, the region proposals generated by the first step RPN are used to train Fast R-CNN and the backbone network connected to it. Note that at this step, RPN and Fast R-CNN do not share backbone network parameters—meaning their respective backbone networks have distinct parameters.
(3) The backbone network parameters connected to the RPN are initialized using those from the Fast R-CNN's backbone network. The backbone network parameters are fixed, and only the layers unique to the RPN are fine-tuned. At this step, RPN and Fast R-CNN share the same backbone network.
(4) The parameters of the shared backbone network are fixed, and only the layers unique to Fast R-CNN are fine-tuned.

The steps of Faster R-CNN in the testing phase are similar to those in the training phase, which also include the above steps. For a test image, Faster R-CNN first uses RPN to generate a series of region proposals, uses NMS to filter these region proposals, and then uses Fast R-CNN to predict the object categories of these region proposals and regress their bounding boxes.

Next, let's look at some details in the code implementation of RPN. In the code, RPN is defined as RegionProposalNetwork, which takes the feature maps extracted from training images using a CNN backbone as input and outputs region proposals on that feature maps.

12.4 RPN Code Framework

First, let's overview the overall framework of the RPN code.

```
class RegionProposalNetwork(torch.nn.Module):
    """
    Implementation of RPN This network is responsible for generating
    region proposals.These regions are then passed to the Fast R-CNN
module
    """


    def __init__(
    self,
      # Module for generating anchor box coordinates
      anchor_generator,
     # Network head for positive/negative classification and bounding
box
      # regression of anchor boxes
      head,
      # IoU threshold for an anchor box to be determined as a positive
anchor box,
      # default value is 0.7
      # If the IoU of the pixel set inside the anchor box and the pixel
set inside
      # any ground-truth bounding box is greater than fg_iou_thresh
      # It is considered that there is an object to be detected in this
anchor box
      fg_iou_thresh,
      # IoU threshold for an anchor box to be determined as a negative
anchor box,
      # default value is 0.3
      # If the IoU of the pixel set inside the anchor box and the pixel
set inside
      # all ground-truth bounding boxes is less than bg_iou_thresh
      # It is considered that there is no object to be detected in this
anchor box
      bg_iou_thresh,
      # Number of anchor boxes sampled per image
      batch_size_per_image,
```

```
    # Proportion of sampled positive anchor boxes
     # Number of positive anchor boxes = batch_size_per_image *
positive_fraction
    positive_fraction,
    # Number of region proposals before NMS
    # Select up to the top pre_nms_top_n region proposals
    pre_nms_top_n,
    # Number of region proposals after NMS
    # Select up to the top post_nms_top_n region proposals to send
to roi_head
    post_nms_top_n,
    # Threshold set during NMS
    nms_thresh,
    # Finally return region proposals with scores greater than
    # this threshold
    score_thresh = 0
  ):
    super(RegionProposalNetwork, self).__init__()

    self.anchor_generator = anchor_generator
    self.head = head

     # Encoder and decoder for encoding and decoding anchor box
coordinates
    self.box_coder = det_utils.BoxCoder(weights = (1.0, 1.0, 1.0,
1.0))

# Define IoU function
    self.box_similarity = box_ops.box_iou

     # Define matcher for matching anchor boxes and ground-truth
bounding boxes
    self.proposal_matcher = det_utils.Matcher(
      fg_iou_thresh,
      bg_iou_thresh,
      allow_low_quality_matches = True,
    )

     # Define positive/negative anchor box sampler to ensure the
balance of
    # positive/negative samples.
   self.fg_bg_sampler = det_utils.BalancedPositiveNegativeSampler(
      batch_size_per_image, positive_fraction.
    )

    self._pre_nms_top_n = pre_nms_top_n
    self._post_nms_top_n = post_nms_top_n
    self.nms_thresh = nms_thresh.
    self.score_thresh = score_thresh
     # Define the threshold for removing region proposalswith too
small area
```

```
        self.min_size = 1e-3

    def pre_nms_top_n(self):
        # Return the number of region proposals before NMS operation
during training
        # or testing phase
            Pass

    def post_nms_top_n(self):
        # Return the number of region proposals after NMS operation
during training
        # or testing phase
        Pass

    def assign_targets_to_anchors(self, anchors, targets):
        # Assign positive/negative labels to each anchor box and match
it with the
        # ground-truth bounding box
            Pass

    def filter_proposals(self, proposals, objectness, image_shapes,
                        num_anchors_per_level):
        # Filter the region proposals to get high-quality region
proposals
            Pass

    def compute_loss(self, objectness, pred_bbox_deltas, labels,
                     regression_targets):
        # Compute the loss function during training
        pass

    def forward(self, images, features, targets = None):
        """
        Forward propagation of RPN. Input images and feature maps to
generate region
        proposals
        Parameters:
        - images: Input images
        - features: Feature maps output by different network layers
computed per
        image, the data structure of this variable is a dictionary
        - targets: Ground-truth bounding boxes in each image. This
parameter can be
        void, if not, the coordinates of each ground-truth bounding
box need to be
        provided

        Returns:
        - boxes: region proposals predicted by RPN
        - losses: Training losses, this item is void during testing
```

```
        """
        # Get the feature maps output from different layers of the
backbone network
        features = list(features.values()).

        # Predict the confidence of each anchor box whether contains an
object and
        # the coordinate offsets of its matched ground-truth bounding
box relative to
        # that anchor
        objectness, pred_bbox_deltas = self.head(features)

        # Generate the coordinates of the anchor boxes
        anchors = self.anchor_generator(images, features)

        num_images = len(anchors)
        num_anchors_per_level_shape_tensors = [o[0].shape for o in
objectness]
        num_anchors_per_level = [s[0] * s[1] * s[2] for s in num_anchors_
per_
                level_shape_tensors]
            objectness, pred_bbox_deltas = concat_box_prediction_
layers(objectness,
                pred_bbox_deltas)
        # Note that the H and W of each layer are not the same here

        # Here we use pred_bbox_deltas.detach to block gradient
propagation
        # This can keep the parameters of RPN unchanged when training
the subsequent
        # network (Fast R-CNN)

        # Decode to get the coordinates of the bounding box of the region
proposal
                proposals = self.box_coder.decode(pred_bbox_
deltas.detach(), anchors)
        proposals = proposals.view(num_images, -1, 4)

        # First, sort by score, select the top pre_nms_top_n, and clip
the out-of-
        # bounds region proposals
        # Filter region proposals and apply NMS to remove redundant
region proposals
        boxes, scores = self.filter_proposals(proposals, objectness,
                images.image_sizes, num_anchors_per_level)

        losses = {}
        # Note: The following steps are only performed during training
        if self.training:
```

```
        # Ensure targets are provided during training
        assert targets is not None
        # Assign labels and matched ground truth bounding boxes to the
anchor boxes
                labels, matched_gt_boxes = self.assign_targets_to_
anchors(anchors,
                 targets)


        # regression_targets are the coordinate offsets of the ground-
truth
            # bounding boxes relative to the matched anchor boxes
            # Encode these offsets
              regression_targets = self.box_coder.encode(matched_gt_
boxes, anchors)


            # Calculate the loss function
                loss_objectness, loss_rpn_box_reg = self.compute_
loss(objectness,
                 pred_bbox_deltas, labels, regression_targets)
            losses = {
              "loss_objectness": loss_objectness,
              "loss_rpn_box_reg": loss_rpn_box_reg,
              }
        return boxes, losses


def concat_box_prediction_layers(box_cls, box_regression):
    """
    Concatenate the results of positive/negative classification of
anchor boxes and
    bounding box regression in the feature maps output by different
levels of the
    network
    """
    box_cls_flattened = []
    box_regression_flattened = []


    for box_cls_per_level, box_regression_per_level in zip(
        box_cls, box_regression
    ):
        N, AxC, H, W = box_cls_per_level.shape
        Ax4 = box_regression_per_level.shape[1]
        A = Ax4 // 4
        C = AxC // A
        box_cls_per_level = permute_and_flatten(
            box_cls_per_level, N, A, C, H, W
        )
        box_cls_flattened.append(box_cls_per_level)


        box_regression_per_level = permute_and_flatten(
          box_regression_per_level, N, A, 4, H, W
        )
```

```
        box_regression_flattened.append(box_regression_per_level)

    box_cls = torch.cat(box_cls_flattened, dim = 1).flatten(0, -2)
      box_regression = torch.cat(box_regression_flattened, dim =
1).reshape(-1, 4)

    # box_cls:[N*levels*A*H*W,1]
    # box_regression:[N*levels*A*H*W,4]
    return box_cls, box_regression
```

Observing the above code, it is not difficult to find that the forward() function is the core part. We can extract its core steps and turn them into the following pseudocode:

```
class RegionProposalNetwork(torch.nn.Module):
    "...omitted parts of the module..."
     def forward(self, images, features, targets = None):
       "...omitted parts of the module..."
      ###---- Code module shared by training and testing phases ----###
       # Predict the confidence of each anchor box whether contains an
object and
        # the coordinate offsets of the matched ground-truth bounding
box relative to
        # that anchor box
objectness, pred_bbox_deltas = self.head(features)
        # Generate the coordinates of the anchor boxes
anchors = self.anchor_generator(images, features)
         # Decode to get the coordinates of the bounding boxes of the
region proposal
      proposals = self.box_coder.decode(pred_bbox_deltas.detach(),
anchors)
         # Filter region proposals and apply NMS to remove redundant
region proposals
          boxes, scores = self.filter_proposals(proposals, object-
ness, images.
                image_sizes, num_anchors_per_level)

        ###---- Code module used only in the training phase ----###
        if self.training:
         # Assign labels and the corresponding ground-truth bounding
boxes
        # to the anchor boxes
                labels, matched_gt_boxes = self.assign_targets_to_
anchors(anchors,
                  targets)

         # regression_targets are the coordinate offsets of the ground-
truth
           # bounding boxes relative to the matched anchor boxes
           # Encode these offsets
             regression_targets = self.box_coder.encode(matched_gt_
boxes, anchors)
           # Calculate the loss function
```

```
            loss_objectness, loss_rpn_box_reg = self.compute_
loss(objectness,
             pred_bbox_deltas, labels, regression_targets)
        losses = {
          "loss_objectness": loss_objectness,
          "loss_rpn_box_reg": loss_rpn_box_reg,
          }
          return boxes, losses
```

It is not difficult to see that both the training and testing phases of RPN require the use of the head, anchor_generator, box_coder, and filter_proposals modules. During training, the assign_targets_to_anchors and compute_loss modules are also needed. First, RPN generates $2k$ confidence scores and $4k$ bounding box coordinate offset parameters from multi-scale feature maps (head module); i.e., it predicts the confidence that the anchor box contains an object and the coordinate offset of the ground-truth bounding box relative to that anchor box. Then, PRN generates a series of anchor box coordinates of different sizes and aspect ratios (anchor_generator module), uses the predicted offsets and generated anchor boxes to decode a series of region proposals (box_coder module), and finally filters these region proposals and applies NMS filtering (filter_proposals module) to obtain high-quality region proposals for the subsequent Fast R-CNN network.

During testing, RPN directly returns the final filtered region proposals; whereas during training, it also needs to assign positive/negative labels and matched ground-truth boxes to each anchor box, and calculate the loss function based on these. We will first introduce the modules that are only needed during training and then introduce the modules that are used in both training and testing.

12.4.1 Training Module

Observe the if self.training part in the RPN code.

```
class RegionProposalNetwork(torch.nn.Module):
  "...omitted modules..."

  def forward(self, images, features, targets = None):
    "...omitted modules..."
          if self.training:
          # Ensure targets are provided during training
          assert targets is not None
        # Assign labels and the corresponding ground-truth bounding
boxes to
          # the anchor boxes
        labels, matched_gt_boxes = self.assign_targets_to_anchors
                (anchors, targets)
           # regression_targets are the coordinate offsets of the
ground-truth
          # bounding boxes relative to the matched anchor boxes
```

```
            # Encode these offsets
            regression_targets = self.box_coder.encode(matched_gt_
boxes,
                        anchors)
                  loss_objectness, loss_rpn_box_reg = self.compute_
loss(objectness,
                        pred_bbox_deltas, labels, regression_targets)
            losses = {
               "loss_objectness": loss_objectness,
               "loss_rpn_box_reg": loss_rpn_box_reg,
            }
      return boxes, losses
```

During training, the RPN first assigns positive/negative labels to each anchor box and assigns it a ground-truth bounding box (self.assign_targets_to_anchors module), then calculates the coordinate offsets of this ground-truth bounding box relative to this anchor box (self.box_coder.encode module). After this, the RPN calculates the classification loss and bounding box regression loss for each anchor box (self.compute_loss module). Let's first look at the self.assign_targets_to_anchors module.

```
class RegionProposalNetwork(torch.nn.Module):
      "...omitted modules..."
     def assign_targets_to_anchors(self, anchors, targets):
      """
     Assign positive/negative labels and coordinates of the matching
ground-truth
      bounding box to each anchor box
      Parameters:
      - anchors: List of anchor boxes, each element corresponds to a
bounding box
            of an anchor box in an image
     - targets: List of ground-truth bounding boxes, each element is
a dictionary
          structure, containing the key "boxes" and its corresponding
ground-
            truth bounding box


      Returns:
     - labels: Label of each anchor box, 0 represents negative anchor
box, 1 represents positive anchor box, -1 represents ignored
     - matched_gt_boxes: Ground-truth bounding box matched with each
anchor box
      """
      Labels = []
      matched_gt_boxes = []
                          for anchors_per_image,    targets_per_
image in zip(anchors, targets):
         gt_boxes = targets_per_image["boxes"]
         print(gt_boxes[0])
         match_quality_matrix = box_ops.box_iou(gt_boxes, anchors_
per_image)
```

```
        matched_idxs = self.proposal_matcher(match_quality_matrix)
        # Get the ground-truth bounding box matched with the positive
anchor box,
        # negative indices (-1, -2) are clamped to 0, i.e., the first
ground-
        # truth bounding box is taken as a placeholder
                matched_gt_boxes_per_image = gt_boxes[matched_
idxs.clamp(min = 0)]

        # Mark positive anchor boxes
        labels_per_image = matched_idxs > = 0
                labels_per_image = labels_per_image.to(dtype =
torch.float32)

        # Mark negative anchor boxes
        bg_indices = matched_idxs = = self.proposal_matcher
                BELOW_LOW_THRESHOLD # Default is -1
        labels_per_image[bg_indices] = torch.tensor(0.0)

        # Mark ignored anchor boxes
        inds_to_discard = matched_idxs = = self.proposal_matcher
                BETWEEN_THRESHOLDS # Default is -2
        labels_per_image[inds_to_discard] = torch.tensor(-1.0)

        labels.append(labels_per_image)
        matched_gt_boxes.append(matched_gt_boxes_per_image)
    return labels, matched_gt_boxes

# Calculate IoU
def box_iou(boxes1, boxes2):
   """
  Calculate the Intersection over Union (IoU) between the pixel sets
inside two
   groups of bounding boxes

   Parameters:
   - boxes1: The first group of bounding boxes, shape is [N,4]
   - boxes2: The second group of bounding boxes, shape is [M,4]

   Returns:
  - IoU matrix, shape is [N,M], representing the IoU of the pixel set
inside each
     bounding box in boxes1 with the pixel set inside each bounding
box in boxes2
   """
   area1 = box_area(boxes1)
   area2 = box_area(boxes2)

  # Calculate the coordinates of the top-left corner of the overlap-
ping region of
```

```
    # the two groups of bounding boxes
    lt = torch.max(boxes1[:, None, :2], boxes2[:, :2])
   # Calculate the bottom-right coordinates of the overlapping region
between two
    # sets of bounding boxes
    rb = torch.min(boxes1[:, None, 2:], boxes2[:, 2:])
   # Calculate the width and height of the overlapping region between
two sets of
    # bounding boxes
    wh = (rb - lt).clamp(min = 0)
    # Calculate the area of the overlapping region between two sets of
bounding boxes
    inter = wh[:, :, 0] * wh[:, :, 1]
    # Calculate IoU
    iou = inter / (area1[:, None] + area2 - inter)


    return iou
```

At this step, positive/negative class labels and the corresponding ground-truth bounding boxes are assigned to each anchor box. The self.proposal_matcher of RPN is defined as the Matcher class.

```
class Matcher(object):
    """
   First, find the ground-truth bounding box with the highest overlap
for each
     anchor box, where overlap is measured by the IoU between their
internal pixel
    sets
    Then, assign positive/negative class labels to the anchor boxes
based on the IoU
    values
    """
    def __init__(self, high_threshold, low_threshold,
                allow_low_quality_matches = False):
        """
        Initialize the matcher


        Parameters:
          - high_threshold (float): IoU threshold for considering an
anchor box as
                positive
      - low_threshold (float): IoU threshold for considering an anchor
box as
                negative
           - allow_low_quality_matches (bool): Whether to allow low-
quality matches
                 When True, ensures that each ground-truth bounding box
matches at
                least one anchor box
        """
```

```
        # The label to be assigned to an anchor when IoU is below the low
threshold
        self.BELOW_LOW_THRESHOLD = -1
        # The label to be assigned to an anchor when IoU is between the
two
        # thresholds
        self.BETWEEN_THRESHOLDS = -2

        # The low threshold must be less than or equal to the high
threshold
        assert low_threshold < = high_threshold

        self.high_threshold = high_threshold
        self.low_threshold = low_threshold
        self.allow_low_quality_matches = allow_low_quality_matches

    def __call__(self, match_quality_matrix):
        """
        Perform the matching process

        Parameters:
        - match_quality_matrix (Tensor): The matrix of IoU between the
internal pixel
            set of each ground-truth bounding box and each anchor box

        Returns:
        - matches (Tensor): The index of the ground-truth bounding box
matched to
          each anchor box, -1 for negative anchor boxes, -2 for ignored
anchor
            boxes
        """

        # Find the ground-truth bounding box that best matches each
anchor box
        matched_vals, matches = match_quality_matrix.max(dim = 0)

        if self.allow_low_quality_matches:
            all_matches = matches.clone()
            # Temporary value, saved before filtering indices with lower
IoU values
        else:
            all_matches = None

        below_low_threshold = matched_vals < self.low_threshold
        between_thresholds = (matched_vals > = self.low_threshold) &
                              (matched_vals < self.high_threshold)

        # Mark negative anchor boxes
```

```
        matches[below_low_threshold] = torch.tensor(self.BELOW_LOW_
THRESHOLD)
        # Mark ignored anchor boxes
          matches[between_thresholds] = torch.tensor(self.BETWEEN_
THRESHOLDS)


        if self.allow_low_quality_matches:
            assert all_matches is not None
            self.set_low_quality_matches_(matches, all_matches,
                                          match_quality_matrix)


        return matches


    def set_low_quality_matches_(self, matches, all_matches,
                                 match_quality_matrix):
        """
          A scenario may occur where the IoU between a ground-truth
bounding box's
          pixel set and all anchor boxes' pixel sets falls below the
threshold,
        implying a ground-truth box might remain unmatched.
        This function prevents such occurrences by guaranteeing every
ground-truth
        bounding box is assigned to at least one anchor box.


"""
        highest_quality_foreach_gt, _ = match_quality_matrix.max(dim
= 1)
        gt_pred_pairs_of_highest_quality = torch.nonzero(
                match_quality_matrix = = highest_quality_foreach_
gt[:, None]
        )


        pred_inds_to_update = gt_pred_pairs_of_highest_quality[:, 1]
        # Ensure that each ground-truth bounding box matches at least
one anchor box,
        # even if the IoU is below the lower threshold.
          matches[pred_inds_to_update] = all_matches[pred_inds_to_
update]
```

There is another detail to note: the ratio of positive anchor boxes to negative anchor boxes is not balanced. Usually, the number of negative anchor boxes is much more than that of positive ones. Therefore, it is necessary to balance the number of both during training. This can be achieved by controlling the ratio through sampling, as implemented below.

```
class BalancedPositiveNegativeSampler(object):
    """
    The sampler for balanced positive and negative anchor boxes.
    """
```

```
    def __init__(self, batch_size_per_image, positive_fraction):
        """
        Initialize the sampler.

        Parameters:
       - batch_size_per_image (int): Total number of anchor box samples
to be
              sampled from each image.
        - positive_fraction (float): The ratio of positive anchor boxes
in all
              samples.
        """
        self.batch_size_per_image = batch_size_per_image
        self.positive_fraction = positive_fraction

    def __call__(self, matched_idxs):
        # type: List[Tensor]
        """
        Perform sampling of positive/negative anchor boxes for
        each image.

        Parameters:
        - matched_idxs (List[Tensor]): List of indices of ground-truth
bounding
              boxes matched by anchor boxes for each image.

        Returns:
          - pos_idx (List[Tensor]): Indices of positive anchor boxes
sampled from each
              image.
          - neg_idx (List[Tensor]): Indices of negative anchor boxes
sampled from each
              image.
        """
        pos_idx = []
        neg_idx = []
        for matched_idxs_per_image in matched_idxs:
                # Determine positive/negative anchor boxes.
          positive = torch.nonzero(matched_idxs_per_image > = 1, as_
tuple = False).
                        squeeze(1)
          negative = torch.nonzero(matched_idxs_per_image = = 0, as_
tuple = False).
                        squeeze(1)

            # Determine the number of positiv/negative anchor boxes to
be
            # sampled.
            num_pos = min(positive.numel(), int(self.batch_size_per_
image * self.
                      positive_fraction))
```

```
    num_neg = min(negative.numel(), self.batch_size_per_image -
num_pos)

        # Randomly sample positive/negative anchor boxes.
         perm1 = torch.randperm(positive.numel(), device = posi-
tive.device)
                    [:num_pos]
         perm2 = torch.randperm(negative.numel(), device = nega-
tive.device)
                    [:num_neg]

        pos_idx_per_image = positive[perm1]
        neg_idx_per_image = negative[perm2]

# Create indices for positive/negative anchor boxes
         pos_idx_per_image_mask = torch.zeros_like(matched_idxs_
per_image,
                                        dtype = torch.bool)
         neg_idx_per_image_mask = torch.zeros_like(matched_idxs_
per_image,
                                        dtype = torch.bool)

        pos_idx_per_image_mask[pos_idx_per_image] = True
        neg_idx_per_image_mask[neg_idx_per_image] = True

        pos_idx.append(pos_idx_per_image_mask)
        neg_idx.append(neg_idx_per_image_mask)

        return pos_idx, neg_idx
```

After understanding the above process, it will be easier for us to understand the compute_loss module.

```
class RegionProposalNetwork(torch.nn.Module):
   "…omitted some modules…"

   def compute_loss(self, objectness, pred_bbox_deltas, labels,
               regression_targets):
     """
     Compute RPN loss, including the positive/negative classifica-
tion loss and

     bounding box regression loss of each anchor box
     Parameters:
      - objectness: Confidence of the presence of an object in the
anchor box,
        i.e., positive/negative classification scores of the anchor
box,
          shape is [total number of anchor boxes, 1]
```

```
        - pred_bbox_deltas: Predicted coordinate offsets of the
bounding box, shape
            is [total number of anchor boxes, 4]
        - labels: Category labels of the anchor boxes, 0 for negative
anchor boxes, 1
            for positive anchor boxes, shape is [total number of anchor
boxes]
        - regression_targets: Coordinate offsets of the ground-truth
bounding box
            relative to the anchor box it matches, shape is [total
number of
            anchor boxes, 4]

    Returns:
        - objectness_loss: Binary cross-entropy loss of positive/
negative
            classification
        - box_loss: L1 loss of bounding box regression
    """
    # Use balanced positive and negative anchor box sampler to select
samples for
    # loss calculation
    sampled_pos_inds, sampled_neg_inds = self.fg_bg_
sampler(labels)

    # Convert sampled positive and negative anchor box indices to
one-dimensional
    # Tensor
    sampled_pos_inds = torch.nonzero(torch.cat(sampled_pos_
inds, dim = 0),
                                     as_tuple = False).squeeze(1)
    sampled_neg_inds = torch.nonzero(torch.cat(sampled_neg_
inds, dim = 0),
                                     as_tuple = False).squeeze(1)

    # Merge positive and negative anchor box indices
    sampled_inds = torch.cat([sampled_pos_inds, sampled_neg_
inds], dim = 0)

    # Flatten score prediction for indexing
    objectness = objectness.flatten()

    # Merge positive/negative labels and regression offsets
    labels = torch.cat(labels, dim = 0)
    regression_targets = torch.cat(regression_targets, dim = 0)

    # Calculate bounding box regression loss of the anchor box, only
for positive
    # anchor boxes
    box_loss = F.l1_loss(pred_bbox_deltas[sampled_pos_inds],
```

```
                         regression_targets[sampled_pos_inds],
                         reduction = "sum") / sampled_inds.numel()

        # Calculate classification loss, for selected positive and
negative anchor
        # boxes
        objectness_loss = F.binary_cross_entropy_with_logits(
                     objectness[sampled_inds], labels[sampled_inds])

        return objectness_loss, box_loss
```

Next, we introduce the code module shared by the RPN training and testing stages.

12.4.2 Head Module

The head module is encapsulated in the RPNHead class.

```
class RPNHead(nn.Module):
    """
    The head of RPN, responsible for positive/negative classification
and bounding
    box regression of anchor boxes in the feature map
    """

def __init__(self, in_channels, num_anchors):
        """
        Initialize the RPN head module

        Parameters:
        - in_channels: Number of channels in the input feature map
        - num_anchors: Number of anchor boxes at each location
        """

        super(RPNHead, self).__init__()
        # Maintain the spatial resolution of the feature map
        self.conv = nn.Conv2d(
        in_channels, in_channels, kernel_size = 3, stride = 1, padding
= 1
        )

        # Perform positive/negative classification and bounding box
regression of
        # anchor boxes separately

            # Category prediction layer, used for positive/negative
classification of
```

```
    # anchor boxes. num_anchors is not multiplied by 2 because binary
cross
      # entropy loss is used, and the output of each anchor box is a
single score
    self.cls_logits = nn.Conv2d(in_channels, num_anchors, kernel_
size = 1,
                                stride = 1)

    # Bounding box regression layer, used to predict the 4 coordinate
offset
      # parameters of the anchor box
      self.bbox_pred = nn.Conv2d(
        in_channels, num_anchors * 4, kernel_size = 1, stride = 1
      )

      # Initialize convolution layer parameters
         for l in self.children():
      # Initialize weights with a normal distribution with a standard
        # deviation of 0.01
        torch.nn.init.normal_(l.weight, std = 0.01)
        # Initialize bias to 0
        torch.nn.init.constant_(l.bias, 0)

def forward(self, x):
        """
Forward propagation

        Parameters:
      - x: List of input multi-scale feature maps, the shape of the
feature map is
          [B, C, H, W]

      Returns:
        - logits: Classification scores of each anchor box in each
feature map, shape
          is [List[B, k, H, W]]
     - bbox_reg: Regression coordinate offsets of each anchor box in
each feature
          map, shape is [List[B, k*4, H, W]]
      """
      logits = []
      bbox_reg = []
      for feature in x:
          # Apply the convolution layer and activation layer to the
input feature
        # map to get the output feature map
        t = F.relu(self.conv(feature))
       # Based on the output feature map, perform classification and
bounding
        # box regression for each anchor box
```

```
            # Classification score, one score for each anchor box
            logits.append(self.cls_logits(t))
            # Coordinate offsets, 4 values for each anchor box
            bbox_reg.append(self.bbox_pred(t))

        return logits, bbox_reg
```

From the code, we can see that the RPN assumes that there are k anchor boxes (where k = num_anchors) at each location in a feature map of size $H \times W$ and predicts the classification scores and coordinate offsets of bounding box regression for these $k \times H \times W$ anchor boxes in total. Here, H and W are the height and width of the feature map, respectively. So how does the RPN generate the coordinates of the anchor boxes? This requires the use of the anchor_generator module.

12.4.3 Anchor Generator Module

The anchor generator module is encapsulated in the AnchorGenerator class.

```
class AnchorGenerator(nn.Module):
    """
    Anchor box coordinate generator, used to generate coordinates of
anchor boxes of
    different sizes and aspect ratios
    """
    def __init__(
        self,
        sizes = ((128, 256, 512),),
        aspect_ratios = ((0.5, 1.0, 2.0),),
    ):
        """
        Initialize the anchor box generator

        Parameters:
        - sizes: The sizes of the anchor boxes
        - aspect_ratios: The aspect ratios of the anchor boxes
        """

        super(AnchorGenerator, self).__init__()

        # Ensure sizes and aspect_ratios are in the correct format for
subsequent
        # processing
            if not isinstance(sizes[0], (list, tuple)):
           # Convert each size into tuple form
           sizes = tuple((s,) for s in sizes)
        # Convert to [(128,), (256,), (512,)]
```

```
        if not isinstance(aspect_ratios[0], (list, tuple)):
            # Copy the same aspect ratio for each size
            aspect_ratios = (aspect_ratios,) * len(sizes)

        # Each size must correspond to an aspect ratio setting
            assert len(sizes) == len(aspect_ratios)

        self.sizes = sizes
        self.aspect_ratios = aspect_ratios

          # Store the anchor boxes under each size and aspect ratio
combination
        self.cell_anchors = [
         self.generate_anchors(size, aspect_ratio) for size, aspect_
ratio in
                  zip(sizes, aspect_ratios)
        ]

    def generate_anchors(self, scales, aspect_ratios, dtype =
torch.float32,
                   device = "cpu"):
        """
      Generate a set of anchor box coordinates, with their centers at
(0,0)
        """
          scales = torch.as_tensor(scales, dtype = dtype, device =
device)
        # aspect_ratios are the aspect ratios
            aspect_ratios = torch.as_tensor(aspect_ratios, dtype =
dtype, device = device)

            # When h_ratios = sqrt(aspect_ratios), w_ratios = 1/
sqrt(aspect_ratios)
        # h_ratios/w_ratios == aspect_ratios
        # Calculate the width and height of the anchor box based on the
aspect ratio
        h_ratios = torch.sqrt(aspect_ratios)
        w_ratios = 1 / h_ratios

        ws = (w_ratios[:, None] * scales[ None, :]).view(-1)
        hs = (h_ratios[:, None] * scales[ None, :]).view(-1)

        # x 1,y1, x 2,y2 (top left and bottom right corners), with the
center point
        # at (0,0)
         # Generate the coordinates of the anchor box centered at the
origin
        base_anchors = torch.stack([-ws, -hs, ws, hs], dim = 1) / 2
        return base_anchors.round()
```

```
    def set_cell_anchors(self, dtype, device):
        # Initialize the anchor boxes
        self.cell_anchors = [cell_anchor.to(dtype = dtype, device =
device)
                             for cell_anchor in self.cell_anchors]


    def grid_anchors(self, grid_sizes, strides):
        """
        Coordinates of the anchor boxes generated at each position of
the feature map


        Parameters:
        - grid_size: Spatial resolution of the feature map
        - strides: Step size for moving the center point of the anchor
box
        """
        anchors = []
      # Import the generated anchor boxes of each size and aspect ratio
combination
        cell_anchors = self.cell_anchors


        # Check if the anchor box is empty
        assert cell_anchors is not None


                for size, stride, base_anchors in zip(grid_
sizes, strides, cell_anchors):
            grid_height, grid_width = size
            stride_height, stride_width = stride
            device = base_anchors.device


            # Calculate the coordinate offset of the anchor box centers
at all
            # positions
                shifts_x = torch.arange(0, grid_width, dtype =
torch.float32, device =
                        device) * stride_width
                shifts_y = torch.arange(0, grid_height, dtype =
torch.float32, device =
                        device) * stride_height
            shift_y, shift_x = torch.meshgrid(shifts_y, shifts_x)


            shift_x = shift_x.reshape(-1)
            shift_y = shift_y.reshape(-1)
            shifts = torch.stack((shift_x, shift_y, shift_x, shift_
y), dim = 1)


           # shifts are offsets: indicating the center of the anchor box
is moved
            # from (0,0) to (shift_x,shift_y)
            # Move the anchor box to all positions
```

```
                anchors.append((shifts.view(-1, 1, 4) + base_
anchors.view(1, -1, 4))
                   reshape(-1, 4))

        return anchors

    def forward(self, image_list, feature_maps):
        """
        Based on the input image list and their corresponding feature
map lists,
       generate the coordinates of the anchor boxes in the feature maps
for all
        images.

        Parameters:
        - image_list: Input image list
        - feature_maps: Feature map list

        Return:
        - anchors: List of anchor box coordinates
        """

        # Spatial resolution of the feature map
        grid_sizes = list([feature_map.shape[-2:] for feature_map in
feature_maps])

        # Size of the input image
        image_size = image_list.tensors.shape[-2:]
       dtype, device = feature_maps[0].dtype, feature_maps[0].device

          # Calculate strides
         strides = [[int(image_size[0] / g[0]), int(image_size[1] /
g[1])]
                 for g in grid_sizes]
         # Generate anchor boxes of different sizes and aspect ratios
centered
        # at (0,0)
        self.set_cell_anchors(dtype, device)
         # Generate the coordinates of the anchor boxes in the feature
maps of
        # different levels
           anchors_over_all_feature_maps = self.grid_anchors(grid_
sizes, strides)

        # Merge the coordinates of the anchor boxes in the feature maps
of
        # different levels
        anchors = []
        for _ in range(len(image_list.image_sizes)):
```

```
        anchors_in_image = [anchors_per_feature_map for anchors_
per_feature_
        map in anchors_over_all_feature_maps]
        anchors.append(anchors_in_image)
      anchors = [torch.cat(anchors_per_image) for anchors_per_
image in anchors]
    return anchors
```

In this module, the aspect ratio and size of the anchor boxes need to be set. Besides, the coordinates for a series of anchor boxes centered at each location in the feature map are generated.

In the anchor box initialization section, the region proposal network (RPN) sets the coordinates for a series of anchor boxes with different aspect ratios at the location (0,0) of the feature maps at different levels. Here, each feature map corresponds to an anchor box size, which represents the base spatial resolution size for generating the anchor box. For example, "size = 128" indicates that the base spatial resolution size for generating the anchor box is 128 pixels. The image features extracted by the backbone network are multi-scale. The deeper the feature map, the richer the semantic information it contains, and the larger the receptive field, making it more suitable for detecting large-size targets. Therefore, anchor boxes with larger base spatial resolution are set in the deepest feature map of the network. As the network level becomes shallower, the base spatial resolution of the set anchor boxes gradually decreases. In practice, the RPN sets the anchor box sizes from large to small as 512 pixels, 256 pixels, and 128 pixels. The aspect_ratios control the shape of the generated anchor boxes. In the code, the size of the anchor box can be directly multiplied by the $\sqrt{\text{aspect\_ratios}}$ and $\frac{1}{\sqrt{\text{aspect\_ratios}}}$ to get the height and width of the anchor boxes of different shapes. For example, when the spatial resolution for generating the anchor box is 32 pixels, and the selected aspect_ratios is 0.5, the height and width of the generated anchor box are 23 pixels and 45 pixels, respectively.

After generating the anchor boxes at location (0,0), the center of the anchor box needs to be moved to other locations of the feature map to generate all the anchor box coordinates for this feature map. The challenge here lies in mapping the positions in the feature map to their corresponding locations in the input image. The core code is as follows:

```
shifts_x = torch.arange(0, grid_width, dtype =
torch.float32, device = device) *
        stride_width
shifts_y = torch.arange(0, grid_height, dtype =
torch.float32, device = device) *
        stride_height
shift_y, shift_x = torch.meshgrid(shifts_y, shifts_x)
```

Here, grid_width and grid_height are the width and height of the feature map, respectively; stride_width and stride_height are stride parameters, defined as the width of the input image divided by the width of the feature map and the height of the input image divided by the height of the feature map, respectively. They represent the distance moved in the original image corresponding to the distance moved in the current feature map by one grid along the x-axis or y-axis direction. For example, if the spatial resolution of the input image is 8 pixels × 8 pixels, and the spatial resolution of the feature map is 2 pixels × 2 pixels, the values of stride_width and stride_width can be calculated as 4, indicating that moving 1 pixel in the feature map in any direction corresponds to moving 4 pixels in the input image in that direction. Specifically, the position coordinates in the feature map are defined as (0,0), (0,1), (1,0), and (1,1), and define that the position (0,0) corresponds to the position (0,0) in the input image. When the center of the anchor box moves from (0,0) to (0,1), its position in the input image moves from (0,0) to (0,4). It is not difficult to conclude that the center points of the anchor boxes generated at (0,0), (0,1), (1,0), and (1,1) of this feature map correspond to the positions (0,0), (0,4), (4,0), and (4,4) in the input image, respectively. Through the above analysis, it can be known that the coordinates of the anchor box are actually determined in the input image based on the correspondence between the feature map and the input image. Therefore, the coordinates of the anchor box are defined in the coordinate system of the input image.

So far, the RPN has generated the coordinates of the anchor boxes at each grid point in the feature map and predicted the coordinate offsets between each anchor box and its matched ground-truth bounding box in the head module. So, how to use the coordinates of the anchor box and the predicted coordinate offsets to get the coordinates of the bounding box of the region proposal? This requires the use of the box_coder module. ###

12.4.4 Box_Coder Module

The box_coder module is used in the forward() function of the RegionProposalNetwork class.

```
# Decode to get the coordinates of the bounding box of the region
proposal
proposals   =   self.box_coder.decode(pred_bbox_deltas.detach(),
anchors)


# Encode the coordinates of the ground-truth bounding box
regression_targets   =   self.box_coder.encode(matched_gt_boxes,
anchors)
```

Let's take a look at how the box_coder module is implemented.

```
class BoxCoder(object):
    """
    This module encodes and decodes the coordinates of bounding boxes
    """

    def __init__(self, weights, bbox_xform_clip = math.log(1000. /
16)):
        """
```

```
        Initialize the bounding box coordinate encoder

        Parameters:
       - weights: Weights used during encoding and decoding to balance
the impact of
             bounding boxes of different sizes
         - bbox_xform_clip: Maximum value to limit coordinate offset
during encoding
             and decoding, preventing instability caused by excessive
offset
        """

        self.weights = weights
        self.bbox_xform_clip = bbox_xform_clip

    # encoder module
    ######################################################
    def encode(self, reference_boxes, proposals):
        boxes_per_image = [len(b) for b in reference_boxes]
        reference_boxes = torch.cat(reference_boxes, dim = 0)
        proposals = torch.cat(proposals, dim = 0)
        targets = self.encode_single(reference_boxes, proposals)

        return targets.split(boxes_per_image, 0)

    def encode_single(self, reference_boxes, proposals):
        """
        Encoding: Calculate the coordinate offset of the bounding box
(proposals)
        relative to the reference bounding box (reference_boxes)
        Parameters:
        - reference_boxes: Coordinates of the reference bounding box
        - proposals: Coordinates of the bounding box to be encoded

        Returns:
        - Encoded offset
        """
        dtype = reference_boxes.dtype
        device = reference_boxes.device
       weights = torch.as_tensor(self.weights, dtype = dtype, device
= device)
        # Call the encode_boxes function to encode the bounding box
        targets = encode_boxes(reference_boxes, proposals, weights)
        return targets

    # decoder module
    ######################################################
    def decode(self, rel_codes, boxes):
        assert isinstance(boxes, (list, tuple))
        assert isinstance(rel_codes, torch.Tensor)
```

```
        boxes_per_image = [b.size(0) for b in boxes]

        concat_boxes = torch.cat(boxes, dim = 0)
        box_sum = 0

        for val in boxes_per_image:
        box_sum += val

        if box_sum > 0:
          rel_codes = rel_codes.reshape(box_sum, -1)

          # Decode the coordinate offset according to the reference
bounding box to get
        # the coordinates of the predicted bounding box
       pred_boxes = self.decode_single(rel_codes.reshape(box_sum, -
1),
                                        concat_boxes)

        if box_sum > 0:
          pred_boxes = pred_boxes.reshape(box_sum, -1, 4)

        return pred_boxes

    def decode_single(self, rel_codes, boxes):
        """
        Decoding: Calculate the coordinates of the predicted bounding
box based on
      the coordinates of the reference bounding box and the coordinate
offset
        """
        boxes = boxes.to(rel_codes.dtype)

        widths = boxes[:, 2] - boxes[:, 0]
        heights = boxes[:, 3] - boxes[:, 1]
        ctr_x = boxes[:, 0] + 0.5 * widths
        ctr_y = boxes[:, 1] + 0.5 * heights

        wx, wy, ww, wh = self.weights
        dx = rel_codes[:, 0::4] / wx
        dy = rel_codes[:, 1::4] / wy
        dw = rel_codes[:, 2::4] / ww
        dh = rel_codes[:, 3::4] / wh

          # The clamp here is to remove excessively large predicted
bounding boxes, but
         # it cannot guarantee that the predicted bounding boxes will
not exceed the
        # border
```

```
        # Therefore, filter_proposal is used later to remove out-of-
border boxes
        dw = torch.clamp(dw, max = self.bbox_xform_clip)
        dh = torch.clamp(dh, max = self.bbox_xform_clip)

        pred_ctr_x = dx * widths[:, None] + ctr_x[:, None]
        pred_ctr_y = dy * heights[:, None] + ctr_y[:, None]
        pred_w = torch.exp(dw) * widths[:, None]
        pred_h = torch.exp(dh) * heights[:, None]

        # Convert to (×1,y1, × 2,y2) format
        pred_boxes1 = pred_ctr_x - torch.tensor(0.5, dtype = pred_
ctr_x.dtype) *
                  pred_w
        pred_boxes2 = pred_ctr_y - torch.tensor(0.5, dtype = pred_
ctr_y.dtype) *
                  pred_h
        pred_boxes3 = pred_ctr_x + torch.tensor(0.5, dtype = pred_
ctr_x.dtype) *
                  pred_w
        pred_boxes4 = pred_ctr_y + torch.tensor(0.5, dtype = pred_
ctr_y.dtype) *
                  pred_h
        pred_boxes = torch.stack((pred_boxes1, pred_boxes2, pred_
boxes3,
                         pred_boxes4), dim = 2).flatten(1)

        return pred_boxes

    ##########################################################

@torch.jit.script.
def encode_boxes(reference_boxes, proposals, weights):
    """
     Encoding: Calculate the offset between an anchor box and its
matched ground-truth
    bounding box
    """
     # These are the weight vectors at __init__, which are used to
balance the
   # bounding box regression loss and classification loss, to prevent
the regression
    # loss from being much smaller than the classification loss
    #

    Wx = weights[0]
    wy = weights[1]
    ww = weights[2]
    wh = weights[3]
```

```
    proposals_x1 = proposals[:, 0].unsqueeze(1)
    proposals_y1 = proposals[:, 1].unsqueeze(1)
    proposals_x2 = proposals[:, 2].unsqueeze(1)
    proposals_y2 = proposals[:, 3].unsqueeze(1)

    reference_boxes_x1 = reference_boxes[:, 0].unsqueeze(1)
    reference_boxes_y1 = reference_boxes[:, 1].unsqueeze(1)
    reference_boxes_x2 = reference_boxes[:, 2].unsqueeze(1)
    reference_boxes_y2 = reference_boxes[:, 3].unsqueeze(1)

    ex_widths = proposals_x2 - proposals_x1
    ex_heights = proposals_y2 - proposals_y1
    ex_ctr_x = proposals_x1 + 0.5 * ex_widths
    ex_ctr_y = proposals_y1 + 0.5 * ex_heights

    gt_widths = reference_boxes_x2 - reference_boxes_x1
    gt_heights = reference_boxes_y2 - reference_boxes_y1
    gt_ctr_x = reference_boxes_x1 + 0.5 * gt_widths
    gt_ctr_y = reference_boxes_y1 + 0.5 * gt_heights

    ttargets_dx = wx * (gt_ctr_x - ex_ctr_x) / ex_widths
    ttargets_dy =    wy * (gt_ctr_y - ex_ctr_y) / ex_heights
targets_dh = wh * torch.log(gt_heights / ex_heights)
    targets_dw = ww * torch.log(gt_widths / ex_widths)

        targets  =  torch.cat((targets_dx, targets_dy, targets_
dw, targets_dh), dim = 1)
    return targets

#######################################################
```

During the training phase of RPN for bounding box regression, it is necessary to calculate the coordinate offset between each anchor box and its matched the ground-truth bounding box. This process is referred to as "encoding", as illustrated by "Encoding" in Fig. 12.11. During the inference phase of the RPN, the RPNHead first predicts the objectness scores and the bounding box coordinate offsets for each anchor box at every grid location. Then, based on these predicted bounding box coordinate offsets and the coordinates of the corresponding anchor boxes, the coordinates of the predicted bounding boxes are obtained. This process is referred to as "decoding", as illustrated by "Decoding" in Fig. 12.11, where $\boldsymbol{t}$ represents the predicted offset. In the decoding process, the coordinates of the anchor box itself are fixed, which is why the anchor box is called an "anchor" box.

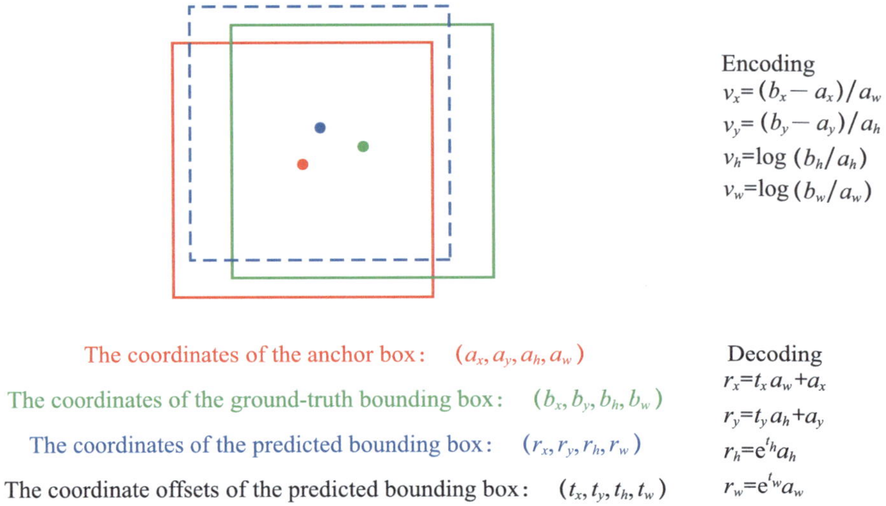

Fig. 12.11 Encoding and decoding of bounding box coordinates

Observing the decode_single part in box_coder:

```
pred_ctr_x = dx * widths[:, None] + ctr_x[:, None]
pred_ctr_y = dy * heights[:, None] + ctr_y[:, None]
pred_h = torch.exp(dh) * heights[:, None]
pred_w = torch.exp(dw) * widths[:, None ]
```

It can be found that these four lines of code correspond to the four formulas in Fig. 12.11 for decoding.

In addition, we will find that the variable passed in the RegionProposalNetwork is pred_bbox_deltas.detach().

```
proposals = self.box_coder.decode(pred_bbox_
deltas.detach(), anchors)
```

This is because Faster R-CNN uses a four-step alternating training method to train the model. When starting to train Fast R-CNN, it freezes RPN to keep its parameters unchanged.

At this point, the RPN obtains a series of region proposals by decoding. Finally, the RPN uses the filter_proposal module to screen these region proposals, obtaining high-quality region proposals which are then passed to the Fast R-CNN.

12.4.5 Filter_Proposal Module

The filter_proposal module filters the obtained region proposals, mainly including the following steps:

(1) Sort the region proposals in descending order according to the confidence of containing the target, and select the top pre_nms_topn region proposals.
(2) Crop the region proposals that exceed the image boundary.
(3) Remove region proposals with too small area.
(4) Perform NMS to remove redundant region proposals.
(5) Sort the results of NMS in descending order according to the confidence, and output the top post_nms_topn region proposals.

```
class RegionProposalNetwork(torch.nn.Module):
   "...omitted parts of the module..."


       def filter_proposals(self, proposals, objectness, image_
shapes, num_
                     anchors_per_level):
      """
      Filter region proposals according to confidence, perform NMS,
and ensure that
      candidate regions do not exceed image borders


      Parameters:
      - proposals: region proposals
     - objectness: confidence of each region proposal containing the
target
      - image_shapes: dimensions of each image, in list form
     - num_anchors_per_level: number of anchor boxes in feature maps
of different
          levels, in list form
      """
      num_images = proposals.shape[0]
      device = proposals.device


      objectness = objectness.detach()
      objectness = objectness.reshape(num_images, -1)
      levels = [
        torch.full((n,), idx, dtype = torch.int64, device = device)
         for idx, n in enumerate(num_anchors_per_level)
         ]
      levels = torch.cat(levels, 0).
      levels = levels.reshape(1, -1).expand_as(objectness)


     # Sort the region proposals generated on the feature map output
from the same
      # level of the backbone network in descending order according
to the
```

```
    # confidence
      # Select up to the top pre_nms_topn (default 2000) region
proposals
    # Return the index
    top_n_idx = self._get_top_n_idx(objectness, num_anchors_per_
level)
    image_range = torch.arange(num_images, device = device)
    batch_idx = image_range[:, None]

    objectness = objectness[batch_idx, top_n_idx]
    levels = levels[batch_idx, top_n_idx]
    proposals = proposals[batch_idx, top_n_idx]

    final_scores = []
    final_boxes = []
    for boxes, scores, lvl, img_shape in zip(proposals, objectness,
                                levels, image_shapes):
        # Prevent region proposals from going out of bounds
        boxes = box_ops.clip_boxes_to_image(boxes, img_shape)
        # Remove region proposals that are too small
        keep = box_ops.remove_small_boxes(boxes, self.min_size)
        boxes, scores, lvl = boxes[keep], scores[keep], lvl[keep]

        # Remove region proposals with too low confidence
        keep = torch.where(scores > = self.score_thresh)[0]
        boxes, scores, lvl = boxes[keep], scores[keep], lvl[keep]

        # Perform NMS operation, note that here the region proposals
generated on
        # the feature map output from different levels of the backbone
network
        # are processed independently
        # The returned keep is the index sorted in descending order
of confidence
        keep = box_ops.batched_nms(boxes, scores, lvl, self.nms_
thresh)

        # Return up to the top post_nms_topn (default 2000) region
proposals
        # If the number of bbox is less than post_nms_topn after NMS,
return all
        keep = keep[:self.post_nms_top_n()]
        boxes, scores = boxes[keep], scores[keep]
        final_boxes.append(boxes)
        final_scores.append(scores)
    return final_boxes, final_scores

  def _get_top_n_idx(self, objectness, num_anchors_per_level):
    """
     Select the top pre_nms_top_n bounding boxes with the highest
confidence in
```

```
        each level
        """
        r = []
        offset = 0
        for ob in objectness.split(num_anchors_per_level, 1):
         # Sort the region proposals generated on the feature map output
from
            # different levels of the backbone network independently
            # ob is a tensor(B,H*W*A)


            num_anchors = ob.shape[1]
            pre_nms_top_n = min(self.pre_nms_top_n(), num_anchors)
            # Region proposals generated on the feature map output from
different
            # levels of the backbone network
             # Sorted in descending order of confidence, select the top
pre_nms_top_n
            # region proposals
            # If the number is less than pre_nms_top_n, return all
            # Record the index
            _, top_n_idx = ob.topk(pre_nms_top_n, dim = 1)
            r.append(top_n_idx + offset)
            offset += num_anchors


                # Return index


                return torch.cat(r, dim = 1)


# Define the batched_nms function outside the class
def batched_nms(boxes, scores, idxs, iou_threshold):
    """
    Perform batched Non-Maximum Suppression (NMS)


    Parameters:
    - boxes: Predicted bounding boxes
     - scores: Classification scores of the predicted bounding boxes
(i.e., confidence
    of containing the target)
     - idxs: Feature level or category index of the predicted bounding
boxes
    - iou_threshold: IoU threshold in NMS
    """
    if boxes.numel() == 0:
            return torch.empty((0,), dtype = torch.int64, device =
boxes.device)
    max_coordinate = boxes.max()
    # idxs have different meanings in rpn and roi_head
    offsets = idxs.to(boxes) * (max_coordinate + 1)


     # Transform the coordinates of the region proposals, shift the
region proposals
```

```
    boxes_for_nms = boxes + offsets[:, None]

    # The returned index is sorted in descending order of scores
    keep = nms(boxes_for_nms, scores, iou_threshold)
    return keep
```

It should be noted that when performing the filtering operation on the region proposals generated in the first step of the above code block, the operation is performed on region proposals located on the feature maps output from the same level of the backbone network. In other words, the region proposals generated from different levels of feature maps are independent of each other. In addition, the values of pre_nms_topn and post_nms_topn are different during training and testing, generally 1000 during testing and 2000 during training. This is easy to understand, as the model needs to balance speed during testing, so fewer region proposals are selected, while more samples need to be trained during training, so more region proposals are selected.

12.5 Running Code Example

Due to the extensive codebase of Faster R-CNN, we will directly call the relevant interfaces for demonstration. First, import the necessary packages and use the ResNet50 pretrained on the MS COCO dataset as the backbone network.

```
import os
import numpy as np
import functools
import matplotlib.pyplot as plt
import cv2
import torch
import torchvision
from torchvision.models.detection.faster_rcnn import FastRCN-
NPredictor
! pip install -U 'git + https://github.com/MS COCOdataset/
MS COCOapi.git#\
   subdirectory = PythonAPI'
! git clone https://github.com/pytorch/vision.git
! cd vision;cp references/detection/utils.py../
! cp references/detection/transforms.py../
! cp references/detection/MS COCO_eval.py../
! cp references/detection/engine.py../
! cp references/detection/MS COCO_utils.py ../

# Load the model, pretrained on MS COCO dataset
model = torchvision.models.detection.fasterrcnn_resnet50_
fpn(pretrained = 'MS COCO')
num_classes = 21
in_features = model.roi_heads.box_predictor.cls_score.in_
features
```

```
model.roi_heads.box_predictor = FastRCNNPredictor(in_features,
num_classes)


device = torch.device('cuda' if torch.cuda.is_available() else
'cpu').
model.to(device)


# Initialize optimizer and learning rate
params = [p for p in model.parameters() if p.requires_grad]
optimizer = torch.optim.SGD(params, lr = 0.001, weight_decay =
0.0005)
lr_scheduler = torch.optim.lr_scheduler.StepLR(optimizer, step_
size = 5, gamma = 0.1)


WEIGHTS_FILE = "../input/fasterrcnn/faster_rcnn_state.pth"
model.load_state_dict(torch.load(WEIGHTS_FILE))
< All keys matched successfully >
```

Next, write the code for model testing.

```
# Test the model
def obj_detector(img):
   img = cv2.imread(img, cv2.IMREAD_COLOR)
   img = cv2.cvtColor(img, cv2.COLOR_BGR2RGB).astype(np.float32)
   # Import and process the image
   img / = 255.0
   img = torch.from_numpy(img)
   img = img.unsqueeze(0)
   img = img.permute(0,3,1,2)


model.eval()


   # Set the threshold
   detection_threshold = 0.70


   img = list(im.to(device) for im in img)
   output = model(img)


   for i, im in enumerate(img):
      boxes = output[i]['boxes'].data.cpu().numpy()
      scores = output[i]['scores'].data.cpu().numpy()
      labels = output[i]['labels'].data.cpu().numpy()


      labels = labels[scores > = detection_threshold]
            boxes    =    boxes[scores     > =    detection_
threshold].astype(np.int32)
      scores = scores[scores >= detection_threshold]


      boxes[:, 2] = boxes[:, 2] - boxes[:, 0]
```

```
        boxes[:, 3] = boxes[:, 3] - boxes[:, 1]

    sample = img[0].permute(1,2,0).cpu().numpy()
    sample = np.array(sample)

    boxes = output[0]['boxes'].data.cpu().numpy()
    name = output[0]['labels'].data.cpu().numpy()
    scores = output[0]['scores'].data.cpu().numpy()

   boxes = boxes[scores > =detection_threshold].astype(np.int32)
    names = name.tolist()

    return names, boxes, sample
```

Test the model on ImageNet.

```
pred_path = "../input/imagenet/imagenet/val/"
pred_files = [os.path.join(pred_path,f) for f in os.listdir(pred_
path)]

classes = {1:'aeroplane', 2:'bicycle', 3:'bird', 4:'boat',
5:'bottle',
      6:'bus', 7:'car', 8:'cat', 9:'chair', 10:'cow',
      11:'diningtable', 12:'dog', 13:'horse', 14:'motorbike',
      15:'person', 16:'pottedplant', 17:'sheep', 18:'sofa',
      19:'train',20:'tvmonitor'}.

plt.figure(figsize = (20, 60))
image_list = [0,11,17,28]
for i, images in enumerate(pred_files):
  if i > 30:
    Break
  if i not in image_list:
    continue

  plt.subplot(10,2,image_list.index(i) + 1)

  names, boxes, sample = obj_detector(images)

  for i,box in enumerate(boxes):
    # Draw bounding boxes
   cv2.rectangle(sample, (box[0], box[1]), (box[2], box[3]), (0,
220, 0), 2)
    cv2.putText(sample, classes[names[i]], (box[0],box[1]-5),
         cv2.FONT_HERSHEY_COMPLEX, 0.7, (220,0,0), 1, cv2.LINE_
AA)

  plt.axis('off')
  plt.imshow(sample)
```

12.6 Summary

This chapter introduced the basic principles of object detection, detailed the most representative object detection models in the era of deep learning—the R-CNN series models and their development trajectory—and implemented the corresponding functions. As one of the most important basic tasks of computer vision, object detection has a wide range of industrial application scenarios, such as the assisted driving system in the automotive industry. Next, we will introduce another important task in image semantic understanding-instance segmentation.

Exercises

(1) The test time for each image in Fast R-CNN does not include the time used for region proposal extraction. Through experimental testing, how much does the test time increase when the region proposal extraction process is included compared to when it is not included?

(2) During training, feeding each anchor box into the RPN's head module produces two vectors: one representing the confidence score that the anchor box contains an object and the other representing the coordinate offsets of the matched ground-truth bounding box relative to the anchor box. If we modify the structure of the RPN's head so that it directly outputs a higher-dimensional vector for each anchor box—formed by concatenating the predictions from the original two vectors—would this enhance object detection performance? Verify through experiments.

(3) In the code implementation, the RPN generates anchor boxes with 3 different scales and aspect ratios. If anchor boxes with more scales or aspect ratios (such as 5 different scales or ratios) are used, will the performance of object detection improve? Verify through experiments.

(4) The Faster R-CNN paper mentions three other different training strategies. Read the paper and explore their differences from the four-step alternating training method adopted by Faster R-CNN, and observe the impact of different training strategies on the model's test effect through experiments.

(5) In Faster R-CNN, the coordinates of the anchor boxes are established on the coordinate system of the input image. Think carefully about whether all the anchor boxes generated by the RPN can cover the entire input image.

References

1. GIRSHICK R, DONAHUE J, DARRELL T, et al. Rich feature hierarchies for accurate object detection and semantic segmentation[C]//IEEE Conference on Computer Vision and Pattern Recognition, 2014: 580–587.
2. ALEXE B, DESELAERS T, FERRARI V. What is an object?[C]//IEEE Computer Society Conference on Computer Vision and Pattern Recognition. IEEE, 2010: 73–80.
3. GIRSHICK R. Fast R-CNN[C]//IEEE International Conference on Computer Vision, 2015: 1440–1448.
4. REN S, HE K, GIRSHICK R, et al. Faster R-CNN: Towards real-time object detection with region proposal networks[J]. Advances in Neural Information Processing Systems, 2015, 28.
5. UIJLINGS J R R, VAN DE SANDE K E A, GEVERS T, et al. Selective Search for Object Recognition[J]. International Journal of Computer Vision, 2013, 104: 154–171.

Chapter 13
Instance Segmentation

13.1 Introduction

The purpose of instance segmentation is to segment the mask of each object instance from the images. Compared with semantic segmentation, instance segmentation not only distinguishes different categories, but also distinguishes different object instances within the same category. As shown in Fig. 13.1, in the results of semantic segmentation, the labels corresponding to different sheep are the same; that is, they are all assigned to the category of "sheep", while in the results of instance segmentation, the category labels of different sheep are the same, but they have different instance numbers; compared with object detection, instance segmentation needs to further segment the mask of the object within each bounding box. Therefore, the task of instance segmentation is a combination of semantic segmentation and object detection. To describe the problem of instance segmentation in mathematical language, we define the image space $\mathbb{I}$ and the category set $\mathcal{C}$.

Given the dataset $\mathcal{D} = \{(\boldsymbol{I}^{(n)}, \boldsymbol{Y}^{(n)})\}_{n=1}^{N}$, where $\boldsymbol{I}^{(n)} \in \mathbb{I}$ is the n th image in the dataset; $\boldsymbol{Y}^{(n)} \in \{\mathcal{C} \times \mathbb{N}\}^{H^{(n)} \times W^{(n)}}$ is its corresponding instance segmentation label map, $H^{(n)}$ and $W^{(n)}$ are the height and width of the image $\boldsymbol{I}^{(n)}$, $\mathbb{N}$ is the set of natural numbers, the i th entry in the instance segmentation label map $\boldsymbol{y}_i^{(n)} = \boldsymbol{Y}^{(n)}(i) = (y_i, z_i)$ is the label corresponding to the i th pixel in the image, $y_i \in \mathcal{C}$ is the category label of this pixel, and $z_i \in \mathbb{N}$ is the instance number of the instance to which this pixel belongs. The task of instance segmentation is to learn a mapping from the image space to the instance segmentation label map space $f : \mathbb{I} \rightarrow \mathcal{Y}$ from $\mathcal{D}$, $\forall n$, $Y^{(n)} \in \mathcal{Y}$ so that for any given test image $\boldsymbol{I}$, the learned mapping function f can be used to predict the instance segmentation label map of this image: $\hat{\boldsymbol{Y}} = f(\boldsymbol{I})$.

In this chapter, we will introduce the classic deep learning-based instance segmentation method Mask R-CNN [1] and implement the corresponding instance segmentation framework.

W. Shen et al., *Hands-On Computer Vision*,
https://doi.org/10.1007/978-981-95-4835-4_13

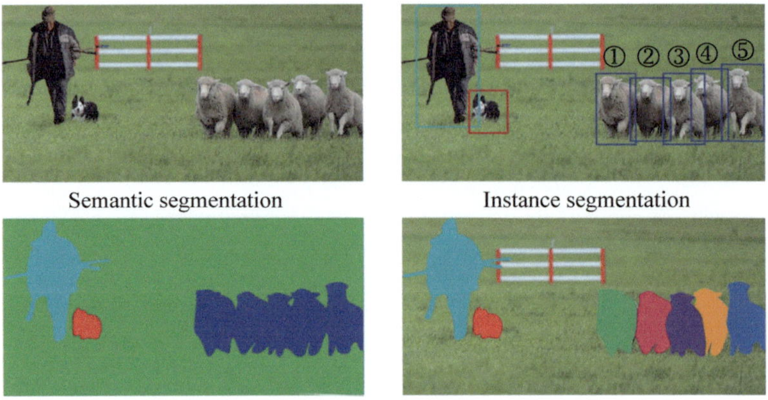

Fig. 13.1 Relationship between instance segmentation and semantic segmentation

13.2 Dataset and Metrics

Due to the close connection between instance segmentation and object detection, the datasets and metrics used for these two tasks are very similar. MS COCO is the most commonly used instance segmentation dataset, and mAP is the evaluation metric for instance segmentation. Different from object detection, the mAP here is measured by Mask IoU. Similar to Box IoU in object detection, for an object in an image, let the pixel set inside its ground-truth mask be $\mathcal{A}$, and the pixel set inside a predicted mask be $\mathcal{B}$, Mask IoU measures the overlap of the two masks by the IoU of the pixel sets inside these two masks: $\text{IoU}(\mathcal{A}, B) = \frac{\mathcal{A} \cap \mathcal{B}}{\mathcal{A} \cup \mathcal{B}}$, that is, the area of the yellow part in Fig. 13.2 divided by the area of the red part. Just like the process of calculating mAP in object detection, for each category, by adjusting the threshold of Mask IoU, we can get the PR curve of the instance segmentation result of this category. The area under the PR curve is the AP of the instance segmentation result of this category, and the average of the AP of the instance segmentation results of all categories is mAP.

13.3 Mask R-CNN

Since instance segmentation combines object detection and semantic segmentation, a very direct idea to implement instance segmentation is to first perform object detection and then perform semantic segmentation in each predicted bounding box. The famous Mask R-CNN [1] model adopts this idea, and it can be seen from the naming of the model that this is an extension of the R-CNN series of work. Mask R-CNN was also proposed by Kaiming He, Georgia Gkioxari, Piotr Dollár, and Ross Girshick, and it won the Marr Prize for the best paper at the 2017 International Conference on Computer Vision (ICCV).

Fig. 13.2 Overlap of two masks is measured by Mask IoU

The structure of Mask R-CNN is shown in Fig. 13.3. It is not difficult to find that Mask R-CNN is an extension of Faster R-CNN. There are three main differences between them:

(1) It introduces the Feature Pyramid Network (FPN) [2] alongside ResNet as the backbone network. FPN, as a method of integrating multi-scale feature information, has a very wide range of applications in the field of vision.
(2) It proposes Region of Interest Alignment (RoIAlign) to replace the RoI Pooling in Faster R-CNN as the feature extractor for target regions. RoIAlign is used to extract features from the entire region proposal and resize the resulting feature map to a fixed size for subsequent prediction.

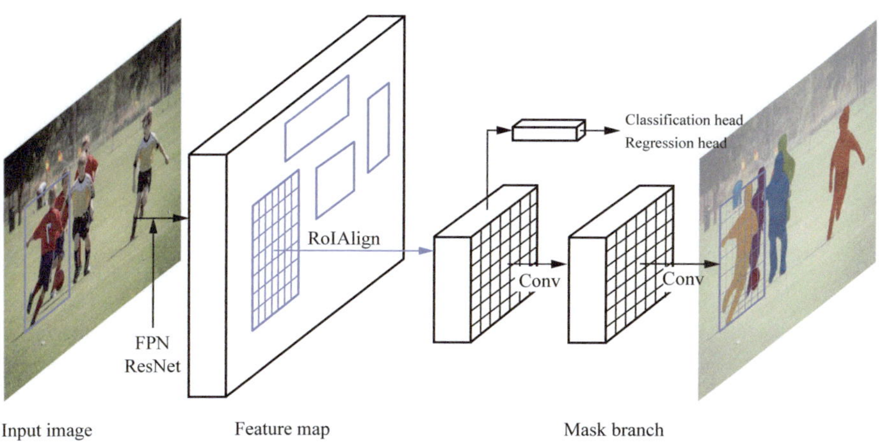

Fig. 13.3 Mask R-CNN (Illustration from reference [1])

(3) It adds a branch for predicting masks. This branch operates in parallel with the classification head and the regression head.

13.3.1 Feature Pyramid Network

Since the sizes of objects in images vary, in order to detect objects of different sizes, object detection models usually require a multi-scale detection architecture. Figure 13.4 shows four different feature extraction frameworks for object detection.

Figure 13.4a is the network architecture adopted by object detection models such as Fast R-CNN and Faster R-CNN. This architecture only performs object detection on the feature map output by the last convolutional layer of the backbone network, so the biggest problem with this architecture is that it does not perform well in detecting small objects. This is because the features of small-scale objects gradually diminish as they undergo successive downsampling through the backbone network layers. By the final layer, only a small amount of feature information remains to support the precise detection of these small objects. Figure 13.4b is the image pyramid structure commonly used in early object detection algorithms. It builds an image pyramid by scaling the input image to different scales, then the backbone network processes these different scale images to obtain feature maps of different scales, and finally performs object detection on each scale feature map. It is not difficult to see that the biggest problem with using an image pyramid is that multiple inferences of the backbone network will lead to a multiple increase in computational overhead.

The network architecture shown in Fig. 13.4c outputs feature maps from multiple levels of the backbone network and then performs independent object detection on feature maps of different spatial resolutions. Obviously, this architecture does not perform feature interaction between different layers, neither giving deep features the ability of shallow features to locate small objects nor giving shallow features

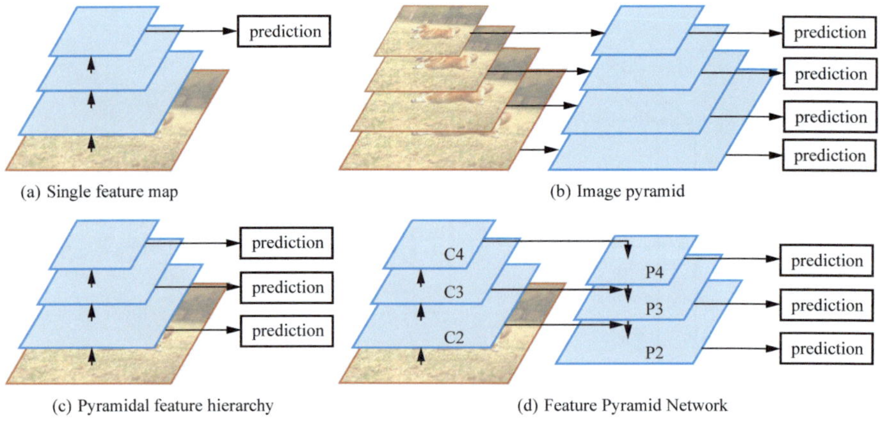

Fig. 13.4 Multi-scale feature extraction and fusion scheme

the semantic information contained in deep layers, so the improvement of object detection effect is limited.

Figure 13.4d shows the architecture of FPN. The main idea of FPN is to build a feature pyramid, integrating feature maps of different levels together, thus achieving the detection of objects of different sizes. Specifically, similar to Fig. 13.4c, FPN first uses a backbone network to obtain the feature map of each level, named from bottom to top as C2, C3, C4, where the numbers 2, 3, 4 (up to l), represent that the spatial resolution of the feature map is $\frac{1}{2^l}$ of the original image. The deep feature map obtained in this way has a small spatial resolution, and the shallow feature map has a large spatial resolution. This process is called bottom-up. After this, FPN builds a top-down path to integrate feature maps of different spatial resolutions. First, FPN directly outputs the feature map with the smallest spatial resolution [the third layer on the right side of Fig. 13.4d, top layer], denoted as P4. Then FPN upsamples P4 by a factor of 2 to make its spatial resolution consistent with the spatial resolution of the C3 feature map. Next, FPN adjusts the number of channels of C3 through 1×1 convolution to make it consistent with the number of channels of P4 and adds the two to get the integrated feature map P3 [the second layer on the right side of Fig. 13.4d]. This process is referred to as lateral connection. This fusion method is iteratively executed at each layer, with the previous layer continuously merging with the next layer, thus achieving a top-down effect. In this way, FPN can obtain features of multiple scales and integrate these features together to form P2, P3, P4, thereby improving the accuracy and efficiency of multi-scale object detection. In addition, in some methods, P4 is processed by a convolutional layer with a stride of 2 to obtain P5, P6, etc.

Let's first look at a piece of FPN code implementation, which implements the fusion process of P5 to P2, corresponding exactly to the feature maps C2 to C5 of the four levels in the ResNet network.

```
class FPN(nn.Module):
    "'
   FPN needs to initialize a list, representing the number of Bottle-
necks in each
    level of ResNet
    "'
def __init__(self, layers):
      super(FPN, self).__init__()
      # Construct C1
      self.inplanes = 64
                  self.conv1  =  nn.Conv2d(in_channels=3,  out_
channels=64, kernel_size=7,
                     stride=2, padding=3, bias=False)
      self.bn1 = nn.BatchNorm2d(64)
      self.relu = nn.ReLU(inplace=True)
                        self.maxpool   =   nn.MaxPool2d(kernel_
size=3, stride=2, padding=1)
      # Constructing C2, C3, C4, C5 from bottom to top
      self.layer1 = self._make_layer(64, layers[0])
      # The stride of the first bottleneck from c2 to c3 is 2
      self.layer2 = self._make_layer(128, layers[1], 2)
```

```
        # The stride of the first bottleneck from c3 to c4 is 2
        self.layer3 = self._make_layer(256, layers[2], 2)
        # The stride of the first bottleneck from c4 to c5 is 2
        self.layer4 = self._make_layer(512, layers[3], 2)
        # Reduce the channels of C5 to get P5
        # 1*1 convolution
        self.toplayer = nn.Conv2d(2048, 256, 1, 1, 0)
                    # Lateral connection, ensuring the consis-
tency of the number of channels in
        # each layer
        self.latlayer1 = nn.Conv2d(1024, 256, 1, 1, 0)
        self.latlayer2 = nn.Conv2d(512, 256, 1, 1, 0)
        self.latlayer3 = nn.Conv2d(256, 256, 1, 1, 0)
        # Smooth processing with 3*3 convolution
        self.smooth = nn.Conv2d(256, 256, 3, 1, 1)
    # Constructing C2 to C5
    def _make_layer(self, planes, blocks, stride=1, downsample =
None ):
                # Before residual connection, ensure the consis-
tency of spatial resolution
        # and the number of channels
                if stride != 1 or self.inplanes != Bottle-
neck.expansion * planes:
            downsample = nn.Sequential(
            nn.Conv2d(self.inplanes, Bottleneck.expansion * planes, 1,
                    stride, bias=False),
                nn.BatchNorm2d(Bottleneck.expansion * planes)
            )
        layers = []
       layers.append(Bottleneck(self.inplanes, planes, stride, down-
sample))
        # Update input and output layers
        self.inplanes = planes * Bottleneck.expansion
       # Add the number of bottlenecks according to the number of blocks
            for i in range(1, blocks):
            # The stride of the later layers is 1
            layers.append(Bottleneck(self.inplanes, planes))
                        # nn.Sequential receives an order-
dict or a series of models, the list needs
        # to be transformed by *
        return nn.Sequential(*layers)
        # Top-down upsampling
    def _upsample_add(self, x, y):
        _, _, H, W = y.shape # b c h w
        # Upsample the features by 2 times (upsample to the size of y)
and add to y
        return F.upsample(x, size=(H, W), mode='bilinear') + y
        def forward(self, x):
        # Bottom-up
        c1 = self.relu(self.bn1(self.conv1(x))) # 1/2
        c2 = self.layer1(self.maxpool(c1)) # 1/4
        c3 = self.layer2(c2) # 1/8
        c4 = self.layer3(c3) # 1/16
        c5 = self.layer4(c4) # 1/32
```

```
        # Top-down, lateral connections
        p5 = self.toplayer(c5)
        p4 = self._upsample_add(p5, self.latlayer1(c4))
        p3 = self._upsample_add(p4, self.latlayer2(c3))
        p2 = self._upsample_add(p3, self.latlayer3(c2))
        # Smoothing
        p5 = p5
        # p5 is directly output
        p4 = self.smooth(p4)
        p3 = self.smooth(p3)
        p2 = self.smooth(p2)
        return p2, p3, p4, p5
```

13.3.2 Region of Interest Alignment

In the ROI pooling layer, to obtain a fixed spatial resolution ROI feature map (such as 7 pixels × 7 pixels) and send it to the subsequent prediction branch, the vertex coordinates of each ROI's bounding box need to be quantized to integer values. In the process of dividing the ROI into 49 sub-windows (7 × 7), each sub-window's coordinates also need to be quantized, as shown in Fig. 13.5.

The reason for quantization is that after mapping the region proposal of the original image to the corresponding ROI in the image feature map, the ROI vertex coordinates may be non-integers, and the coordinates of each sub-window may also be non-integers. However, the coordinates of each position on the extracted feature map are integers. Therefore, it is usually necessary to quantize the floating-point coordinates to the nearest integer coordinates. However, since this is an approximation, it will introduce errors, which will affect the performance of the detection algorithm. To solve this problem, RoIAlign no longer uses quantization to handle non-integer coordinates, but directly uses these coordinates, as shown in Fig. 13.6.

How to handle non-integer coordinates and get the corresponding values on the feature map? Recall the previously learned bilinear interpolation, for any position in

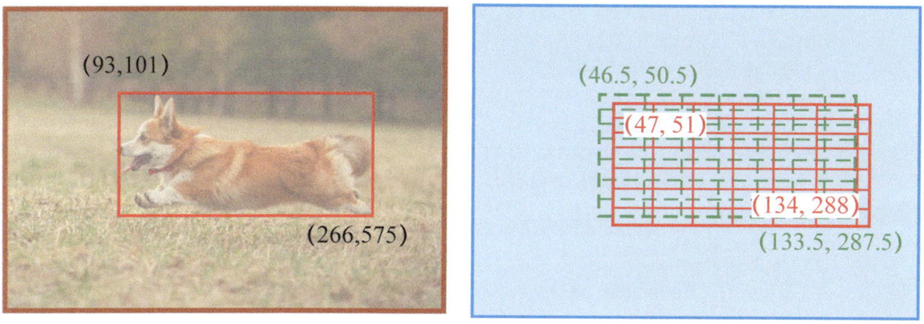

Fig. 13.5 Quantization effect in the ROI pooling process

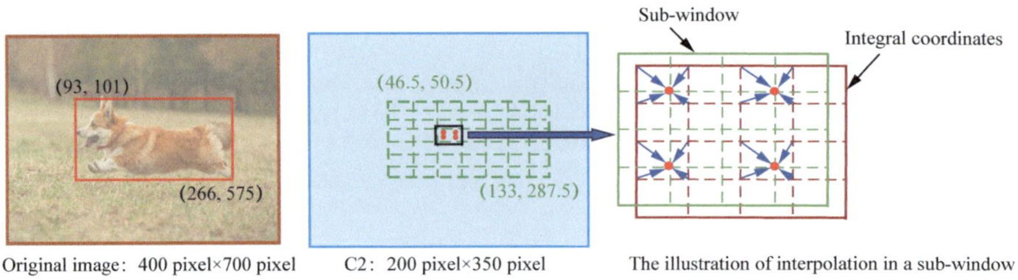

Fig. 13.6 RoIAlign uses bilinear interpolation to calculate the feature values at 4 non-integer coordinates in each sub-window

the feature map, its corresponding value can be obtained using bilinear interpolation. This process does not involve quantization; thus it will not introduce offset errors caused by coordinate quantization, which is beneficial to the improvement of instance segmentation accuracy. Similar to ROI pooling, in RoIAlign, each ROI will be evenly divided into $M \times N$ sub-windows (7×7 in the figure). Then, each sub-window is divided into 4 smaller sub-windows. The feature value at each center point of these 4 smaller sub-windows is computed via bilinear interpolation using the feature values at the nearest integer coordinates within the feature map. A max pooling or average pooling operation is then applied to these four interpolated values to obtain the feature value for the original sub-window. Finally, a spatial resolution of M pixels $\times$ N pixels ROI feature map can be obtained. Next, we will introduce how to implement RoIAlign with code.

```
import torch
import torch.nn as nn
import torch.nn.functional as F
class PyramidROIAlign(nn.Module):
    def __init__(self, pool_shape):
     super(PyramidROIAlign, self).__init__()
     self.pool_shape = tuple(pool_shape)
    def forward(self, inputs):
                 # The input includes necessary informa-
tion, such as bounding box coordinates
     # and original image information
     # Get bounding box coordinates
     boxes = inputs[0]
     # Get image metadata
     image_meta = inputs[1]
     # Get feature map information [batch, height, width, channels]
     feature_maps = inputs[2:]
     # Get the width and height of the bounding box
     y1, x1, y2, x2 = torch.split(boxes, 1, dim=2)
     h = y2 - y1
     w = x2 - x1
     # Obtain the size of the image
    image_shape = parse_image_meta(image_meta)['image_shape'][0]
   # Determine the level of the feature pyramid to which the bounding
box
```

```
        # belongs based on its size
        image_area = float(image_shape[0] * image_shape[1])
            ROI_level = torch.log2(torch.sqrt(h * w) / (224.0 /
torch.sqrt(torch.
                    tensor(image_area))))
                ROI_level = torch.clamp(4 + torch.round(ROI_
level), min=2, max=5).int()
                # Compress axis=2 from shape [batch, num_
boxes, 1] to [batch, num_boxes]
        ROI_level = torch.squeeze(ROI_level, dim=2)
        pooled = []
        box_to_level = []
       # The second to fifth levels of the network compress the original
        # image size to 1/4, 1/8, 1/16, and 1/32 respectively
          for i, level in enumerate(range(2, 6)):
            # Extract bounding boxes that match the current level
            ix = torch.nonzero(ROI_level == level, as_tuple= False )
            level_boxes = boxes[ix[:, 0], ix[:, 1]]
    # Specify which image in the batch the current bounding box belongs to
            box_to_level.append(ix)
            box_indices = ix[:, 0].int()
            # Stop gradient descent
            level_boxes = level_boxes.detach()
            box_indices = box_indices.detach()
            ##########################################
           # Use bilinear interpolation to crop and scale the feature map
            # [batch * num_boxes, pool_height, pool_width, channels]
            ##########################################
            pooled.append(
              F.interpolate(
                  roi_align(feature_maps[i], level_boxes, self.pool_
shape,
                        box_indices, method='bilinear'),
                size=self.pool_shape,
                mode='bilinear',
                align_corners=False
              )
            )
        pooled = torch.cat(pooled, dim=0)
        box_to_level = torch.cat(box_to_level, dim=0)
       box_range = torch.arange(box_to_level.size(0)).unsqueeze(1)
        box_to_level = torch.cat([box_to_level, box_range], dim=1)
        ''
        Since the ROIs extracted by RPN are corrected,
        their sizes do not strictly follow RPN_ANCHOR_SCALES,
                    this will cause the order of pooled_
features to be different from the
        original boxes, so they need to be reordered.
        ''
        # The sorting principle is to sort by batch first, then by box_
index
          sorting_tensor = box_to_level[:, 0] * 100000 + box_to_
level[:, 1]
        ix = torch.argsort(sorting_tensor, descending= False )
```

```
      # Get the index of the image
      ix = box_to_level[:, 2][ix]
      pooled = pooled[ix]
     # Reshape back to [batch, num_ROIs, POOL_SIZE, POOL_SIZE, chan-
nels]
      shape = torch.cat([torch.tensor(boxes.shape[:2]),
                    torch.tensor(pooled.shape[1:])], dim=0)
      pooled = pooled.view(*shape)
      return pooled
     def compute_output_shape(self, input_shape):
return input_shape[0][:2] + self.pool_shape + (input_shape[2][-
1], )
# Additional Helper Functions
def parse_image_meta(image_meta):
   # Placeholder function for parsing image metadata
   # Replace with actual implementation as needed
return {'image_shape': image_meta}
def log2_graph(x):
return torch.log(x) / torch.log(torch.tensor(2.0))
def    roi_align(feature_map,    boxes,    pool_shape,    box_
indices, method='bilinear'):
   # Placeholder function for ROI alignment
   # Replace with actual implementation as needed
     return  torch.zeros(len(boxes),  feature_map.size(1),  pool_
shape[0],
                    pool_shape[1])
```

After obtaining the ROI feature maps with fixed spatial resolution using the ROIAlign layer, these feature maps can be used for subsequent tasks. Similar to Faster R-CNN, Mask R-CNN uses fully connected layers in the classification and regression branches to classify the category of the ROI and perform bounding box regression. Unlike Faster R-CNN, Mask R-CNN adds a branch specifically for predicting masks, as shown in Fig. 13.3. In this branch, the size of the ROI feature map is 14 pixels $\times$ 14 pixels, which first goes through 4 convolutional layers to adapt to the segmentation task, and then undergoes 2 $\times$ upsampling to obtain a feature map with a spatial resolution of 28 pixels $\times$ 28 pixels. This is because feature maps with larger spatial resolution have a positive impact on improving segmentation accuracy. Finally, a convolutional layer is used to predict the final segmentation result. The code implementation of subsequent tasks is as follows:

```
# Category prediction and bounding box regression
def fpn_classifier_graph(ROIs, feature_maps, image_meta, pool_
size, num_classes,
                    train_bn=True, fc_layers_size=1024):
   # First, get the ROI with fixed spatial resolution
   x = PyramidROIAlign([pool_size, pool_size])([ROIs, image_meta]
+ feature_maps)
   # x: [batch, num_ROIs, POOL_SIZE, POOL_SIZE, channels]
   # POOL_SIZE is 7, the size of x is 7*7*256
   # Use convolution to integrate features
  x = TimeDistributed(nn.Conv2d(fc_layers_size, (pool_size, pool_
size),
```

```
                padding="valid"))(x)
            x    =    TimeDistributed(nn.BatchNorm2d(fc_layers_
size))(x, training=train_bn)
    x = F.relu(x)
    # x: [batch, num_ROIs, 1, 1, fc_layers_size]
    x = TimeDistributed(nn.Conv2d(fc_layers_size, (1, 1)))(x)
            x    =    TimeDistributed(nn.BatchNorm2d(fc_layers_
size))(x, training=train_bn)
    x = F.relu(x)
    # x: [batch, num_ROIs, 1, 1, fc_layers_size]
    shared = torch.squeeze(torch.squeeze(x, 3), 2)
    # x: [batch, num_ROIs, fc_layers_size]
    # Classification head
    # Predict the category of the object in the bounding box
      mrcnn_class_logits  =  TimeDistributed(nn.Linear(fc_layers_
size, num_classes))
                                    (shared)
    # mrcnn_probs: [batch, num_ROIs, num_classes]
    mrcnn_probs = F.softmax(mrcnn_class_logits, dim=-1)
    # Regression head
    # Bounding box regression
x     =     TimeDistributed(nn.Linear(fc_layers_size,     num_
classes * 4))(shared)
        x   =   TimeDistributed(nn.Linear(fc_layers_size,   num_
classes * 4))(shared)
    # mrcnn_bbox: [batch, num_ROIs, num_classes, 4]
    mrcnn_bbox = x.view(-1, x.size(1), num_classes, 4)
      return mrcnn_class_logits, mrcnn_probs, mrcnn_bbox
# Mask prediction
# Perform ROI alignment
# Semantic Segmentation Based on ROI
#----------------------------------------------#
def build_fpn_mask_graph(ROIs, feature_maps, image_meta, pool_
size, num_classes,
                train_bn=True):
    # First, align the feature maps with the ROI to get ROIs with the
same spatial
    # resolution
    x = PyramidROIAlign([pool_size, pool_size])([ROIs, image_meta]
+ feature_maps)
   # x: [batch, num_ROIs, MASK_POOL_SIZE, MASK_POOL_SIZE, channels]
    # Then, input the ROI into 4 convolutional layers
    x = TimeDistributed(nn.Conv2d(256, (3, 3), padding="same"))(x)
   x = TimeDistributed(nn.BatchNorm2d(256))(x, training=train_bn)
    x = F.relu(x)
    x = TimeDistributed(nn.Conv2d(256, (3, 3), padding="same"))(x)
   x = TimeDistributed(nn.BatchNorm2d(256))(x, training=train_bn)
    x = F.relu(x)
    x = TimeDistributed(nn.Conv2d(256, (3, 3), padding="same"))(x)
   x = TimeDistributed(nn.BatchNorm2d(256))(x, training=train_bn)
    x = F.relu(x)
    x = TimeDistributed(nn.Conv2d(256, (3, 3), padding="same"))(x)
   x = TimeDistributed(nn.BatchNorm2d(256))(x, training=train_bn)
    x = F.relu(x)
```

```
    # x: [batch, num_ROIs, MASK_POOL_SIZE, MASK_POOL_SIZE, 256]
    # x: 14*14*256
    # Use deconvolution for upsampling, doubling the number of chan-
nels in the
    # feature map
    x = TimeDistributed(nn.ConvTranspose2d(256, (2, 2), strides=2,
                                activation="relu"))(x)
    # x: [batch, num_ROIs, 2xMASK_POOL_SIZE, 2xMASK_POOL_SIZE, 256]
    # x: 28*28*256
          #   After   deconvolution,   perform   1x1   convolu-
tion again to adjust the number of
    # channels in the feature map, so that the final number is numclasses
    # It's not hard to see that the above code block is actually an FCN
    x = TimeDistributed(nn.Conv2d(num_classes, (1, 1), strides=1,
                            activation="sigmoid"))(x)
       # x: [batch, num_ROIs, 2xMASK_POOL_SIZE, 2xMASK_POOL_
SIZE, numclasses]
    return x
```

The training and testing phases of Mask R-CNN are basically the same as Faster R-CNN. The difference is that in the training stage; the loss function of Mask R-CNN L is defined as follows:

$$L = L_{\text{cls}} + L_{\text{reg}} + L_{\text{mask}}.$$

In addition to the same classification loss L_{cls} and bounding box regression loss L_{reg} as Faster R-CNN, Mask R-CNN adds a mask segmentation loss L_{mask} to optimize the binary mask of the object. For each category, it uses per-pixel binary cross-entropy loss to measure the deviation between the predicted mask of the category and the ground-truth mask corresponding to the category.

In the testing phase, Mask R-CNN predicts the bounding box of the region proposal and simultaneously predicts the mask of the object within the bounding box. In addition, Mask R-CNN also needs to perform NMS processing on the predicted bounding boxes, remove redundant bounding boxes, and return the final results.

13.4 Running Code Example

Due to the extensive codebase of Mask R-CNN, we will directly call the relevant interfaces for demonstration. First, import the necessary packages.

```
! git clone https://github.com/matterport/Mask_RCNN.git
! cd Mask_RCNN
import os
import sys
sys.path.append('Mask_RCNN')
os.chdir('./Mask_RCNN')
os.getcwd()
! python setup.py install
```

```
from mrcnn.config import Config
from mrcnn import model as modellib
from mrcnn import visualize
import cv2
import colorsys
import argparse
import imutils
import random
import os
import numpy as np
import matplotlib.pyplot as plt
import tensorflow as tf
```

Next, import the model. We pretrain the model using the MS COCO dataset.

```
class SimpleConfig(Config):
   # Set name
   NAME = "coco_inference"
   # Set nunmber of GPU, and asign the number of images on each GPU
   GPU_COUNT = 1
   IMAGES_PER_GPU = 1
   # The number of class in MS COCO
   NUM_CLASSES = 81
config = SimpleConfig()
config.display()
model = modellib.MaskRCNN(mode="inference", config=config, model_
dir=os.getcwd())
model.load_weights("mask_rcnn_coco.h5", by_name=True)
Configurations:
BACKBONE                      resnet101
BACKBONE_STRIDES                [4, 8, 16, 32, 64]
BATCH_SIZE                    1
BBOX_STD_DEV                   [0.1 0.1 0.2 0.2]
COMPUTE_BACKBONE_SHAPE          None
DETECTION_MAX_INSTANCES         100
DETECTION_MIN_CONFIDENCE        0.7
DETECTION_NMS_THRESHOLD         0.3
FPN_CLASSIF_FC_LAYERS_SIZE      1024
GPU_COUNT                     1
GRADIENT_CLIP_NORM              5.0
IMAGES_PER_GPU                 1
IMAGE_CHANNEL_COUNT              3
IMAGE_MAX_DIM                  1024
IMAGE_META_SIZE                 93
IMAGE_MIN_DIM                  800
IMAGE_MIN_SCALE                 0
IMAGE_RESIZE_MODE               square
IMAGE_SHAPE                   [1024 1024   3]
LEARNING_MOMENTUM               0.9
LEARNING_RATE                  0.001
LOSS_WEIGHTS             {'rpn_class_loss': 1.0, 'rpn_bbox_loss': 1.0,
'mrcnn_class_loss':  1.0,  'mrcnn_bbox_loss':  1.0,  'mrcnn_mask_
loss': 1.0}
MASK_POOL_SIZE                  14
```

```
MASK_SHAPE                [28, 28]
MAX_GT_INSTANCES            100
MEAN_PIXEL                [123.7 116.8 103.9]
MINI_MASK_SHAPE             (56, 56)
NAME                    coco_inference
NUM_CLASSES               81
POOL_SIZE                7
POST_NMS_ROIS_INFERENCE      1000
POST_NMS_ROIS_TRAINING      2000
PRE_NMS_LIMIT              6000
ROI_POSITIVE_RATIO          0.33
RPN_ANCHOR_RATIOS           [0.5, 1, 2]
RPN_ANCHOR_SCALES           (32, 64, 128, 256, 512)
RPN_ANCHOR_STRIDE           1
RPN_BBOX_STD_DEV            [0.1 0.1 0.2 0.2]
RPN_NMS_THRESHOLD           0.7
RPN_TRAIN_ANCHORS_PER_IMAGE   256
STEPS_PER_EPOCH            1000
TOP_DOWN_PYRAMID_SIZE        256
TRAIN_BN                 False
TRAIN_ROIS_PER_IMAGE         200
USE_MINI_MASK              True
USE_RPN_ROIS               True
VALIDATION_STEPS            50
WEIGHT_DECAY               0.0001
2023-01-05 12:27:25.556772: I tensorflow/core/platform/cpu_
feature_guard.cc:141]
Your CPU supports instructions that this Tensor-
Flow binary was not compiled to
use: AVX2 FMA
2023-01-05 12:27:25.583159: I tensorflow/core/platform/profile_
utils/cpu_utils.
cc:94] CPU Frequency: 2300090000 Hz
2023-01-05 12:27:25.589540: I tensorflow/compiler/xla/service/
service.cc:150]
XLA service 0x302a000 executing computations on plat-
form Host. Devices:
2023-01-05 12:27:25.589584: I tensorflow/compiler/xla/service/
service.cc:158]
StreamExecutor device (0): <undefined>, <undefined>
```

After this, you can use Mask R-CNN for instance segmentation. Import an image and use Mask R-CNN to perform instance segmentation on it.

```
class_names = ['BG', 'person', 'bicycle', 'car', 'motorcycle',
         'airplane','bus', 'train', 'truck', 'boat',
         'traffic light', 'fire hydrant', 'stop sign',
         'parking meter', 'bench', 'bird', 'cat', 'dog',
         'horse', 'sheep', 'cow', 'elephant', 'bear', 'zebra',
         'giraffe', 'backpack', 'umbrella', 'handbag', 'tie',
        'suitcase', 'frisbee', 'skis', 'snowboard', 'sports ball',
         'kite', 'baseball bat', 'baseball glove', 'skateboard',
         'surfboard', 'tennis racket', 'bottle', 'wine glass',
         'cup', 'fork', 'knife', 'spoon', 'bowl', 'banana',
```

```
            'apple', 'sandwich', 'orange', 'broccoli', 'carrot',
            'hot dog', 'pizza', 'donut', 'cake', 'chair', 'couch',
            'potted plant', 'bed', 'dining table', 'toilet', 'tv',
            'laptop', 'mouse', 'remote', 'keyboard', 'cell phone',
            'microwave', 'oven', 'toaster', 'sink', 'refrigerator',
            'book', 'clock', 'vase', 'scissors', 'teddy bear',
            'hair drier', 'toothbrush']
image = cv2.imread('1.png')
image = cv2.cvtColor(image, cv2.COLOR_BGR2RGB)
image = imutils.resize(image, width=512)
# Forward, and get prediction
print("[INFO] making predictions with Mask R-CNN...")
result = model.detect([image], verbose=1)
r1 = result[0]
visualize.display_instances(image,   r1['ROIs'],   r1['masks'],
r1['class_ids'],
 class_names, r1['scores'])
```

As can be seen, Mask R-CNN can capture each individual object and use a mask to describe the specific shape of the object.

13.5 Summary

This chapter introduces the fundamental principles of instance segmentation and implements a representative model of instance segmentation—Mask R-CNN. Mask R-CNN is an extension of Faster R-CNN for instance segmentation tasks. Compared to Faster R-CNN, Mask R-CNN adds a branch for mask prediction. More importantly, Mask R-CNN achieves more refined feature extraction: it introduces FPN to fuse multi-scale features; it uses ROI alignment instead of ROI pooling to avoid coordinate quantization errors that occur during region feature extraction.

Exercises

(1) What is the difference between the ROIAlign layer and the ROI pooling layer? What are the advantages of the ROIAlign layer?
(2) In Mask R-CNN, the mask branch calculates the loss between the predicted mask and the true mask for each category. How would you design the corresponding module and loss function if you want to train a category-independent mask branch?
(3) In Mask R-CNN, the feature map with a resolution of 14 pixels by 14 pixels is finally upsampled through the mask branch to a resolution size of 28 pixels by 28 pixels. This is because increasing its resolution can improve segmentation accuracy. Will further upsampling improve segmentation accuracy? Verify through experiments.
(4) In Mask R-CNN, ROIAlign is used to solve the quantization error introduced by ROI pooling. Besides this, from what other perspectives can the advantages of ROI alignment be explained (Hint: translation-equivariance property)?

References

1. HE K, GKIOXARI G, DOLLAR P, et al. Mask r-cnn[C]//IEEE International Conference on Computer Vision, 2017:2961–2969.
2. LIN T Y, DOLLAR P, GIRSHICK R, et al. Feature pyramid networks for object detection [C]// IEEE Conference on Computer Vision and Pattern Recognition, 2017:2117–2125.
3. TIAN Z, SHEN C, CHEN H. Conditional convolutions for instance segmentation[C]//European Conference on Computer Vision, 2020:282–298.

Chapter 14
Human Pose Estimation

14.1 Introduction

Human pose estimation is a crucial task in computer vision, aiming to identify human actions and postures, which is vital for many applications such as sports analysis, virtual reality, and human–computer interaction. In virtual reality, human pose estimation technology helps track user movements, making the virtual reality experience more realistic. In human–computer interaction, human pose estimation technology aids devices in better recognizing user commands, thereby making the interaction smoother.

Generally speaking, human pose estimation can be categorized into two-dimensional pose estimation and three-dimensional pose estimation. There are obvious differences between them. Two-dimensional pose estimation is used to detect the key point coordinates of the human body in images, outputting two-dimensional coordinates. Therefore, two-dimensional pose estimation is similar to visual recognition tasks such as semantic segmentation and object detection, requiring techniques such as image feature extraction and coordinate regression. Three-dimensional pose estimation is used to identify the key point coordinates of the human body in three-dimensional space, outputting three-dimensional coordinates. Therefore, three-dimensional pose estimation usually requires scene reconstruction techniques, such as stereo vision and motion estimation.

In this chapter, we mainly introduce two-dimensional pose estimation. Let us describe the task in mathematical language, i.e., predefining K joints, given N images, defining image space $\mathbb{I}$, given dataset $\mathcal{D} = \{(\boldsymbol{I}^{(n)}, \boldsymbol{y}^{(n)})\}_{n=1}^{N}$, where $\boldsymbol{I}^{(n)} \in \mathbb{I}$ is the n th image in the dataset; $\boldsymbol{y}^{(n)} = \left(\boldsymbol{y}_1^{(n)}, \ldots \boldsymbol{y}_j^{(n)}, \ldots \boldsymbol{y}_K^{(n)}\right)$ is the ground-truth coordinate vector of the human body joints in this image, also known as the pose vector, $\boldsymbol{y}_j^{(n)} \in \mathbb{R}^2$ represents the two-dimensional image coordinates of the n th joint in the j th image. The task of pose estimation is to learn a mapping f from the image space to the coordinate vector space of human body joints from $\mathcal{D}$, so that given any test image $\boldsymbol{I}$,

W. Shen et al., *Hands-On Computer Vision*,
https://doi.org/10.1007/978-981-95-4835-4_14

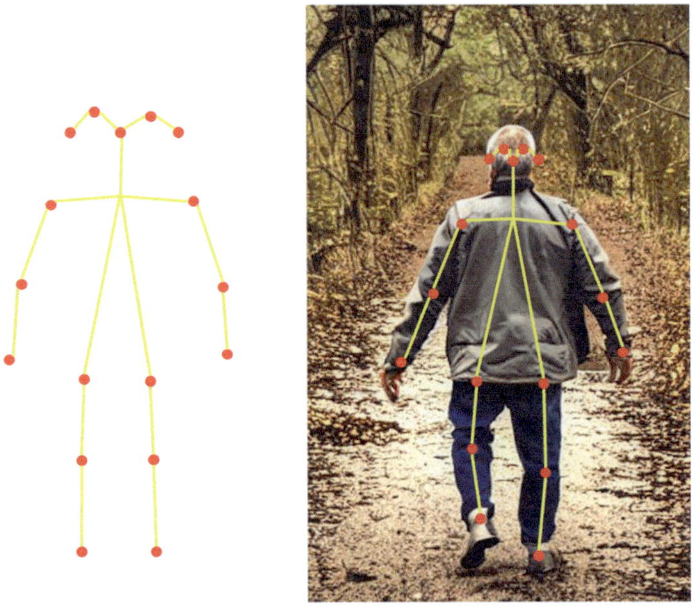

Fig. 14.1 Schematic of human pose estimation

its label can be predicted with the learned mapping function f: $\boldsymbol{y}^* = f(\boldsymbol{I})$. According to the human body structure, the joints can be connected to form a human skeleton (as shown in Fig. 14.1), so human pose estimation is also called human skeleton estimation.

14.2 Dataset and Metrics

This section will introduce the datasets and evaluation metrics related to human pose estimation.

14.2.1 Dataset

In human pose estimation, the following commonly used datasets are usually selected for model training and testing.

(1) Leeds Sports Pose (LSP) [1]: A total of 2000 full-body posture images are included, divided into eight categories (athletics, badminton, baseball, gymnastics, parkour, football, tennis, and volleyball). Each human image has 14 joints.

(2) Frames Labeled In Cinema (FLIC) [2]: A total of 5003 images are included, which come from 30 famous Hollywood movies. Human body detection is performed every 10 frames of each movie, obtaining about 20,000 human body region proposals. These region proposals are published on the crowdsourcing platform Amazon Mechanical Turk for annotation. Each region proposal acquires ground-truth coordinates for 10 upper-body joints. Finally, images with severe occlusion or non-frontal views are subsequently removed through manual screening.

(3) Max Planck Institute for Informatics (MPII) Human Pose [3]: About 25,000 images are contained, including more than 40,000 people with annotated joints. The entire dataset covers 410 human activities. The images in the dataset come from YouTube, covering indoor and outdoor scenes and various imaging conditions, so the dataset has high diversity in appearance. Researchers provide rich annotations for the collected images, including the positions of body joints, 3D views of the head and torso, and the positions of the eyes and nose. In addition, the visibility of all body joints and parts is annotated.

(4) Microsoft Common Objects in Context (MS COCO) [4]: The MS COCO dataset is not only used for tasks such as object detection, segmentation, but also for human pose estimation. MS COCO annotates 17 joints for each human body instance, including the nose, eyes, ears, shoulders, elbows, wrists, hips, knees, and ankles. Compared to the MPII dataset, MS COCO provides richer and more diverse annotations for facial structures.

14.2.2 Evaluation Metrics

The following evaluation metrics are commonly used in human pose estimation.

(1) Percentage of Correct Keypoints (PCK), sometimes also referred to as the percentage of correct keypoints, is the proportion of predicted joint coordinates where the normalized distance to their corresponding ground-truth coordinates is less than a predefined threshold.

$$\text{PCK}_j = \frac{1}{N}\sum_{n=1}^{N} 1\left(\frac{\left\|\hat{\boldsymbol{y}}_j^{(n)} - \boldsymbol{y}_j^{(n)}\right\|_2}{S} \le \alpha\right),$$

where I is the indicator function; $\hat{\boldsymbol{y}}_j^{(n)}$ is the predicted coordinate of the j th joint in the n th image; $\boldsymbol{y}_j^{(n)}$ is the corresponding ground-truth coordinate; N is the total number of images; S is the scale factor, which is usually the diameter of the human head; and α is the threshold, which is usually set to 0.5, meaning that the prediction is considered correct when the distance between the predicted joint and the ground-truth joint is less than half the size of the human body. At this time, PCK is also written as PCK@0.5.

(2) Object Keypoint Similarity (OKS). The specific calculation formula is

$$\text{OKS} = \frac{\sum_j^{\Sigma\left(-\left(\left\|\hat{y}_j^{(n)} - y_j^{(n)}\right\|_2\right)/2S^2\sigma_j^2\right)(v_j>0)} \exp}{\sum_j 1\left(v_j > 0\right)},$$

where I is the indicator function; v_j is the visibility flag of the key point, $v_j = 1$ indicates that this joint is unobstructed and has been annotated, $v_j = 2$ indicates that the joint is obstructed but has been annotated; S is the scale factor, but here S is usually set to the square root of the area of the human detection box $\sqrt{H \times W}$, H and W are the height and width of the human detection box; σ_j represents the normalization factor of this joint, which is usually determined based on the distribution of joint annotation errors in the dataset, reflecting the annotation accuracy of the current joint. The larger the value, the worse the annotation effect of this joint, and vice versa. It can be seen that OKS takes into account the visibility of the joint, the scale factor, and the annotation effect of the joint, and thus can more comprehensively evaluate the performance of human pose estimation.

14.3 Human Pose Estimation Model—DeepPose

Early human pose estimation methods were based on predicting joint coordinates from image patches and constraining them with knowledge of human anatomy [3]. However, it is difficult to accurately predict joints-based solely on local image information. For example, it is difficult to determine which part of the human body they represent from the two image patches on the left side of Fig. 14.2, so a method is needed that can take the entire image as input and directly predict all keypoints. As we know from the previous chapters, deep neural networks can achieve this function. Thus, DeepPose [5], a method based on deep neural networks, emerged.

Next, we will detail the network architecture and training process of DeepPose.

14.3.1 Human Pose Estimation Based on Deep Neural Networks

Before training DeepPose, the data needs to be preprocessed. In the dataset, joint coordinates are usually given in absolute image coordinates, but this representation is not ideal for network learning. Therefore, DeepPose converts joint coordinates into relative coordinates, i.e., normalizes the joint coordinates relative to the human bounding box. Specifically, given an image $\boldsymbol{I}$, define the bounding box $\boldsymbol{b} = \left(b_x, b_y, b_h, b_w\right)$. For the coordinate $\mathbf{y}_j^{(n)}$ of a human body joint, its normalization relative to the bounding box can be represented as

Fig. 14.2 It is difficult to effectively predict poses-based solely on local information

$$\mathrm{norm}\left(\boldsymbol{y}_j^{(n)}; \boldsymbol{b}\right) = \begin{bmatrix} \frac{1}{b_w} & 0 \\ 0 & \frac{1}{b_h} \end{bmatrix} \left(\boldsymbol{y}_i^{(n)} - \begin{bmatrix} b_x \\ b_y \end{bmatrix}\right).$$

Further, the same normalization can be applied to all elements of the pose vector $\boldsymbol{y}^{(n)}$, resulting in $\mathrm{norm}(\boldsymbol{y}^{(n)}; \boldsymbol{b}) = (\mathrm{norm}\left(\boldsymbol{y}_1^{(n)}; \boldsymbol{b}\right), \ldots, \mathrm{norm}\left(\boldsymbol{y}_j^{(n)}; \boldsymbol{b}\right), \ldots, \mathrm{norm}\left(\boldsymbol{y}_K^{(n)}; \boldsymbol{b}\right))$. For convenience of description, here we use $\mathrm{crop}(\boldsymbol{I}; \boldsymbol{b})$ to represent the local image obtained by cropping image $\boldsymbol{I}$ based on bounding box $\boldsymbol{b}$. DeepPose formulates the pose estimation problem as a regression task, mapping a given image $\boldsymbol{I}$ to a normalized pose vector by training and utilizing a pose regressor $\psi(\boldsymbol{I}; \boldsymbol{\theta})$, where $\boldsymbol{\theta}$ represents the parameters of the pose regressor. Therefore, according to the normalization transformation mentioned above, the predicted pose vector $\mathbf{y}^*$ in the absolute coordinates of the image is represented as

$$\boldsymbol{y}^* = \mathrm{norm}^{-1}(\psi(\mathrm{crop}(\boldsymbol{I}; \boldsymbol{b}); \boldsymbol{\theta}); \boldsymbol{b}),$$

where $\mathrm{norm}^{-1}(\cdot)$ is the inverse transformation of normalization, defined as

$$\mathrm{norm}^{-1}\left(y'; b\right) = \begin{bmatrix} b_w & 0 \\ 0 & b_h \end{bmatrix} y' + \begin{bmatrix} b_x \\ b_y \end{bmatrix},$$

where $y' = \psi(\mathrm{crop}(I; b); \theta)$. The objective of the pose regressor ψ is to minimize the error between the predicted pose vector $\boldsymbol{y}^*$ and the ground-truth pose vector $\boldsymbol{y}$. Here, DeepPose uses a deep neural network with a fixed input size of 220 pixels × 220 pixels as the pose regressor. As a regression task, DeepPose trains the network by minimizing the mean square error loss function to predict the pose vector. Since the ground-truth pose vector is defined in the absolute coordinates of the image, and the pose sizes in different images are different, DeepPose uses the normalization method defined above to normalize the training set $\mathcal{D}$:

$$\mathcal{D}_N = \{(\mathrm{crop}(\boldsymbol{I}; \boldsymbol{b}), \mathrm{norm}(\boldsymbol{y}; \boldsymbol{b}))|(\boldsymbol{I}, \boldsymbol{y}) \in \mathcal{D}\}.$$

The mean square error loss function used to train DeepPose is defined as

$$\sum_{(\boldsymbol{I},\boldsymbol{y})\in\mathcal{D}_N} \sum_{j=1}^{K} \boldsymbol{y}_j - \psi(\boldsymbol{I}; \boldsymbol{\theta})_2^2$$

It should be noted that even if not all joints are marked in some images, the above loss function can still be used. In this case, the corresponding items in the sum will be ignored.

14.3.2 Cascade Regression

The method introduced in Sect. 14.3.1 has a problem, i.e., the input image size of the network is fixed at 220 pixels × 220 pixels, which limits the network's ability to capture details. To solve this problem, DeepPose proposes a method of cascade regression. In the initial stage, DeepPose estimates an initial pose. In the subsequent refinement stages, an additional pose regressor is trained for each joint to predict the displacement of the joint from the position predicted in the previous stage to the ground-truth position. Each refinement stage uses the joint positions predicted in the previous stage to focus on the relevant parts of the joints in the image, i.e., to crop the local image around the joint position predicted in the previous stage, and apply the pose regressor to predict the refined position of the joints on this local image, as shown in Fig. 14.3. This method of cascade regression can improve the network's perception of details and thus improve the accuracy of pose estimation.

DeepPose uses the same network architecture for all stages, but learns different network parameters. For stage $c \in \{1, \cdots, C\}$ in a total of C cascade stages, the pose regressor for the c th stage for the j th joint is represented as $\psi\left(\mathrm{crop}(\boldsymbol{I}; b); \boldsymbol{\theta}_j^c\right)$, where $\boldsymbol{\theta}_j^c$ represents its network parameters. For a given joint coordinate $\boldsymbol{y}_j$, consider a joint bounding box $\boldsymbol{b}_j$, which captures the local image around the joint coordinate $\boldsymbol{y}_j$: $\boldsymbol{b}_j = \left(\mathbf{y}_j, H_j, W_j\right)$, where H_j and W_j represent the predefined bounding box size for the jth joint, depending on the physical meaning of the joint and the distribution of the dataset. In DeepPose $H_j = W_j$.

In the first stage (initial stage), i.e., $c = 1$, DeepPose starts detection from the initial bounding box $\boldsymbol{b}^0$, which can be the entire image or obtained by a human body object detector. The initial joint coordinates are predicted from the bounding box $\boldsymbol{b}^0$:

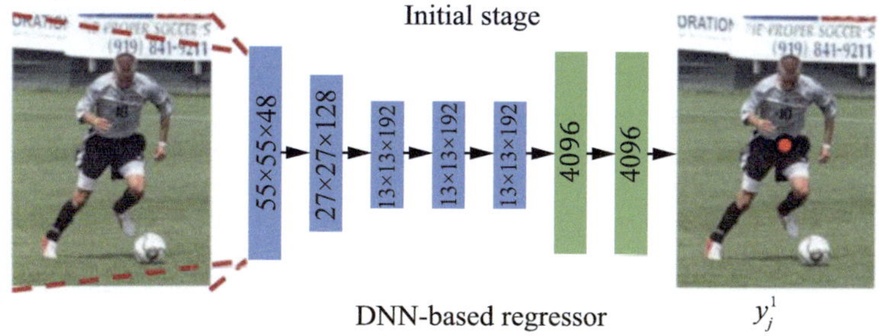

(a) The illustration of initial stage

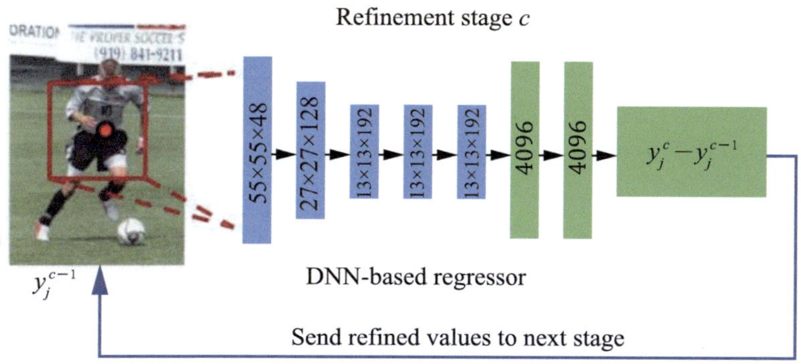

(b) The illustration of refinement stage

Fig. 14.3 Schematic view of DeepPose (illustration from reference [5])

$$\boldsymbol{y}^1 = \text{norm}^{-1}(\psi(\text{crop}(\boldsymbol{I}; \boldsymbol{b}^0); \boldsymbol{\theta}_1); \boldsymbol{b}^0).$$

In each subsequent stage, i.e., $c \geq 2$, for all joints $j \in \{1, \cdots, K\}$, DeepPose first uses the joint coordinates $\mathbf{y}_j^{c-1}$ regressed in the previous stage to define the local image, obtains the corresponding bounding box $\boldsymbol{b}_j^{c-1}$, and then uses a corresponding pose regressor ψ to predict the refined displacement of joints $\boldsymbol{y}_j^c - \boldsymbol{y}_j^{c-1}$:

$$\boldsymbol{y}_j^c \leftarrow \boldsymbol{y}_j^{c-1} + \text{norm}^{-1}\left(\psi\left(\text{crop}\left(\boldsymbol{I}; \boldsymbol{b}_j^{c-1}\right); \boldsymbol{\theta}_j^c\right); \boldsymbol{b}_j^{c-1}\right).$$

Thus, we can obtain the bounding box of joints at the refinement stage c $\boldsymbol{b}_j^c$:

$$\boldsymbol{b}_j^c \leftarrow \left(\boldsymbol{y}_j^c, H_j, W_j\right).$$

In the experiments, DeepPose uses $C = 3$ cascade stages.

DeepPose also performs data augmentation for joints. The specific method is to randomly offset the ground-truth position of the joint j. The offset follows a two-dimensional normal distribution $N(\mu, \sigma)$, where μ and σ are equal to the mean and variance of the observed offsets $\left(\boldsymbol{y}_j^{c-1} - \boldsymbol{y}_j\right)$ of all samples in the training data. In this way, the augmented training data and the real data can be used together for the training stage c of the pose regressor. The augmented training data can be represented as

$$\mathcal{D}_A^c = \left\{\left(\text{crop}\left(\boldsymbol{I}; \boldsymbol{b}_j^{c-1}\right), \text{norm}\left(\boldsymbol{y}_j; \boldsymbol{b}_j^{c-1}\right)\right) | (\boldsymbol{I}, \boldsymbol{y}_j) \sim \mathcal{D},\right.$$
$$\left.\left\| \delta \sim N(\mu, \sigma), \boldsymbol{b}_j^{c-1} = \left(\boldsymbol{y}_j + \delta, H_j, W_j\right)\right\}.$$

The training target of the cascade stage c is

$$\min_{\boldsymbol{\theta}_j^c} \sum_{(\boldsymbol{I}, \boldsymbol{y}_j) \in \mathcal{D}_A^c} \left\| \boldsymbol{y}_j - \psi_j\left(\boldsymbol{I}; \boldsymbol{\theta}_j^c\right)\right\|_2^2$$

DeepPose has the following innovations compared to previous methods based on image patches.

(1) For the problem of how to obtain the coordinates of joints from a global perspective, DeepPose proposes to use deep neural networks as global feature extraction and take the entire image as input.
(2) Human body joints themselves inherent spatial distribution patterns, but their absolute coordinates in the image coordinate system show no consistent regularity. Therefore, DeepPose introduces a method that transforms absolute coordinates into normalized coordinates with distribution characteristics by selecting local bounding boxes around each joint and computing the joint coordinates within these boxes at every stage.
(3) In order to achieve higher accuracy coordinate calculation, DeepPose proposes a cascaded deep neural network. After obtaining the inital coordinates of the joints, a certain local region is selected in the original image according to the coordinates to achieve higher accuracy coordinate calculation.

Through this series of designs, DeepPose successfully became the state-of-the-art (SOTA) at that time and led the trend of deep learning in the field of human pose estimation. Next, let's write DeepPose and test the prediction effect on the MS COCO dataset.

14.4 DeepPose Code Implementation

Since the cascading process of DeepPose requires training a regressor for each joint, this process is very time-consuming. As described in the DeepPose paper, it takes 7 days to train each cascading refinement stage. Therefore, we adopt a more efficient approach here: at each stage, the joint coordinates predicted in the previous stage and the feature map extracted from the image are concatenated, then the refinement of the joint coordinates at this stage is based on this concatenated features. Compared with the cascading refinement process of DeepPose, this method eliminates the cropping operation, does not need to calculate image features multiple times, and is therefore much more efficient; in addition, since the concatenated feature map contains the position information of the joint predicted in the previous stage, it can make the network pay more attention to the local image region around this position, thereby achieving the refinement of the joint coordinates.

First, let's write the code for DeepPose.

```
import torch
import torch.nn as nn
import torchvision.models as models
class DeepPose(nn.Module):
      def __init__(self, num_keypoints=17, pretrained=True, num_
stages=3):
          super(DeepPose, self).__init__()
          self.num_keypoints = num_keypoints
          self.num_stages = num_stages
          # Load the pre-trained ResNet model for feature extraction
          self.backbone = models.resnet50(pretrained=pretrained)
   self.backbone = nn.Sequential(*list(self.backbone.children())[:-
2])
          # Define regression layers for each cascade stage
          self.regression_layers = nn.ModuleList([
             self._make_regression_layer() for _ in range(num_stages)
          ])
      # The final fully connected layer of each cascade stage, used for
joint
          # prediction
          self.fc_layers = nn.ModuleList([
           nn.Linear(2048, num_keypoints * 2) for _ in range(num_stages)
          ])
    def _make_regression_layer(self):
           # Define the regression layer, composed of several convolu-
tional layers
          return nn.Sequential(
             nn.Conv2d(2048, 512, kernel_size=3, padding=1),
             nn.BatchNorm2d(512),
             nn.ReLU(inplace=True),
             nn.Conv2d(512, 512, kernel_size=3, padding=1),
             nn.BatchNorm2d(512),
             nn.ReLU(inplace=True),
             nn.Conv2d(512, 2048, kernel_size=1)
          )
```

```
    def forward(self, x):
        # Use the backbone network to extract features
        features = self.backbone(x)
        # Initialize joint prediction to zero
                keypoint_preds = torch.zeros(x.size(0), self.num_
keypoints * 2).
                                to(x.device)
        for i in range(self.num_stages):
         # Concatenate the joint prediction results with the feature map
            keypoint_map = keypoint_preds.view(x.size(0), self.num_
keypoints, 2,
                                1, 1)
                    keypoint_map = keypoint_map.expand(-1, -1, -
1, features.size(2),
                                features.size(3))
            features_with_keypoints = torch.cat([features,
                keypoint_map.view(x.size(0), -1, features.size(2),
                 features.size(3))], dim=1)
            # Refine through the regression layer
             regression_output = self.regression_layers[i](features_
with_keypoints)
        # Flatten the regression output and pass it through the fully
connected
            # layer
            regression_output = regression_output.view(x.size(0), -1)
            keypoint_preds += self.fc_layers[i](regression_output)
        # Return the final positions of the joints
        return keypoint_preds.view(x.size(0), self.num_keypoints, 2)
```

Next, we train it on the MS COCO dataset. We first import the necessary repositories and library functions.

```
!git clone https://github.com/Naman-ntc/Pytorch-Human-Pose-Est
imation.git
pip install -r requirements.txt
```

Set up the model settings and the path of the MS COCO dataset, and start training the model.

```
!python main.py -DataConfig conf/datasets/coco.defconf -
ModelConfig /
conf/models/DeepPose.defconf
```

```
==> |################################ | train Epoch: [1][9363/9364]| Total: 0:07:27 | ETA: 0:00:01 | Loss: 0.027381 (0.014873)| PCK: 0.146 (0.246)
==> |################################ | train Epoch: [2][9363/9364]| Total: 0:07:19 | ETA: 0:00:01 | Loss: 0.021852 (0.038345)| PCK: 0.233 (0.160)
==> |################################ | train Epoch: [3][9363/9364]| Total: 0:07:21 | ETA: 0:00:01 | Loss: 0.020009 (0.010192)| PCK: 0.273 (0.305)
==> |#################################| val Epoch: [3][397/397]| Total: 0:00:11 | ETA: 0:00:01 | Loss: 0.007666 (0.012200)| PCK: 0.336 (0.172)
==> |################################ | train Epoch: [4][9363/9364]| Total: 0:07:24 | ETA: 0:00:01 | Loss: 0.018659 (0.015728)| PCK: 0.298 (0.347)
==> |################################ | train Epoch: [5][9363/9364]| Total: 0:07:21 | ETA: 0:00:01 | Loss: 0.018105 (0.022155)| PCK: 0.317 (0.379)
Reducing learning rate of group 0 from 0.000250 to 0.000175
==> |################################ | train Epoch: [6][9363/9364]| Total: 0:07:22 | ETA: 0:00:01 | Loss: 0.016398 (0.025791)| PCK: 0.357 (0.299)
==> |#################################| val Epoch: [6][397/397]| Total: 0:00:10 | ETA: 0:00:01 | Loss: 0.024147 (0.035195)| PCK: 0.328 (0.171)
==> |################################ | train Epoch: [7][9363/9364]| Total: 0:07:23 | ETA: 0:00:01 | Loss: 0.015652 (0.019737)| PCK: 0.369 (0.440)
==> |################################ | train Epoch: [8][9363/9364]| Total: 0:07:18 | ETA: 0:00:01 | Loss: 0.015587 (0.006113)| PCK: 0.379 (0.406)
==> |################################ | train Epoch: [9][9363/9364]| Total: 0:07:21 | ETA: 0:00:01 | Loss: 0.015239 (0.007124)| PCK: 0.386 (0.452)
==> |#################################| val Epoch: [9][397/397]| Total: 0:00:10 | ETA: 0:00:01 | Loss: 0.006615 (0.008718)| PCK: 0.412 (0.271)
```

As the training output is quite long, only the output at the beginning of the training stage is shown here. Finally, we test the model on the test set and find that the final PCK can reach 57.5%.

```
loading annotations into memory...
Done (t=7.90s)
creating index...
index created!
loading annotations into memory...
Done (t=0.21s)
creating index...
index created!
==> |##################################| val Epoch: [-1][397/397]| Total: 0:00:15 | ETA: 0:00:01 | Loss: 0.005509 (0.013679)| PCK: 0.575 (0.446)
```

14.5 Summary

This chapter introduced the pioneering work of human pose estimation using deep learning—DeepPose, and trained and tested it on the MS COCO dataset. Human pose estimation is a fundamental problem in the field of computer vision. Only by accurately estimating the pose of the human body in the image can we enable subsequent operations such as motion capture in movies, animation production, trajectory tracking, human–computer interaction, and motion analysis. Next, we will continue to introduce how to recognize motion from videos.

Exercises

(1) Implement Object Keypoint Similarity (OKS) and re-evaluate the experimental results using OKS.
(2) DeepPose treats the problem of human pose estimation as a precise regression problem, without considering the uncertainty of human pose. Consider how to introduce uncertainty information to improve the robustness of the model.
(3) In the cascade regression, if the initially estimated joint position is far from the ground-truth joint position, subsequent iterations cannot correct the initial error. Consider how to solve this problem.
(4) In Chap. 12, the bounding box regressor in the Faster R-CNN object detector is essentially regressing coordinates. Can the idea of cascade regression in this chapter be applied to Faster R-CNN? If so, briefly describe how to implement it.

References

1. JOHNSON S, EVERINGHAM M. Clustered pose and nonlinear appearance models for human pose estimation[C]//British Machine Vision Conference, 2010, 2(4): 5.
2. SAPP B, TASKAR B. MODEC: Multimodal decomposable models for human pose estimation [C]//IEEE Conference on Computer Vision and Pattern Recognition, 2013: 3674–3681.

3. ANDRILOUKA M, PISCHCHULIN L, GEHLER P, et al. 2D human pose estimation: New benchmark and state of the art analysis[C]//IEEE Conference on Computer Vision and Pattern Recognition, 2014: 3686–3693.
4. LIN T Y, MAIRE M, BELONGIE S, et al. Microsoft COCO: Common objects in context[C]// European Conference on Computer Vision, 2014: 740–755.
5. TOSHEV A, SZEGEDY C. DeepPose: Human pose estimation via deep neural networks [C]// IEEE Conference on Computer Vision and Pattern Recognition, 2014: 1653–1660.

Chapter 15
Action Recognition

15.1 Introduction

In previous chapters, readers have learned a variety of analysis techniques for images, including object detection, instance segmentation, and even human pose estimation. However, in the real world, everything is in motion, so it is necessary to master techniques for video streams. In this chapter, we will try to understand this world of motion, specifically, we will introduce human action recognition. As the name suggests, human action recognition refers to the recognition of human actions in videos, which can infer the intentions and states of the characters, providing important information for understanding video content. For example, in the field of video surveillance, human action recognition can be used to detect crimes and security incidents; in sports events, it can be used to analyze player techniques and tactics; in entertainment and advertising, it can be used to analyze audience reactions and engagement. It should be noted that the discussion here is about narrow-sense action recognition, which is understood as a video classification task, as shown in Fig. 15.1, while broad-sense action recognition includes more fine-grained recognition tasks, such as detecting certain action frames from a video.

The narrow-sense human action recognition task can be described in mathematical language as follows: predefine K action labels $\mathcal{L} = \{l_1, l_2, \cdots, l_K\}$, define the video sequence space $\mathbb{S}$, given the dataset $\mathcal{D} = \{(\boldsymbol{S}^{(n)}, l^{(n)})\}_{n=1}^{N}$, where $\boldsymbol{S}^{(n)} \in \mathbb{S}$ is the n th video sequence in the dataset, $l^{(n)}$ is the corresponding action label for this video sequence. $\boldsymbol{S}^{(n)}$ can usually be represented as a high-order tensor. If the video image is a grayscale image, it is a three-order tensor. If the video image is a color image, it is a four-order tensor. The task of human action recognition is to learn a mapping f from the video sequence space to the human action label space from $\mathcal{D}$, so that given any test video sequence $\boldsymbol{S}$, the learned mapping function f can be used to predict its label: $\hat{l} = f(\boldsymbol{S})$.

In this chapter, we will first introduce the dataset and evaluation metrics, and then learn the classic method in action recognition—C3D [1].

W. Shen et al., *Hands-On Computer Vision*,
https://doi.org/10.1007/978-981-95-4835-4_15

Fig. 15.1 Action recognition can be considered as a classification task for video sequences

15.2 Dataset and Metrics

This section will introduce the commonly used datasets and metrics for action recognition.

15.2.1 Dataset

The commonly used datasets for human action recognition include the following three.

(1) UCF101 [2]: The UCF101 dataset was released in 2012. It consists of some real-world videos from YouTube and includes 101 different action categories. These categories can be divided into five types: human motion, human–human interaction, human-object interaction, playing instruments, and sports. The UCF101 dataset has a total of 13,320 video clips, with a total duration of over 27 h, and all videos have a fixed frame rate of 25 frames per second.
(2) Sports-1M [3]: Sports-1M was released in 2014 and is the first large-scale video action dataset, consisting of over one million YouTube videos, with 487 sports categories labeled. Due to the small granularity of the categories, the differences between the categories are small.
(3) DeepMind Kinetics Human Action Dataset: The Kinetics family is currently the most widely used benchmark dataset. The Kinetics-400 [4] released in 2017 contains about 240,000 training videos and 20,000 validation videos, covering

400 human action categories. Each action category has at least 400 video clips, and each video clip lasts about 10 s. Over time, the Kinetics family has been continuously expanding, with the Kinetics-600 [5] released in 2018 containing over 490,000 videos, and the Kinetics-700 [6] released in 2019 containing over 650,000 videos.

15.2.2 *Evaluation Metrics*

The commonly used evaluation metrics in human action recognition tasks are as follows.

(1) Accuracy: Accuracy is the most commonly used evaluation metric for classification tasks, which represents the proportion of correctly classified samples to the total number of samples.
(2) Hit Rate (hit@ k): Whether the correct label is included in the top k results predicted by the model. The specific definition is as follows:

$$\text{hit@}k = \frac{1}{M}\sum_{m=1}^{M} 1\left(l^{(m)} \in \left\{\hat{l}_{\text{top1}}^{(m)}, \hat{l}_{\text{top2}}^{(m)}, \cdots, \hat{l}_{\text{top}k}^{(m)}\right\}\right),$$

where M is the number of video sequences in the test set; $l^{(m)}$ is the actual action label of the m-th video sequence; $\left\{\hat{l}_{\text{top1}}^{(m)}, \hat{l}_{\text{top2}}^{(m)}, \cdots, \hat{l}_{\text{top}k}^{(m)}\right\}$ is the set of the first k labels predicted by the model for the m-th video sequence; 1 is the indicator function.

15.3 Action Recognition Model—C3D

Video data differs from image data as it is a continuous sequence. To recognize actions in a video, we need to consider temporal information. In this section, we will introduce a classic action recognition model—C3D [1] (Convolutional 3D), which uses a three-dimensional convolutional network to extract spatio-temporal features from video data, thereby achieving high-precision action recognition.

15.3.1 *Three-Dimensional Convolution*

Before introducing C3D, let's first understand its core component—three-dimensional convolution. Three-dimensional convolution is a natural extension of two-dimensional convolution. In two-dimensional convolution, the convolution kernel slides over the input two-dimensional data (such as an image), calculating the weighted sum of the neighboring region. In three-dimensional convolution, in

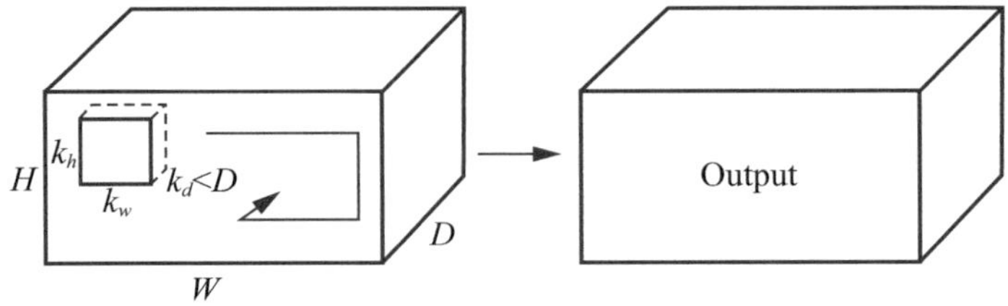

Fig. 15.2 Schematic of three-dimensional convolution

addition to sliding in width (W) and height (H), the convolution kernel also slides in depth (D), as shown in Fig. 15.2. Here, depth usually corresponds to the temporal dimension of video frames. Given a video sequence S (assuming the images in it are all grayscale), it can be understood as a third-order tensor. The mathematical expression for performing three-dimensional convolution on it is

$$G(i,j,k) = \sum_{m=1}^{k_d} \sum_{n=1}^{k_h} \sum_{p=1}^{k_w} K(m,n,p) \cdot S(i-m, j-n, k-p),$$

where K is the three-dimensional convolution kernel; G is the output tensor; k_d, k_h, and k_w represent the dimensions of the convolution kernel in spatial width, height, and temporal depth, respectively. The padding, stride, and other operations of three-dimensional convolution are similar to those of two-dimensional convolution, thus the detailed elaboration of them is omitted here.

Below is a simple example of three-dimensional convolution.

```
import numpy as np
import pprint as pp
def generate_increasing_volume(d, h, w):
 """
  Generate an increasing tensor, where the value of each element is
its index value
   in the tensor plus 1
   Parameters:
  - d, h, w: The depth, height, and width of the tensor to be generated
   Returns:
   - volume: The generated increasing tensor
   """
return np.arange(1, d*h*w + 1).reshape(d, h, w)
def conv3d(input_volume, kernel):
   """
      Use a specified convolution kernel to perform 3D convolu-
tion on the given input
      Tensor
   Parameters:
      - input_volume: A three-dimensional numpy array, dimen-
sions correspond to depth,
      height, and width
```

```
    - kernel: A three-dimensional numpy array, dimensions are smaller
  than the input
        tensor, and each dimension size is odd
    Returns:
   -output_volume: A three-dimensional numpy array, the output tensor
  of the
        Convolution operation
    """
    d, h, w = input_volume.shape
    kd, kh, kw = kernel.shape
    # Calculate the order of the output tensor
    output_d = d - kd + 1
    output_h = h - kh + 1
    output_w = w - kw + 1
    # Initialize the output tensor
    output_volume = np.zeros((output_d, output_h, output_w))
    # Compute the three-dimensional convolution
    for i in range(output_d):
        for j in range(output_h):
            for k in range(output_w):
                sub_volume = input_volume[i:i+kd, j:j+kh, k:k+kw]
                output_volume[i, j, k] = np.sum(sub_volume * kernel)
    return output_volume
# Generate a 4×4×4 increasing order tensor
input_volume_increasing = generate_increasing_volume(4, 4, 4)
kernel = np.array([[[1, 1], [1, 1]], [[1, 1], [1, 1]]]) # A 2×2×
2 kernel
#      Perform      three-dimensional      convolution      opera-
tion on the increasing tensor
output_volume_increasing          =          conv3d(input_volume_
increasing, kernel)
print("Part of the input tensor:")
pp.pprint(input_volume_increasing[0:2, 0:2, 0:2])
print("Kernel:")
pp.pprint(kernel)
print("Part of the output tensor:")
print(output_volume_increasing[0, 0, 0])
Part of the input tensor:
array([[[1, 2],
[5, 6]],
[[17, 18],
[21, 22]]])
Kernel:
array([[[1, 1],
[1, 1]],
[[1, 1],
[1, 1]]])
Part of the output tensor:
92.0
```

In this example, we use a $2 \times 2 \times 2$ all-ones convolution kernel to perform a three-dimensional convolution operation on an incrementally increasing $4 \times 4 \times 4$ tensor. The convolution kernel slides over the input tensor, performing multiplication and summation operations on each local tensor, resulting in a $3 \times 3 \times 3$ output tensor.

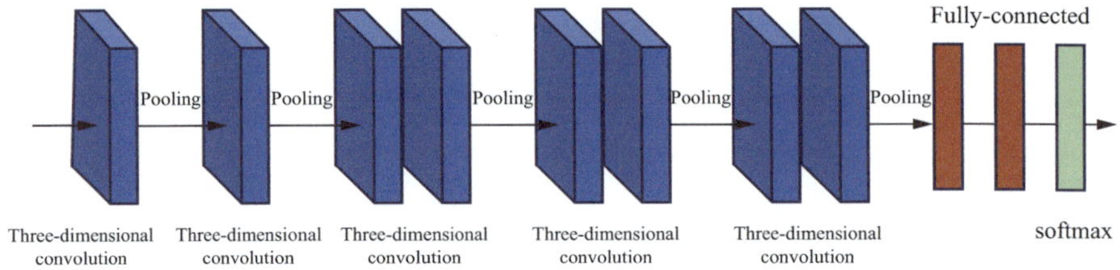

Fig. 15.3 Schematic of the C3D model

The main advantage of three-dimensional convolution over two-dimensional convolution is that it can directly process the temporal dimension information of video data. Two-dimensional convolution only operates in space, so after convolution on the image, a method to fuse time information needs to be designed. However, three-dimensional convolution can directly capture the temporal continuity of video sequences, thereby more effectively identifying and analyzing dynamic scenes and behaviors. This gives three-dimensional convolution a significant advantage in action recognition and other video analysis tasks.

15.3.2 C3D Model

Because of the advantages of three-dimensional convolution, Tran et al. [1] proposed in 2014 to directly use three-dimensional convolution networks to extract spatio-temporal features from video data, thereby achieving high-precision video action recognition. Their proposed C3D model is an end-to-end three-dimensional convolution network, consisting of 8 convolution layers, 5 pooling layers, 2 fully connected layers, and 1 softmax layer. Its network architecture is shown in Fig. 15.3.

The input to the C3D model is $16 \times 112 \times 112 \times 3$ video data, where 16 represents the length of the input video sequence, 112 represents the width and height of the video frame, and 3 represents the number of channels of the video frame. According to the research on two-dimensional convolutional neural networks [7], the best results can be obtained with a small receptive field (3×3 convolution kernel) and a deeper network architecture. Therefore, in the architecture search research of C3D, Du Tran et al. fixed the spatial receptive field to 3×3, only changed the temporal depth of the three-dimensional convolution kernel, and found through experiments that the $3 \times 3 \times 3$ convolution kernel works best.

Du Tran et al. qualitatively evaluated the generalization of C3D by visualizing the features learned on another dataset, confirming whether these features are suitable for video analysis. Specifically, they randomly selected 100,000 video sequences from the UCF101 dataset, used C3D to extract the features of these sequences, and used t-SNE [8] to map the features to a two-dimensional space. Figure 15.4 shows the results, with sequences of the same action displaying the same color. The results

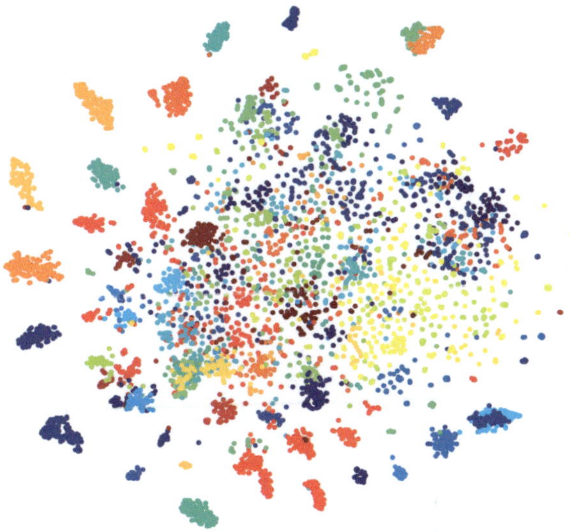

Fig. 15.4 t-SNE visualization (illustration from reference [1])

show that the features extracted by C3D are clearly distinguishable, indicating that it can effectively extract spatio-temporal features from video data.

15.4 C3D Code Implementation

We have already introduced three-dimensional convolution and the C3D model, next we start to implement a C3D model and train and test it on the UCF101 dataset.

```
Import torch.nn as nn
Class C3D(nn.Module):
    """
C3D, Convolution 3D, i.e., three-dimensional convolution
    """
    def __init__(self):
        super(C3D, self).__init__()
                        # Notice that the kernel is three-
dimensional, which meets the requirements
        # of three-dimensional convolution
                        self.conv1 = nn.Conv3d(3, 64, kernel_
size=(3, 3, 3), padding=(1, 1, 1))
                            self.pool1 = nn.MaxPool3d(kernel_
size=(1, 2, 2), stride=(1, 2, 2))
                       self.conv2 = nn.Conv3d(64, 128, kernel_
size=(3, 3, 3), padding=(1, 1, 1))
                            self.pool2 = nn.MaxPool3d(kernel_
size=(2, 2, 2), stride=(2, 2, 2))
                      self.conv3a = nn.Conv3d(128, 256, kernel_
size=(3, 3, 3), padding=(1, 1, 1))
```

```
                        self.conv3b = nn.Conv3d(256, 256, kernel_
size=(3, 3, 3), padding=(1, 1, 1))
                                self.pool3 = nn.MaxPool3d(kernel_
size=(2, 2, 2), stride=(2, 2, 2))
                        self.conv4a = nn.Conv3d(256, 512, kernel_
size=(3, 3, 3), padding=(1, 1, 1))
                        self.conv4b = nn.Conv3d(512, 512, kernel_
size=(3, 3, 3), padding=(1, 1, 1))
                                self.pool4 = nn.MaxPool3d(kernel_
size=(2, 2, 2), stride=(2, 2, 2))
                        self.conv5a = nn.Conv3d(512, 512, kernel_
size=(3, 3, 3), padding=(1, 1, 1))
                        self.conv5b = nn.Conv3d(512, 512, kernel_
size=(3, 3, 3), padding=(1, 1, 1))
                                sclf.pool5 = nn.MaxPool3d(kernel_
size=(2, 2, 2), stride=(2, 2, 2),
                           padding=(0, 1, 1))
    self.fc6 = nn.Linear(8192, 4096)
    self.fc7 = nn.Linear(4096, 4096)
    self.fc8 = nn.Linear(4096, 487)
    self.dropout = nn.Dropout(p=0.5)
    self.relu = nn.ReLU()
    self.softmax = nn.Softmax()
  def forward(self, x):
    h = self.relu(self.conv1(x))
    h = self.pool1(h)
    h = self.relu(self.conv2(h))
    h = self.pool2(h)
    h = self.relu(self.conv3a(h))
    h = self.relu(self.conv3b(h))
    h = self.pool3(h)
    h = self.relu(self.conv4a(h))
    h = self.relu(self.conv4b(h))
    h = self.pool4(h)
    h = self.relu(self.conv5a(h))
    h = self.relu(self.conv5b(h))
    h = self.pool5(h)
    h = h.view(-1, 8192)
    h = self.relu(self.fc6(h))
    h = self.dropout(h)
    h = self.relu(self.fc7(h))
    h = self.dropout(h)
    logits = self.fc8(h)
    probs = self.softmax(logits)
    return probs
```

We will implement video action recognition in the UCF101 dataset based on C3D. Here, we will directly call the completed code, which can be viewed in detail in the GitHub link.

```
!git clone https://github.com/Niki173/C3D
```

After setting up the UCF101 dataset and the pre-trained weights of the model, we can conduct the training of C3D.

```
!python train.py
```

Here, only part of the training process is shown.

```
100%|██████████| 8460/8460 [08:10<00:00, 17.25it/s]
[train] Epoch: 19/20 Loss: 0.13226544890879774 Acc: 0.9595744680851064
Execution time: 490.36240720096976

100%|██████████| 2159/2159 [01:02<00:00, 34.49it/s]
[val] Epoch: 19/20 Loss: 0.11561366206690023 Acc: 0.9689671144048171
Execution time: 62.59326391783543

100%|██████████| 8460/8460 [08:12<00:00, 17.17it/s]
[train] Epoch: 20/20 Loss: 0.12648103022828842 Acc: 0.9601034840335697
Execution time: 492.60593162314035

100%|██████████| 2159/2159 [01:02<00:00, 34.75it/s]
[val] Epoch: 20/20 Loss: 0.1177274482070989 Acc: 0.9597035664659564
Execution time: 62.13380773481913
```

Finally, we test on the testing set, achieving an accuracy of 96%.

```
100%|██████████| 2701/2701 [01:16<00:00, 35.14it/s]
[test] Epoch: 20/20 Loss: 0.12571397957808705 Acc: 0.9603850425768234
Execution time: 76.86971226101741
```

15.5 Summary

This chapter introduces the basic principles of human action recognition, commonly used datasets and evaluation metrics, and provides a detailed analysis of a classic action recognition model—C3D. The C3D model uses a three-dimensional convolutional network to extract spatiotemporal features from video data, thereby achieving high-precision action recognition. Finally, we demonstrated how to train and validate the C3D model on the UCF101 dataset, achieving good results. Looking back at our hands-on learning journey, from basic image processing to semantic understanding of images and videos, we are constantly approaching the real world, which is three-dimensional. Therefore, we will introduce scene reconstruction next, exploring the application of computer vision algorithms in the three-dimensional world.

Exercises

(1) Assume the video data size is $16 \times 512 \times 512 \times 3$, what is the output size after convolution with a $3 \times 3 \times 3$ convolution kernel?
(2) In Exercise (1), considering both the padding size and the stride are 2, what is the output size?
(3) Implement a three-dimensional pooling layer to correspond with the three-dimensional convolution.
(4) Can we extract features from each frame image using two-dimensional convolution, then fuse them in time order to achieve an effect similar to three-dimensional convolution?

(5) We will introduce optical flow computation for videos in Chap. 17. Is optical flow computation helpful for action recognition? If so, how can optical flow computation be combined with three-dimensional convolution?

References

1. TRAN D, BOURDEV L, FERGUS R, et al. Learning spatiotemporal features with 3D convolutional networks[C]//IEEE International Conference on Computer Vision, 2015:4489–4497.
2. SOOMRO K, ZAMIR A R, SHAH M. UCF101: A dataset of 101 human actions classes from videos in the wild[EB/OL]. (2012–12–03)[2024–09–25]. arXiv:1212.0402.
3. KARPATHY A, TODERICI G, SHETTY S, et al. Large-scale video classification with convolutional neural networks[C]//IEEE Conference on Computer Vision and Pattern Recognition, 2014:1725–1732.
4. KAY W, CARREIRA J, SIMONYAN K, et al. The Kinetics human action video dataset[EB/OL]. (2017–05–19)[2024–09–25]. arXiv:1705.06950.
5. CARREIRA J, NOLAND E, BANKI-HORVATH A, et al. A short note about Kinetics- 600[EB/OL]. (2018–08–03)[2024–09–25]. arXiv:1808.01340.
6. CARREIRA J, NOLAND E, HILLIER C, et al. A short note on the Kinetics-700 human action dataset[EB/OL]. (2020–10–17)[2024–09–25]. arXiv:1907.06987.
7. SIMONYAN K, ZISSERMAN A. Very deep convolutional networks for large-scale image recognition[EB/OL]. (2015–04–10)[2024–09–25]. arXiv:1409.1556.
8. VAN DER MAATEN L, HINTON G. Visualizing data using t-SNE[J]. Journal of Machine Learning research, 2008, 9(11).

Part IV
Scene Reconstruction

Chapter 16
Camera Calibration

16.1 Introduction

Capturing images serves as a primary means of capturing and recording the world, playing an indispensable role in our three-dimensional world. An image is a visual record $\boldsymbol{I}$ projected onto a two-dimensional plane by the camera imaging function f from the real-world scene $\boldsymbol{S}$, providing us with a window to observe and understand the world. However, the real world is three-dimensional, and the recorded images are two-dimensional with limited resolution, so this conversion process inevitably involves information loss. Despite this, we still hope to reconstruct the scene described in the image.

To move toward this goal, we must first deeply understand the camera imaging function f. Only by fully mastering the principle of how the camera projects the three-dimensional world onto a two-dimensional image can we possibly reverse this process and achieve the reconstruction from image to scene, i.e., the recovery of three-dimensional information from two-dimensional information. In this chapter, we will first introduce the basic principles of camera imaging, i.e., how the camera establishes the mapping relationship between a point in the real three-dimensional space and its projection point on the two-dimensional image, and then introduce how to calculate the parameters in the camera imaging process through camera calibration.

16.2 Camera Imaging Principle

Although the optical system of a camera in the real world is extremely complex, the core principle of the camera imaging function f is not much different from the simplified model. For ease of calculation and explanation, we use simplified pinhole camera models and lens camera models to approximate the working principle of actual cameras. The pinhole camera model, as a basic and efficient theoretical model,

W. Shen et al., *Hands-On Computer Vision*,
https://doi.org/10.1007/978-981-95-4835-4_16

explains the process of light passing through a small hole and forming an image on the screen (imaging plane) on the other side. Although theoretically, pinhole imaging can produce clear images, as the pinhole only allows a very small amount of light to enter, the imaging brightness is very low. This not only limits the use of pinhole imaging in low light conditions, but also requires a longer exposure time to obtain clear images. The lens camera model uses a convex lens to replace the small hole in the pinhole model for imaging, which is closer to the cameras we actually use. It should be noted that the manufacturing and assembly process of the lens may introduce certain deviations, which will cause the light ray to not propagate exactly along the expected path, thereby causing image distortion. Through camera calibration, we can model these distortions and effectively correct them.

16.2.1 Camera Model

Before introducing the principle of camera imaging, it is necessary to understand some related terms.

- Optical Center: The center of the lens. Light rays pass through the optical center without any deviation.
- Optical Axis: A straight line perpendicular to the lens that passes through the optical center.
- Focal Point: The point where light rays parallel to the optical axis converge after passing through the lens, usually located on the optical axis.
- Focal Length: Generally refers to the distance from the optical center to the focal point.

Next, we use the candle projection experiment from middle school physics class to introduce the lens camera model. As shown in Fig. 16.1, a lit candle is located at point A on the horizontal axis. To the right of the candle is a convex lens, its optical center is at point O, and the focal point of the lens is at point B. If we place a screen at point C on the right side of the convex lens, then the light from the candle will form an inverted candle image on the screen after passing through the convex lens. In this case, define the object distance $OA = n$, focal length $OB = f$, and image distance $OC = m$ on the optical axis.

Then, according to the refraction principle of the convex lens, we can get

$$mn = mf + nf.$$

That is:

$$\frac{1}{f} = \frac{1}{m} + \frac{1}{n}.$$

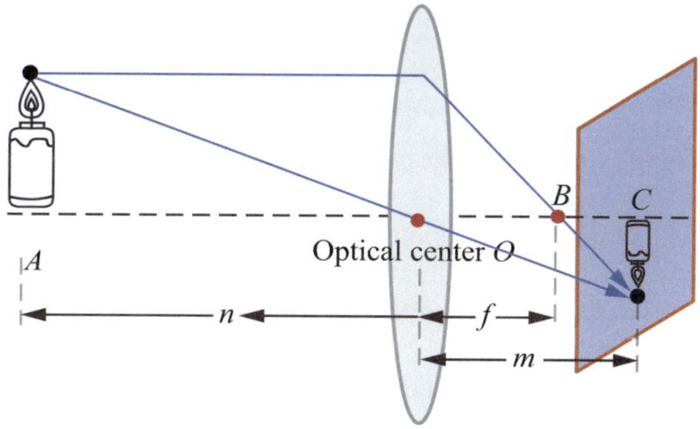

Fig. 16.1 Candle projection experiment

Generally, we consider that the object distance is much larger than the image distance, i.e., $n >> m$, so $m \approx f$, which can be approximately considered that the physical locations of B point and C point are the same. In this case, the lens camera model can be approximated as the pinhole camera model, m is also known as the effective focal length of the pinhole camera model.

16.2.2 Definition of Coordinate Systems

In Chap. 8, we have introduced the homogeneous coordinate system and the matrix form of spatial transformations. Based on this, we define different coordinate systems.

- World Coordinate System: A three-dimensional coordinate system used to describe the absolute position of spatial points in the real world. Any spatial point has a unique coordinate in the world coordinate system. Since the camera itself exists in three-dimensional space, we use the world coordinate system to record the spatial coordinates of the camera. The unit of the world coordinate system is usually meters (m).
- Camera Coordinate System: A three-dimensional coordinate system defined to conveniently describe the position of spatial points from the camera's perspective. The camera coordinate system is a coordinate system with the camera's optical center as the origin, which can be obtained from the world coordinate system through translation and rotation. The unit of the camera coordinate system is usually meters (m).
- Image Coordinate System: A two-dimensional coordinate system with the upper left corner of the imaging plane as the origin, usually represented by (u, v) coordinates. The unit of the image coordinate system is pixels.

16.2.3 Camera Extrinsic Parameters

As shown in Fig. 16.2, a point P in space falls on a point P' on the imaging plane after being projected by the camera. Let the coordinates of point P in the world coordinate system be $\boldsymbol{p}_w : (x_w, y_w, z_w)$, its homogeneous coordinate form is $\tilde{\boldsymbol{p}}_w : (x_w, y_w, z_w, 1)$; the coordinates of point P in the camera coordinate system are $\boldsymbol{p}_c : (x_c, y_c, z_c)$, its homogeneous coordinate form is $\tilde{\boldsymbol{p}}_c : (x_c, y_c, z_c, 1)$, their transformation relationship can be described by the rotation and translation relationship between the two coordinate systems.

Given the optical center O of the camera in the world coordinate system, and the rotation matrix from the world coordinate system to the camera coordinate system:

$$\boldsymbol{R} = \begin{bmatrix} r_{11} & r_{12} & r_{13} \\ r_{21} & r_{22} & r_{23} \\ r_{31} & r_{32} & r_{33} \end{bmatrix}, \boldsymbol{R} \in \mathbb{R}^{3\times 3}$$

For any point P in space, we have:

$$\boldsymbol{p}_c^{\mathrm{T}} = \boldsymbol{R}(\boldsymbol{p}_w - \mathbf{o})^{\mathrm{T}} = \boldsymbol{R}\boldsymbol{p}_w^{\mathrm{T}} - \boldsymbol{R}\boldsymbol{o}^{\mathrm{T}}$$

Let $-\boldsymbol{R}\boldsymbol{o}^{\mathrm{T}}$ be denoted as $\boldsymbol{t}$:

$$\boldsymbol{t} = -\boldsymbol{R}\boldsymbol{o}^{\mathrm{T}} = \begin{bmatrix} t_1 \\ t_2 \\ t_3 \end{bmatrix}, \boldsymbol{t} \in \mathbb{R}^{3\times 1}$$

The homogeneous form is:

$$\tilde{\boldsymbol{p}}_c^{\mathrm{T}} = \begin{bmatrix} \boldsymbol{R} & \boldsymbol{t} \\ 0^{\mathrm{T}} & 1 \end{bmatrix} \tilde{\boldsymbol{p}}_w^{\mathrm{T}}.$$

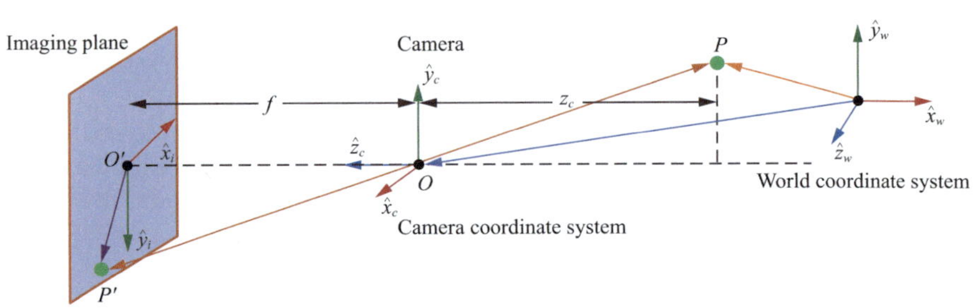

Fig. 16.2 Schematic of camera projection

In the above equation, 0^Trepresents a 1×3 row zero vector. In this way, we obtain the transformation matrix $[\boldsymbol{R}|\boldsymbol{t}]$ from the world coordinate system to the camera coordinate system, usually referred to as the camera extrinsics matrix.

16.2.4 Camera Intrinsic Parameters

The camera extrinsics matrix describes the coordinate transformation between the world coordinate system and the camera coordinate system. Knowing the camera's extrinsics matrix can transform the coordinates of a point in the real three-dimensional space from the world coordinate system to the camera coordinate system. Next, we need to calculate the transformation relationship between the coordinates of this point in the camera coordinate system and the coordinates of its projection point on the imaging plane in the image coordinate system. Let's continue with the previous definition. The coordinates of this point in the camera coordinate system are $\boldsymbol{p}_c$::(x_c, y_c, z_c), and the projection point on the imaging plane is P'. We assume that the imaging plane is perpendicular to the z-axis of the camera coordinate system, and the imaging plane is located in the negative direction of the z-axis. Then the intersection of the z-axis of the camera coordinate system and the imaging plane is the projection point of the optical center O on the imaging plane O'; the x-axis and y-axis of the camera coordinate system are parallel to the horizontal (x-axis) and vertical (y-axis) axes of the imaging plane, respectively. Let the coordinates of point P' in the camera coordinate system be $(x_i, y_i, -f)$, where f is the effective focal length of the camera. As shown in Fig. 16.2, point P is projected through O to point P', so based on similar triangles we can get

$$\frac{z_c}{f} = -\frac{x_c}{x_i} = -\frac{y_c}{y_i}.$$

Thus, it is not difficult to obtain.

$$\begin{cases} x_i = -f\frac{x_c}{z_c} \\ y_i = -f\frac{y_c}{z_c} \end{cases}.$$

The negative sign in the formula indicates that the image formed is inverted. The actual imaging plane is shown in Fig. 16.3a. To simplify the model, we can mirror the imaging plane to the front of the camera and place it on the same side of the camera coordinate system as the three-dimensional space point, as shown in Fig. 16.3b. In fact, in daily life, the images we see are upright, because the camera has automatically corrected the inverted image in the actual output process. Therefore, this not only removes the negative sign in the formula, making the formula more concise, but also more closely aligns with the observations in daily life.

After removing the negative sign, the matrix form of the above equation is

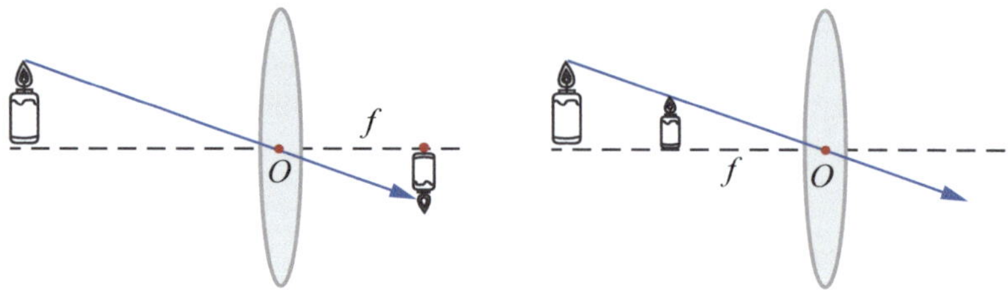

(a) Actual imaging plane (b) Mirrored imaging plane

Fig. 16.3 Schematic diagram of the imaging plane

$$\begin{bmatrix} z_c x_i \\ z_c y_i \\ z_c \end{bmatrix} = \begin{bmatrix} f & 0 & 0 & 0 \\ 0 & f & 0 & 0 \\ 0 & 0 & 1 & 0 \end{bmatrix} \begin{bmatrix} x_c \\ y_c \\ z_c \\ 1 \end{bmatrix}.$$

For points on the imaging plane, their z-axis coordinates in the camera coordinate system are the same, so we can use only the x-axis and y-axis coordinates to describe their spatial position. Since the imaging plane is perpendicular to the optical axis, the projection of the optical center O on the imaging plane is O', so the x-axis and y-axis coordinates (x_i, y_i) of point P′ in the camera coordinate system can be regarded as being defined in a coordinate system constructed on the imaging plane with O' as the origin. The image coordinate system, as shown in Fig. 16.4, has its origin in the upper left corner of the imaging plane, so a translation transformation is needed for the coordinates (x_i, y_i) to make O' coincide with the origin of the image coordinate system. In addition, the unit of coordinates (x_i, y_i) is m, while the image coordinate system uses pixels as the unit, so a scale factor is needed to describe the actual physical length corresponding to a single pixel. Since the scale factor of the camera's pixels may be different in the horizontal and vertical directions, we need two different scale factors to describe this scale transformation.

Here, we set the scale factor of the image coordinate system on the u-axis (horizontal axis) as α, and the scale factor on the v-axis (vertical axis) as β. At the same time, the displacement of O' relative to the origin of the image coordinate system is $\left(c_x, c_y\right)$. Then, the relationship between the coordinates of P' in the camera coordinate system and its coordinates (u, v) in the image coordinate system is

$$\begin{cases} u = \alpha \times f \frac{x_c}{z_c} + c_x \\ v = \beta \times f \frac{y_c}{z_c} + c_y \end{cases}.$$

Combining $\alpha \times f$ in the above equation into f_x, and $\beta \times f$ into f_y, we can get the complete matrix:

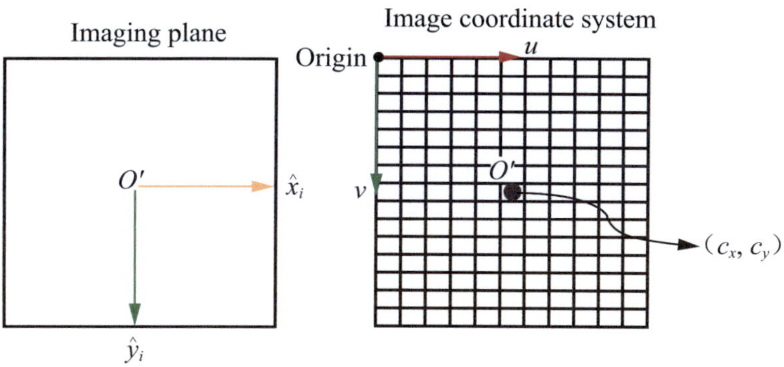

Fig. 16.4 Imaging plane and image coordinate system

$$\begin{bmatrix} z_c u \\ z_c v \\ z_c \end{bmatrix} = \begin{bmatrix} f_x & 0 & c_x \\ 0 & f_y & c_y \\ 0 & 0 & 1 \end{bmatrix} \begin{bmatrix} x_c \\ y_c \\ z_c \end{bmatrix}.$$

In the above equation, we generally call the middle 3 × 3 matrix the camera intrinsics matrix $\boldsymbol{K}$. Generally, the camera intrinsics can be considered as fixed and will not change significantly during use. Some manufacturers will directly tell users the camera intrinsics, but most of the time we need to calibrate the camera intrinsics ourselves. Sometimes we will see that there is a parameter s in the intrinsics matrix given by some manufacturers, which is used to describe the non-orthogonality of pixels:

$$\begin{bmatrix} z_c u \\ z_c v \\ z_c \end{bmatrix} = \begin{bmatrix} f_x & s & c_x \\ 0 & f_y & c_y \\ 0 & 0 & 1 \end{bmatrix} \begin{bmatrix} x_c \\ y_c \\ z_c \end{bmatrix}.$$

However, in most cases, considering the existing technology and simplifying calculations, we can assume that $s = 0$, i.e., the pixels are orthogonal.

16.2.5 Projection Matrix

According to Sects. 16.2.3 and 16.2.4, with known camera intrinsic and extrinsic parameters, the coordinates of any point in space in the image coordinate system can be calculated. Therefore, we can combine the camera intrinsic and extrinsic parameters to obtain a 3 × 4 matrix, which is called the projection matrix. The definition of the projection matrix is as follows:

$$P = K[R|t] = \begin{bmatrix} p_{11} & p_{12} & p_{13} & p_{14} \\ p_{21} & p_{22} & p_{23} & p_{24} \\ p_{31} & p_{32} & p_{33} & p_{34} \end{bmatrix}.$$

In order to obtain an invertible projection matrix, an additional row is usually considered to construct a 4×4 homogeneous matrix:

$$\tilde{P} = \begin{bmatrix} K & 0 \\ 0^{\mathrm{T}} & 1 \end{bmatrix} \begin{bmatrix} R & t \\ 0^{\mathrm{T}} & 1 \end{bmatrix}.$$

Given the projection matrix and the homogeneous coordinates of the space point, its coordinates in the image coordinate system can be obtained through matrix multiplication:

$$\tilde{p}_i^{\mathrm{T}} = \tilde{P}\tilde{p}_w^{\mathrm{T}},$$

where $\tilde{p}_i$ is the homogeneous coordinates of point P in the image coordinate system.

16.2.6 Distortion

As mentioned earlier, the amount of light entering through a pinhole is insufficient, so we usually use lenses instead of pinholes for imaging. However, the manufacturing and assembly process of the lens may introduce some deviations, which will cause the light ray to not propagate exactly as expected, resulting in image distortion. There are two types of these distortions:

- Distortions caused by lens design and optical characteristics are called radial distortions.
- Distortions caused by the lens not being strictly parallel to the imaging plane are called tangential distortions.

Next, we will introduce the causes of radial and tangential distortions and their correction methods.

1. Radial Distortion

Ideally, the lens should make the incoming light rays precisely converge at a specific point on the imaging plane. However, in practice, the light rays do not always perfectly focus on a point when passing through the lens, especially when passing through the edge of the lens. This phenomenon is called spherical aberration of the lens. Near the center of the lens, light rays can be focused more accurately. However, as the distance from the point where a ray enters the lens to the lens center increases, the focusing error of the ray also increases. This results in the corresponding point on the image no longer being a true mapping of the incident

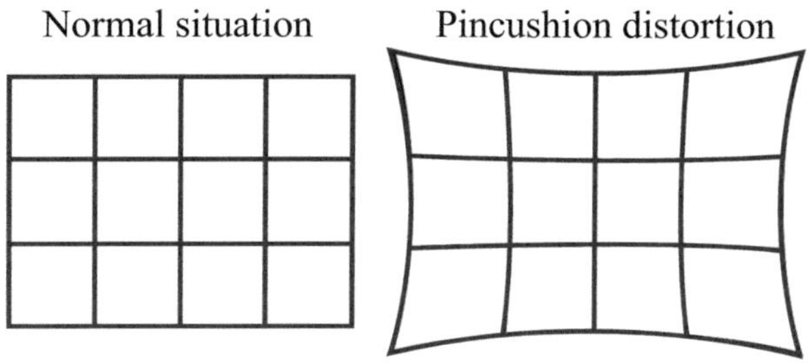

Fig. 16.5 Radial distortion

ray, but instead being shifted inward or outward, forming what is known as radial distortion. Radial distortion usually manifests in two forms: barrel distortion and pincushion distortion. Pincushion distortion makes the borders of the image sink towards the center, while barrel distortion makes the borders of the image bulge outwards, as shown in Fig. 16.5. The degree of distortion usually increases with the distance from the center of the lens.

2. Tangential Distortion

To ensure that light rays are focused uniformly on the imaging plane, the lens and the imaging plane should ideally be perfectly parallel. However, due to manufacturing defects, assembly errors, and other factors, the lens may not be perfectly parallel to the imaging plane, as shown in Fig. 16.6. This non-parallelism causes light rays to arrive at the imaging plane at an angle, resulting in stretching or compression phenomena in certain regions of the image. The border regions of the image are particularly susceptible to the effects of lens tilt or misalignment, because the changes in the light path in these regions are the most significant. The resulting distortion is called tangential distortion, which mainly affects the borders of the image, making straight lines appear curved, thereby affecting the image quality.

3. Distortion Correction

As shown in Fig. 16.7, radial distortion can be understood as the actual imaging point moving along the radial direction, while tangential distortion can be understood as the actual imaging point moving along the tangent direction. Therefore, we can use polynomial functions to describe the coordinate changes brought by distortion, thereby achieving distortion correction.

First, let's use mathematical language to describe the formation of radial distortion: given the coordinates of a point in the camera coordinate system as (x_c, y_c, z_c), if the lens does not have distortion, we can directly obtain the coordinates of the projection point (pixel point) on the imaging plane under ideal conditions in the image coordinate system according to similar triangles. From Sect. 16.2.4, we can get

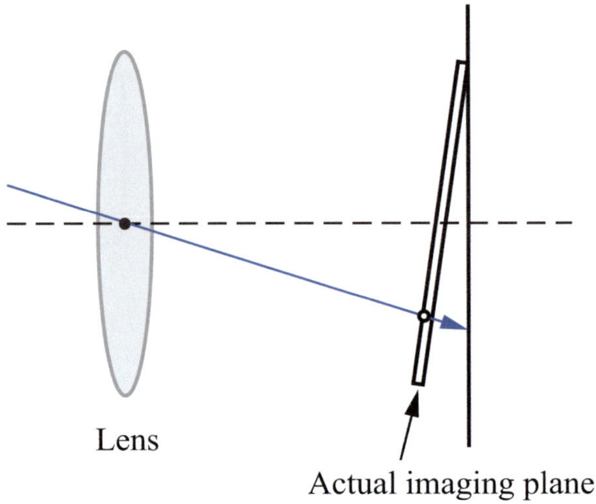

Fig. 16.6 Tangential distortion

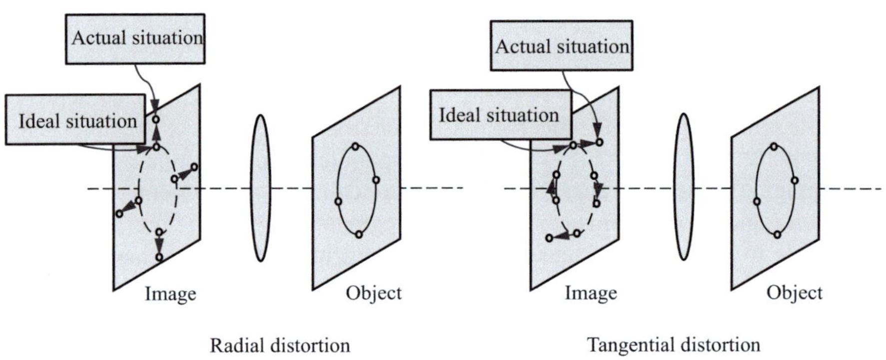

Fig. 16.7 Displacement of the imaging point during distortion

$$\begin{bmatrix} u \\ v \\ 1 \end{bmatrix} = \begin{bmatrix} f_x & 0 & c_x \\ 0 & f_y & c_y \\ 0 & 0 & 1 \end{bmatrix} \begin{bmatrix} x_c' \\ y_c' \\ 1 \end{bmatrix}$$

where x_c' and y_c' are, respectively, equal to $\frac{x_c}{z_c}$ and $\frac{y_c}{z_c}$. However, due to lens distortion, the actually observed pixel locations are shifted radially, and the magnitude of this shift is dependent on the distance from the pixel to the image center. Therefore, we can use a polynomial function to describe the correction for radial distortion:

$$\begin{cases} x_{\text{cor}} = x_c'\left(1 + k_1 r^2 + k_2 r^4 + k_3 r^6 + \ldots\right) \\ y_{\text{cor}} = y_c'\left(1 + k_1 r^2 + k_2 r^4 + k_3 r^6 + \ldots\right) \end{cases},$$

where $r^2 = x'_{c^2} + y'_{c^2}$. Here, $k_1, k_2, k_3, \ldots$ are the distortion coefficients of radial distortion, which are obtained through camera calibration. In general lenses, using the first two coefficients (k_1 and k_2) can handle distortion well; for lenses with large distortion, such as fisheye lenses, we need to add k_3 term or even higher order terms to correct the distortion. Similarly, tangential distortion can be seen as a change in the coordinate point along the tangent direction, so we can introduce two additional parameters p_1 and p_2 to correct the tangential distortion:

$$\begin{cases} x_{\text{cor}} = x'_c + 2p_1 x'_c y'_c + p_2\left(r^2 + 2x'_{c^2}\right) \\ y_{\text{cor}} = y'_c + p_1\left(r^2 + 2y'_{c^2}\right) + 2p_2 x'_c y'_c \end{cases}.$$

After the above studying, we have initially understood the correction models of radial distortion and tangential distortion. In real scenarios, radial distortion and tangential distortion usually coexist, so we need to combine the correction equations of radial distortion and tangential distortion:

$$\begin{cases} x_{\text{cor}} = x'_c\left(1 + k_1 r^2 + k_2 r^4 + k_3 r^6 + \ldots\right) + 2p_1 x'_c y'_c + p_2\left(r^2 + 2x'_{c^2}\right) \\ y_{\text{cor}} = y_{c'}\left(1 + k_1 r^2 + k_2 r^4 + k_3 r^6 + \ldots\right) + p_1\left(r^2 + 2y'_{c^2}\right) + 2p_2 x'_c y'_c \end{cases}.$$

Then, based on the camera's intrinsic matrix $\boldsymbol{K}$, convert $(x_{cor}, y_{cor})^{\mathrm{T}}$ to $(u_{cor}, v_{cor})^{\mathrm{T}}$, so we get the corrected image coordinate system coordinates:

$$\begin{cases} u_{\text{cor}} = f_x x_{\text{cor}} + c_x \\ v_{\text{cor}} = f_y y_{\text{cor}} + c_y \end{cases}.$$

Since different cameras have different characteristics, these five parameters can be freely combined in practical use, and not all need to be considered.

So far, we have fully introduced the camera imaging model, which can well describe the imaging process of the camera and correct radial and tangential distortions. In practical applications, we need to obtain the values of the parameters in the model through camera calibration.

16.3 Implementation of Camera Calibration

In Sect. 16.2, we delved into the principles of camera imaging, the concepts of intrinsic and extrinsic parameters, and the distortion correction model. Given the camera's intrinsic and extrinsic parameters as well as the distortion parameters, the projected coordinates of any point in 3D space on the imaging plane can be precisely calculated. Conversely, can we solve the camera's intrinsic and extrinsic parameters, as well as the distortion parameters, from the projected coordinates of three-dimensional points on the image plane? This question is the camera calibration problem. The answer is yes. This process is essentially a parameter estimation

Fig. 16.8 Checkerboard calibration board

problem, which can be realized through mathematical optimization methods. Specifically, we can collect a series of known three-dimensional space points and their corresponding two-dimensional image projection point coordinates. Then, we can use these coordinates as input, and solve the camera parameters by minimizing the reprojection error, i.e., the coordinate differences between the points projected from the three-dimensional points to the two-dimensional imaging plane and the points actually observed in the image. This method usually requires multiple sets of data to ensure the stability and accuracy of the solution process. Through this method, we can obtain the intrinsic parameters, extrinsic parameters, and distortion parameters of the camera, thereby achieving camera calibration.

16.3.1 Calibration Board

Before introducing the calibration process, let's first understand the calibration board. The calibration board is an indispensable tool in the camera calibration process. It typically consists of a pattern with high contrast, whose geometric sizes and layout are precisely known. Figure 16.8 shows a common calibration board. Its pattern is composed of a series of black and white alternating checkerboards, hence known as a checkerboard calibration board. We will use the checkerboard calibration board as an example to explain how to calibrate the camera.

16.3.2 Calibration Process

First, we take pictures of the calibration board from multiple different angles. These captured images should meet the following requirements:

- The calibration board should be clearly visible and unobstructed.
- The calibration board should be roughly in the center of the image.
- The corners of the calibration board should be clearly visible.

After obtaining an image of the calibration board, we use the corner detection algorithm mentioned in Chap. 6 to get coordinates of each corner $\left(u^{(i)}, v^{(i)}, 1\right)$ in the image coordinate system. The next problem is how to obtain the coordinates of the corresponding three-dimensional points of these pixels in the world coordinate system. The checkerboard calibration board itself is a plane, thus we can regard it as a two-dimensional plane. We can set the world coordinate system fixed on the checkerboard, with the z-axis perpendicular to the checkerboard plane, and the x-axis and y-axis parallel to the checkerboard plane. Furthermore, since the exact sizes of the checkerboard pattern are known, we can calculate the coordinates of each corner $\left(x_w^{(i)}, y_w^{(i)}, z_w^{(i)}\right)$ in the world coordinate system. In this way, we obtain the image coordinate system coordinates and world coordinate system coordinates of each corner in this calibration board image.

We start with the case of a single image. In this case, we do not consider distortion parameters first. According to the projection matrix, we can obtain the projection equation:

$$\begin{bmatrix} u^{(i)} \\ v^{(i)} \\ 1 \end{bmatrix} = \begin{bmatrix} p_{11} & p_{12} & p_{13} & p_{14} \\ p_{21} & p_{22} & p_{23} & p_{24} \\ p_{31} & p_{32} & p_{33} & p_{34} \end{bmatrix} \begin{bmatrix} x_w^{(i)} \\ y_w^{(i)} \\ z_w^{(i)} \\ 1 \end{bmatrix}.$$

Converting the matrix form into an equation form, we have

$$\begin{aligned} u^{(i)} &= \frac{p_{11}x_w^{(i)} + p_{12}y_w^{(i)} + p_{13}z_w^{(i)} + p_{14}}{p_{31}x_w^{(i)} + p_{32}y_w^{(i)} + p_{33}z_w^{(i)} + p_{34}} \\ v^{(i)} &= \frac{p_{21}x_w^{(i)} + p_{22}y_w^{(i)} + p_{23}z_w^{(i)} + p_{24}}{p_{31}x_w^{(i)} + p_{32}y_w^{(i)} + p_{33}z_w^{(i)} + p_{34}}. \end{aligned}$$

In theory, all points in the same image share the same projection matrix, thus we only need to input multiple different points into the above formula to solve the projection equation.

$$\begin{bmatrix} x_w^{(1)} & y_w^{(1)} & z_w^{(1)} & 1 & 0 & 0 & 0 & 0 & -u^{(1)}x_w^{(1)} & -u^{(1)}y_w^{(1)} & -u^{(1)}z_w^{(1)} & -u^{(1)} \\ 0 & 0 & 0 & 0 & x_w^{(1)} & y_w^{(1)} & z_w^{(1)} & 1 & -v^{(1)}x_w^{(1)} & -v^{(1)}y_w^{(1)} & -v^{(1)}z_w^{(1)} & -v^{(1)} \\ x_w^{(2)} & y_w^{(2)} & z_w^{(2)} & 1 & 0 & 0 & 0 & 0 & -u^{(2)}x_w^{(2)} & -u^{(2)}y_w^{(2)} & -u^{(2)}z_w^{(2)} & -u^{(2)} \\ 0 & 0 & 0 & 0 & x_w^{(2)} & y_w^{(2)} & z_w^{(2)} & 1 & -v^{(2)}x_w^{(2)} & -v^{(2)}y_w^{(2)} & -v^{(2)}z_w^{(2)} & -v^{(2)} \\ \vdots & \vdots & \vdots & \vdots & \vdots & \vdots & \vdots & \vdots & \vdots & \vdots & \vdots & \vdots \\ x_w^{(n)} & y_w^{(n)} & z_w^{(n)} & 1 & 0 & 0 & 0 & 0 & -u^{(n)}x_w^{(n)} & -u^{(n)}y_w^{(n)} & -u^{(n)}z_w^{(n)} & -u^{(n)} \\ 0 & 0 & 0 & 0 & x_w^{(n)} & y_w^{(n)} & z_w^{(n)} & 1 & -v^{(n)}x_w^{(n)} & -v^{(n)}y_w^{(n)} & -v^{(n)}z_w^{(n)} & -v^{(n)} \end{bmatrix}$$

$$\begin{bmatrix} p_{11} \\ p_{12} \\ p_{13} \\ p_{14} \\ p_{21} \\ p_{22} \\ p_{23} \\ p_{24} \\ p_{31} \\ p_{32} \\ p_{33} \\ p_{34} \end{bmatrix} = \begin{bmatrix} 0 \\ 0 \\ 0 \\ 0 \\ \vdots \\ 0 \\ 0 \end{bmatrix}.$$

Simplify the above formula into the form of a system of homogeneous linear equations $\boldsymbol{A}\boldsymbol{p} = 0$. According to the solution method of the system of homogeneous linear equations, we can assume $\overline{\boldsymbol{p}}$ is the general solution of the system of equations, then any $k\overline{\boldsymbol{p}}$ can be used as the solution of the above equation. Therefore, for the convenience of calculation, we directly assume $\overline{\boldsymbol{p}}$ satisfies $\|\overline{\boldsymbol{p}}\|_2 = 1$, then the above formula can be written as

$$\min_{\boldsymbol{p}} \|\boldsymbol{A}\boldsymbol{p}\|^2 \quad \text{s.t.} \quad \|\overline{\boldsymbol{p}}\|_2 = 1.$$

This is a quadratic programming problem. The specific solution method for it can refer to the method introduced in Sect. 8.6. The eigenvector corresponding to the smallest eigenvalue of the matrix $\boldsymbol{A}^{\mathrm{T}}\boldsymbol{A}$ is the approximate solution of this system of equations. However, it should be noted that all corners are on a calibration board plane. Review our configuration of the world coordinate system: we fix the world coordinate system on the chessboard, with the z-axis perpendicular to the checkerboard plane, and the x-axis and y-axis parallel to the checkerboard plane. In this case, the physical coordinates of any point on the chessboard satisfy $z_w^{(i)} = 0$. At this time, there are multiple columns in the matrix $\boldsymbol{A}$ that are all zero, such as the third column, the seventh column, and the eleventh column. Then, the values in the corresponding dimensions in $\boldsymbol{P}$ cannot be determined, thus the previous method should not be used for solution. In this case, the previous projection equation becomes

$$\begin{bmatrix} u^{(i)} \\ v^{(i)} \\ 1 \end{bmatrix} = \begin{bmatrix} f_x & 0 & c_x \\ 0 & f_y & c_y \\ 0 & 0 & 1 \end{bmatrix} \begin{bmatrix} r_{11} & r_{12} & r_{13} & t_x \\ r_{21} & r_{22} & r_{23} & t_y \\ r_{31} & r_{32} & r_{33} & t_z \end{bmatrix} \begin{bmatrix} x_w^{(i)} \\ y_w^{(i)} \\ 0 \\ 1 \end{bmatrix}.$$

It is not difficult to find that, r_{13}, r_{23}, r_{33}, these three unknowns cannot be solved in the above formula. Let's remove this column and get

$$\begin{bmatrix} u^{(i)} \\ v^{(i)} \\ 1 \end{bmatrix} = \begin{bmatrix} f_x & 0 & c_x \\ 0 & f_y & c_y \\ 0 & 0 & 1 \end{bmatrix} \begin{bmatrix} r_{11} & r_{12} & t_x \\ r_{21} & r_{22} & t_y \\ r_{31} & r_{32} & t_z \end{bmatrix} \begin{bmatrix} x_w^{(i)} \\ y_w^{(i)} \\ 1 \end{bmatrix}.$$

Take $[r_{11}\ r_{21}\ r_{31}]^{\mathrm{T}}$ as a whole, denoted as $\mathbf{r}_1$, and $[r_{12}\ r_{22}\ r_{32}]^{\mathrm{T}}$ is denoted as $\mathbf{r}_2$, then the above formula can be written as

$$\begin{bmatrix} u^{(i)} \\ v^{(i)} \\ 1 \end{bmatrix} = \boldsymbol{K}\begin{bmatrix} \boldsymbol{r}_1 & \boldsymbol{r}_2 & \boldsymbol{t} \end{bmatrix} \begin{bmatrix} x_w^{(i)} \\ y_w^{(i)} \\ 1 \end{bmatrix}.$$

The above $\boldsymbol{K}[\boldsymbol{r}_1 \quad \boldsymbol{r}_2 \quad \boldsymbol{t}]$ is denoted as $\boldsymbol{H} = [\boldsymbol{h}_1 \quad \boldsymbol{h}_2 \quad \boldsymbol{h}_3]$, where $\boldsymbol{h}_1 = \boldsymbol{K}\boldsymbol{r}_1, \boldsymbol{h}_2 = \boldsymbol{K}\boldsymbol{r}_2, \boldsymbol{h}_3 = \boldsymbol{K}\boldsymbol{t}$. Here, $\boldsymbol{H}$ is the homography matrix we mentioned in Chap. 8. $\boldsymbol{H}$ matrix itself is a 3×3 matrix, with eight degrees of freedom (the last degree of freedom is the scale factor, which can be determined by normalization), thus at least four pairs of points are needed to construct a system of linear equations containing eight unknowns for solving $\boldsymbol{H}$. After obtaining the homography matrix $\boldsymbol{H}$, the next problem to consider is how to solve $\mathbf{K}, \mathbf{R}, \boldsymbol{t}$ from $\boldsymbol{H}$. Here we need to use the properties of the rotation matrix, that is, the rotation matrix is an orthogonal matrix, thus we have $\boldsymbol{r}_1^{\mathrm{T}}\boldsymbol{r}_2 = 0, \boldsymbol{r}_1^{\mathrm{T}}\boldsymbol{r}_1 = \boldsymbol{r}_2^{\mathrm{T}}\boldsymbol{r}_2 = 1$. Also, because $\boldsymbol{r}_1 = \boldsymbol{K}^{-1}\boldsymbol{h}_1, \boldsymbol{r}_2 = \boldsymbol{K}^{-1}\boldsymbol{h}_2$, then we can get

$$\begin{cases} \boldsymbol{h}_1^{\mathrm{T}}\boldsymbol{B}\boldsymbol{h}_1 - \boldsymbol{h}_2^{\mathrm{T}}\boldsymbol{B}\boldsymbol{h}_2 = 0 \\ \boldsymbol{h}_1^{\mathrm{T}}\boldsymbol{B}\boldsymbol{h}_2 = 0 \end{cases}$$

In the above formula, $\boldsymbol{B} = \boldsymbol{K}^{-\mathrm{T}}\boldsymbol{K}^{-1}$. Obviously $\boldsymbol{B}$ is a symmetric semi-positive definite matrix, and hence contains six unknown elements. Since each image of the calibration board from a different views can provide the aforementioned system of equations, i.e., two equations, we need at least three images of the calibration board from different views to solve for $\boldsymbol{B}$. Note that the intrinsic matrix $\boldsymbol{K}$ is an invertible upper right triangular matrix, thus $\boldsymbol{K}^{-\mathrm{T}}$ and $\boldsymbol{K}^{-1}$ are, respectively, lower left triangular matrix and upper right triangular matrix, then $\boldsymbol{B}$ is a symmetric positive definite matrix. Therefore, we only need to solve for $\boldsymbol{B}$, and then we can solve for the camera intrinsic matrix $\boldsymbol{K}$ through Cholesky decomposition. After obtaining the intrinsic matrix, we can solve for $\boldsymbol{t}$ through $\boldsymbol{K}^{-1}\boldsymbol{h}_3$, and finally solve for the first two columns of the rotation matrix through $\mathbf{r}_1 = \boldsymbol{K}^{-1}\boldsymbol{h}_1$, $\mathbf{r}_2 = \boldsymbol{K}^{-1}\boldsymbol{h}_2$. The calculated $\boldsymbol{r}_1$ and $\boldsymbol{r}_2$ do not satisfy orthogonality, thus we need to orthogonalize them, usually using Schmidt orthogonalization. According to the properties of the rotation matrix, its third column can be obtained by cross multiplying the first two columns, i.e., $\boldsymbol{r}_3 = \boldsymbol{r}_1 \times \boldsymbol{r}_2$. Here, we need to check whether the direction of $\mathbf{r}_3$ is correct, i.e., $det(\boldsymbol{R}) = 1$, if not, we need to take its opposite. At this point, we have obtained the camera intrinsic matrix $\boldsymbol{K}$ and the extrinsic matrix $[\boldsymbol{R}|\boldsymbol{t}]$, but don't forget, these derivations are all based on the premise that the image has no distortion, thus we still need to consider the distortion term. First, assume that the just obtained intrinsic matrix $\boldsymbol{K}$ is correct, according to the distortion model in Sect. 16.2.6, we can get

$$\begin{bmatrix} x_{cor} \\ y_{cor} \end{bmatrix} = \left(1 + k_1 r^2 + k_2 r^4 + k_3 r^6\right) \begin{bmatrix} x \\ y \end{bmatrix} + \begin{bmatrix} 2p_1 xy + p_2\left(r^2 + 2x^2\right) \\ p_1\left(r^2 + 2y^2\right) + 2p_2 xy \end{bmatrix}$$
$$\text{s.t.} \quad x^2 + y^2 = r^2$$

We assume that the lens is unbiased, then through the projection matrix we can get the expected coordinates $(\overline{x}, \overline{y})$ of the corners in the image coordinate system. We can obtain

$$\min_{\mathbf{k}} \| \{x_{\text{cor}} - \overline{x}, y_{\text{cor}} - \overline{y}\} \|^2,$$

Where $\boldsymbol{k} = \begin{bmatrix} k_1 & k_2 & p_1 & p_2 & k_3 \end{bmatrix}^{\mathrm{T}}$. This equation has become an optimization problem. We can apply the method used in solving the intrinsic parameters directly: by substituting the observed results from different images and iteratively solving for $\boldsymbol{k}$. When calculating the distortion parameters, it is assumed that the camera intrinsic parameters are correct. This assumption is reasonable when there is no distortion, but it is not reasonable when considering distortion. Therefore, to get the final result, we need to perform alternating iterative optimization between the intrinsic parameter matrix and the distortion parameters.

Through alternating iterative optimization, we finally obtain the result of camera calibration $\{k_1, k_2, p_1, p_2, k_3\}$, $\{f_x, f_y, c_x, c_y\}$. In the actual calibration process, the above convergence process is relatively slow. Generally, the complete set of parameter estimates is obtained by minimizing the following function:

$$\sum_{i=1}^{n} \sum_{j=1}^{m} \left\| \boldsymbol{m}_{ij} - \boldsymbol{m}\left(\boldsymbol{K}, k_1, k_2, k_3, p_1, p_2, \boldsymbol{R}_i, \boldsymbol{t}_i, \boldsymbol{M}_j\right) \right\|^2.$$

In the above equation, $\boldsymbol{m}\left(\boldsymbol{K}, k_1, k_2, k_3, p_1, p_2, \boldsymbol{R}_i, \boldsymbol{t}_i, \boldsymbol{M}_j\right)$. This optimization problem is a nonlinear least squares problem, which can be solved by the Gauss–Newton method or the Levenberg–Marquardt method.

16.3.3 Code Implementation

Next, we introduce the code implementation of camera calibration. For ease of understanding, we do not consider the impact of camera distortion. The entire process includes extracting corners from the calibration board image, calculating the homography matrix, solving the intrinsic matrix, solving the extrinsic matrix, and finally evaluating the accuracy of the calibration through reprojection error. Here, we use the calibration images in the OpenCV sample as examples. Readers can also obtain calibration board images by taking pictures from printed or purchased calibration boards.

```
# First clone the corresponding repository
! git clone https://github.com/boyu-ai/Hands-on-CV.git
```

```
Cloning into 'Hands-on-CV'...
remote: Enumerating objects: 9, done.
remote: Counting objects: 100% (9/9), done.
remote: Compressing objects: 100% (4/4), done.
remote: Total 9 (delta 1), reused 5 (delta 0), pack-reused 0
Receiving objects: 100% (9/9), done.
Resolving deltas: 100% (1/1), done.
```

```
Import cv2
Import glob
Import numpy as np
Import matplotlib.pyplot as plt
% matplotlib inline
```

```
# Get image path
image_dirs = sorted(glob.glob("./Hands-on-CV/Sec-16/
left*.jpg"),
          key=lambda x: int(x.split("/")[-1].split(".")[0][4:]))
```

```
# Visualize 4 checkerboard images
plt.figure()
for I in range(4):
plt.subplot(2, 2, i+1)
img = cv2.imread(image_dirs[i], 0)
plt.imshow(img, cmap="gray")
plt.axis("off")
```

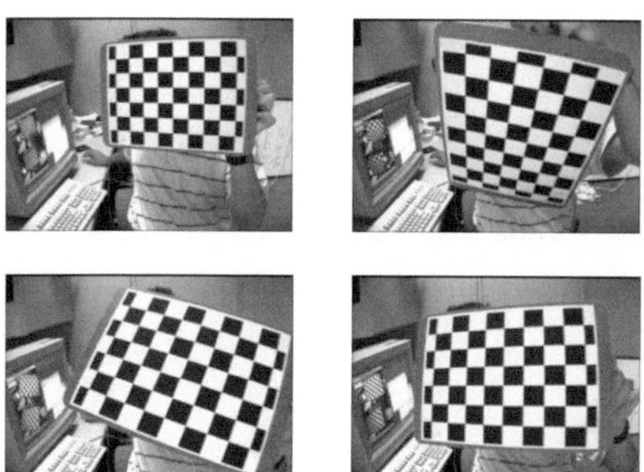

We can obtain the coordinates of the corners of the checkerboard in the above images through the corner detection algorithm. OpenCV provides the cv2.findChessboardCorners() function to help us detect the corners of the checkerboard.

```
def detect_corner(image_dirs):
   """
      Detect corners in the image and return, meanwhile visual-
izing the corner
   Detection results
   """
  # Determine the number of corners used for calibration based on the
   # calibration board. Here take (7, 6) as an example
   num_corner = (7, 6)
      # Create a list to save the three-dimensional coordi-
nates of the corners in each
   # image
   objpoints = []
      # Create a list to save the two-dimensional coordi-
nates of the corners in each
   # image
   imgpoints = []

   # Define three-dimensional coordinates: [row, col, z]
   objp = np.zeros((6*7,3), np.float32)
   objp[:,:2] = np.mgrid[0:num_corner[0], \
         0:num_corner[1]].T.reshape(-1,2)

   # Traverse all images to find corners
   for fname in image_dirs:
      img = cv2.imread(fname)
      # Convert the image to grayscale to facilitatecorner detection
      gray = cv2.cvtColor(img, cv2.COLOR_BGR2GRAY)
               # Use corner detection to find corner coordi-
nates, if found ret returns True
      # The top-left corner is the origin
            ret, corners = cv2.findChessboardCorners(gray, num_
corner, None)
      # Record corners based on the status of ret
      if ret == True:
         objpoints.append(objp[:, :2])


         imgpoints.append(corners.reshape(-1, 2))
         # Use OpenCV's built-in drawing function to visu-
alize the corner detection #
   # results, starting from red and ending in purple
   cv2.drawChessboardCorners(img, (7,6), corners, ret)
   plt.imshow(cv2.cvtColor(img, cv2.COLOR_BGR2RGB))
   plt.show()

   return objpoints, imgpoints, gray
# Call the detect_corner function to detect the corners of each image
objpoints, imgpoints, gray = detect_corner(image_dirs)
```

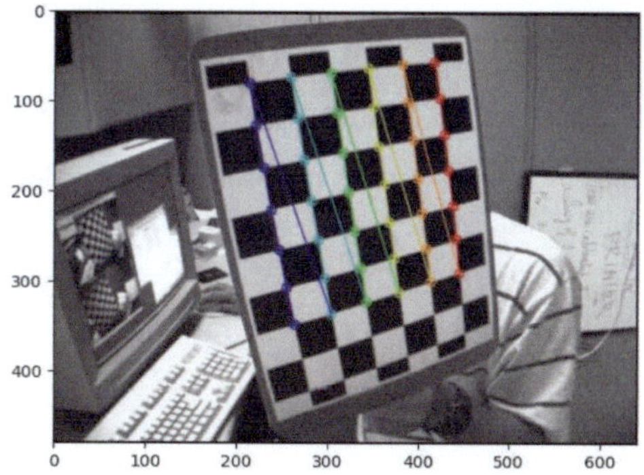

At this point, we have obtained the image coordinates of the corners in the image and their corresponding coordinates in the world coordinate system. Next, we can use the correspondence between these coordinates to solve for the homography matrix ***H***.

```
Def normalizing_input_data(coor_data):
   # Calculate the mean of the coordinates
   x_avg = np.mean(coor_data[:, 0])
   y_avg = np.mean(coor_data[:, 1])
  # Calculate the standard deviation of the coordinates and use it to
     # calculate the scale factor, so that the standard devia-
tion of the normalized
   # coordinates is sqrt(2)
   sx = np.sqrt(2) / np.std(coor_data[:, 0])
   sy = np.sqrt(2) / np.std(coor_data[:, 1])
  # Construct the normalization matrix, which is used to normalize the
coordinates
   # so that the mean is 0 and the standard deviation is sqrt(2)
norm_matrix = np.array([[sx, 0, -sx * x_avg],
   norm_matrix = np.array([[sx, 0, -sx * x_avg],
                  [0, sy, -sy * y_avg],
                  [0, 0, 1]])
   return norm_matrix


def compute_homography(pic_coor, real_coor):
   """
   Compute the homography matrix H


   Parameters:
   - pic_coor: The coordinates in the image coordinate system
   - real_coor: The coordinates in the world coordinate system


   Returns:
   - H: Homography matrix
   """
   pic_norm_mat = normalizing_input_data(pic_coor)
   real_norm_mat = normalizing_input_data(real_coor)
```

```
A = [] # Build the system of linear equations for solving H
  for i in range(len(pic_coor)):
          # Convert the coordinates of current image coordi-
nate system and world
      # coordinate system into homogeneous coordinates
            single_pic_coor = np.array([pic_coor[i][0], pic_
coor[i][1], 1])
          single_real_coor = np.array([real_coor[i][0], real_
coor[i][1], 1])
      # Normalize the coordinates
      pic_norm = np.dot(pic_norm_mat, single_pic_coor)
      real_norm = np.dot(real_norm_mat, single_real_coor)


      # Construct the rows of matrix A based on the normalized coor-
dinates
      # This part implements the process of converting the
constraints of the
      # homography matrix H into linear equations
     A.append(np.array([-real_norm.item(0), -real_norm.item(1), -
1, 0, 0, 0,
         pic_norm.item(0) * real_norm.item(0), pic_norm.item(0) *
            real_norm.item(1), pic_norm.item(0)]))
         A.append(np.array([0, 0, 0, -real_norm.item(0), -real_
norm.item(1), -1,
         pic_norm.item(1) * real_norm.item(0), pic_norm.item(1) *
            real_norm.item(1), pic_norm.item(1)]))


  # Use singular value decomposition (SVD) to solve h in Mh=0,
which is the
  # vectorized form of the homography matrix H
 U, S, VT = np.linalg.svd((np.array(A, dtype='float')).reshape((-
1, 9)))
  H = VT[-1].reshape((3, 3)) # Reshape the singular vector corre-
sponding to the


                      # smallest singular value into a 3x3 matrix
  # Denormalize H
  H = np.dot(np.dot(np.linalg.inv(pic_norm_mat), H), real_norm_
mat)
  H = H / H[-1, -1] # Normalize to ensure the last element of H is 1


  return H


H_list = []
for i in range(len(objpoints)):
  H = compute_homography(imgpoints[i], objpoints[i])
  H_list.append(H)
  if i < 3:


 print("Homography matrix for the {}th image is:\n{}".format(i+1, H))
Homography matrix for the 1st image is:
```

```
[[-2.90500492e+01 -2.05911540e+00 4.76529133e+02]
[ 2.28048296e+00 -3.63192023e+01 2.64694023e+02]
[ 1.49422654e-02 -5.06829993e-03 1.00000000e+00]]
Homography matrix for the 2nd image is:
[[-1.28830042e+01 3.91039199e+01 2.53736256e+02]
[-4.27973766e+01 7.39439498e+00 3.09778969e+02]
[-4.92899678e-02 -3.79194108e-03 1.00000000e+00]]
Homography matrix for the 3rd image is:
[[-4.25026982e+01 2.84366906e+01 5.00044815e+02]
[-1.26971800e+01 -4.04613414e+01 3.75934812e+02]
[ 1.57645215e-02 2.74643346e-02 1.00000000e+00]]
```

After obtaining $\boldsymbol{H}$ corresponding to each calibration board image, we first need to extract the constraint equations for solving matrix $\boldsymbol{B}$ from each homography matrix $\boldsymbol{H}$, then solve $\boldsymbol{B}$ through SVD, and finally solve the camera intrinsic matrix $\boldsymbol{K}$ through Cholesky decomposition.

```
def compute_B_matrix(H_list):
    """
    Compute B matrix from the list of homography matrices H
    Parameters:
    - H_list: List of homography matrices H
    Returns:
    - B: B matrix
    """
    V = []
    for H in H_list:
        # Decompose H matrix to get its column vectors
        h1, h2, _ = H[:,0], H[:,1], H[:,2]
         # Construct rows of V matrix based on the orthogonality prop-
erty of the
        # rotation matrix
        # v_ij is the vector form of constructing the equation hi^T * B
* hj = 0
        # Since h = K * r, we can use h to replace r
        # The first equation comes from r1^T * r2 = 0 -> (h1^T * B * h2 =
0)
                  v12    =    np.array([h1[0]*h2[0],    h1[0]*h2[1]    +
h1[1]*h2[0], h1[1]*h2[1],
                     h1[2]*h2[0]   +  h1[0]*h2[2],  h1[2]*h2[1]   +
h1[1]*h2[2], h1[2]*h2[2]])


        # The second equation comes from r1^T * r1 = r2^T * r2 ->
        # ((h1^T * B * h1) - (h2^T * B * h2) = 0)
        # ((h1^T * B * h1) - (h2^T * B * h2) = 0)
          v11_v22 = np.array([h1[0]**2 - h2[0]**2, 2*(h1[0]*h1[1] -
h2[0]*h2[1]),
                 h1[1]**2 - h2[1]**2, 2*(h1[2]*h1[0] - h2[2]*h2[0]),
                2*(h1[2]*h1[1] - h2[2]*h2[1]), h1[2]**2 - h2[2]**2])


        # Add the parameters of these two equations to the V matrix
        V.append(v12)
```

```
    V.append(v11_v22)
  V = np.array(V)

  # Use SVD to solve for b, where b is the vector form of the 6 unknowns
in the B
  # matrix
  U, S, Vt = np.linalg.svd(V)
          b   =   Vt[-1]      #   Singular   vector   corre-
sponding to the smallest singular value

  # Reconstruct the B matrix based on b
  B = np.array([[b[0], b[1], b[3]],
         [b[1], b[2], b[4]],
         [b[3], b[4], b[5]]])

  return B

B = compute_B_matrix(H_list)
print("The B matrix is:\n{}".format(B))
The B matrix is:
[[ 2.16451749e-06  7.58169969e-09 -7.67824576e-04]
[ 7.58169969e-09  2.15556058e-06 -4.90907403e-04]
[-7.67824576e-04 -4.90907403e-04  9.99999585e-01]]
```

Next, use Cholesky decomposition to solve for the camera intrinsic matrix $\boldsymbol{K}$.

```
def cholesky_solve(B):
  """
Solve for the K matrix using Cholesky decomposition
  """
  # Check if B is a symmetric matrix
  if not np.allclose(B, B.T):
   raise ValueError("B is not a symmetric matrix")

  # Perform Cholesky decomposition
  L = np.linalg.cholesky(B)

  # L is a lower triangular matrix, while K is an upper trian-
gular matrix
  # The last element of the K matrix is 1
  K = K / K[-1, -1]
  return K

  # Directly solve
  K = cholesky_solve(B)
  print("The K matrix is:\n{}".format(K))

The K matrix is:
[[533.92350191  -1.87407784 353.93909352]
[  0.       535.03494272 226.49511563]
```

```
[ 0.          0.          1.        ]]
```

Next, calculate the camera extrinsic matrix $[\boldsymbol{R}|\boldsymbol{t}]$ from the homography matrix.

```
def get_extrinsics_param(H, intrinsics_param):
   """
            Calculate the extrinsic matrix and transla-
tion vector t from the homography
    matrix H and intrinsic matrix K, and ensure that the determi-
nant of R is 1


   Parameters:
   - H: List of homography matrices H
   - intrinsics_param: Intrinsic matrix K


   Returns:
  -extrinsics_param: List containing extrinsic matrices R and trans-
lation vectors t
   """
extrinsics_param = []
   inv_intrinsics_param = np.linalg.inv(intrinsics_param)
   for i in range(len(H)):
      h0 = (H[i].reshape(3, 3))[:, 0]
      h1 = (H[i].reshape(3, 3))[:, 1]
      h2 = (H[i].reshape(3, 3))[:, 2]


         scale_factor = 1 / np.linalg.norm(np.dot(inv_intrinsics_
param, h0))
      r0 = scale_factor * np.dot(inv_intrinsics_param, h0)
      r1 = scale_factor * np.dot(inv_intrinsics_param, h1)
      t = scale_factor * np.dot(inv_intrinsics_param, h2)
      r2 = np.cross(r0, r1)


      # Construct an approximate rotation matrix
      R_approx = np.array([r0, r1, r2]).transpose()
        # Use SVD to correct R, ensuring it conforms to the proper-
ties of a rotation
      # matrix
      U, _, Vt = np.linalg.svd(R_approx)
      R_corrected = np.dot(U, Vt)


      # Ensure the determinant of R is 1
      if np.linalg.det(R_corrected) < 0:
         U[:, -1] *= -1 # Adjust the last column of U
         R_corrected = np.dot(U, Vt) # Recalculate R


      extrinsics = np.column_stack((R_corrected, t))
      extrinsics_param.append(extrinsics)


   return extrinsics_param
```

```
extrinsics_param = get_extrinsics_param(H_list, K)
for i in range(len(extrinsics_param)):
  print("The extrinsic matrix for the {}th image is:\n{}".format(i+1,
extrinsics_param[i]))
   if i == 2:
   break
```

```
The extrinsic matrix for the 1st image is:
[[-9.73670749e-01 9.02344992e-04 2.27957142e-01 3.47913167e+00]
[-1.90344917e-02 -9.96821819e-01 -7.73559911e-02 1.08066170e+00]
[ 2.27162851e-01 -7.96583141e-02 9.70593423e-01 1.51363433e+01]]
The extrinsic matrix for the 2nd image is:
[[ 0.11529592 0.97966689 0.16419391 -2.41686208]
[-0.76215049 0.19325491 -0.61788281 2.01046147]
[-0.63705061 -0.0539011 0.7689351 12.91567438]]
The extrinsic matrix for the 3rd image is:
[[-0.9339432 0.35280444 0.05726373 2.84741705]
[-0.31749332 -0.89247809 0.32043853 2.89596682]
[ 0.16415876 0.28109053 0.94553689 10.36835246]]
```

Next, we can project points in three-dimensional space to the image coordinate system according to the calculated intrinsic and extrinsic parameters, and then calculate the reprojection error to evaluate the accuracy of our calibration.

```
def reproject_error(K, extrinsic, pixel_coor, real_coor):
   """
   Calculate the reprojection error


   Parameters:
   - K: Intrinsic Matrix
   - extrinsic: Extrinsic Matrix
   - pixel_coor: Pixel Coordinate System
    - real_coor: World Coordinate System


   Returns:
   - error: Reprojection Error
  """
   # Calculate the projection matrix
   P = np.dot(K, extrinsic)


         # Convert the coordinates of the world coordi-
nate system to the homogeneous
   # coordinates
     real_coor = np.column_stack((real_coor, np.zeros(len(real_
coor)),
                       np.ones(len(real_coor))))
   # Calculate reprojected coordinates
   reprojected_coor = np.dot(P, real_coor.T).T
     reprojected_coor = reprojected_coor[:, :2] / reprojected_
coor[:, 2:3]
   # Calculate reprojection error
   error = np.linalg.norm(reprojected_coor - pixel_coor, axis=1)
```

```
    return error.mean()

# Convert both intrinsic and extrinsic matrices by repre-
senting them in terms of homogeneous coordinates
K_homo = np.column_stack((K, np.zeros(3)))
K_homo = np.row_stack((K_homo, [0, 0, 0, 1]))

# Calculate the mean reprojection error of all images
mean_error = 0
for j in range(len(imgpoints)):
                extrinsic_homo    =    np.row_stack((extrinsics_
param[j], [0, 0, 0, 1]))

# Calculate the reprojection error of each image
              error    =    reproject_error(K_homo,    extrinsic_
homo, imgpoints[j], objpoints[j])
  mean_error += error
# Get the average reprojection error
mean_error /= len(imgpoints)
print("The average reprojection error is: {}".format(mean_error))

The average reprojection error is: 2.2527822694246837
```

At this point, we have completed the basic camera calibration process. Based on the reprojection error, the camera parameters we calculated are quite accurate, with an average error of 2.25 pixels. In practical applications, we often directly use OpenCV's calibration function to calibrate the camera:

```
# Convert to the format required by OpenCV
objpoints_cv= [np.hstack((i, np.zeros((i.shape[0], 1)))).astype(
        np.float32) for i in objpoints]
imgpoints_cv = [i[:,None ,:] for i in imgpoints]

# Use OpenCV's calibration function to calibrate the camera
ret, mtx, dist, rvecs, tvecs = cv2.calibrateCamera(objpoints_cv,
                    imgpoints_cv, gray.shape[::-1], None, None)

print("Camera intrinsic parameters:")
# Camera intrinsic parameters, whose output format is [[fx,0,cx],
[0,fy,cy], [0,0,1]]
print(mtx, "\n")

print("Distortion parameters:")
# k1,k2,p1,p2,k3
print(dist)

Camera intrinsic parameters:
[[530.16217137 0. 341.48703364]
 [ 0. 530.21111757 230.10277488]
```

```
 [ 0. 0. 1. ]]
Distortion parameters:
[[-3.60236613e-01 8.54966618e-01 5.79031024e-04 -4.97455055e-04
-2.16444973e+00]]
```

```
# Initialize error
mean_error = 0
for i in range(len(objpoints_cv)):
    # Reproject points using intrinsic, extrinsic, and distor-
tion parameters
    imgpoints2, _ = cv2.projectPoints(objpoints_cv[i],
                        rvecs[i], tvecs[i], mtx, dist)
   # Calculate the error between the reprojected points and the orig-
inal points,
    # measured by Euclidean distance
    error = cv2.norm(imgpoints_cv[i], imgpoints2,
                        cv2.NORM_L2) / len(imgpoints2)
    # Accumulate error
    mean_error += error
# Get the L2 norm of the average pixel offset per point
mean_error /= len(objpoints_cv)
print("The average reprojection error obtained by OpenCV is:
 {}".format(mean_error))
```

```
The average reprojection error obtained by OpenCV is:
0.062162126761103303
```

It can be seen that the calibration results obtained by our simple algorithm and the calibration function directly using OpenCV are generally consistent. The main reason for the difference in the results of the two algorithms is that our simple algorithm does not consider the impact of distortion parameters, while OpenCV's algorithm fully considers the impact of radial and tangential distortions.

16.4 Summary

This chapter mainly introduces the basic principles of camera imaging, as well as important parameters in the camera model: intrinsic parameters, extrinsic parameters, and distortion parameters. This chapter also introduces how to calibrate the camera using a calibration board, and implements camera calibration through code. The calibrated camera, like a bridge connecting the three-dimensional world and the two-dimensional image plane, allows us to reversely calculate the information of the three-dimensional space through the image, providing an important foundation for subsequent computer vision applications.

Exercises

(1) If the side length of each square on the chessboard calibration board is assumed to be 1m during the camera calibration process, instead of its actual physical length, will this affect the calibration results? Why?

(2) Which is more common, radial distortion or tangential distortion? Why?

(3) The chessboard calibration board is commonly used in camera calibration. In practical applications, can other forms of calibration boards be used for calibration? Give examples.

(4) The accuracy of corner detection will affect the calibration results. How to reduce the impact of its error.

Chapter 17
Motion Field and Optical Flow

17.1 Introduction

In a constantly moving world, our eyes and brain can naturally perceive the motion of the surrounding environment. Correspondingly, a challenge faced by computer vision technology is how to extract motion information from acquired image sequences. Through motion field and optical flow estimation, we can reconstruct motion information from videos.

The motion field describes the projection of the motion of points in the three-dimensional world on the two-dimensional imaging plane, as shown in Fig. 17.1. The motion field is the field formed by the two-dimensional projection velocity vectors, on the imaging plane, of the three-dimensional velocity vectors corresponding to all pixels in the image. The motion field is an ideal representation of three-dimensional motion on a two-dimensional imaging plane. It is directly related to the actual physical motion of the object, but we cannot directly observe this motion from the image. We can only approximate the motion field by analyzing the optical flow in the image sequence.

Optical flow is defined as the manifestation of pixel brightness changes over time in an image sequence caused by changes in objects, cameras, or lighting. It is calculated from changes in image intensity and is considered an approximation of the two-dimensional projection velocity vector of pixels. The optical flow vectors of all pixels on the entire image plane form the optical flow field, which describes the motion pattern at the image level and is an approximation of the two-dimensional motion field. However, the optical flow field does not always coincide with the actual motion field, as optical flow may be affected by non-motion factors such as changes in lighting.

American psychologist James J. Gibson first proposed the concept of optical flow in the 1940s [1]. Since then, optical flow estimation has become a research hotspot in the field of computer vision and has been widely used in motion analysis, target tracking, image registration, and three-dimensional reconstruction.

W. Shen et al., *Hands-On Computer Vision*,
https://doi.org/10.1007/978-981-95-4835-4_17

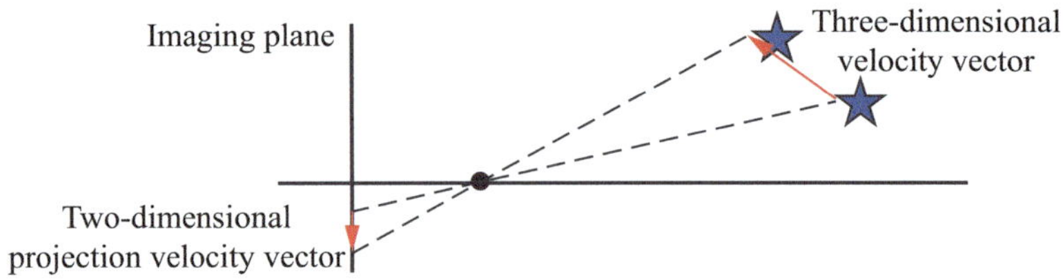

Fig. 17.1 Correspondence between three-dimensional velocity vectors and their two-dimensional projections

This chapter will delve into the basic principles and classic methods of optical flow estimation. By understanding and applying these methods, we can better reconstruct motion information from videos, making the motion of objects constructed from two-dimensional images closer to the motion of targets in the real three-dimensional physical world.

17.2 Motion Field

First, we derive the mathematical representation of the motion field on the two-dimensional imaging plane from the three-dimensional velocity vector. To simplify the calculation, assume that the world coordinate system coincides with the camera coordinate system. Consider a point $P(t)$ in space moving to point $P(t+\delta t)$ after time δt. Correspondingly, its projection point $P'(t)$ on the imaging plane moves to point $P'(t+\delta t)$, as shown in Fig. 17.2. Let $\boldsymbol{p} : (x, y, z)^{\mathrm{T}}$ and $p' : \left(x', y', f\right)^{\mathrm{T}}$ be the coordinates of the spatial point P and its projection point P', the velocity vector in space is $\boldsymbol{v} : \left(v_x, v_y, v_z\right)^{\mathrm{T}}$, and the velocity vector on the imaging plane is $\boldsymbol{v}' : \left(v_{x'}, v_{y'}, v_{z'} = 0\right)^{\mathrm{T}}$. Assuming the camera's focal length f is known, then according to the camera imaging principle, we have

$$\boldsymbol{p}' = f\frac{\boldsymbol{p}}{z},$$

where z is the depth of point P in the camera coordinate system. Further, the velocity vector $\boldsymbol{v}'$ on the imaging plane can be obtained by differentiating the above formula:

$$\boldsymbol{v}' = f\frac{z\boldsymbol{v} - v_z\boldsymbol{p}}{z^2} = \frac{f\boldsymbol{v} - v_z\boldsymbol{p}'}{z}$$

That is:

$$v_x' = \frac{fv_x - v_z x'}{z}$$

$$v'_y = \frac{fv_y - v_z y'}{z}$$

$$v'_z = \frac{fv_z - v_z f}{z} = 0$$

Here, it can be seen that, $\mathbf{v}'$ on the imaging plane along the x-axis and y-axis components are inversely proportional to the depth z of the spatial point, reflecting the principle of "near objects move fast, far objects move slow". This is consistent with what we observe in daily life, for example, during driving, distant objects move relatively slowly, while nearby objects appear to move faster.

Figure 17.3 shows the corresponding motion fields on the imaging plane when the scene remains stationary and the camera undergoes several typical motions. We can refer to Fig. 17.2 to better understand how the projection points on the imaging plane respond to different types of motion (translation and rotation), and how they are reflected in the two-dimensional motion field.

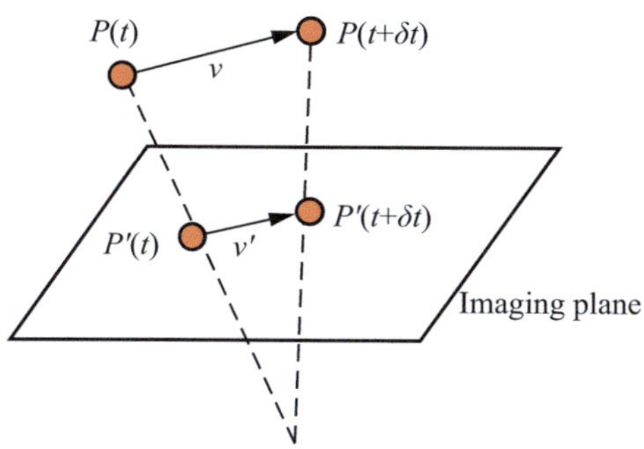

Fig. 17.2 Relationship between three-dimensional motion and two-dimensional motion field

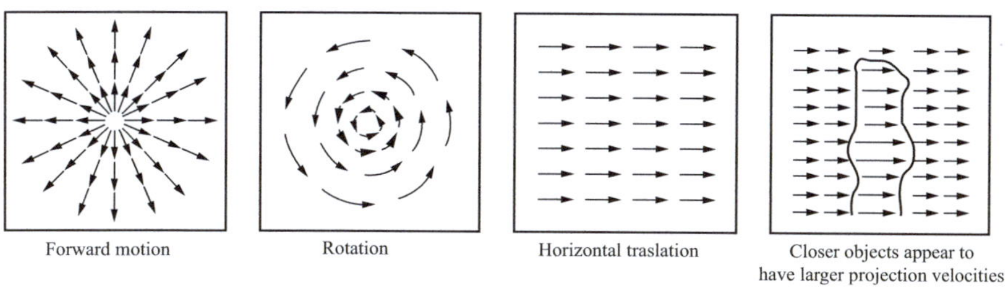

Fig. 17.3 Projections of several typical motions on the imaging plane

17.3 Optical Flow

The previous section introduced the mathematical representation of deriving a two-dimensional motion field from a three-dimensional velocity vector. However, in most cases, it is not feasible to directly calculate the motion field of an object. We usually use the method of calculating optical flow to approximate the estimation of the motion field of an object. Next, we will explore the basic principles and common calculation methods of optical flow estimation.

17.3.1 Feature Point Method

Optical flow is essentially a two-dimensional pixel change caused by image brightness changes, thus it can be calculated by tracking feature points in the image. As described in Chap. 7, extracting visual features (such as corners and blob-like regions) from images and tracking the correspondence of these feature points between consecutive frames is one method of calculating optical flow. This feature point-based optical flow estimation produces sparse optical flow. Although it is robust in expressing the motion relationship between multiple frames and is particularly suitable for describing large relative movements, it has the following limitations.

(1) High Computational Cost: The process of extracting feature points and calculating descriptors is very time-consuming. For example, the SIFT algorithm cannot achieve real-time computation when running on a CPU, and the ORB [2] algorithm also requires about 20 ms of computation time.
(2) Insufficient Use of Information: When using the feature point method, all information in the image other than the feature points is ignored. An image may contain hundreds of thousands of pixels, while the number of feature points is usually only a few hundred, which means that a large amount of potentially useful image information is discarded.
(3) Feature-Poor Scenes: The camera may sometimes move to scenes lacking distinct features, such as facing a white wall or an empty corridor. In these scenes, the number of feature points may significantly decrease, making it difficult to find enough matching points to accurately calculate the optical flow and the motion of the camera.

17.3.2 Direct Method

The direct method uses pixel brightness information in the image to estimate motion, without the need to calculate feature points and descriptors. This allows it to effectively estimate motion in situations where features are missing. As long as there are brightness changes in the scene (no matter they are gradual change or changes insufficient to form local image gradients), the direct method remain applicable. Unlike

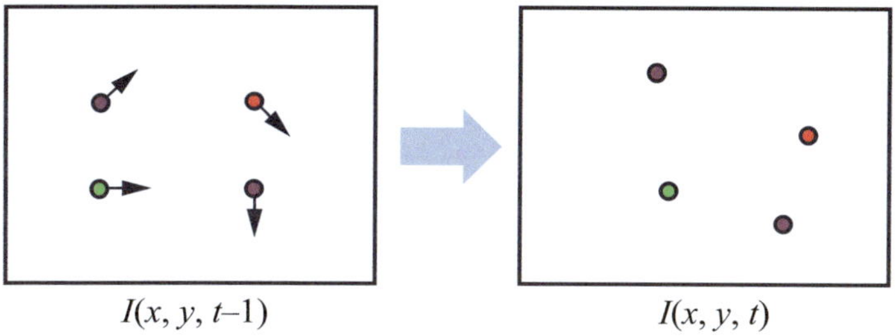

Fig. 17.4 Direct method for calculating optical flow

the feature point method, which can only re construct sparse optical flow, the direct method can construct sparse, dense, or semi-dense optical flow based on the number of available pixels. However, the direct method is more sensitive to changes in image appearance (such as brightness changes) and may mistakenly interpret these changes as motion. Therefore, this type of method is more suitable for calculating optical flow in videos where the motion amplitude is small.

Next, we will introduce how to calculate optical flow using the direct method. As shown in Fig. 17.4, given two frames $I(x, y, t-1)$ and $I(x, y, t)$ before and after motion, our goal is to find the correspondence between pixels in the image to obtain the optical flow of each pixel. To directly find the correspondence between pixels at the pixel level, the following assumptions need to be introduced.

(1) Brightness Constancy: It assumes that the intensity of a pixel corresponding to a point in three-dimensional space remains unchanged over time in the two-dimensional image. This means that the pixel intensities with this correspondence remain invariant across consecutive frames.
(2) Small Motion: It is assumed that the movement of a three-dimensional point is small in a short period of time.

According to the brightness constancy assumption, i.e., the intensity of the pixel corresponding to a three-dimensional point in the two-dimensional image at time $t-1$ and time t remains unchanged, we can get

$$I(x, y, t-1) = I(x + \delta x, y + \delta y, t),$$

where (x, y) and $(x + \delta x, y + \delta y)$ are the coordinates of the projection point of the same three-dimensional point on the imaging plane at time $t-1$ and time t, respectively. Also, according to the small motion assumption, both δx and δy are very small. Therefore, the right side of the above equation can be expanded into a Taylor series:

$$I(x + \delta x, y + \delta y, t) \approx I(x, y, t) + \frac{\partial I}{\partial x}\delta x + \frac{\partial I}{\partial y}\delta y$$

From which we can get

$$I(x, y, t) + \frac{\partial I}{\partial x}\delta x + \frac{\partial I}{\partial y}\delta y - I(x, y, t-1) = 0.$$

Also, according to the first-order Taylor expansion in time, we get

$$I(x, y, t) - I(x, y, t-1) \approx \frac{\partial I}{\partial t}(\delta t = 1).$$

Here, $\delta t = 1$ as the frame difference between two consecutive images is 1, from which we get

$$I_x \cdot u + I_y \cdot v + I_t = 0,$$

where I_x and I_y and I_t represent the gradients of the image along the x-axis, y-axis and t-axis, i.e., $I_x = \frac{\partial I}{\partial x}$, $I_y = \frac{\partial I}{\partial y}$, $I_t = \frac{\partial I}{\partial t}$; u and v represent the motion velocities of pixels along the x axis and y axis, respectively, i.e., $u = \frac{\delta x}{\delta t}$, $v = \frac{\delta y}{\delta t}$. The above equation can be rewritten as.

$$\nabla I \cdot (u, v) + I_t = 0.$$

The (u, v) in the above equation is the optical flow vector we need to solve. Written in matrix form as.

$$\begin{bmatrix} I_x \ I_y \end{bmatrix}\begin{bmatrix} u \\ v \end{bmatrix} = -I_t.$$

This equation expresses the relationship between the spatial gradient and the temporal gradient of image brightness. It can be used to estimate the motion of pixel brightness over time, i.e., optical flow, hence it is also called the optical flow equation. However, there are two unknowns u and v in this equation, and a definite solution cannot be obtained from this equation alone. It needs to be solved through additional constraints or optimization methods.

17.3.3 Lucas-Kanade Optical Flow Method

To solve the underdetermined problem in the above equation, the Lucas-Kanade optical flow method [3] introduces the assumption of spatial consistency, that is, it assumes that adjacent points on the same surface in the scene have similar motion. These points remain adjacent when projected onto the imaging plane, and their motion velocities are also similar. This means that if we consider a feature point and the points in its neighborhood, we can assume that the velocities of these points along the x-axis and y-axis (u and v) are the same.

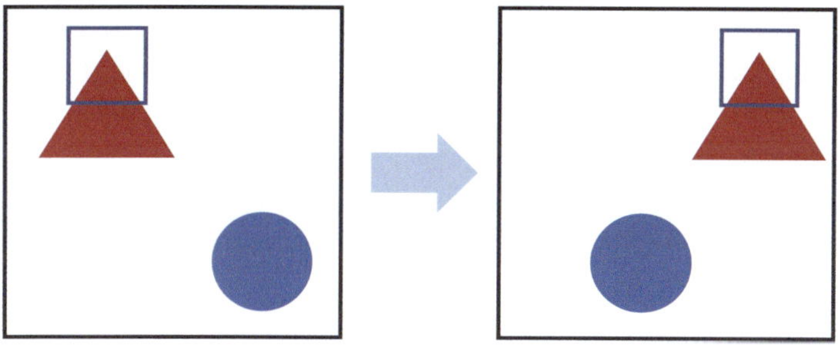

Fig. 17.5 Spatial consistency assumption

Taking Fig. 17.5 as an example, within a neighborhood, such as the region marked by the box, all optical flow vectors can be considered consistent. Therefore, by applying the optical flow equation in such a characteristic area, we can set up multiple equations to solve the uniform velocities u and v in this area.

Specifically, assuming a 5×5 window is used as the spatial coherence region, then an optical flow equation can be computed for each pixel within this window, yielding a total of 25 equations., i.e.,

$$\begin{bmatrix} I_x(p_1) & I_y(p_1) \\ I_x(p_2) & I_y(p_2) \\ \vdots & \vdots \\ I_x(p_{25}) & I_y(p_{25}) \end{bmatrix} \begin{bmatrix} u \\ v \end{bmatrix} = - \begin{bmatrix} I_t(p_1) \\ I_t(p_2) \\ \vdots \\ I_t(p_{25}) \end{bmatrix}.$$

For convenience of description, it is abbreviated as

$$\boldsymbol{A}\,\boldsymbol{d} = -\boldsymbol{b} \rightarrow \min \|\boldsymbol{A}\boldsymbol{d} + \boldsymbol{b}\|^2.$$

Obviously, this is another overdetermined linear equation about u, v, traditionally solved using the least squares method:

$$\begin{bmatrix} \sum I_x I_x & \sum I_x I_y \\ \sum I_x I_y & \sum I_y I_y \end{bmatrix} \begin{bmatrix} u \\ v \end{bmatrix} = - \begin{bmatrix} \sum I_x I_t \\ \sum I_y I_t \end{bmatrix}$$

That is

$$\boldsymbol{A}\boldsymbol{A}^{\mathrm{T}} \begin{bmatrix} u \\ v \end{bmatrix} = -\boldsymbol{A}^{\mathrm{T}}\boldsymbol{b}.$$

Then it can be solved to get

$$\begin{bmatrix} u \\ v \end{bmatrix}^* = -(\boldsymbol{A}^{\mathrm{T}}\boldsymbol{A})^{-1}\boldsymbol{A}^{\mathrm{T}}\boldsymbol{b}.$$

We introduced the Harris corner detection algorithm in Chap. 6. By comparison, we can find that the form of the above equation is very similar to the Harris algorithm, thus it is not difficult to derive the conditions for the solution of the above equation:

(1) $\boldsymbol{A}^{\mathrm{T}}\boldsymbol{A}$ is invertible.
(2) The eigenvalues of $\boldsymbol{A}^{\mathrm{T}}\boldsymbol{A}$, i.e., λ_1, λ_2, cannot be too small.
(3) $\boldsymbol{A}^{\mathrm{T}}\boldsymbol{A}$ is a well-conditioned matrix, sensitive to small perturbations of data, i.e., λ_1 and λ_2 should be as close as possible.

The regions that meet these conditions are generally corner regions, thus the Lucas-Kanade optical flow method works best at corners.

17.3.4 Improvement of the Lucas-Kanade Optical Flow Method

The constraints of the Lucas-Kanade optical flow method are its three assumptions: brightness constancy, small motion, and spatial coherence. Although these assumptions are valid in many cases, they also bring some limitations, especially when dealing with fast-moving objects or scenes with significant brightness changes. To improve the algorithm's versatility and robustness, researchers and engineers have done a lot of subsequent work [4]. Here, we briefly introduce some practical improvement methods.

(1) The iterative method calculates the optical flow by gradually estimating the optical flow and then updating it. As shown in Fig. 17.6, the iterative method starts with displacement estimation in the initial stage, obtains a preliminary estimated velocity vector $\hat{d}$, and updates the vector $d_1 = d_n + \hat{d}$ using the Lucas-Kanade optical flow method. Then, the first frame image is warped according to the current displacement result to make it closer to the brightness distribution of the second frame image. By continuously iterating this process, calculating new estimates and accumulating the velocity vectors obtained from each iteration, the final accurate optical flow estimate is obtained, making the brightness of the warped first frame almost identical to the brightness of the second frame.

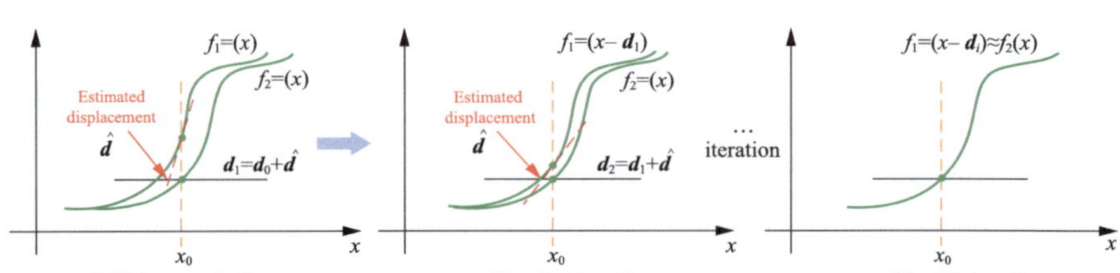

Fig. 17.6 Iterative method

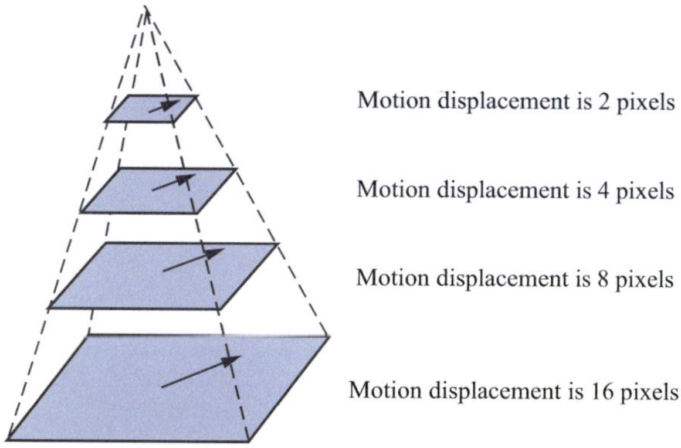

Fig. 17.7 Image pyramid

(2) Multi-scale Image Method (image pyramid method): For situations where the object's motion displacement between two frames is large, the image resolution is reduced by constructing an image pyramid, thereby reducing pixel displacement (as shown in Fig. 17.7), making the small motion assumption valid again. For example, if the original image resolution is 400 pixels × 400 pixels, the pixel's motion displacement on the image plane is 16 pixels; when the image resolution is reduced to 200 pixels × 200 pixels, the motion displacement becomes 8 pixels; further when the image resolution is reduced to 100 pixels × 100 pixels, the motion displacement becomes 4 pixels.

17.4 Code Implementation

Next, let's implement the Lucas-Kanade optical flow method. First, we create a noise image and rotate it clockwise by 1°.

```
import cv2
import numpy as np
import matplotlib.pyplot as plt
import random
import math
# Rotate the image according to the angle
def rotate_image(img, angle):
   # Calculate the rotation center
   center = tuple(np.array(img.shape[1::-1]) / 2)
   # Calculate the rotation matrix
   rot_mat = cv2.getRotationMatrix2D(center, angle, 1.0)
   # Rotate the image
   rotated = cv2.warpAffine(img, rot_mat,
               img.shape[1::-1], flags=cv2.INTER_LINEAR)
   return rotated
# Create a 200*200 random array and convert it to float32 type
img_t0 = np.random.rand(200, 200).astype(np.float32)
# Copy the contents of img_t0 to img_t1
```

```
img_t1 = img_t0.copy()
# Rotate img_t1 by -1°
img_t1 = rotate_image(img_t1, -1)
# Visualization
fig1, (ax_1, ax_2) = plt.subplots(1, 2)
# Display img_t0 in ax_1
ax_1.imshow(img_t0)
ax_1.set_title("Frame t0")
# Display img_t1 in ax_2
ax_2.imshow(img_t1)
ax_2.set_title("Frame t1")
# Display the image
plt.show()
```

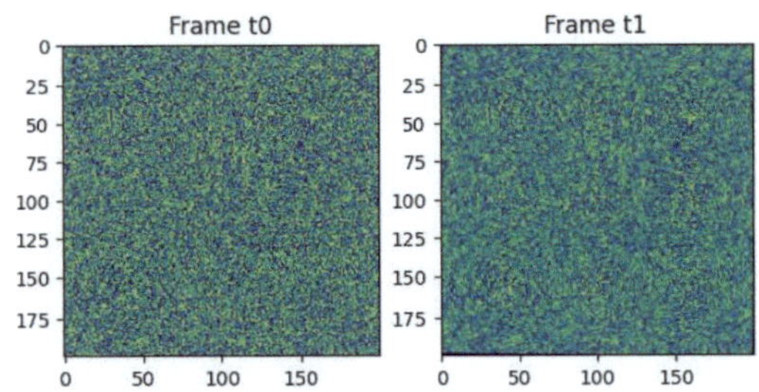

Next, we implement a Gaussian filter to blur the image to reduce the impact of noise, and then calculate the image gradient.

```
def smooth(img, sigma):
    """
    Gaussian blur function, returns the blurred image
    Parameters:
    - img: Input image
    - sigma: Standard deviation of the Gaussian kernel
    """
    # Create x array, range is [-3sigma,3sigma]
    x = np.array(list(range(math.floor(-3.0 * sigma + 0.5),
                      math.floor(3.0 * sigma + 0.5) + 1)))
    # Calculate Gaussian kernel G
    G = np.exp(-x ** 2 / (2 * sigma ** 2))
    G = G / np.sum(G)
    # Perform two-dimensional convolution on the image
    return cv2.sepFilter2D(img, -1, G, G)
def gaussderiv(img, sigma):
    """
    Gaussian derivative function
    Parameters:
    - param img: Input image
    - param sigma: Standard deviation of the Gaussian kernel
    Returns:
    - Dx: Derivative image in the x-axis direction
    - Dy: Derivative image in the y-axis direction
    """
```

```
# Create x array, range is [-3sigma,3sigma]
 x = np.array(list(range(math.floor(-3.0 * sigma + 0.5),
                    math.floor(3.0 * sigma + 0.5) + 1)))
   # Calculate Gaussian kernel G
   G = np.exp(-x ** 2 / (2 * sigma ** 2))
   G = G / np.sum(G)
   # Calculate Gaussian derivative kernel D
   D = -2 * (x * np.exp(-x ** 2 / (2 * sigma ** 2))) / ( \
                    np.sqrt(2 * math.pi) * sigma ** 3)
   D = D / (np.sum(np.abs(D)) / 2)
   # Perform two-dimensional convolution on the image along the x-
axis and y-axis
   # respectively
   Dx = cv2.sepFilter2D(img, -1, D, G)
   Dy = cv2.sepFilter2D(img, -1, G, D)
   return Dx, Dy
def calculate_derivatives(img1, img2, smoothing, derivation):
   """
   Calculate the derivatives of the image
   Parameters:
   - img1: Previous frame image
   - img2: Next frame image
   - smoothing: Standard deviation of Gaussian blur
   - derivation: Standard deviation of Gaussian derivative
   Returns:
   - i_x: Derivative image in the x-axis direction
   - i_y: Derivative image in the y-axis direction
   - i_t: Derivative image in the time direction
   """
   # Calculate derivative in the t direction
   i_t = smooth(img2 - img1, smoothing)
   # Calculate derivatives in the x and y directions
   i_x, i_y = gaussderiv(smooth(np.divide(img1 + \
                     img2, 2), smoothing), derivation)
   return i_x, i_y, i_t
```

Then, based on the obtained gradient, calculate the optical flow within each block.

```
def sum_kernel(x, N):
   "'
   Calculate the sum within the block
   "'
   return cv2.filter2D(x, -1, np.ones((N, N)))
def lucas_kanade(img1, img2, N, smoothing=1, derivation=0.4):
   """
   Lucas-Kanade Algorithm
   Parameters:
   - img1: Previous frame image
   - img2: Next frame image
   - N: Block size
   - smoothing: Standard deviation of Gaussian blur
   - derivation: Standard deviation of Gaussian derivative
Returns:
   - u: Velocity image in the x-axis direction
```

```
    - v: Velocity image in the y-axis direction
    """
    # Calculate image derivatives
    i_x, i_y, i_t = calculate_derivatives(img1, img2, smoothing, deriva-
tion)
    # Calculate i_x_t and i_y_t
    i_x_t = sum_kernel(np.multiply(i_x, i_t), N)
    i_y_t = sum_kernel(np.multiply(i_y, i_t), N)
    # Calculate the square of the gradient
    i_x_2 = sum_kernel(np.square(i_x), N)
    i_y_2 = sum_kernel(np.square(i_y), N)
    i_x_y = sum_kernel(np.multiply(i_x, i_y), N)
    # Calculate the sum of squares
    D = np.subtract(
        np.multiply(i_x_2, i_y_2),
        np.square(i_x_y)
    )
    D += 1e-5
    # Calculate u, v within each block
    u = np.divide(
        np.add(
            np.multiply(-i_y_2, i_x_t),
            np.multiply(i_x_y, i_y_t)
        ),
        D
    )
    v = np.divide(
        np.subtract(
            np.multiply(i_x_y, i_x_t),
            np.multiply(i_x_2, i_y_t)
        ),
        D
    )
    return u, v
```

At this point, we have obtained the velocity vectors between the two frames, and will visualize them next.

```
def show_flow(U, V, ax):
    """
    Draw optical flow based on provided U, V
    """
    # Control the size of the blocks
    scaling = 0.1
    # Process the optical flow with Gaussian blur
    u = cv2.resize(smooth(U, 1.5), (0, 0), fx=scaling, fy=scaling)
    v = cv2.resize(smooth(V, 1.5), (0, 0), fx=scaling, fy=scaling)
    # Generate coordinate matrices for x, y
    x_ = (np.array(list(range(1, u.shape[1] + 1))) - 0.5) / scaling
    y_ = -(np.array(list(range(1, u.shape[0] + 1))) - 0.5) / scaling
    x, y = np.meshgrid(x_, y_)
    # Draw arrows
    ax.quiver(x, y, -u * 5, v * 5)
    ax.set_aspect(1.)
```

```
def draw_optical_flow(image_1, image_2,
                normalizeImages=True, win_size=10):
    """
    Calculate the optical flow between images and display it
    """
    # Normalize images
     if normalizeImages:
      image_1 = image_1 / 255.0
      image_2 = image_2 / 255.0
    # Calculate optical flow
    U_lk, V_lk = lucas_kanade(image_1, image_2, win_size)
    # Predefine canvas for visualization
    fig2, (ax_11, ax_12, ax_13) = plt.subplots(1, 3, dpi=200)
  # First frame
    ax_11.imshow(image_1)
    ax_11.set_title("Frame t0")
    ax_11.axis('off')
    # Second frame
    ax_12.imshow(image_2)
    ax_12.set_title("Frame t1")
    ax_12.axis('off')
    # Optical flow
    show_flow(U_lk, V_lk, ax_13)
    ax_13.set_title("Lucas-Kanade")
    ax_13.axis('off')
    # Canvas layout
    fig2.tight_layout()
    plt.show()
```

We call the draw_optical_flow() method on the noise image we created earlier and the image rotated 1° clockwise to calculate the optical flow.

```
draw_optical_flow(img_t0, img_t1, normalizeImages = False)
```

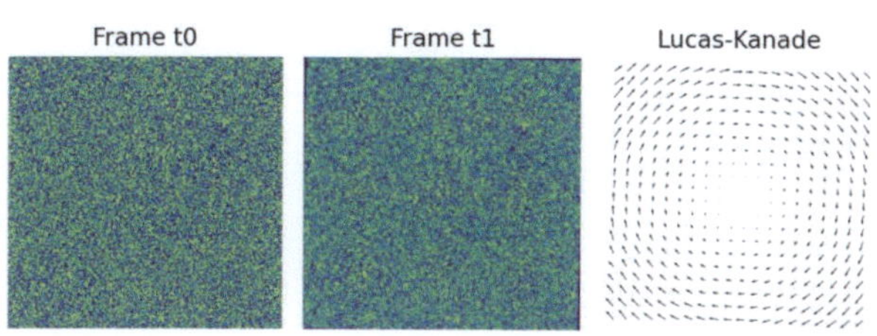

It can be seen that the Lucas-Kanade optical flow method can achieve good results when the motion displacement is small. Next, let's see how the Lucas-Kanade algorithm performs when the motion displacement is large.

```
img_t0 = np.random.rand(200, 200).astype(np.float32)
img_t1 = img_t0.copy()
# Test the case with large motion amplitude (rotation of 8°)
img_t1 = rotate_image(img_t1, -8)
draw_optical_flow(img_t0, img_t1, normalizeImages= False )
```

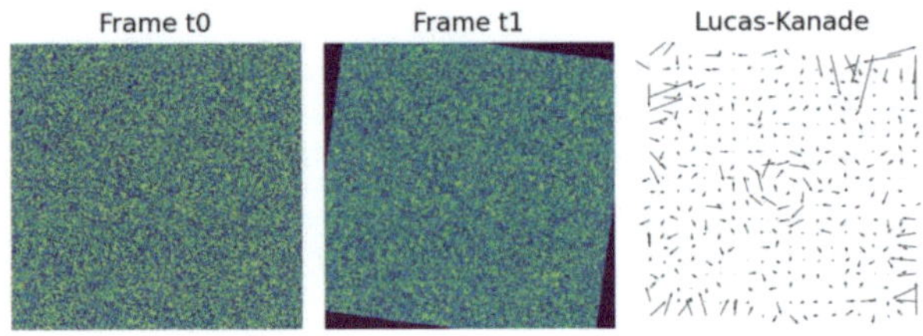

It can be seen that when the motion displacement is large, the effect of the Lucas-Kanade optical flow method is not as ideal as when the motion displacement is small. Next, we test the effect of the Lucas-Kanade optical flow method on real images.

```
!git clone https://github.com/boyu-ai/Hands-on-CV.git
image_1 = cv2.imread("learncv_img/Sec-17/frame_0001.png",
              cv2.IMREAD_GRAYSCALE).astype(np.float32)
image_2 = cv2.imread("learncv_img/Sec-17/frame_0002.png",
              cv2.IMREAD_GRAYSCALE).astype(np.float32)
# Draw the optical flow map
draw_optical_flow(image_1, image_2, normalizeImages= True , win_
size=15)
```

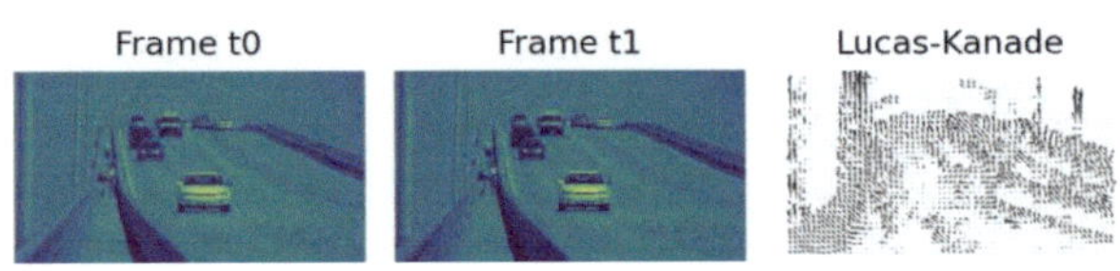

What we have implemented above is the calculation of optical flow on all pixels. In practice, corner points are usually detected first, and then the optical flow is calculated. Next, we use OpenCV's calcOpticalFlowPyrLK function to calculate the optical flow.

```
import cv2 as cv
import numpy as np
import matplotlib.pyplot as plt
%matplotlib inline
# Read a video clip for optical flow calculation
cap = cv.VideoCapture(
   "./learncv_img/Sec-17/slow_traffic_small.mp4")
# ShiTomasi corner detection parameters
feature_params = dict(maxCorners = 100,
                qualityLevel = 0.3,
                minDistance = 7,
                blockSize = 7 )
# Lucas-Kanade optical flow method parameters
lk_params = dict( winSize = (15, 15),
   maxLevel = 2,
   criteria = (cv.TERM_CRITERIA_EPS | cv.TERM_CRITERIA_COUNT,
         10, 0.03))
# Generate random colors for describing optical flow
color = np.random.randint(0, 255, (100, 3))
# Read the first frame and find the corners
```

```
ret, old_frame = cap.read()
old_gray = cv.cvtColor(old_frame, cv.COLOR_BGR2GRAY)
p0 = cv.goodFeaturesToTrack(old_gray,
              mask = None, **feature_params)mask = None , **feature_
params)
# Create a mask for drawing trajectories
mask = np.zeros_like(old_frame)
while(1):
   ret, frame = cap.read()
     if not ret:
      print('No frames grabbed!')
      break
   frame_gray = cv.cvtColor(frame, cv.COLOR_BGR2GRAY)
   # Calculate optical flow, and return the points p1 that success-
fully tracked the
   # optical flow, tracking status st, and tracking difference err
   p1, st, err = cv.calcOpticalFlowPyrLK(old_gray, frame_gray,
                              p0, None, **lk_params)
   # Select good tracking points
   if p1 is not None :
      # Filter out the points that have been successfully tracked
      good_new = p1[st==1]
      good_old = p0[st==1]
   # Draw trajectories
     for i, (new, old) in enumerate(zip(good_new, good_old)):
      a, b = new.ravel()
      c, d = old.ravel()
      mask = cv.line(mask, (int(a), int(b)), (int(c), int(d)), \
                 color[i].tolist(), 2)
      frame = cv.circle(frame, (int(a), int(b)), 5, \
                   color[i].tolist(), -1)
   img = cv.add(frame, mask)
   # Update the image and tracking points of the previous frame
   old_gray = frame_gray.copy()
   p0 = good_new.reshape(-1, 1, 2)
# Display the result
plt.imshow(cv.cvtColor(img, cv.COLOR_BGR2RGB))
plt.axis('off')
plt.show()
```

17.5 Summary

This chapter delves into the core concepts and theoretical foundations of motion fields and optical flow, revealing the powerful capabilities of optical flow in describing and analyzing object motion. The uniqueness of optical flow technology lies in its ability to estimate the possible motion of objects by analyzing image sequences without prior knowledge of the scene. This feature not only makes the optical flow method applicable under camera motion states, but also makes optical flow an important means of capturing information about moving objects and the three-dimensional structure of the scene.

Exercises

(1) Briefly explain the relationship between motion fields and optical flow.

(2) The Lucas-Kanade optical flow method introduces the spatial consistency assumption to solve the problem of insufficient constraints. Can other assumptions be introduced to provide constraints?

(3) Barber shops usually hang a rotating sign with red, blue, and white stripes outside (as shown in Fig. 17.8). This rotating sign itself spins around a vertical axis, but we visually have an illusion that the stripes on the rotating sign are moving from the bottom right to the top-left. Explain this illusion based on the calculation method of optical flow.

Fig. 17.8 Barber shop rotating sign

(4) Why is Gaussian blur applied to the image when implementing the Lucas-Kanade optical flow method? What are the benefits of doing this for calculating optical flow?

(5) Calculate the optical flow in Fig. 17.9.

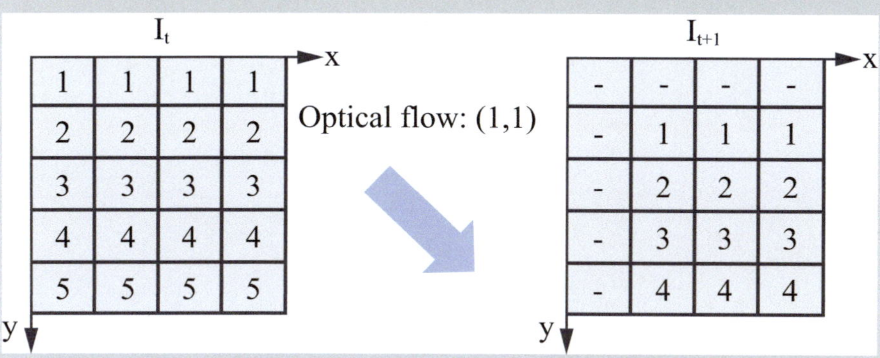

Fig. 17.9 Exercise (5) Schematic

References

1. GIBSON J J. The perception of the visual world[M]. Boston: Houghton Mifflin, 1950.
2. RUBLEE E, RABAUD V, KONOLOGIE K, et al. ORB: An efficient alternative to SIFT or SURF[C]//International Conference on Computer Vision. IEEE, 2011:2564–2571.
3. LUCAS B D, KANADE T. An iterative image registration technique with an application to stereo vision[C]//7th International Joint Conference on Artificial Intelligence. 1981, 2:674–679.
4. BOUGUET J Y. Pyramidal implementation of the affine Lucas Kanade feature tracker description of the algorithm[R]. 2001.

Chapter 18
Parallel Binocular Vision

18.1 Introduction

Camera imaging is a process that maps the three-dimensional world onto a two-dimensional image. If we want to recover the information of the three-dimensional world from the image, we need to solve a crucial problem: recovering the depth information lost during the camera imaging process. Given a single image, we cannot determine the coordinates of the point in the three-dimensional space corresponding to each pixel. This is because all points in the three-dimensional space along the ray from the camera's optical center to the imaging plane can be projected onto the same pixel. Only when we know the depth corresponding to a pixel can we accurately determine its spatial position in the three-dimensional space. In this chapter, we will introduce the structure and imaging principle of parallel binocular cameras, as well as how to use parallel binocular cameras to obtain depth information of the scene.

18.2 Parallel Binocular Camera

The parallel binocular camera is currently the most common depth camera. It consists of two independent cameras placed horizontally, each with its own optical center and imaging plane. Next, we will introduce the structure and working principle of the parallel binocular camera. To simplify the description, unless otherwise specified, the binocular cameras mentioned in this chapter are all parallel binocular cameras.

W. Shen et al., *Hands-On Computer Vision*,
https://doi.org/10.1007/978-981-95-4835-4_18

18.2.1 Concept Definition

Placing two cameras side by side and making their optical axes parallel can form a system similar to human binocular vision. This configuration is called a parallel binocular vision system. These two cameras are referred to as parallel binocular cameras, and the two photos they take constitute a pair of binocular images. The mainstream parallel binocular cameras are arranged horizontally, with the left and right cameras corresponding to the human left and right eyes, as shown in Fig. 18.1. Of course, vertical binocular cameras can also be realized in principle (readers can imagine such a strange shape).

In this left–right stereo camera system, the two cameras can be regarded as pinhole camera models with the same characteristics. They are placed horizontally, which means that the optical centers of the two cameras are both on the x-axis, and their optical axes are parallel. The horizontal line connecting the optical centers of the two cameras is called the baseline of the stereo camera, whose length is represented by b, which is a key parameter for measuring the geometric configuration of the binocular camera. The length of the baseline is crucial for calculating the disparity between images and ultimately determining the depth information of objects in the scene.

Now, consider a point P in the three-dimensional space, its coordinates in the left camera coordinate system are (x, y, z), and it is projected to two image points through

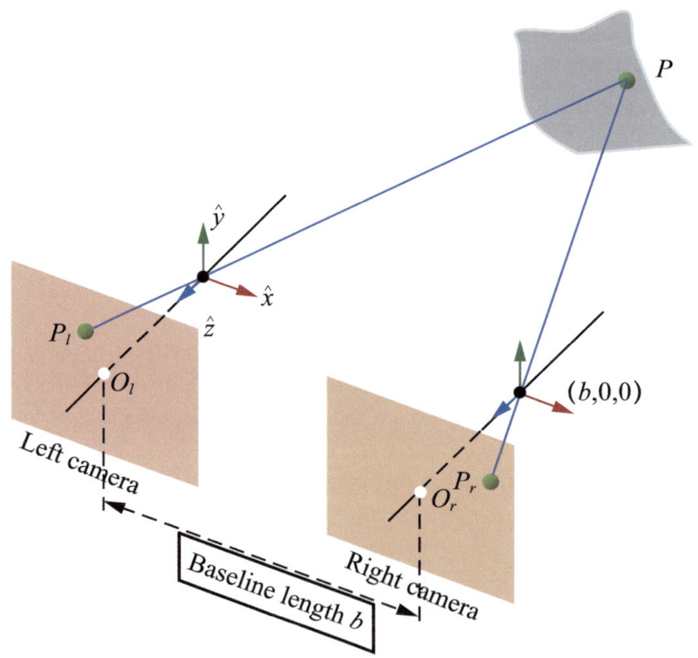

Fig. 18.1 Parallel stereo camera

the left and right cameras, denoted as P_l and P_r, respectively. Ideally, since the left and right cameras only differ in the positions on the x-axis, the two projections of P also only differ in the positions on the x-axis (corresponding to the u axis of the image). We denote the pixel coordinates of the projection in the left image P_l as (u_l, v_l), and the pixel coordinates of that in the right image P_r as (u_r, v_r).

18.2.2 Disparity

As shown in Fig. 18.2, the point P in the three-dimensional space, the optical center O_l and O_r of the left and right cameras, as well as the point P and its projection points P_l and P_r on the left and right imaging planes form similar triangles $\triangle PO_lO_r \sim\triangle PP_lP_r$. Usually, the baseline length b of the binocular cameras is known and the intrinsic parameters of the left and right cameras are exactly the same. According to the imaging principle of the camera, we can get

$$u_l = \frac{f \times x}{z} + c_x,\ v_l = \frac{f \times y}{z} + c_y.$$

Since the difference in the coordinates on the x-axis between the optical centers of the right camera and the left camera is the baseline length b, we have

$$u_r = \frac{f \times (x - b)}{z} + c_x,\ v_r = \frac{f \times y}{z} + c_y.$$

Arrange the above two equations into

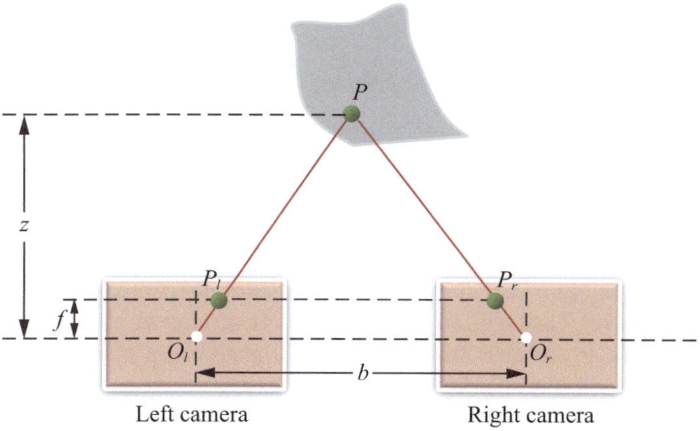

Fig. 18.2 Disparity calculation

$$u_l - u_r = \frac{f \times b}{z}.$$

Let $d = u_l - u_r$, then we have

$$z = \frac{f \times b}{d}.$$

Here, d is the difference in the x-coordinates (horizontal axis) between the projection in the left image and that in the right image, known as disparity; z is the depth of the point. Observing these expressions, it is not difficult to find that in a horizontally placed binocular camera, the v-coordinates (vertical axis) of a three-dimensional point's projections on the imaging planes of the two cameras are the same. The depth of the point determines its disparity. The formula shows that disparity is inversely proportional to depth; the greater the disparity, the smaller the depth. We can use disparity to estimate the depth information of objects in the scene. It should also be noted that the calculation of disparity is based on pixel coordinates, and pixel coordinates are discrete; thus disparity is also discrete. The minimum measurable depth change (division value) of a binocular vision system has a theoretical maximum value, which is $f \times b$. When the camera parameters are fixed, the longer the baseline, the larger the depth range that the binocular vision system can measure, and the larger the division value of depth measurement; conversely, the shorter the baseline, the smaller the measurable depth range, the smaller the division value of depth measurement, but the measurement precision is improved. The disparity calculated for each pixel is plotted at the pixel coordinates to obtain the corresponding disparity map. The disparity of each pixel is converted into depth through the aforementioned formula to obtain the depth map, which can intuitively reflect the depth information of objects in the scene.

18.2.3 Binocular Feature Matching

Although the formula for calculating depth using disparity is straightforward, the process of obtaining disparity is relatively complex. This process requires us to accurately determine the corresponding pixel in the right image for a certain pixel in the left image, which is the process of binocular feature matching. Chapters 4 and 7 introduced template matching and feature point matching, which can be used to calculate disparity. However, in a binocular camera system, the situation is more special: since the two cameras are horizontally aligned, the projection of any three-dimensional point on the imaging planes of these two cameras will have the same vertical coordinates. Therefore, in the feature matching process, we only need to search along the horizontal direction to find the corresponding matching points.

A straightforward method is to select any pixel in the left image and then search for its corresponding pixel on the row where the pixel is located in the right image.

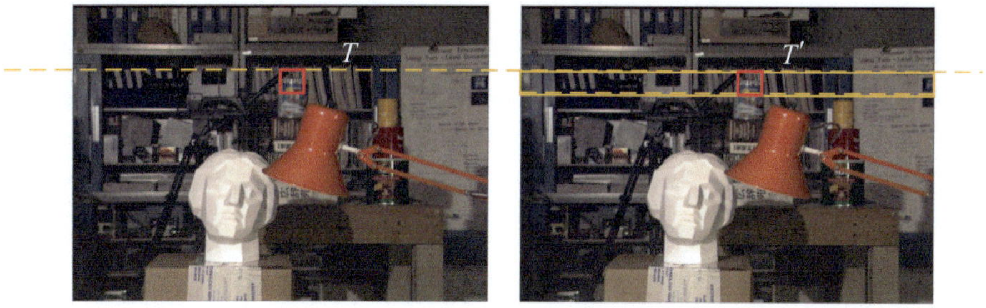

(a) Orignial Image $\boldsymbol{I}_l$ (b) Image to be matched $\boldsymbol{I}_r$

Fig. 18.3 Images taken by a stereo camera

However, single pixel matching has a great deal of uncertainty. For example, a single-colored object may have several identical pixels on a row. To reduce this uncertainty, we can consider not directly matching pixels, but matching image patches, i.e., patch matching. An image patch of size $w \times w$ is selected around the pixel to be matched, and then many image patches of the same size are selected around each pixel on the corresponding row for comparison, which can improve distinguishability to a certain extent.

In the original image $\boldsymbol{I}_l$ of Fig. 18.3a, the template image patch T is selected, then its corresponding image patch T' is requested to be found in region at the corresponding height in the image to be matched $\boldsymbol{I}_r$ in Fig. 18.3b. This is the template matching problem discussed in Chap. 4.

For clarity, let's define the image patch to be matched as $\boldsymbol{A} \in \mathbb{R}^{w \times w}$, and the n image patches to be matched on the corresponding row as $\boldsymbol{B}_k$, where $k = 1, 2, \cdots, n$. The difference between image patches can be measured using the following matching algorithms.

(1) Sum of Absolute Difference (SAD), as the name suggests, is the sum of the absolute values of the differences between the two image patches:

$$S(\boldsymbol{A}, \boldsymbol{B})_{SAD} = \sum_{i,j} | A(i, j) - B(i, j)| .$$

(2) Sum of Squared Difference (SSD) calculates the sum of the squared differences between the two image patches:

$$S(\boldsymbol{A}, \boldsymbol{B})_{SSD} = \sum_{i,j} (A(i, j) - B(i, j))^2 .$$

(3) Normalized Cross-Correlation (NCC) calculates the correlation between the two image patches:

$$S(\boldsymbol{A}, \boldsymbol{B})_{NCC} = \frac{\sum_{i,j} A(i,j)B(i,j)}{\sqrt{\sum_{i,j} A(i,j)^2 \sum_{i,j} B(i,j)^2}} .$$

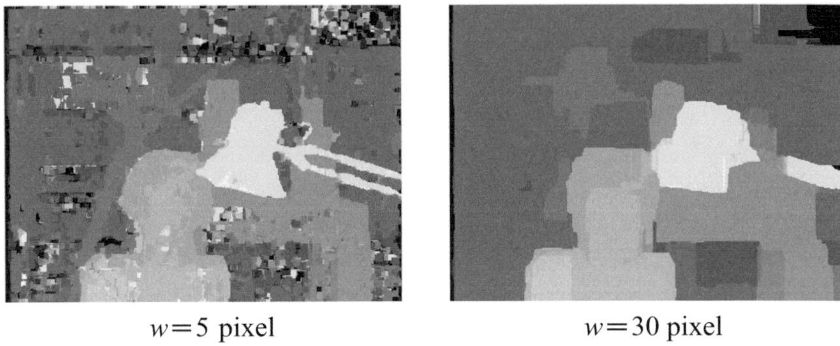

Fig. 18.4 Disparity maps under different patch sizes

In addition to basic matching algorithms, preprocessing can be applied to each image patch, such as removing the mean value of each image patch, to implement mean-removed SSD, mean-removed NCC, etc. The advantage of mean removal is that it can eliminate brightness differences between image patches, thereby improving the accuracy of matching. Specifically, mean removal can make the grayscale values of image patches closer, ensuring the accuracy of matching even if there are overall brightness differences in the image patches. Each method has its characteristics and limitations: SAD is the fastest but very sensitive to local brightness changes; SSD is medium speed and sensitive to brightness offset; while NCC is the slowest, its advantage lies in its insensitivity to contrast and brightness changes. Therefore, in practical applications, the choice of matching algorithm should be determined based on specific requirements and characteristics of the scene.

In patch matching algorithms, the size of the selected patch directly affects the efficiency of matching and the quality of the results. As shown in Fig. 18.4, different patch sizes will produce disparity maps of different qualities. Generally, smaller patch sizes can capture more detail information, but this may also lead to more matching errors and noise. Conversely, larger patch sizes can produce smoother disparity maps, but this method may overlook some important detail information. To balance the impact of patch size on matching results, an effective strategy is to use a multi-scale patch matching method. For each pixel, we do not just use a single size patch for matching, but try multiple different size patches. Then, the disparity corresponding to the best similarity measure is selected as the final result.

18.2.4 Global Optimization

In the methods discussed previously, the depth of each pixel is calculated independently, which may lead to significant depth differences between adjacent pixels. However, in the real world, the depths of adjacent pixels are usually similar, and depth changes are less frequent. Based on this prior knowledge, a spatial regularization term can be introduced to improve depth estimation, making the predicted depth map smoother. Therefore, the binocular feature matching problem can be transformed into a global optimization problem. We first define what constitutes excellent binocular feature matching results. Excellent binocular feature matching results should have the following characteristics. (1) High matching quality: Ensure that each pixel has a high-quality matching point in the corresponding image. (2) Depth smoothness: Require that the disparity changes between adjacent pixels remain consistent. Based on the above objectives, we can construct a matching cost function $E(d) = E_d(d) + \lambda E_s(d)$. Where, $E_d(d)$ represents the quality of single pixel matching, which can usually be measured by the difference between image patches introduced in Sect. 18.2.3; $E_s(d)$ represents the smoothness term, used to measure the smoothness of adjacent pixels. $E_d(d)$ is mainly obtained by various matching algorithms, while $E_s(d)$ is mainly calculated by the disparity difference of neighboring pixels. Let's define a set $\mathcal{E}$, each element of which is a pair of neighboring pixels: (p, q). Then given $(p, q) \in \mathcal{E}$, we have

$$E_s(d) = \sum_{(p,q)\in\mathcal{E}} V\left(d_p, d_q\right)$$

Here, d_p and d_q represent the disparities of pixels p and q, respectively, and V represents the measurement function for calculating the smoothness term. Common functions include L_1 distance function and discriminative function. The L_1 distance is defined as

$$V\left(d_p, d_q\right) = \left|d_p - d_q\right|.$$

The discriminative function is defined as

$$V\left(d_p, d_q\right) = \begin{cases} 0, \ if \ \left|d_p = d_q\right. \\ 1, \ if \ \left|d_p \neq d_q\right. \end{cases}|$$

It should be noted that this optimization problem is NP-hard; thus it usually needs to be solved by approximate algorithms such as dynamic programming. For related solutions, see reference [1].

18.3 Code Implementation

In Sect. 18.2, we introduced the construction of binocular cameras and the principle of depth calculation. Next, we will move on to the implementation part, implementing how to obtain disparity maps from a pair of binocular images.

```
# First, clone the corresponding code repository
! git clone https://github.com/boyu-ai/Hands-on-CV.git
```

```
Cloning into 'learncv_img'...
remote: Enumerating objects: 89, done.
remote: Counting objects: 100% (8/8), done
remote: Compressing objects: 100% (8/8), done
remote: Total 89 (delta 0), reused 0 (delta 0), pack-reused 81
Receiving objects: 100% (89/89), 14.23 MiB | 1023.00 KiB/s, done.
Resolving deltas: 100% (10/10), done.
```

First, we read the left and right images and perform a simple visualization.

```
import os
import time
import cv2 as cv
from PIL import Image
import numpy as np
from matplotlib import pyplot as plt
# Get the image from the left camera
limg_raw = np.asanyarray(Image.open(
r"./learncv_img/Sec-18/scene1.row3.col1.ppm"))
# Get the image from the right camera
rimg_raw = np.asanyarray(Image.open(
r"./learncv_img/Sec-18/scene1.row3.col3.ppm"))
# Convert the images to grayscale
limg = cv.cvtColor(limg_raw, cv.COLOR_BGR2GRAY)
rimg = cv.cvtColor(rimg_raw, cv.COLOR_BGR2GRAY)
# Convert the images to double type
limg = np.asanyarray(limg, dtype = np.double)
rimg = np.asanyarray(rimg, dtype = np.double)
# Define an array of the same size as the input image
img_size = np.shape(limg)[0:2]
# Simple visualization of the left and right images
plt.figure(dpi = 100)
plt.title("binocular images")
plt.imshow(np.hstack([limg_raw, rimg_raw]))
plt.axis('off')
plt.show()
```

Next, we implement a function to generate a disparity map. This function first calculates the overall disparity between the left and right images, then performs disparity search for each pixel, and selects the disparity corresponding to the minimum matching cost as the final disparity.

```
def get_disp_map(max_D, win_size, img_size, match_mode = "SAD"):
    """
```

```
    Get the disparity map based on the left and right images
    Parameters:
    - max_D: The maximum possible disparity between the left and right
images
    - win_size: Patch size
    - img_size: Size of the binocular images
    - match_mode: Matching mode, can be "SAD" or "SSD"
    """
    # Record the initial time
    t1 = time.time()
    # Initialize the disparity map
    imgDiff = np.zeros((img_size[0], img_size[1], max_D))
    def SAD(x, y, error_map, win_size):
        return np.sum(error_map[(x - win_size):(x + win_size),
            (y - win_size):(y + win_size)])
    def SSD(x, y, error_map, win_size):
        return np.sum(np.square(error_map[
(x - win_size):(x + win_size), (y - win_size):(y + win_size)]))
    # Traverse all possible disparity values
    for i in range(0, max_D):
     # Record the overall difference between the left and right images
when the
        # disparity is i
      e = np.abs(rimg[:, 0:(img_size[1]-i)] - limg[:, i:img_size[1]])
        e2 = np.zeros(img_size)
        # Traverse all pixels
        for x in range(0, img_size[0]):
            for y in range(0, img_size[1]):
                # Calculate the matching cost based on the matching mode
                if match_mode == "SAD":
                    # Calculate SAD value
                    e2[x, y] = SAD(x, y, e, win_size)
                elif match_mode == "SSD":
                    # Calculate SSD value
                    e2[x, y] = SSD(x, y, e, win_size)
                else:
                    raise NotImplemented
            # Store the matching cost in imgDiff
            imgDiff[:,:, i] = e2
        # Initialize the disparity map
        dispMap = np.zeros(img_size)
        for x in range(0, img_size[0]):
            for y in range(0, img_size[1]):
                # Sort the matching costs
                val = np.sort(imgDiff[x, y,:])
                # Simple check for boundary conditions
                if np.abs(val[0]-val[1]) > 10:
                  # Find the index of the smallest matching cost disparity
                    val_id = np.argsort(imgDiff[x, y,:])
                    # Map the disparity to the range 0 ~ 255
                    dispMap[x, y] = val_id[0] / max_D * 255
        # Print the execution time.
        print("Execution time:", time.time() - t1)
        # Display the disparity map
```

```
        plt.figure("Disparity Map")
        plt.imshow(dispMap)
        plt.show()
        # Return the disparity map
        return dispMap
    # Maximum disparity
    max_D = 25
    # Sliding window size
    win_size = 5
    # Visualize the SAD matching effect with a block size of 5 pixels
    _ = get_disp_map(max_D, win_size, img_size).
Execution time: 11.269958972930908.
```

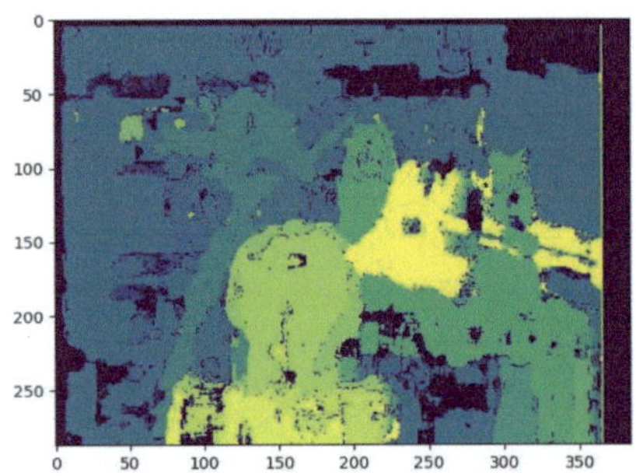

By generating the disparity map of binocular images, we can observe some intuitive phenomena. For example, the lamp appears brighter in the disparity map, indicating that its disparity value is relatively large, while the background is darker, indicating a smaller disparity value. The brightness variation in the disparity map directly reflects the relative depth differences between objects and the camera: brighter regions (larger disparity) indicate that the object is relatively closer to the imaging plane, while darker regions (smaller disparity) indicate that the object is relatively further away. Therefore, using the disparity map, we can effectively estimate the depth information of various objects in the scene.

Next, let's look at the effect of increasing the patch size in the patch matching.

```
# Testing larger patch sizes.
win_size = 30.
# SAD matching result, patch size is 30 pixels.
_ = get_disp_map(max_D, win_size, img_size).
Time used: 14.947252035140991.
```

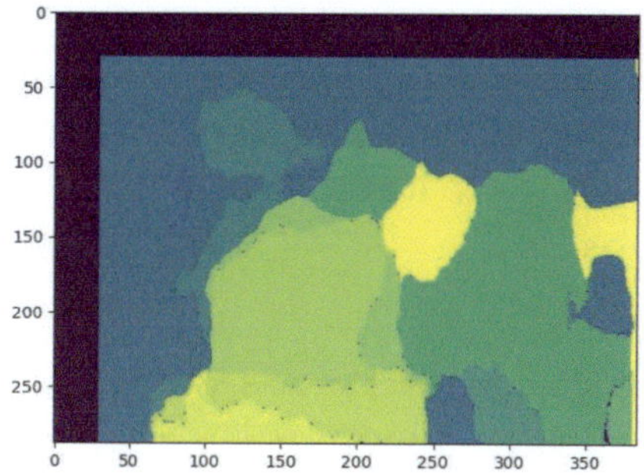

It is not difficult to find that the larger the patch size, the smoother the predicted disparity map, but the more severe the loss of detail, and the increase in computation time.

Next, let's look at the effect of SSD.

```
win_size = 5
# SSD matching result, patch size is 5 pixels
_ = get_disp_map(max_D, win_size, img_size, match_mode = "SSD")
Time used: 13.194314956665039
```

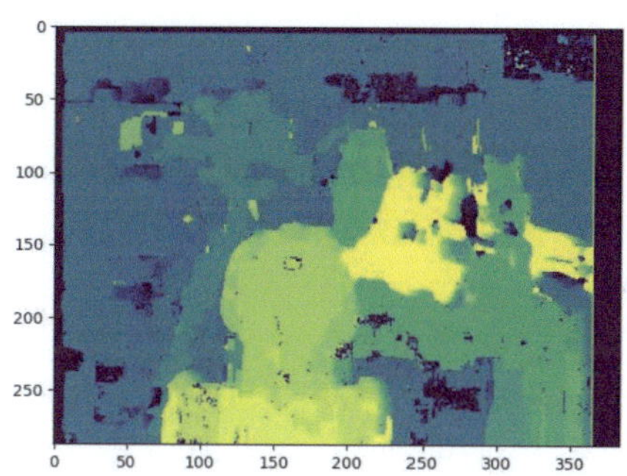


```
win_size = 30
# SSD matching result, patch size is 30 pixels
_ = get_disp_map(max_D, win_size, img_size, match_mode = "SSD")
Time used: 18.293694019317627
```

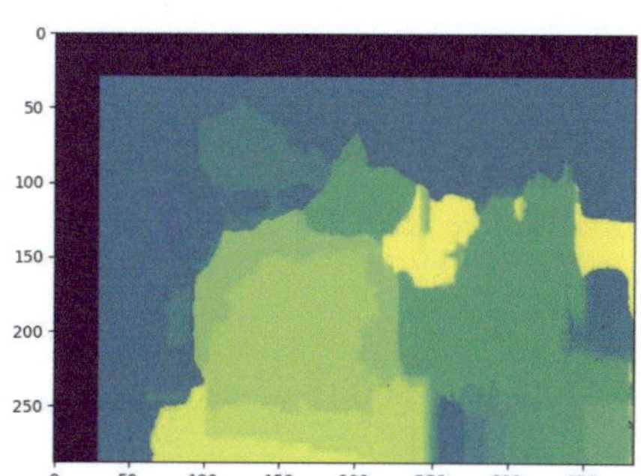

Comparing the effects of SAD and SSD, we can find that SSD retains more details, but it also takes more time.

18.4 Summary

In this chapter, we discussed how to calculate disparity information of a scene using binocular images. After obtaining the disparity, we can further calculate the depth of each point in the image by combining the intrinsic parameters and baseline length of the binocular camera. Depth, as a key element of 3D vision, is directly related to the geometric structure of the scene. Accurate depth information is the basis for scene reconstruction.

In Chap. 19, we will explore how to perform 3D reconstruction of a scene based on a non-parallel binocular vision system.

Exercises

(1) The depth measurement of the binocular system has theoretical limits in terms of resolution and range. Try to design a "trinocular" system based on the binocular system to enhance the depth measurement range of the binocular system and reduce its resolution.
(2) Binocular cameras can also be placed vertically. Please provide the disparity map calculation equation for vertically placed binocular cameras.
(3) Given a binocular camera with a baseline of 10 cm, the resolution of the captured image is 1920 pixels by 1080 pixels, and the camera focal length is 560 mm, try to calculate the maximum measurement distance of this stereo camera and the actual distance corresponding to one pixel.
(4) Implement a binocular depth estimation algorithm based on mean-removed NCC matching. Note that NCC calculates correlation, and the higher the correlation, the higher the match.
(5) In Sect. 18.2.3, to alleviate the impact of patch size during patch matching, we introduced a multi-scale patch matching method. Please implement an adaptive SAD matching algorithm and experience the difference in quality and speed between it and the ordinary SAD algorithm.

Reference

1. BROWN M Z, BURSCHKA D, HAGER G D. Advances in computational stereo[J]. TPAMI, 2003, 25(8):993-1008

Chapter 19
3D Reconstruction

19.1 Introduction

The previous chapters introduced camera calibration, optical flow computation, and parallel binocular vision, all of which explore how to extract three-dimensional information from two-dimensional images. With this foundation, this chapter will finally introduce how to reconstruct three-dimensional scenes from images (3D reconstruction) taken in our daily life.

First, consider the case of a single image. Since a single image cannot provide depth information, it is impossible to accurately estimate the real size of the imaged object, resulting in visual illusions as shown in Fig. 19.1.

To reconstruct the geometric structure of a scene, multiple images are often required. Chapter 18 introduced the parallel binocular vision system. Through disparity, we can recover the depth information of the scene from the images taken by the parallel binocular camera. However, in real life, the multiple images we obtain are often not taken by parallel binocular cameras. In many cases, these images are taken from different angles by the same camera. Imagine we see an exquisite roly-poly toy on a tabletop. Using the same camera, we take two photographs from different viewpoints, as depicted in Fig. 19.2. Obviously, these two images do not satisfy the assumption of parallel optical axes required for a parallel binocular vision system. Therefore, we cannot directly employ the methods introduced for parallel binocular vision systems to calculate depth information.

To recover the three-dimensional information of the scene from these images, we need to use the constraints between the camera models to infer the geometric structure of the scene.

This chapter will introduce how to recover the geometric information of the scene from images taken by a non-parallel binocular vision system, mainly focusing on epipolar geometry and triangulation.

W. Shen et al., *Hands-On Computer Vision*,
https://doi.org/10.1007/978-981-95-4835-4_19

Fig. 19.1 Visual illusion caused by the inability of a single image to provide depth information

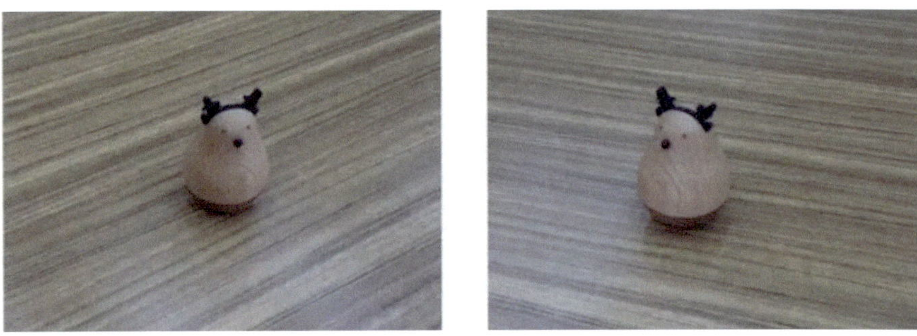

Fig. 19.2 Roly-poly toy taken from different angles

19.2 Epipolar Geometry

Before introducing epipolar geometry, let's review the parallel binocular vision system. In the parallel binocular vision system, two cameras are placed horizontally and their optical axes are parallel. In this case, since the positions of the left and right cameras only differ on the x-axis, the projections of a point in the three-dimensional space on the imaging planes of the left and right cameras also only differ on the x-axis (corresponding to the horizontal axis of the image), which is the disparity. In the non-parallel binocular vision system, the optical axes of the two cameras are no longer parallel, but have a certain degree of convergence, as shown in Fig. 19.3.

In this case, we can no longer find corresponding points on the left and right imaging planes along the horizontal axis, but must consider more complex geometric relationships. We will introduce in this section how to solve this problem through epipolar geometry.

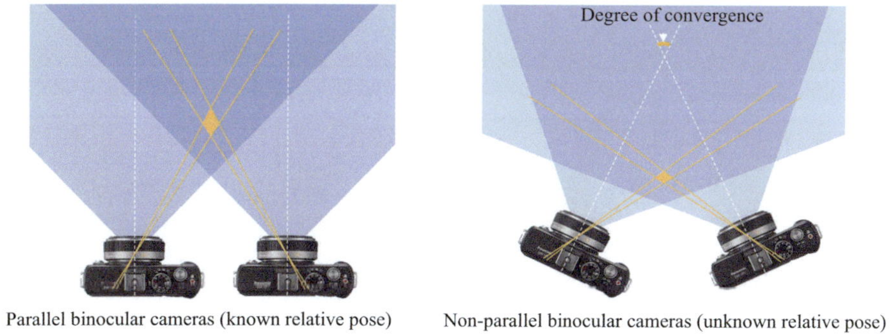

Fig. 19.3 Parallel binocular vision system and non-parallel binocular vision system

19.2.1 Mathematical Definition

As shown in Fig. 19.4, we consider a non-parallel binocular vision system. The two cameras in this vision system are referred to as the left camera and the right camera. Their optical axes are not parallel. Their respective imaging planes are referred to as the left imaging plane and the right imaging plane. The corresponding camera coordinate systems are the left camera coordinate system and the right camera coordinate system. The images taken from the two cameras are the left image and the right image. Note that if these two cameras have exactly the same intrinsic parameters, they can be equivalent to the same camera placed at different viewpoints. For simplicity, we align the world coordinate system with the camera coordinate system of the left camera. Suppose the optical centers of these two cameras are located at points O_l and O_r, respectively. The coordinates of a point P in three-dimensional space in the left and right camera coordinate systems are $\boldsymbol{x}_l$ and $\boldsymbol{x}_r$, respectively. The coordinates of the two projection points P_l and P_r of this point on the left and right imaging planes are $\boldsymbol{u}_l$ and $\boldsymbol{u}_r$ in the left and right image coordinate systems, respectively.

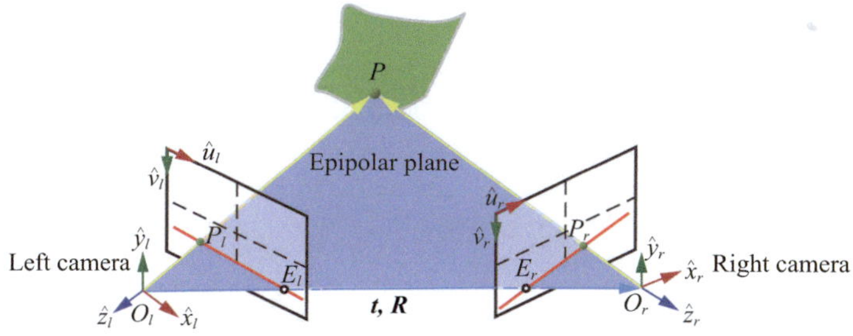

Fig. 19.4 Epipolar geometry of non-parallel binocular cameras

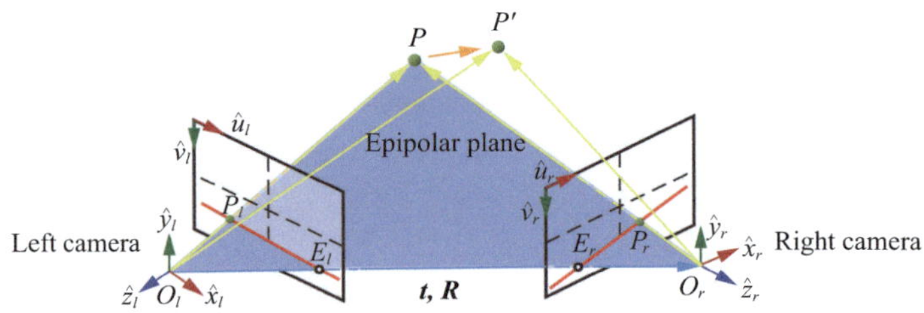

Fig. 19.5 Uniqueness of the epipole

Next, we define some terms to describe spatial geometric relationships: Ray O_lP_l and Ray O_rP_r intersect at point P in three-dimensional space, then these three points O_r, O_l, P can determine a plane, called the epipolar plane. As defined in the parallel binocular vision system, the line connecting the two optical centers O_lO_r is called the baseline. The intersection points of the baseline with the two imaging planes are respectively E_l and E_r. It is not difficult to find that, E_l and E_r are the projections of the optical center O_r on the left imaging plane and the optical center O_l on the right imaging plane, respectively. The points E_l and E_r are referred to as epipoles, and the intersection lines P_lE_l and P_rE_r of the epipolar plane with the two imaging planes are referred to as epipolar lines.

It should be noted that, when the position and orientation of the camera remain unchanged, the position of the epipole is unique. As shown in Fig. 19.5, besides the spatial point P, other points P' in the three-dimensional space can also construct a new polar plane O_lO_rP'. Regardless of how the position of the spatial point changes, the corresponding epipolar plane always contains the baseline O_lO_r; thus it always intersects with the imaging plane at E_l and E_r. We can also understand the uniqueness of the epipole from its physical meaning: the epipole is the projection of the optical center onto the opposite imaging plane. Once the position and orientation of the camera are determined, the positions of the epipoles E_l and E_r are also determined.

Figure 19.6 shows a key concept in epipolar geometry: for a point P_l on the left imaging plane, its corresponding three-dimensional space point P must be projected onto an epipolar line on the right imaging plane. This phenomenon is called the epipolar constraint. Specifically, if we have a set of non-parallel binocular images, the positional relationship between the projected pixel of each point in three-dimensional space in the left image and its projected pixel in the right image is not random, but is constrained by the geometric configuration (especially their relative position and orientation) between the two cameras. This constraint allows us to infer the relative position and attitude of the cameras by finding the correspondence between pixels on the left and right images, thereby recovering the three-dimensional information of the scene.

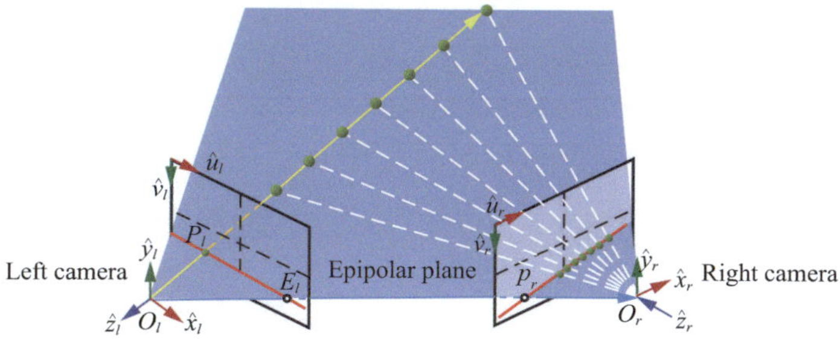

Fig. 19.6 Epipolar constraint

19.2.2 Essential Matrix

In Sect. 19.2.1, we intuitively understood the epipolar constraint through geometry. In this section, we will derive the mathematical representation of the epipolar constraint.

Define the coordinates of the right camera's optical center in the left camera's coordinate system as $\boldsymbol{t} \in \mathbb{R}^{3\times 1}$, and the rotation matrix from the right camera's coordinate system to the left camera's coordinate system as $\boldsymbol{R} \in \mathbb{R}^{3\times 3}$. $\mathbf{x}_l$ and $\mathbf{x}_r$ are respectively the coordinates of the point P in the left and right camera coordinate systems, then we can get the relationship between $\boldsymbol{x}_l$ and $\boldsymbol{x}_r$:

$$\boldsymbol{x}_l = \boldsymbol{R}\boldsymbol{x}_r + \boldsymbol{t}.$$

Expand it to

$$\begin{bmatrix} x_l \\ y_l \\ z_l \end{bmatrix} = \begin{bmatrix} r_{11} & r_{12} & r_{13} \\ r_{21} & r_{22} & r_{23} \\ r_{31} & r_{32} & r_{33} \end{bmatrix} \begin{bmatrix} x_r \\ y_r \\ z_r \end{bmatrix} + \begin{bmatrix} t_x \\ t_y \\ t_z \end{bmatrix}.$$

Next, consider the geometric relationship on the epipolar plane. As shown in Fig. 19.7, the vectors $\boldsymbol{t}$, $\boldsymbol{x}_l$ and $\boldsymbol{x}_r$ are coplanar, we can use the cross product of vectors $\boldsymbol{t}$ and $\boldsymbol{x}_i$ to represent the normal vector of the epipolar plane $\boldsymbol{n}$, which is perpendicular to vectors $\boldsymbol{t}$, $\boldsymbol{x}_l$ and $\boldsymbol{x}_r$.

Then we can get an identity:

$$\boldsymbol{x}_l^{\mathrm{T}} \cdot (\boldsymbol{t} \times \boldsymbol{x}_l) = 0.$$

According to the definition of the cross product, we can get

$$\begin{bmatrix} x_l & y_l & z_l \end{bmatrix} \begin{bmatrix} t_y z_l - t_z y_l \\ t_z x_l - t_x z_l \\ t_x y_l - t_y x_l \end{bmatrix} = 0\,.$$

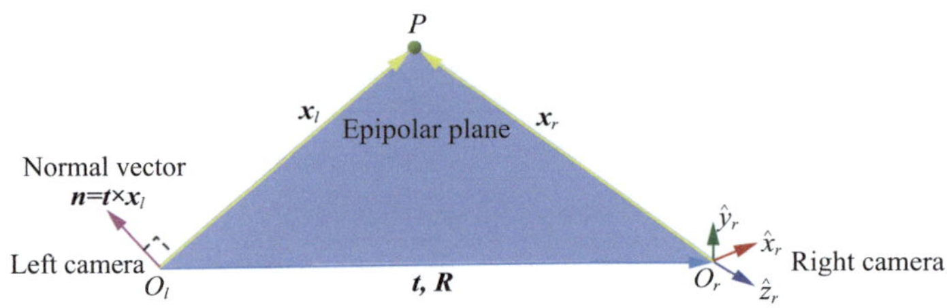

Fig. 19.7 Geometric relationship of the epipolar constraint

The above equation can be transformed into a form of matrix and vector multiplication:

$$\begin{bmatrix} x_l & y_l & z_l \end{bmatrix}\begin{bmatrix} 0 & -t_z & t_y \\ t_z & 0 & -t_x \\ -t_y & t_x & 0 \end{bmatrix}\begin{bmatrix} x_l \\ y_l \\ z_l \end{bmatrix} = 0..$$

The cross product of two vectors can always be written as the product of a skew-symmetric matrix, composed of elements from one of the vectors, and the other vector. Here, the middle matrix is a skew-symmetric matrix, denoted as $\boldsymbol{T}_{\times}$. So, we can get

$$\boldsymbol{x}_l^{\mathrm{T}}\boldsymbol{T}_{\times}\boldsymbol{x}_l = 0.$$

Express the right side $\boldsymbol{x}_1$ with $\boldsymbol{Rx}_r + \boldsymbol{t}$:

$$\boldsymbol{x}_l^{\mathrm{T}}\boldsymbol{T}_{\times}\boldsymbol{Rx}_r + \boldsymbol{x}_l^{\mathrm{T}}\boldsymbol{T}_{\times}\boldsymbol{t} = 0.$$

Obviously, theross product of $\boldsymbol{t}$ with itself $\mathbf{t} \times \mathbf{t}$ is 0, so we get

$$\boldsymbol{x}_l^{\mathrm{T}}\begin{bmatrix} 0 & -t_z & t_y \\ t_z & 0 & -t_x \\ -t_y & t_x & 0 \end{bmatrix}\begin{bmatrix} r_{11} & r_{12} & r_{13} \\ r_{21} & r_{22} & r_{23} \\ r_{31} & r_{32} & r_{33} \end{bmatrix}\boldsymbol{x}_r = 0.$$

We simplify the middle part of the above equation $\boldsymbol{T}_{\times}\boldsymbol{R}$ as $\boldsymbol{E}$, then we get $\boldsymbol{x}_l^{\mathrm{T}}\boldsymbol{Ex}_r = 0$. In this equation, $\boldsymbol{x}_l$ is the coordinate of the spatial point P in the left camera coordinate system, $\boldsymbol{x}_r$ is the coordinate of the spatial point P in the right camera coordinate system, and the middle matrix $\boldsymbol{E}$ links the coordinates of points in three-dimensional space under different camera coordinate systems. This matrix is called the essential matrix.

Next, consider expressing the coordinate relationship with the camera's intrinsic parameters, assuming the intrinsic parameters of the left and right cameras are $\boldsymbol{K}_l$, $\boldsymbol{K}_r$. According to the derivation above, we already know the relationship between the coordinates of the same three-dimensional point in different camera coordinate systems as well as the pose of the camera:

$$\begin{bmatrix} x_l & y_l & z_l \end{bmatrix} \begin{bmatrix} e_{11} & e_{12} & e_{13} \\ e_{21} & e_{22} & e_{23} \\ e_{31} & e_{32} & e_{33} \end{bmatrix} \begin{bmatrix} x_r \\ y_r \\ z_r \end{bmatrix} = 0.$$

According to the transformation relationship from the camera coordinate system to the image coordinate system, the above equation can be written in the form of multiplying the camera's internal parameters:

$$\begin{bmatrix} u_l & v_l & 1 \end{bmatrix} \left(\boldsymbol{K}_{\mathrm{l}}^{-1}\right)^{\mathrm{T}} \boldsymbol{E} \boldsymbol{K}_r^{-1} \begin{bmatrix} u_r \\ v_r \\ 1 \end{bmatrix} = 0.$$

Let $\boldsymbol{F} = \left(\boldsymbol{K}_{\mathrm{l}}^{-1}\right)^{\mathrm{T}} \boldsymbol{E} \boldsymbol{K}_r^{-1}$, then we get

$$\begin{bmatrix} u_l & v_l & 1 \end{bmatrix} \begin{bmatrix} f_{11} & f_{12} & f_{13} \\ f_{21} & f_{22} & f_{23} \\ f_{31} & f_{32} & f_{33} \end{bmatrix} \begin{bmatrix} u_r \\ v_r \\ 1 \end{bmatrix} = 0.$$

That is,

$$\tilde{\boldsymbol{u}}_l^{\mathrm{T}} \boldsymbol{F} \tilde{\boldsymbol{u}}_r = 0.$$

Up to this point, we have established the relationship between the coordinates of the projection points of a point in three-dimensional space on the left and right imaging planes in the image coordinate system. $\boldsymbol{F}$ is generally referred to as the fundamental matrix.

19.2.3 Solving the Fundamental Matrix Using the Eight-Point Method

From the identity $\tilde{\boldsymbol{u}}_l^{\mathrm{T}} \boldsymbol{F} \tilde{\boldsymbol{u}}_r = 0$, we know that the essential matrix $\boldsymbol{E}$ and the fundamental matrix $\boldsymbol{F}$ only differ by a matrix related to the camera's intrinsic parameters. Therefore, as long as we can solve the matrix $\boldsymbol{F}$ and combine it with the known camera intrinsic parameters (even if the camera intrinsic parameters are unknown, they can be calibrated using the method introduced in Chap. 16), we can obtain the relative pose between the cameras. $\boldsymbol{F}$ is a 3×3 matrix, theoretically having 9 parameters, but since the fundamental matrix is determined only up to a scale factor (i.e., the fundamental matrix does not change with the multiplication of any nonzero scalar), only 8 independent parameters need to be solved. Therefore, at least 8 pairs of matching points are needed to solve the fundamental matrix using the "eight-point method".

These matching points can be obtained based on the feature detection method introduced in Chap. 7. Next, we will introduce how to solve the fundamental matrix using the eight-point method.

First, assume that we have obtained the coordinate pairs of matched pixels on the left and right images through feature detection, denoted as $\left(\left(u_l^{(i)}, v_l^{(i)}\right), \left(u_r^{(i)}, v_r^{(i)}\right)\right)$, where $i = 1, 2, \ldots, m$ and $m \geq 8$. Then we have

$$\begin{bmatrix} u_l^{(i)} & v_l^{(i)} & 1 \end{bmatrix} \begin{bmatrix} f_{11} & f_{12} & f_{13} \\ f_{21} & f_{22} & f_{23} \\ f_{31} & f_{32} & f_{33} \end{bmatrix} \begin{bmatrix} u_r^{(i)} \\ v_r^{(i)} \\ 1 \end{bmatrix} = 0.$$

Expand it to get

$$\begin{aligned} &\left(f_{11}u_r^{(i)} + f_{12}v_r^{(i)} + f_{13}\right)u_l^{(i)} + \left(f_{21}u_r^{(i)} + f_{22}v_r^{(i)} + f_{23}\right)v_l^{(i)} \\ &\quad + f_{31}u_r^{(i)} + f_{32}v_r^{(i)} + f_{33} = 0. \end{aligned}$$

Substitute different pixel coordinates to form a homogeneous system of linear equations:

$$\begin{bmatrix} u_l^{(1)}u_r^{(2)} & u_l^{(1)}v_r^{(2)} & u_l^{(1)} & v_l^{(1)}u_r^{(1)} & v_l^{(1)}v_r^{(1)} & v_l^{(1)} & u_r^{(1)} & v_r^{(1)} & 1 \\ u_l^{(2)}u_r^{(2)} & u_l^{(2)}v_r^{(2)} & u_l^{(2)} & v_l^{(2)}u_r^{(2)} & v_l^{(2)}v_r^{(2)} & v_l^{(2)} & u_r^{(2)} & v_r^{(2)} & 1 \\ \vdots & \vdots & \vdots & \vdots & \vdots & \vdots & \vdots & \vdots & \vdots \\ u_l^{(m)}u_r^{(m)} & u_l^{(m)}v_r^{(m)} & u_r^{(m)} & v_l^{(m)}u_r^{(m)} & v_l^{(m)}v_r^{(m)} & v_l^{(m)} & u_r^{(m)} & v_r^{(m)} & 1 \end{bmatrix} \begin{bmatrix} f_{11} \\ f_{12} \\ f_{13} \\ f_{21} \\ f_{22} \\ f_{23} \\ f_{31} \\ f_{32} \\ f_{33} \end{bmatrix} = \begin{bmatrix} 0 \\ 0 \\ \vdots \\ 0 \end{bmatrix}$$

Does this equation look familiar? We saw similar equation $\boldsymbol{A} \cdot \boldsymbol{f} = 0$ when we introduced camera calibration in Chap. 16, i.e., calculating $\min_f \|\boldsymbol{A}\boldsymbol{f}\|^2$ s.t.$\|\boldsymbol{f}\|^2 = 1$. The specific solution process can be referred to Chap. 16 and will not be repeated here.

19.2.4 Solving Camera Pose from the Essential Matrix

In Sect. 19.2.3, we have already solved the fundamental matrix $\boldsymbol{F}$ using the eight-point method. Next, we will solve the essential matrix $\boldsymbol{E}$ from the fundamental matrix $\boldsymbol{F}$ and further determine the pose of the camera. As introduced in Sect. 19.2.3, $\boldsymbol{E}$ has a fixed expression form $\boldsymbol{E} = \boldsymbol{T}_\times \boldsymbol{R}$, where $\boldsymbol{T}_\times$ is a skew-symmetric matrix, representing the translation vector of the camera, and $\boldsymbol{R}$ is an orthogonal matrix, representing the rotation matrix of the camera. Since $\boldsymbol{T}_\times$ and $\boldsymbol{R}$ have specific properties, we can separate them from $\mathbf{E}$ using singular value decomposition (SVD). Let the SVD form of $\boldsymbol{E}$ be $\boldsymbol{E} = \boldsymbol{U}\boldsymbol{\Sigma}\boldsymbol{V}^{\mathrm{T}}$, where $\boldsymbol{U}$ and $\boldsymbol{V}$ are orthogonal matrices, and $\boldsymbol{\Sigma}$ is a singular value matrix, which gives

$$\boldsymbol{E} = \begin{bmatrix} u_{11} & u_{12} & u_{13} \\ u_{21} & u_{22} & u_{23} \\ u_{31} & u_{32} & u_{33} \end{bmatrix} \begin{bmatrix} \sigma_1 & 0 & 0 \\ 0 & \sigma_2 & 0 \\ 0 & 0 & \sigma_3 \end{bmatrix} \begin{bmatrix} v_{11} & v_{12} & v_{13} \\ v_{21} & v_{22} & v_{23} \\ v_{31} & v_{32} & v_{33} \end{bmatrix}^{\mathrm{T}}.$$

Based on $\boldsymbol{E} = \boldsymbol{T}_\times\boldsymbol{R}$ and $\boldsymbol{E} = \boldsymbol{U}\boldsymbol{\Sigma}\boldsymbol{V}^{\mathrm{T}}$, we can solve for the suitable $\boldsymbol{R}$ and $\boldsymbol{t}$:

$$\left\{\begin{array}{ll} \boldsymbol{R} = \left(\det UWV^{\mathrm{T}}\right)UWV^{\mathrm{T}} & \boldsymbol{t} = \boldsymbol{u}_3 \\ \boldsymbol{R} = \left(\det UWV^{\mathrm{T}}\right)UWV^{\mathrm{T}} & \boldsymbol{t} = -\boldsymbol{u}_3 \\ \boldsymbol{R} = \left(\det UW^{\mathrm{T}}V^{\mathrm{T}}\right)UW^{\mathrm{T}}V^{\mathrm{T}} & \boldsymbol{t} = \boldsymbol{u}_3 \\ \boldsymbol{R} = \left(\det UW^{\mathrm{T}}V^{\mathrm{T}}\right)UW^{\mathrm{T}}V^{\mathrm{T}} & \boldsymbol{t} = -\boldsymbol{u}_3 \end{array}\right|.$$

In the above equation, $\boldsymbol{u}_3$ represents the third column of $\boldsymbol{U}$; $\boldsymbol{W}$ is an auxiliary matrix, specifically

$$\boldsymbol{W} = \begin{bmatrix} 0 & -1 & 0 \\ 1 & 0 & 0 \\ 0 & 0 & 1 \end{bmatrix}.$$

It is not difficult to find that the four solutions mathematically represent the four relative pose relationships among two cameras and a point in space, as shown in Fig. 19.8. According to the definition of a pinhole camera, any point observable by the camera (i.e., lying in front of the camera) must have a positive z-coordinate (z-axis) in the camera coordinate system. Therefore, we need to calculate the depth of any point in three-dimensional space under these four combinations of $\boldsymbol{R}$ and $\boldsymbol{t}$ (using the triangulation method introduced in Sect. 19.3). If the calculated depth of the point in both camera coordinate systems is positive, the corresponding combination of $\boldsymbol{R}$ and $\boldsymbol{t}$ is the correct relative pose between the two cameras.

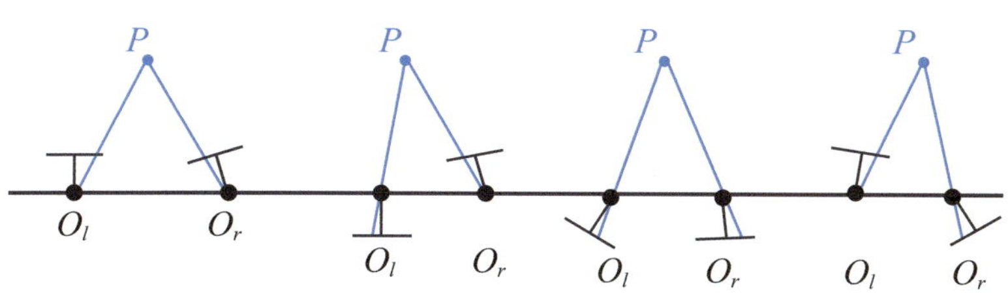

Fig. 19.8 Relative poses of the three-dimensional space point and the left and right cameras represented by the four solutions

19.3 Triangulation

After obtaining the relative pose between two cameras, triangulation can be employed to determine the depth of each pixel's corresponding three-dimensional point, thereby achieving the final three-dimensional reconstruction. Given two or more cameras and the projection points of the same point on the imaging planes of these cameras, a ray is emitted from the optical center of each camera that passes through the corresponding projection point on the imaging plane. These rays theoretically intersect at the same point in space, which is the position of the three-dimensional point we want to solve. This process is called triangulation.

Taking Fig. 19.4 as an example, according to the perspective projection rules, we can get

$$z_l \begin{bmatrix} u_l \\ v_l \\ 1 \end{bmatrix} = \begin{bmatrix} f_x^{(l)} & 0 & o_x^{(l)} & 0 \\ 0 & f_y^{(l)} & o_y^{(l)} & 0 \\ 0 & 0 & 1 & 0 \end{bmatrix} \begin{bmatrix} x_l \\ y_l \\ z_l \\ 1 \end{bmatrix}$$

and

$$z_r \begin{bmatrix} u_r \\ v_r \\ 1 \end{bmatrix} = \begin{bmatrix} f_x^{(r)} & 0 & o_x^{(r)} & 0 \\ 0 & f_y^{(r)} & o_y^{(r)} & 0 \\ 0 & 0 & 1 & 0 \end{bmatrix} \begin{bmatrix} x_r \\ y_r \\ z_r \\ 1 \end{bmatrix}$$

where f_x, f_y, o_x, o_y represent the focal length of the camera on the x-axis, the focal length of the camera on the y-axis, the x-coordinate and the y-coordinate of the intersection point of the optical axis and the imaging plane in the image coordinate system. The superscripts (l) and (r) indicate whether these parameters belong to the left or right camera. Since the relative pose between the two cameras is known, we have:

$$\begin{bmatrix} x_l \\ y_l \\ z_l \\ 1 \end{bmatrix} = \begin{bmatrix} r_{11} & r_{12} & r_{13} & t_x \\ r_{21} & r_{22} & r_{23} & t_y \\ r_{31} & r_{32} & r_{33} & t_z \\ 0 & 0 & 0 & 1 \end{bmatrix} \begin{bmatrix} x_r \\ y_r \\ z_r \\ 1 \end{bmatrix}.$$

By combining these, we get:

$$z_l \begin{bmatrix} u_l \\ v_l \\ 1 \end{bmatrix} = \begin{bmatrix} f_x^{(l)} & 0 & o_x^{(l)} & 0 \\ 0 & f_y^{(l)} & o_y^{(l)} & 0 \\ 0 & 0 & 1 & 0 \end{bmatrix} \begin{bmatrix} r_{11} & r_{12} & r_{13} & t_x \\ r_{21} & r_{22} & r_{23} & t_y \\ r_{31} & r_{32} & r_{33} & t_z \\ 0 & 0 & 0 & 1 \end{bmatrix} \begin{bmatrix} x_r \\ y_r \\ z_r \\ 1 \end{bmatrix}.$$

This can be abbreviated as:

$$\tilde{u}_l \propto \boldsymbol{M}_l \tilde{\boldsymbol{x}}_r$$

where $\tilde{u}_l$ represents the homogeneous coordinates of $\boldsymbol{u}_l$; $\boldsymbol{M}_l$ represents the product of the two middle matrices; $\tilde{\boldsymbol{x}}_r$ represents the homogeneous coordinates of $\boldsymbol{x}_r$; the proportionality symbol $\propto$ indicates that the two homogeneous coordinate vectors are proportional. Also, because:

$$\tilde{\boldsymbol{u}}_r \propto \boldsymbol{P}_r \tilde{\boldsymbol{x}}_r$$

where $\boldsymbol{P}_r$ represents the projection matrix of the right camera. By combining these two equations, we can obtain the system of equations for x_r, y_r, z_r:

$$\begin{bmatrix} u_r p_{31} - p_{11} & u_r p_{32} - p_{12} & u_r p_{33} - p_{13} \\ v_r p_{31} - p_{21} & v_r p_{32} - p_{22} & v_r p_{33} - p_{23} \\ u_l m_{31} - m_{11} & u_l m_{32} - m_{12} & u_l m_{33} - m_{13} \\ v_l m_{31} - m_{21} & v_l m_{32} - m_{22} & v_l m_{33} - m_{23} \end{bmatrix} \begin{bmatrix} x_r \\ y_r \\ z_r \end{bmatrix} = \begin{bmatrix} p_{14} - p_{34} \\ p_{24} - p_{34} \\ m_{14} - m_{34} \\ m_{24} - m_{34} \end{bmatrix}.$$

The above equation can be abbreviated as:

$$\boldsymbol{A}\boldsymbol{x}_r = \boldsymbol{b}.$$

This is an overdetermined inhomogeneous system of linear equations, whose least-squares solution can be expressed using the pseudoinverse matrix:

$$\boldsymbol{A}^{\mathrm{T}}\boldsymbol{A}x_r = \boldsymbol{A}^{\mathrm{T}}b \quad x_r = \left(\boldsymbol{A}^{\mathrm{T}}\boldsymbol{A}\right)^{-1}\boldsymbol{A}^{\mathrm{T}}\boldsymbol{b}.$$

The final $\left(\boldsymbol{A}^{\mathrm{T}}\boldsymbol{A}\right)^{-1}\boldsymbol{A}^{\mathrm{T}}\boldsymbol{b}$ is the desired (x_r, y_r, z_r), i.e., the three-dimensional coordinates of the spatial point corresponding to the specified pixel in the right camera coordinate system. Then, based on the relative pose, its three-dimensional coordinates in the left camera coordinate system can be calculated. Considering that there may be many mismatches in feature point matching, we need to use epipolar constraints to further filter out incorrect matches. How to use epipolar constraints? Given a calculated fundamental matrix, two images (left and right), and a pixel coordinate $[u_l \;\; v_l]$ on the left image, according to the definition of epipolar constraints, we can get:

$$[u_l \;\; v_l \;\; 1] \begin{bmatrix} f_{11} & f_{12} & f_{13} \\ f_{21} & f_{22} & f_{23} \\ f_{31} & f_{32} & f_{33} \end{bmatrix} \begin{bmatrix} u_r \\ v_r \\ 1 \end{bmatrix} = 0$$

where $[u_r \;\; v_r]$ is the coordinate of the corresponding pixel on the right image (unknown). Expanding the equation, we can get:

$$(f_{11}u_l + f_{21}v_l + f_{31})u_r + (f_{12}u_l + f_{22}v_l + f_{32})v_r + (f_{13}u_l + f_{23}v_l + f_{33}) = 0.$$

This can be abbreviated as:

$$a'u_r + b'v_r + c' = 0.$$

At this point, we have obtained the expression of the epipolar line in the right image corresponding to the pixel in the left image. Similarly, we can obtain the expression of the epipolar line in the left image corresponding to the pixel in the right image. According to the epipolar constraint, the matched points on in the left and right images should fall on their respective corresponding epipolar lines; i.e., the distance from a matched point to the corresponding epipolar line should be 0. By setting an appropriate distance threshold, we can select high-quality matched points that meet the epipolar constraints. Using these selected matched points for triangulation, we can get more accurate 3D reconstruction results. In addition, there are nonlinear methods for triangulation. The core idea is to find a point *P'* in the three-dimensional space, so that the distance (reprojection error) between its projection points on the left and right cameras and the currently known pixel points is minimized. This will not be detailed here.

19.4 Code Implementation

We have already understood the basic concepts and mathematical derivations of epipolar constraints, as well as how to solve the fundamental matrix and perform triangulation through epipolar constraints. Next, we will learn how to calculate the fundamental matrix between two given images captured from different views and perform triangulation.

```
# First, clone the corresponding code repository
!git clone https://github.com/boyu-ai/Hands-on-CV.git
```

```
Cloning into 'learncv_img'...
remote: Enumerating objects: 89, done.
remote: Counting objects: 100% (8/8), done.
remote: Compressing objects: 100% (8/8), done.
Receiving objects: 100% (89/89), 14.23 MiB | 32.00 KiB/s, done.
remote: Total 89 (delta 0), reused 0 (delta 0), pack-reused 81
Resolving deltas: 100% (10/10), done.
```

```
import os, cv2, random
import matplotlib.pyplot as plt
import numpy as np
% matplotlib inline
class FeatureExtractor:
```

```
    """
    Class for extracting SIFT features
    """
    def __init__(self, image):
        """
        Initialize the FeatureExtractor class
        Parameters:
        - image: (np.ndarray): Image in RGB format
        """
        self.image = image
        # Convert the image to grayscale
        self.gray = cv2.cvtColor(self.image, cv2.COLOR_BGR2GRAY)
        self.keypoints = None
        self.descriptors = None
    def extract_features(self):
        """
         Extract SIFT features from the image using OpenCV's built-in
function
        Returns:
        - keys: (list): List of keypoints
        - descriptors: (np.ndarray): Descriptors
        """
        sift = cv2.SIFT_create()
        keys, descriptors = sift.detectAndCompute(self.gray, None)
        # If the number of keypoints is less than 20, return None
        if len(keys) <= 20:
            return None, None
        else:
            self.keypoints = keys
            self.descriptors = descriptors
            return keys, descriptors
def vis_imgs(imgs):
    """
    Visualize multiple images
    Parameters:
    - imgs: List of images to visualize
    """
    # Calculate the number of images
    num_imgs = len(imgs)
    # Create a canvas
    fig = plt.figure(figsize=(10, 10))
    # Iterate over each image
    for i in range(num_imgs):
        # Add a subplot
        ax = fig.add_subplot(1, num_imgs, i + 1)
        # Display the image
        ax.imshow(imgs[i])
        # Turn off the axis
        ax.axis('off')
    # Show the canvas
    plt.show()
```

For convenience, the camera intrinsic parameters (data from the camera itself) are provided here, but you can also obtain the intrinsic parameters obtained by the camera calibration method introduced in Chap. 16.

```
def load_instrinsic(path):
    """
    Directly read intrinsic parameters from the file
    """
    return np.loadtxt(path).astype(np.float32)
def construct_img_info(img_root):
    """
    Extract feature information from the image
    """
    imgs = []
    feats = []
    K = []
    for _, name in enumerate(os.listdir(img_root)):
        if '.jpg' in name or '.JPG' or '.png' in name:
            # Read the image
            path = os.path.join(img_root, name)
            img = cv2.cvtColor(cv2.imread(path), cv2.COLOR_BGR2RGB)
            imgs.append(img)
            # Extract features
            feature_ext = FeatureExtractor(img)
            kpt, des = feature_ext.extract_features()
            # Read intrinsic parameters
            K = load_instrinsic(os.path.join(
                os.path.dirname(img_root), 'K.txt'))
            feats.append({'kpt': kpt, 'des': des})
    return imgs, feats, K
```

Next, calculate the correspondence between two images, query and match the features between them.

```
def get_matches(des_query, des_train):
    """
    Match related image features
    Parameters:
    - des_query: (np.ndarray): Query descriptors
    - des_train: (np.ndarray): Training descriptors
    Returns:
    - goods: (list): Match results
    """
    # Create a matcher
    bf = cv2.BFMatcher(cv2.NORM_L2)
    # Get match results
    matches = bf.knnMatch(des_query, des_train, k=2)
    # Create a goods list to store useful match results
    goods = []
    # Iterate through all match results
    for m, m_ in matches:
        # Set the threshold to 0.65 to retain more features
        if m.distance < 0.65 * m_.distance:
            goods.append(m)
    return goods
def get_match_point(p, p_, matches):
    """
    Find matched keypoints
```

```
    Parameters:
    - p: (list[cv2.KeyPoint]): Query keypoints
    - p_: (list[cv2.KeyPoint]): Training keypoints
    - matches: (list[cv2.DMatch]): Matching information
    Returns:
    - points_query: (np.ndarray): Query keypoints
    - points_train: (np.ndarray): Training keypoints
    """
    # Find matched keypoints from query keypoints
    points_query = np.asarray([p[m.queryIdx].pt for m in matches])
    # Find matched keypoints from training keypoints
    points_train = np.asarray([p_[m.trainIdx].pt for m in matches])
    # Return matched query and training keypoints
    return points_query, points_train
def homoco_pts_2_euco_pts(pts):
    """
    Convert homogeneous coordinates to Euclidean coordinates
    """
    if len(pts.shape) == 1:
        pts = pts.reshape(1, -1)
    res = pts / pts[:, -1, None]
    return res[:, :-1].squeeze()
def euco_pts_2_homoco_pts(pts):
    """
    Convert Euclidean coordinates to homogeneous coordinates
    """
    if len(pts.shape) == 1:
        pts = pts.reshape(1, -1)
    one = np.ones(pts.shape[0])
    res = np.c_[pts, one]
    return res.squeeze()
def normalize(pts, T=None):
    """
    Normalize the point set
    """
    # If the T parameter is empty
    if T is None:
        # Calculate the mean of the point set
        u = np.mean(pts, 0)
        # Calculate the sum of the distances between each point in the
set and the
        # origin
        d = np.sum(np.sqrt(np.sum(np.power(pts, 2), 1)))
        # Calculate the normalization matrix
        T = np.array([
                [np.sqrt(2) / d, 0, -(np.sqrt(2) / d * u[0])],
                [0, np.sqrt(2) / d, -(np.sqrt(2) / d * u[1])],
                [0, 0, 1]
        ])
    # Normalize the point set
    return homoco_pts_2_euco_pts(np.matmul(T,
            euco_pts_2_homoco_pts(pts).T).T), T
```

At this point, we have obtained the corresponding pixel relationship between the two images. Next, we use the eight-point method to solve the fundamental matrix.

```
def estimate_fundamental(pts1, pts2, num_sample=8):
   """
   Solve the fundamental matrix
   Parameters:
    - pts1: (np.ndarray): Training point set obtained from matched
features
     - pts2: (np.ndarray): Query point set obtained from matched
features
   Return:
   - f: (np.ndarray): Fundamental matrix
   """
   n = pts1.shape[0]
   pts_index = range(n)
   sample_index = random.sample(pts_index, num_sample)
   p1 = pts1[sample_index, :]
   p2 = pts2[sample_index, :]
   n = len(sample_index)
   # Normalize the coordinates of the points in the set
   p1_norm, T1 = normalize(p1, None)
   p2_norm, T2 = normalize(p2, None)
   w = np.zeros((n, 9))
   # Construct matrix A
   for i in range(n):
      w[i, 0] = p1_norm[i, 0] * p2_norm[i, 0]
      w[i, 1] = p1_norm[i, 1] * p2_norm[i, 0]
      w[i, 2] = p2_norm[i, 0]
      w[i, 3] = p1_norm[i, 0] * p2_norm[i, 1]
      w[i, 4] = p1_norm[i, 1] * p2_norm[i, 1]
      w[i, 5] = p2_norm[i, 1]
      w[i, 6] = p1_norm[i, 0]
      w[i, 7] = p1_norm[i, 1]
      w[i, 8] = 1
   # SVD
   U, sigma, VT = np.linalg.svd(w)
   f = VT[-1, :].reshape(3, 3)
   U, sigma, VT = np.linalg.svd(f)
   sigma[2] = 0
   f = U.dot(np.diag(sigma)).dot(VT)
   # Inverse normalization
   f = T2.T.dot(f).dot(T1)
   # There exists noise and mismatches in randomly selected matched
points, which
   # cause significant errors in the computed the F matrix, thus the
function
   # (RANSAC) in OpenCV is used to compute the F matrix
   pts1 = pts1.astype(np.float32)
   pts2 = pts2.astype(np.float32)
   f, mask = cv2.findFundamentalMat(pts1, pts2, cv2.FM_RANSAC)
   return f
def convert_F_to_E(F_single, K):
   """
   Calculate the E matrix based on the F matrix
   """
   inverse_K = np.linalg.inv(K)
```

```
    E_single = inverse_K.T.dot(F_single).dot(inverse_K)
    return E_single
def get_Rt_from_E(E_single,K,pts1,pts2):
    """
   Calculate Rt based on the E matrix, using the recoverPose function
in OpenCV
    """
    # The recoverPose function in OpenCV has automatically removed
the 3 unreasonable
    # solutions
    _, R, t, _ = cv2.recoverPose(E_single, pts1, pts2, K)
    return R, t
def build_F_E_matrix(feats, K):
    """
    Calculate the fundamental matrix F and the essential matrix E,
separate Rt from E
    and return
    """
    pair = dict()
    match = dict()
    Rts = dict()
    for i in range(len(feats)):
        for j in range(i + 1, len(feats)):
            matches = get_matches(
                feats[i]['des'], feats[j]['des'])
            pts1, pts2 = get_match_point(
                feats[i]['kpt'], feats[j]['kpt'], matches)
            assert pts1.shape == pts2.shape
            # At least 8 points are needed to calculate the F matrix
            if pts1.shape[0] < 8:
                continue
            # Calculate the F matrix
            F_single = estimate_fundamental(pts1, pts2)
            # Calculate the E matrix based on the F matrix
            E_single = convert_F_to_E(F_single, K)
            # Get the relative pose from the E matrix
            R, t = get_Rt_from_E(E_single, K, pts1, pts2)
            if pts1.shape[0] < 8:
                continue
            pair.update({(i, j): {'pts1': pts1, 'pts2': pts2}})
            match.update({(i, j): {'match': matches}})
            Rts.update({(i, j): {'R': R, 't': t}})
    return F_single, E_single, pair, match, Rts
```

After obtaining the fundamental matrix, we can calculate the coordinates of the three-dimensional point through triangulation.

```
def filter_matches_by_epipolar(pts1, pts2, F, threshold = 3.0):
    """
    Filter matched points using epipolar constraint
    Parameters:
    - pts1, pts2: pair of matched points
    - F: Fundamental Matrix
    - threshold: epipolar error threshold
```

```
    Returns:
    - pts1_filtered, pts2_filtered: filtered matching points
    """
    pts1_reshaped = pts1.T.reshape(-1,1,2)
    pts2_reshaped = pts2.T.reshape(-1,1,2)
    # Calculate the epipolar lines of two images
    lines1 = cv2.computeCorrespondEpilines(pts2_reshaped, 2, F)
    lines2 = cv2.computeCorrespondEpilines(pts1_reshaped, 1, F)
    dist1 = np.abs(np.sum(lines1.reshape(-1,3) *
          np.hstack((pts1.T, np.ones((pts1.shape[1],1)))), axis=1))
    dist2 = np.abs(np.sum(lines2.reshape(-1,3) *
          np.hstack((pts2.T, np.ones((pts2.shape[1],1)))), axis=1))
    mask = (dist1 < threshold) & (dist2 < threshold)
    return pts1[:,mask], pts2[:,mask]
img_root = 'learncv_img/Sec-19/images'
imgs, feats, K = construct_img_info(img_root) # visualize images
vis_imgs(imgs)
F, E, pair, match, Rts = build_F_E_matrix(feats, K)
print(The Fundamental Matrix is:\n, F)
print(The Essential Matrix is:\n, E)
# The first image is assumed to define the world coordinate system
R_t_0 = np.array([
    [1, 0, 0, 0],
    [0, 1, 0, 0],
    [0, 0, 1, 0]
])
R_t_1 = np.empty((3, 4))
R_t_1[:, :3] = Rts[(0, 1)]['R']
R_t_1[:, 3] = Rts[(0, 1)]['t'].reshape(3)
P_0 = K.dot(R_t_0)
P_1 = K.dot(R_t_1)
print(The camera matrix of the first image is:\n, P_0)
print(The camera matrix of the second image is:\n, P_1)
pts1 = np.transpose(pair[(0,1)]['pts1'])
pts2 = np.transpose(pair[(0,1)]['pts2'])
# Filter matched points
pts1_filtered,      pts2_filtered      =      filter_matches_by_
epipolar(pts1, pts2, F)
print("Number  of  matched  points  before  filtering:  ",  pts1  .
shape[1])
print("Number of matched points after filtering: ", pts1_filtered
.
shape[1])
# Triangulate to get the coordinates of the spatial point
points_3d = cv2 . triangulatePoints(P_0, P_1, pts1_filtered, pts2_
filtered)
# The values in the last row of homogeneous coordinates should be 1.
Division by the
# values in the last row is required.
points_3d /= points_3d[3]
points_3d = points_3d[:3, :] . T
print("The obtained 3D points are:\n", points_3d)
# Calculate the proportion of valid points to all pixels
```

```
print("The proportion of detected points to image pixels
is: {:02f}%" . format(
  points_3d . shape[0] / len(imgs[0][ ... ,0] . flatten()) * 100))
```

```
Number of matched points before filtering: 16
Number of matched points after filtering: 13
The obtained 3D points are:
[[-0.60458395 -0.01198244 0.0969504 ]
[-0.58099777 -0.21461379 0.05341815]
[-0.47523613 -0.39286399 -0.15945556]
[-0.56740703 -0.24286074 -0.00477856]
[-0.49754951 -0.36653935 -0.14429421]
[-0.47079379 -0.40467599 -0.19146369]
[-0.55889738 -0.26988774 -0.09548055]
[-0.60761656 -0.14041958 -0.12032324]
[-0.56458993 -0.29775277 -0.2171921 ]
[-0.6082215 -0.14859759 -0.13404173]
[-0.43299244 -0.4819224 -0.33418579]
[-0.5657818 -0.3328847 -0.29034157]
[-0.5657818 -0.3328847 -0.29034157]]
The detected points account for 0.004757% of the image pixels.
```

It can be observed that some matched points do not strictly follow the epipolar constraint. Next, we will visualize the epipolar lines and matched points.

```
def draw_epipolar_lines(pts1, pts2, img1, img2, F):
  """
  Draw epipolar lines
  Parameters:
  - pts1: (np.ndarray): Matched points in the first image
  - pts2: (np.ndarray): Matched points in the second image
  - img1: (np.ndarray): The first image
  - img2: (np.ndarray): The second image
  - F: (np.ndarray): Fundamental matrix
  """
  # Convert point coordinates to integers
  pts1 = np.int32(pts1)
  pts2 = np.int32(pts2)
  # Select the first 8 points for visualization
  idx = np.arange(8)
  pts1 = pts1[idx]
  pts2 = pts2[idx]
  # Calculate the corresponding epipolar lines
       lines1 = cv2.computeCorrespondEpilines(pts2.reshape(-
1,1,2), 2, F)
  lines1 = lines1.reshape(-1,3)
  # Draw epipolar lines
  img1, imgr = drawlines(img1, img2, lines1, pts1, pts2)
  # Concatenate the two images
  vis = np.concatenate((img1, imgr), axis=1)
  # Display the image
  plt.figure(figsize=(10, 10))
```

```
    plt.imshow(vis)
    plt.axis('off')
    plt.show()
def drawlines(img1, img2, lines, pts1, pts2):
    """
    Draw epipolar lines
    Parameters:
    - img1: (np.ndarray): Left image
    - img2: (np.ndarray): Right image
    - lines: (np.ndarray): Epipolar lines
    - pts1: (np.ndarray): Matched points in the left image
    - pts2: (np.ndarray): Matched points in the right image
    """
    # Get image size
    r, c, _ = img1.shape
    for r, pt1, pt2 in zip(lines, pts1, pts2):
        color = tuple(np.random.randint(0, 255, 3).tolist())
        # Calculate two points on the line
        x0, y0 = map(int, [0, -r[2]/r[1]])
        x1, y1 = map(int, [c, -(r[2]+r[0]*c)/r[1]])
        # Draw the line in img1
        img1 = cv2.line(img1, (x0, y0), (x1, y1), color, 1)
        # Draw corresponding feature points in img1
        img1 = cv2.circle(img1, tuple(pt1), 5, color, -1)
        # Draw corresponding feature points in img2
        img2 = cv2.circle(img2, tuple(pt2), 5, color, -1)
    return img1, img2
# Visualize the corresponding epipolar lines on the original image
draw_epipolar_lines(pair[(0,1)]['pts1'], pair[(0,1)]['pts2'],
imgs[0], imgs[1], F)
```

It can be seen that the epipolar lines we drew are quite accurate.

19.5 Summary

This chapter discussed the basics of 3D reconstruction, focusing on the principles of epipolar geometry and triangulation. We solved the fundamental matrix through epipolar constraints and further decomposed it to obtain the pose of the camera, then used triangulation to determine the three-dimensional coordinates of spatial points. Although we only obtained the three-dimensional coordinates of very sparse spatial points, these coordinates are highly reliable, providing necessary three-dimensional structural support for the scene and laying a solid foundation for subsequent in-depth analysis and applications.

Recovering three-dimensional structure from two-dimensional images is undoubtedly a challenging task. Although the content introduced in this chapter only covers some basic 3D reconstruction methods, these methods lay an important foundation for understanding and building more complex 3D vision systems. It is hoped that readers can grasp the core ideas of 3D reconstruction from these preliminary concepts and further explore and expand on this basis.

Exercises

(1) If one of the two cameras has its imaging plane parallel to the baseline, in this case, do the corresponding epipole and epipolar line of this camera exist? If they exist, provide their locations.

(2) Review the parallel binocular vision system in Chap. 18, its division value of disparity is limited by the baseline length and camera intrinsic parameters. In the non-parallel binocular vision system introduced in this chapter, is its division value of disparity still subject to this limitation?

(3) Prove that the $\boldsymbol{F}$ matrix is a rank 2 singular matrix.

(4) Assume that the $\boldsymbol{F}$ of a known image pair is

$$\boldsymbol{F} = \begin{bmatrix} -0.003 & -0.028 & 13.19 \\ -0.003 & -0.008 & -29.2 \\ 2.97 & 56.38 & -9999 \end{bmatrix}.$$

Find the epipolar line of the pixel coordinate $\tilde{\boldsymbol{u}}_l = [343 \quad 221 \quad 1]^{\mathrm{T}}$.

(5) As shown in Fig. 19.9, $\boldsymbol{M}_1$ and $\boldsymbol{M}_2$ are the projection matrices of the left and right cameras, assuming $\boldsymbol{M}_1 = [\boldsymbol{I}|0]$ and $\boldsymbol{M}_2 = [\boldsymbol{A}|\boldsymbol{a}]$, where $\boldsymbol{A}$ is a non-singular matrix of 3×3. Prove:

(a) The fundamental matrix $\boldsymbol{F} = [\boldsymbol{a}_\times]\boldsymbol{A}$.

(b) $\boldsymbol{a}$ is the coordinate of a certain epipole.

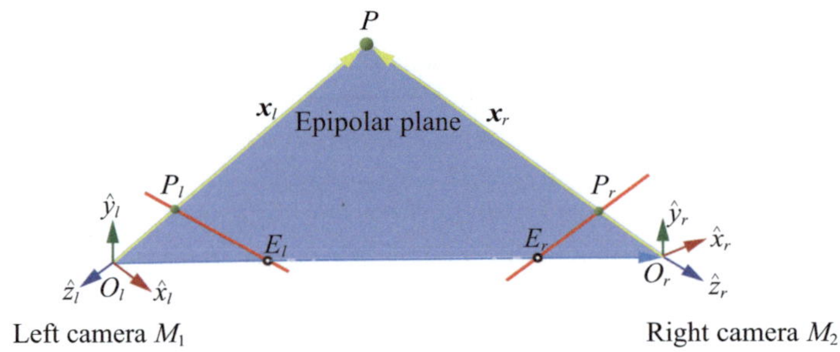

Fig. 19.9 Schematic of Exercise (5)

Summary and Prospects

Dear reader, you have completed the study of the content of this book, including:

- Image processing in computer vision.
- Visual recognition methods in computer vision, especially those based on deep learning.
- Scene reconstruction in computer vision.

By now, you have mastered the basic knowledge of computer vision and gained firsthand experience in coding for computer vision. However, it should be noted that this book is just the beginning of exploring the vast world of computer vision. On the one hand, as there are many problems involved in computer vision, this book does not cover all subfields of computer vision; on the other hand, the development of computer vision is advancing rapidly, but the content introduced in this book is relatively classic computer vision algorithms, not covering the latest developments in the field of computer vision. With the advent of the era of big data and large models, the field of computer vision is facing significant revolution. At the end of this book, the author makes some prospects for the development of computer vision technology in the era of big data with his limited knowledge.

- The rise of large visual models. In terms of models, deep convolutional neural networks are no longer the only dedicated backbone network model in computer vision. Transformers, originally used for natural language processing, are also widely used in computer vision. Compared with convolutional neural networks, Transformers introduce a self-attention mechanism, which is more advantageous when dealing with image structures with long-range dependencies; at the same time, there is no explicit parameter sharing in the self-attention mechanism, which can better capture the relationship between inputs, thereby improving the model's generalization ability. This makes Transformers have stronger fitting ability for big data. Therefore, in the era of big data, Transformers are gradually becoming large visual models used to solve computer vision tasks.
- The popularity of unsupervised pretraining paradigms. In the era of big data, data is often unlabeled, and thus the previous pretraining paradigm for visual

W. Shen et al., *Hands-On Computer Vision*,
https://doi.org/10.1007/978-981-95-4835-4

models, which relied on labeled data, has become ill-suited to the progress of the times. Instead, the unsupervised pretraining paradigm based on unlabeled big data has taken its place. In fact, unsupervised pretraining paradigms, such as masked language modeling, have achieved great success in the field of natural language processing. Similar methods, such as masked image modeling, will also be widely used in computer vision. Large visual models based on unsupervised pretraining can fit large-scale image datasets, giving the large visual models strong generalization ability, and can also be fine-tuned for specific tasks. This method will accelerate the development and deployment of computer vision tasks.
- The development of multimodal fusion and cross-modal learning. With the development of large models, cross-modal learning (such as learning between images and text) will become more important. By jointly learning different modal data and effectively integrating multimodal information, a more comprehensive and accurate visual understanding can be obtained. This will enable deeper interaction between images and text, thereby driving the convergence and collaborative development of fields like computer vision and natural language processing.
- The demand for high-performance hardware accelerators. Large visual models require a lot of computational resources for training and inference, including but not limited to hardware computing power, memory capacity, parallel computing ability, real-time inference, and energy efficiency. The further development of computer vision technology will inevitably increase the demand for high-performance hardware accelerators.

In summary, the era of big data and large models will bring many opportunities and challenges to computer vision technology. Through large-scale data and powerful computing capabilities, we can expect more practical applications of computer vision technology in scenarios such as autonomous driving, human-computer interaction, video surveillance, and medical image-assisted diagnosis.

MIX
Papier aus verantwortungsvollen Quellen
Paper from responsible sources
FSC® C105338

If you have any concerns about our products,
you can contact us on
ProductSafety@springernature.com

In case Publisher is established outside the EU,
the EU authorized representative is:
Springer Nature Customer Service Center GmbH
Europaplatz 3, 69115 Heidelberg, Germany

Printed by Libri Plureos GmbH
in Hamburg, Germany